THE MOUNTAIN MEN
and the Fur Trade of the Far West
III

OTHER PUBLICATIONS BY LEROY R. HAFEN –

1926 – *The Overland Mail, 1849-1869*
1927 – editor, *History of Colorado*, 3 volumes
1931 – *Broken Hand: the Life of Thomas Fitzpatrick* (with W. J. Ghent)
1932 – editor, *Villard's Past and Present of the Pike's Peak Region*
1933 – *Colorado, the Story of a Western Commonwealth*
1938 – *Fort Laramie and the Pageant of the West* (with F. M. Young)
1941 – *Western America* (with C. C. Rister); revised, 1950
1941-1942 – editor, *Southwest Historical Series*, volumes IX, X, XI
1943 – *Colorado: a Story of the State and its People* (with Ann W. Hafen)
1948 – *Colorado and its People*, 2 volumes
1950 – editor, *Ruxton of the Rockies*
1951 – editor, *Ruxton's Life in the Far West*
1953 – *The Colorado Story* (with Ann W. Hafen)
1924-1954 – editor, *The Colorado Magazine*
1954 – *The Old Spanish Trail* (with Ann W. Hafen)
1954-1962 – editor, *The Far West and Rockies Series*, 15 volumes (with
    Ann W. Hafen)
1960 – *Handcarts to Zion* (with Ann W. Hafen)
1962 – compiler and editor, *The Hafen Families of Utah*
1965 – *The Mountain Men and Fur Trade of the Far West*, vols. 1-2

Also contributions to numerous other publications and journals. For further
detail see *LeRoy R. and Ann W. Hafen, their writings and their notable
collection of Americana given to Brigham Young University Library* (1962,
109 pages)

A Fur Trade Rendezvous Scene

As depicted in an illustration in F. F. Victor's *River of the West*, 1870.

THE MOUNTAIN MEN
and the Fur Trade
of the Far West

biographical sketches of the participants
by scholars of the subject
and with introductions by the editor

under the editorial supervision of

LeRoy R. Hafen

State Historian of Colorado, Emeritus
Professor of History, Brigham Young University

Volume III

THE ARTHUR H. CLARK COMPANY
Glendale, California
1966

Contents

Illustrations

For the map of the "Fur Country of the Far West,"
see the first volume of this series, at page 20.

Preface

In this, the third volume of the Mountain Men Series, will be found biographical sketches of thirty-six more of the men engaged in the trans-Mississippi fur trade of the first half of the nineteenth century.

The sketches in this volume, as in the first two, are arranged alphabetically under the surname of the subject person. This same format will be used in all volumes of the Series, with an index-guide in the final volume.

The reader is referred to the summary history of the fur trade, presented in the first section of volume I, for the general background history and the contribution of the fur men in advancing the frontier. Likewise, for the area concerned, the large map which appears at page 20 of volume I, will be of value in connection with the text of all volumes.

Again we express sincere thanks to the scholars of the fur trade era, for their cooperation in contributing the valuable biographies presented in this work.

Gratitude is also extended to all those who have assisted in furnishing copy for the portraits and illustrations. These persons include the authors of the articles, the personnel of several historical societies and other archives in Western states, and with help from the collections of Mr. Fred Rosenstock of Denver, and Mr. Robert J. Woods of Los Angeles. A few of the portraits are from other publications, as indicated in the captions.

JAMES BAKER
Courtesy, Fred Rosenstock, Denver.

HENRY A. BOLLER
At the age of 22, before departing
for the West. Courtesy of State
Historical Society of North Dakota.

WILLIAM M. DOUGHTY
Courtesy, Oregon Historical Society.

JOSEPH DOYLE
From Conard's *Wootton*, 1890.

ISAAC GRAHAM
Courtesy, California State Library.

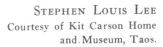

STEPHEN LOUIS LEE
Courtesy of Kit Carson Home
and Museum, Taos.

JACOB PRIMER LEESE
Courtesy, California State Library,
from *The Hesperian*, June 1859.

PETER SKENE OGDEN
From Chittenden's *Fur Trade*, 1935.
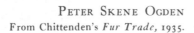

RUFUS B. SAGE
From an 1888 photograph.

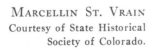

MARCELLIN ST. VRAIN
Courtesy of State Historical
Society of Colorado.

GEORGE S. SIMPSON
Courtesy of State Historical
Society of Colorado.

COURTNEY M. WALKER
From an old photograph.

SETH E. WARD
Courtesy of Native Sons
of Kansas City, Missouri.

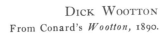

DICK WOOTTON
From Conard's *Wootton*, 1890.

Marcelino Baca

by JANET LECOMPTE
Colorado Springs, Colorado

As a rule, native New Mexicans did not make good trappers. Trapping was a solitary occupation and New Mexicans preferred the safety of numbers, an attitude bred into them by their forebears' precarious existence in an isolated Spanish colony surrounded for two centuries by savage tribes. During the 1830s, it is true, there were many New Mexicans employed at trading posts on the Missouri, Platte, and Arkansas rivers, and even in the roaming trapping brigades, but almost invariably as muleteers or packers. It was a rare native of New Mexico who chose to make his living as a trapper, often alone and protected only by his rifle, his wit, and his reflexes.

Marcelino Baca was one of these rare New Mexican trappers.[1] Born about 1808 at Taos, the son of Salvador and Tomasa Silva Baca, Marcelino grew up tall and strong, handsome and intelligent, and contemptuous of the race from which he had sprung. George F. Ruxton described him thus:

> Marcellin — who, though a Mexican, despised his people and abjured his blood, having been all his life in the mountains with the white hunters — looked down easily upon six feet and odd inches. In form a Hercules, he had the symmetry of an Apollo; with strikingly handsome features, and masses of long black hair hanging from his slouching beaver over the shoulders of his buckskin hunting shirt. He, as he was wont to say, was "no dam Spaniard, but 'mountainee man,' wagh!"[2]

[1] Joseph Meek remembered another, named Loretta, who with his Blackfoot wife became interpreter to an American Fur Company post among the Blackfoot. F. F. Victor, *The River of the West* (Hartford, 1870), 134-35.

[2] *Life in the Far West* (New York, 1849), 193. Ruxton ends his novel, of which

"Mountainee man" he surely was, and in later years he boasted of the nine years he had spent in the mountains, living on meat alone and tasting neither salt nor bread.[3]

Marcelino Baca probably learned to trap in one of the many companies of American trappers who made Taos their headquarters and outfitting point during the 1820s. He also spent some time working with his father in a gold mine (probably at the *Real de Dolores* [Old Placer], discovered in 1828 south of Santa Fe) where he learned to pan gold in wooden bowls. When in later years he showed up at Fort Laramie with a vial of gold dust he had panned on the Chugwater, it was the first gold the trappers had ever seen. But the West was more interested in fur than in gold at that time, and his discovery went unnoticed.[4]

Marcelino probably began his nine years as a trapper in 1832 or 1833. By 1835 he was a member of James Bridger's American Fur Company brigade and well on his way to acquiring his reputation of "the best trapper and hunter in the mountains and ever first in the fight."[5] His Mexican background, always mentioned by those who wrote about him, was on one occasion a decided asset to the brigade. On the Humboldt River in 1835, Marcelino spied a Digger Ute creeping towards the trappers' horses. Throwing his lasso – hardly a standard piece of trapping equipment – he caught the Indian around the neck, wheeled his horse and galloped through the greasewood, dragging the remains of the unfortunate Digger behind him.[6]

he says "there is no incident in it which has not actually occurred" (p. x), with an account of a party of mountaineers, "Marcellin" being the only one named, finding the frozen body of Bill Williams in "New Park" (Middle Park, Colo.). This did not actually occur, however, since Ruxton died a year before Bill Williams did.

[3] Lieut. E. G. Beckwith's report, *Report of Explorations and Surveys for a Railroad Route from the Mississippi River to the Pacific Ocean,* II (Washington, D.C., 1855), 35.

[4] James B. Marsh, *Four Years in the Rockies, or, The Adventures of Isaac P. Rose* (New Castle, Pa., 1884; reprint, Columbus, Ohio, n.d.), 215.

[5] Ruxton, *op. cit.,* 23.   [6] Marsh, *op. cit.,* 89.

Marcelino had the well-developed flair for self-preservation that marked a successful Mountain Man. While serving in Bridger's brigade on the Yellowstone River, he went to reconnoiter a Blackfoot fort on top of a bluff above the trappers' camp. Near the top of the hill Marcelino was fired on from the fort, the charge striking and breaking his ankle. He fell to the ground, and as the Indians rushed from the fort to finish him off, he coiled himself into a ball and rolled down the snow-covered slope into camp.[7] Another account of this episode on the Yellowstone dates it February 22, 1837, and refers to its hero only as "a Spaniard."[8] Still with Bridger's brigade in the winter of 1837-8, Marcelino was one of those sent from camp on Powder River to Fort Laramie for supplies, returning to camp in January.[9]

Around the end of 1838, Marcelino blundered into Pawnee lands on the Platte River. The Pawnees took him captive and prepared him for a peculiarly unpleasant ritual sacrifice: After tying the captive to a post, the Indians would build a fire nearby and dance; as they danced, they would approach the victim, cut off a strip of flesh, roast it in the fire and eat it, the captive perishing miserably in the meantime. While the handsome trapper was being fattened for such a feast, the chief's daughter fell in love with him and begged her father to spare his life. Her wish was granted and Marcelino was released. He took his Pawnee Pocahontas to wife, giving her his mother's name of Tomasa or Tomacita.[10] If she was beautiful, the legend does not say so, but fifteen years later she was at least possessed of "matronly grace and dignity."[11] Their eldest son, José, was born on the

---

[7] *Ibid.*, 144.

[8] Osborne Russell, *Journal of a Trapper* (Boise, Idaho, 1921), 53.

[9] *Ibid.*, 79f. Isaac P. Rose says Bridger's camp was on Wind River. Rose, Tom Biggs and Marcelino went to Fort Laramie for supplies, says Rose, and did not return to Bridger's camp until spring. Marsh, *op. cit.*, 215-17.

[10] F. W. Cragin's notes of an interview with José de Jesús Valdez, Walsenburg, Colo., Dec. 9, 1907, Cragin Collection, Pioneers' Museum, Colorado Springs, Colo.

[11] Lieut. Beckwith's report, *loc. cit.*, 35.

South Platte River near present Denver in 1839; their second son, Luis, was born at Fort Laramie in 1841; their only daughter, Elena, was born at the Hardscrabble settlement in 1846, and later married a son of Charles Autobees. After the birth of Elena, Marcelino took his wife and children to Taos where he had the children baptized and at the same time was married in the Catholic church to their mother. Tomasa outlived Marcelino, dying in 1871.[12]

When the beaver trade went to pieces, Marcelino joined other trappers who found refuge from the wreck of their occupation at Pueblo, the Arkansas River trading post and agricultural settlement at the mouth of Fountain River. In the spring of 1844 he moved with George Simpson and others to Hardscrabble Creek, thirty miles west of Pueblo, and made a new settlement. For three or four years Marcelino lived at Hardscrabble, trading with Indians and trapping occasionally, probably more for fun than profit, for by now the Indian trade had made him a wealthy man.[13]

In 1847 or 1848 the Hardscrabble settlement began to decline, and Marcelino moved to the lovely valley of the Greenhorn River, south of the Arkansas, where he kept cattle and grew corn, wheat, beans and watermelons, not only for his family's consumption, but to trade to the Indians.[14] In 1852 the Utes swooped down on Greenhorn, killing some of Marcelino's cattle, destroying his grain and

---

[12] F. W. Cragin's notes of an interview with Elena Baca Autobees, Pueblo, Colo., Nov. 8, 1907, Cragin Collection.

[13] Janet S. Lecompte, "The Hardscrabble Settlement, 1844-1848," *Colorado Magazine*, XXXI, no. 2 (April, 1954).

[14] Lieut. Beckwith's report, *loc. cit.*, 34-35; Cragin's notes of an interview with Elena Baca Autobees, cited. Charles Autobees testified in 1873 that Marcelino Baca, along with Archibald Metcalf, John Brown, and William New, occupied land on the Greenhorn in 1841 or 1842. If so, this early occupation was sporadic, perhaps only to grow a crop of corn, or pasture stock there for a short period. Testimony of Charles Autobees, Jan. 16, 1873, Pueblo, Colo.; "Vigil and St. Vrain Grant," Correspondence, 1868-1914, Records of the General Land Office, RG 49, National Archives, Wash., D.C.

stealing his horses. He decided to move back to the deserted Pueblo and live in the old fort while he was building a log house a mile east across Fountain River. He moved onto his new ranch and in the spring of 1853 he dug a ditch from the Fountain and planted a cornfield, but a flood washed it out.[15] Before summer he put in another crop on the Greenhorn and while he was engaged in farming it, he was hired as a guide over the Sangre de Cristo Pass to Fort Massachusetts by the party surveying a route for a railroad to the Pacific. As a guide he performed adequately; Captain Gunnison described him as an intelligent man with thirty years' experience in the mountains.[16]

In the fall of 1853, Marcelino moved back to his log house on the east side of Fountain River, where he had built ten or twelve other houses for his peons, as well as corrals for his cattle and horses (he was said to have had as many as 500 head of cattle and 50 horses). At the same time the old Pueblo was fixed up and occupied by a group of Mexicans from Taos, who in the spring and summer of 1854 put in a cornfield and did a little trading with the Utes, notably with Chief Blanco's band of Muaches.

In the early morning of December 24, 1854, Chief Blanco and his men, apparently friendly as usual, paid Marcelino's ranch a visit, asking to come inside the house. Marcelino would have let the Utes in, but an old man named Barela vehemently objected, and his wise advice prevailed. As the Indians went away, crossing the Fountain towards Pueblo, they drove off all Marcelino's cattle and horses that had not been secured in the corrals. At Pueblo the Indians were admitted, and immediately began a massacre of the seventeen men in the fort, not one of whom escaped alive.[17] Mar-

---

[15] Charles Irving Jones, "William Kroenig, New Mexico Pioneer," *New Mexico Historical Review*, XIX (Oct., 1944), 292, 296f.

[16] Beckwith's report, *loc. cit.*, 120.

[17] Janet Lecompte, "Pueblo Massacre," *Denver Westerners' Brand Book*, 1954 (Boulder, Colo., 1955), 41-48.

celino's loss of 73 head of cattle, 13 horses, and 2 mules amounted to over $4000.[18]

A month later the Utes returned to the Arkansas and killed Marcelino's brother, Benito, near Pueblo. By then Marcelino had had enough. He moved his family to New Mexico, to the little frontier village of Rio Colorado (now Red River), where he spent the remaining years of his life. When the Civil War broke out, he enlisted in the New Mexico Volunteers and was killed by a shot in the forehead during the battle with invading Texans at Valverde, N.M., on February 21, 1862.[19]

---

[18] "Claims for Indian Depredations in New Mexico," *H. exec. doc. 123,* 35 Cong., 1 sess. (ser. 959).

[19] F. W. Cragin's notes of interviews with José de Jesús Valdez and Elena Baca Autobees, cited.

James Baird

by REX W. STRICKLAND
Texas Western College, El Paso

For almost a century and a half, since the day James Baird died on a borrowed mattress in the ancient town of El Paso del Norte (Ciudad Juárez), the story of the last years of the Santa Fe trader, Spanish prisoner, and free trapper has been an enigma, unsolved for want of data. Only now has the acquisition by Texas Western College of microfilms of the *Documentos de Ciudad Juárez* made it possible to write the finale to his checkered legend of near success and ultimate failure.

Baird was a Pennsylvanian by birth and upbringing. Born in 1767, he was of middle-age before he emigrated from Pittsburgh to St. Louis in 1810. There he earned a living by hammering out beaver traps in his blacksmith shop. St. Louis already had become a point of departure for a burgeoning fur trade that stretched up the muddy Missouri and toward the borders of Spanish America. While they waited in Baird's shop for traps, shaggy hunters told tales of the far country to a man not content to grow old at his forge. In 1812 he formed a partnership with Robert McKnight (one of the Irish gang),[1] Benjamin Shreve, and Michael McDonogh, organized with the aim of entering into the trade with New Mexico. Five hired men – Samuel Chambers, Thomas Cook, William Mines, Alfred Allen, and Peter Baum – and an interpreter, Carlos Miers, made up the remainder of the party.[2]

---

[1] Frederic L. Billon, *Annals of St. Louis in Territorial Days* (St. Louis, 1888), 232.

[2] I am indebted to Frank B. Golley, "James Baird, Early Santa Fe Trader," in Missouri Historical Society *Bulletin,* xv (Apr. 1959), 171-93, for the details of Baird's life until his release from imprisonment in October 1821.

As is well known, Baird and his associates were not the first Americans to essay the trade with New Mexico. In 1810 Reuben Smith, James Patterson and Joseph McLanahan had gone to Santa Fe, where their goods were confiscated and they themselves sent to Chihuahua as prisoners.[3] Just two years later they were released by Nemesio Salcedo, commandant-general of the *Provincias Internas,* and returned to the United States. Their arrival at Natchitoches was reported by John Sibley, Indian agent, in a letter written April 27, 1812.[4] But Baird could hardly have been aware of the liberation of the luckless trio, for his departure from St. Louis took place within a day or two of the date of the captives' return to distant Natchitoches. Probably news of Hidalgo's thrust at independence in New Spain had trickled into St. Louis and convinced him that the mercantile policy of the Spaniards had been relaxed.

April, 1812, was running to a close as the party left St. Louis with a pack train of goods designed, it would seem, to catch the fancy of the women of New Mexico. The mules were laden with silks, velvets, linens, and sheer muslins – the value of the cargo has been placed at ten thousand dollars. The adventure went well enough until the party came down Raton Pass to Taos. The governor of New Mexico was Jose Manrrique, a suspicious satrap, influenced by his greed or egotism in the interpretation of the laws of trade. He arrested the party and herded them into the capital, Santa Fe. Their goods were confiscated and sold. After a brief interval the prisoners were sent to Chihuahua and incarcerated in the old military hospital.[5]

---

[3] José Manrrique to Salcedo, Mar. 31, 1810, Santa Fe, M.N.M., Spanish Archives, 2311.

[4] Julia Kathryn Garrett (ed.), "Dr. Sibley and the Louisiana Texas Frontier, 1803-1815," in *Southwestern Historical Quarterly,* LXIX (Jan. 1946), 406.

[5] In 1884 the penitentiary at Chihuahua was demolished to make way for a new building; on a cell wall were scratched the names of Allen, Baird, and Chambers and the date, September 28, 1812. *Lone Star* (El Paso), Jan. 30, 1881. It seems logical to assume that this record was left during the first days of confinement.

The story of their nine years in Mexico has been told well by Frank B. Golley.[6] The men were not kept closely confined at all times, though scattered documents show that they were subjected to restraint whenever their custody promised a gratuity. In time they scattered: Baird was leased as a bond servant to Don Francisco Velasco of Durango;[7] Robert McKnight mined and merchandized on the eastern slopes of the Sierra Madre at Galeana; with him was Alfred Allen; William Mines went to Mexico City; Michael McDonogh joined the Order of the Friars Minor and was domiciled in the College for the Propagation of the Faith at Zacatecas; Thomas Cook died in Mexico; of Peter Baum, Benjamin Shreve, and Samuel Chambers we know only that they lived to return to the United States.[8]

In 1820, Ferdinand VII of Spain was obliged to grant a constitution to his subjects and in May he issued a decree directing the liberation of all foreigners imprisoned in the viceroyalty of Mexico. The order reached Chihuahua in September and Alejo Conde Garcia, commandant general of the Western Provinces,[9] gave the Americans their freedom. Most of the men left immediately for home; there were a number of persons detained in Nueva Vizcaya. The first party was composed of Baum, Chambers, and Shreve – accompanied by Simon McCoy (Cooley?) and Charles King (Keene?), captured in east Texas with Nolan in 1801; William Meeks, arrested with Pike's party in March, 1807; and John Stephanson, William Gray, and Charles Mint (the times of their seizure being unknown). This group reached Ft. Smith on the Arkansas River in January or February, 1821.[10]

---

[6] *Op. cit.*, 182-89.

[7] A letter of James Baird from Durango, Mexico, Sept. 12 ,1820, to his son in St. Louis, published in the *St. Louis Enquirer,* Mar. 31, 1821.

[8] *Ibid.*

[9] Francisco R. Almada, *Resumen de Historia del Estado de Chihuahua* (Mexico, 1955), 157.

[10] *St. Louis Enquirer,* Mar. 31, 1821.

Baird and McKnight did not return to Missouri immediately after their release. Baird, we know, remained in
Chihuahua until the middle of October 1821; on the 10th
of that month he answered a letter he had received from
Stephen F. Austin, written in San Antonio on August 17,
but delayed in its delivery in the postoffice at Durango. He
acknowledged the receipt of two letters, enclosed by Austin,
from his son (actually his nephew, whom he had adopted),
James Baird, Jr.; expressed his sorrow over the news of the
death of Austin's father; and concluded by saying that he
intended to leave for the United States at the beginning of
the following week.[11]

The legend that Baird returned alone across the prairies
seems to be verified by the letter to Austin. An addendum to
his saga of travel asserts that he traveled from Mexico to St.
Louis, thence to Pittsburgh and back to St. Louis by the end
of December 1821. The period of time seems too short for so
long a journey nor does there appear to be any logical reason
why he was obliged to cover the distance during the interval
assigned to him.

Back in St. Louis he evolved plans to re-enter the New
Mexican trade. Probably he felt financial gain lay in that
quarter; nor can we discount the fact that the United States
was laggard in reimbursing the traders for their losses in
1812 – we know McKnight was galled by its close-fisted
policy.[12] No doubt Baird must have had much the same
feeling of frustration. Moreover, perhaps the fires of adventure had not burned quite down to the ashes.

To secure money and goods for the venture, Baird formed
a partnership with William Anderson, senior, Paul Anderson, junior, John Foughlin, and Wilson McGunnigle under

---

[11] James Baird to Stephen F. Austin, Chihuahua, Oct. 10, 1821, American Historical Association, *Annual Report, 1919*, II: Eugene C. Barker (ed.) *Austin Papers*,
vol. I, part 1, p. 416.

[12] Thomas James, *Three Years among the Indians and Mexicans* (Chicago,
1962), 98.

the name of James Baird and Company.[13] Surely the commission merchants provided the finances and Baird contributed the know-how for the enterprise. Samuel Chambers, Baird's comrade in captivity, accompanied the party, probably as an *engagé;* certainly he was not a signatory of the articles of incorporation, and he disappeared from the legend as soon as the group reached New Mexico.

The *St. Louis Enquirer* of September 2, 1822, reported the venture:

> About twenty individuals with sixty pack horses and mules, set out from this place last week with an adventure of merchandise to Santa Fe. Messrs. Baird and Chambers, who were prisoners in the internal provinces for near ten years, are of the party.

The snows caught them on the Arkansas. They holed up a few miles west of the present site of Dodge City and waited out the winter. Most of their horses and mules perished of cold and hunger, and when spring came to the valley they left their goods cached while they journeyed to Taos to buy pack animals. Although they were successful in retrieving their wares, the delay was only the first of a series of misfortunes that dogged their enterprise until the fall of 1823. The Mexican officials sought to hinder their trade with the Indians (it appears that they were not engaged in the Santa Fe trade *per se*), and the proprietors grew tired of a losing business.

The company dissolved at Taos, September 1, 1823.[14] Most of the members of the expedition returned to St. Louis to report that the prospects of trade were not entirely hopeless, despite the interference of the Mexican authorities.[15] The final liquidation of the partnership was announced in St. Louis, December 13, with a notice that all debts due the

[13] *St. Louis Enquirer,* Dec. 13, 1823.

[14] *Ibid.,* Dec. 1, 1823. This notice of dissolution was signed by William Anderson, junior; Paul Anderson, junior; John Foughlin and Wilson McGunnigle.

[15] *Missouri Gazette,* Nov. 8, 1823.

concern were to be paid to James Baird, William Anderson, senior, Paul Anderson, junior, John Foughlin, and/or Wilson McGunnigle.[16]

Baird apparently remained in New Mexico during the winter of 1823-24, as did Paul Anderson the younger. In the late spring of 1824 he accompanied a party of New Mexicans from Santa Fe to Council Bluff (Grove?), acting as interpreter for the group, who sought some arrangement with the American traders that would facilitate and protect the commerce with the United States.[17] However, by September he had returned to Mexico and had joined an expedition recruited to drive Indian invaders out of Chihuahua.

The Opatas under Ignacio Dorame had pronounced for the restoration of the Spanish monarchy, crossed the Sierra Madres and seized Moris and Jesus Maria.[18] It was this episode that gave rise to the report that Baird had joined Iturbide's army in 1823-24. In reality, he served with the republican forces – Iturbide had fallen from power in February, 1823. Citing his service as proof of his loyalty to his adopted country, Baird applied for Mexican citizenship in October, 1824, and received the commendation of the territorial delegation (New Mexico) for his assistance "in the late trouble with the barbarous tribes."[19] Thus he cut all ties with home and country and lived out the rest of his days as an expatriate.

It is reasonable to assume that the young partner mentioned in the Baird family records was Paul Anderson,

16 *St. Louis Enquirer,* Dec. 13, 1823.

17 J. E. B. Austin to Stephen F. Austin, Sept. 6, 1824, Amer. Hist. Assn., *Annual Report, 1919, op. cit.,* part 1, p. 891.

18 Cuenta y manifesta lo fecha me resta de finado Anglo Americano Santiago Bairs irle vivo conmigo y asistencia en su enfermidad, Nov. 12, 1826, *Documentos de Ciudad Juárez* (microfilm, Texas Western College), reel 50/0429; Almada, *op. cit.,* 179; Edward H. Spicer, *Cycles of Conquest* (Tucson, 1962), 101.

19 "Minutes of the territorial delegation in New Mexico," State Historical Society, Santa Fe.

junior.[20] From time to time Baird's presence was noted in Santa Fe and El Paso del Norte; it was in the latter town that he had his headquarters during the last year of his life. His career as a trapper (Mountain Man) comprised no more than two seasons, the winters of 1824-25 and 1825-26, when he engaged in the beaver hunt *(caza de nutria)* on the sources of the Gila River in the Mogollon Mountains. His search for pelts antedated the coming of Ceran St. Vrain to the region by at least two years. Cautiously it may be suggested that he was the first American to engage in the enterprise, but historical dogmatism can be dangerous, for we are probing a frontier that reveals its secrets reluctantly.

Baird spent the last months of his life in El Paso del Norte preparing for another season's hunt on the Gila. On the eve of his departure for the beaver country, he wrote to Alejandro Ramirez, prefect of the District Bravo, protesting the anticipated invasion of the area by American trapping parties authorized by Antonio Narbona, governor of New Mexico. He pointed out that he had become a Mexican citizen so that he could engage in the beaver hunt under the protection of the laws of his adopted country. He had, he said, invested his small means with the hope of systematically building up a business that would be of profit to himself and his fellow citizens (Mexicans) either by birth or adoption.[21] His insistence on his love for his new country, one feels, was not entirely an expression of patriotism. His hope to enjoy a monopoly of the pelts of the Gila basin may have contributed measurably to his zeal.

This, Baird's last letter, was written October 26, 1826. Within a day or two he left for the fur fields accompanied

20 I. (Samuel) McClure to Baird's family, Franklin, Mo., Oct. 13, 1827, quoted in Golley, *op. cit.*

21 James Baird to Alejandro Ramirez, El Paso del Norte ,Oct. 26, 1826, Archivo de Gobernacion (Mexico), Comercio, Expediente 44, cited by Thomas M. Marshall, "St. Vrain's Expedition to the Gila in 1826," in *Southwestern Historical Quarterly,* XIX (Jan. 1916), 256-57.

by a small party of hired men: Juan Bautista Chelifre and his brother; Pedro Chelifre, Frenchman; and Luciano Grijalva.[22] Perhaps Paul Anderson was a member of the group. Baird got as far as Ojo de Samalayuca (thirty-five miles below El Paso del Norte on the road to Chihuahua) where he became too ill to ride and turned back, leaving the hired men to continue their way. He reached El Paso mortally sick and took to his bed – a borrowed mattress, sheet, and pillow. He died on the morning of November 3 in the presence of eight to ten Americans.

Julian Bernal, first *alcalde* of El Paso del Norte, had been Baird's patron, perhaps partner, during his residence on the Rio Grande. Indeed, it was Bernal's solicitude for his accounts that preserved the record of the trapper's last days. The file of papers (*expediente numero 753*, Tomo II, Ano de 1826, *Documentos de Ciudad Juárez*) reveals that no sooner was Baird dead than Bernal assembled the American residents to assist him in making an inventory of the deceased man's goods, first in Spanish,[23] and the next day in English.[24] The lists were drawn with the aid of John W. Rogers in the presence of William Aiken, John G. Parrish, Edward Beavers, Paul Anderson, and Samuel McClure, each of whom signed the documents.[25]

Bernal also made the arrangements for Baird's burial and charged the costs against his meager estate. Eighteen pesos were paid Jose Ignacio for making the coffin; three pesos bought a swatch of black cloth to cover the crude box; two

---

[22] Interrogacion, Sub-prefectura de Janos, Jan. 17, 1827, *Documentos de Ciudad Juárez*, reel 50/0432. Conjecture makes the brothers to be Jean Baptiste and Pierre Charlefoux, one of whom later went to California. *California Pioneer Register and Index* (Baltimore, 1964), 98.

[23] Inventario y manifesta los muebles y Estado . . . de Anglo Americano Santiago Baires, Nov. 3, 1826, *Docs. de C. Juárez*, 50/0427.

[24] List of the goods and chattels belonging to the late James Baird taken immediately after his death by Julian Bernal and John W. Rogers, Nov. 4, 1826, *Docs. de C. Juárez*, 50/0425.

[25] See appendix for the list in English.

pesos purchased the coffin nails; a peso went for the death watch over the body; four *mozos* dug the grave for a peso each; the *cura* charged fourteen pesos for a grave plot in the churchyard of Nuestra Senora de Guadalupe; and a peso procured two pieces of paper on which the inventory was written.[26]

Bernal continued to present claims against Baird's estate during the month that followed his death. These assessments are valuable because they throw light upon his trapping operations in previous seasons. Bernal had provided two horses and two pack mules for one expedition at the rate of four pesos per month for the horses and five per month for the mules. Once at Baird's order he had advanced two pesos to Jorge Mondragon and Company for powder; another item mentions twenty pesos paid to a cooper, Andres Herrera, for two barrels made in his shop.[27]

The last chapter in Baird's story was written at Janos, January 27, 1827, when Julian Bernal appeared before Francisco Perea, first *regidor* of the *ayuntamiento,* and sought permission to interrogate Juan and Pedro Chelifre, then incarcerated in the local jail, concerning the whereabouts of the dead man's pack animals. Upon presentation in open court, they testified that they had left El Paso del Norte with Baird's party at "the end of October" en route to the Gila; at Ojo de Samalayuca the *patron* became too sick to go further and returned to El Paso. Luciano Grijalva was left in charge of the pack train and they had gone with him to Tucson (for what purpose they did not say), from whence they started back to Janos by the way of San Bernardino. Near Janos they separated from Grijalva, who

---

[26] Cuenta fecha de nuestro de los pagamentos hecho de dinero por cuenta del finado Anglo Americano Santiago Baires, Nov. 18, 1826, *Docs. de C. Juárez,* 50/0428.

[27] Cuenta y manifesta lo fecha me resta de finado Anglo Americano Santiago Bairs irle vivo conmigo y asistencia en su enfermidad, Nov. 18, 1826, *Docs. de C. Juárez,* 50/0429.

announced it was his intention to go to the Gila. He carried
with him the horses and mules that Baird had leased from
Bernal: one dark-bay horse, one light-bay horse, one dapple-
gray mule and one light-gray mare mule.[28] Further the
witnesses said not. And with this negative note the saga of
James Baird comes to an uncertain end.

APPENDIX

List of the chattels and goods belonging to the Estate of the late James
Baird, deceased:

One pair of saddlebags containing cash $47.75

A small book containing papers
of agreement.

Obligation, receipts &c to the
amount of nineteen

Strand white beads

Nutmegs

One Cwt (?) of thread

One silk strand

Razors, a hone strope and shaving box

A small valice containing pantaloons –
  1 neck handkerchief
  1 bed comforter
  1 green flannel shirt
  1 *guinga* (gingham) shirt
  2 flannel shirts
  2 pr flannel drawers
  2 dozen woollen stockings
  1 hone
  1 small bag shot

A small buffalo skin containing –
  21 butcher knives
  1 flask gunpowder
  1 small bag coffee
  1 pound neck beads
  2 pieces shaving soap
  1 dozen common combs

Pieces soap

Phial calomel

Pr suspenders

Box sewing needles

Two foot rool (rule)

Empty phials

Small shaving glass

Gun, bullet moulds, shot bag
and powder horn

Pistol, butcher knife & bullet
mould

Small bag of ground coffee

  1 bottle mustard
  1 dozen awls
  1 file
  1 paper fish hooks
  1 small paper camphor
  1 small paper cream tartar
  1 bottle snuff
  half quire writing paper

  2 boxes containing four nutmegs
  8 small iron handled pocket
  knives
  1 dozen pen knives
  1 small canister tea

[28] Interrogación, Sub-prefectura de Janos, Jan. 17, 1827, *Docs. de C. Juárez*,
50/0432.

1 paper thread
4 pocket combs
Saddle, bridle and spurs
Buffalo robe
Blanket
Hat
Coat
Vest

1 spring lancet
1 hand clock
Pr pantaloons
Pr drawers
Pr stockings
Pr shoes
2 black silk handkerchiefs
2 mules

This inventory was taken in the presence of the undersigned immediately after the death of the late James baird, El Paso, November 4, 1826.

John W. Rogers   John G. Parrish
W. Aitken   Edward Beavers
Julian Bernal   Paul Anderson
          Samuel McClure

James Baker

by NOLIE MUMEY
Denver, Colorado

James Baker was one of the "reckless breed of men" who ventured into the mountains in the days before the vanguard of gold seekers invaded the region. He was born in Belleville, Illinois, December 19, 1818, of Scottish ancestry,[1] and lived through more than half a century of the most turbulent history of the West.

He was an impressive-looking man, tall and lean. In his late years he wore a goatee and had long, curly, reddish hair that hung in ringlets to his shoulders. He was unconventional in his habits, drank, played at various games of chance, swore, and was involved in many Indian romances. Though with a rough exterior, he was unselfish, faithful to duty, and achieved fame as a hunter, trapper, scout, guide, and Indian fighter. (A portrait of Baker appears at page 13 of this volume.)

James Baker, better known as Jim Baker, had little formal education. Tales of frontier life in the mountains appealed to his imaginative nature and caused him to leave his home. "I didn't like to go to school," he told a Denver reporter, "so I ran away and went in the employ of the American Fur Company. I enlisted for eighteen months."[2]

Baker's first journey began in the spring of 1838, when he boarded the steamer "St. Peter" to go up the Missouri

---

[1] I. W. Brewster, "Unknown Makers of History" (manuscript in possession of the author). Brewster interviewed Baker on several occasions and wrote his paper, in first person, from stories he gathered from the old scout. The first and only book-length biography of Baker is Nolie Mumey, *The Life of Jim Baker, 1818-1898* (Denver, 1931).

[2] The *Denver Tribune-Republican*, July 10, 1886.

River. They cruised to the mouth of the Kaw River, near the present site of Kansas City. A little west of the city, at the Kaw Indian Agency, their supplies were put on carts and their journey began across the prairie. They followed the Platte River, reached Fort Laramie, and continued on to the Wind River, where, at its confluence with the Popo Agie, the rendezvous was held.

Baker spent the years 1838 and 1839 trapping and hunting along the Green River and in the nearby mountains. His first two years were formative, and free of any romance or unusual experience. His contract with the American Fur Company expired in 1840 and he returned to his home in Illinois. But he was not content with the quiet life among civilized people, living in a small village. He longed for the freedom of the outdoors. So, in the spring of 1841, he began his second journey to the mountains, a journey from which he would never return to his native state. He joined the first caravan of emigrants that traveled the Oregon Trail,[3] a party led by the old Mountain Man Thomas Fitzpatrick. When they reached the Green River, Baker left the Oregon-bound travelers and joined Jim Bridger's band of trappers.

Being worried over Indians on the warpath, Bridger wanted to notify his partner, Henry Fraeb, and a band of trappers who were camped on the Little Snake River of northern Colorado, to abandon their site and seek refuge in some safe place. Baker and two other men volunteered to go in search of the party, and after two days of hard riding they came to Fraeb's camp.

Not long afterward, Fraeb's party was attacked by a large band of Indians. The red men, covered with war paint and armed with flintlock muskets and arrows, were led, it was said, by an Arapaho princess garbed in war dress. She was

[3] See John Bidwell's account of this emigrant train in his *Journey to California,* etc. (San Francisco, 1937).

a picturesque figure leading the redskins in their murderous attack, chanting a weird war song, urging the Indians on, driving them into a frenzied state of excitement.[4] The Indians demanded horses from the trappers, who refused to give up their stock. The first assault began in the afternoon of August 21 with the red men making short runs up the hill, firing, then retreating. Baker gave a description of the battle to a newspaper reporter in Denver in 1886:

> Shortly after I came out here the second time we were camped on the very creek where I live now – Battle Creek, Snake River we called it then – and there we had a lively fight with a party of about 500 Sioux, Cheyenne and Arapahoes. The Arapahoes didn't do so much fighting, but they urged the others on. There were twenty-three in our party, and I can give you the names of every one of them. Old Frapp [Fraeb] was in command. The Indians made about forty charges on us, coming up within ten to fifteen paces of us every time. Their object was to draw our fire, but Old Frapp kept shouting, "Don't shoot till you're sure! One at a time!" And so some of us kept loaded all the time.
>
> We made breastworks of our horses and hid behind stumps. Old Frapp was killed . . . and when the fighting was over there were about a hundred dead Indians. There were three of our party killed.[5]

Baker was modest in relating the story of the battle in which he was a hero. After the death of Fraeb, he sprang to the front, took command, and began giving orders. He kept half of the rifles in action while the other half were reloading. The fight ended when the princess had her horse shot out from under her. This seemed to strike terror in the hearts of the red men and they retreated under cover of darkness, which gave the trappers a chance to abandon their fortified hill. They made a hurried departure for Bridger's camp on the Green River, arriving there on the 27th of August, 1841.[6]

---

[4] Brewster manuscript.

[5] *Denver Tribune-Republican,* July 10, 1886.

[6] Brewster manuscript.

During the years 1841 to 1846 Baker was engaged in trapping on various streams and was associated with the Bannock Indians, who were on friendly terms with the white trappers. Baker became attached to these Shoshones and was adopted into their tribe in 1847; he was referred to as the "Red Headed Shoshone." He took an active part in all of their sports and accompanied the braves on their hunts. He was quick to adopt the habits and customs of the Shoshones and adhered to their superstitions, believing in the miraculous cures of the medicine men.[7]

In the fall of 1847, Baker accompanied the braves of his adopted tribe on a buffalo hunt, leaving the squaws, children, and the chief behind. When the party left the camp the women stood waving good-bye, wishing them a good hunt. The daughter of the chief seemed to direct all her good wishes to Baker.

While the braves and Baker were away on the hunt the Shoshone camp was attacked by Blackfeet, who carried away the chief's daughter and others as captives. After the Shoshone hunters returned they organized a pursuit party, including Baker. He played the leading role in a successful rescue and won the princess as wife.[8]

Baker lived in the Shoshone village for two years with his wife, carrying on trapping activities. But the fur trade had declined with the advent of the silk hat.

Baker is said to have been one of a party of Kit Carson men who went on a final trapping excursion in 1852. Upon his return to his Shoshone home he found that his wife, Marina, had died during his absence. He became depressed and moved about from place to place.

One time while he was setting traps along the Grand River with Jim Bridger, they came upon two young grizzly bears.

[7] *Ibid.*

[8] The story, with detailed elaborations, including the chief's words in the marriage ceremony, is told in the fictional account prepared by Brewster, cited above.

Baker suggested: "Let's pitch in and skulp the varmints with our knives. It would be a trick worth telling about." The two men rushed in toward the bears. Baker circled around his beast trying to get behind it, but the bear kept turning with him and finally rushed in for a clinch. Jim thrust his long knife under the ribs of the grizzly and it went down. In the meantime, his trapper friend was not doing so well with his bear. He yelled to Baker for help, then ran away from the scene, leaving his friend with the second bear. This one rushed in with a terrific blow, tearing the shirt and arm of Baker, and the two finally went into a clinch. A wrestling match ensued; first Baker and then the bear seemed to be winning. Finally Jim was able to thrust his knife into a vital spot and the second grizzly went down. Baker firmly resolved to "never fight narry nother grizzly without a good shootin-iron in his paws." [9]

Jim could speak several Indian dialects and his services were valuable to any expedition among the red men. He was an interpreter and guide for Captain Randolph B. Marcy on his march to Fort Union, New Mexico, to procure reenforcements for Johnston's army bound for Utah. They left Bridger's Fort on November 24, 1857, and took a direct course over mountain ranges where they encountered deep snow. It was necessary for the men to go ahead of the animals and break the trail through the heavy drifts. They had to kill some of their animals for food, and by New Year's Day of 1858 they were in a serious predicament. The men's clothes had worn out and their food supply was low, but finally they reached Fort Massachusetts, in the San Luis Valley of Colorado.

When they reached Taos, New Mexico, Baker "cast aside his leggins, moccasins, and other mountain gear, and adopted a civilized wardrobe." Later, when he met Marcy,

---

[9] As told by Baker to Capt. R. B. Marcy in 1858. See Marcy, *Thirty Years of Army Life on the Border* (New York, 1866), 409.

he said, "Confound these yere store butes, Cap.; they choke
my feet like hell." [10] It was the first time in twenty years that
he had worn anything but moccasins upon his feet, and they
were not prepared for the severe torture.

The Marcy expedition, including Baker, eventually
reached Fort Union, then made the return trip to Fort
Bridger, reaching there on June 8, 1858.

Baker's next venture was in a business he established on
the Mormon Trail at the Green River crossing. He established a small trading post where he did a good business
with the Indians and the passing emigrants. A Frenchman
arrived and set up a rival post. Baker became incensed over
the competition and challenged the Frenchman to a duel.
Both men started drinking. They would appear in their
cabin doors, fire their revolvers, then go back and drink
more between each round of shots. They became so intox-
icated that they were rendered harmless.

Captain Marcy, returning from Utah, met Baker here and
inquired the cause of the disturbance. "He replied, 'That
thar yaller-bellied toad-eatin *parlyvoo* over thar and me,
we've been havin a small exchange of a skrimmage today,
we have, Cap.' I remonstrated with him upon his folly, but
he continued: 'The sneakin polecat, I'll raise his har yet.
I'll skulp him, Cap., ef he don't quit these yeare diggins.'" [11]
The next morning Baker felt better and expressed regret at
what had transpired.

Baker settled in Colorado during the gold rush of 1859
and pre-empted the northwest quarter of Section 18,
Township 3 S., R. 68 W. on June 3, 1859, and proved up
on the land under the Homestead Act. He officially filed
on December 3, 1863.[12] He built an adobe house at what is
now West 53rd Avenue and Tennyson Street in Denver, at

---

[10] *Ibid.*, 406.   [11] *Ibid.*, 410-11.
[12] Application no. 96, Homestead Certificate no. 102, Denver City, Colorado, May
30, 1862. Vol. I, p. 109, U.S. Certificate Land Office.

a point where an old road to Boulder crossed the stream. The dwelling was located on a high grassy hill with a commanding view of the surrounding country. The ford at Clear Creek came to be known as Baker's Crossing. During the spring run-off in 1859, Clear Creek became high and deep, so that the crossing was dangerous. Baker built and operated a toll bridge over the stream and ran a small store in connection with the enterprise.[13]

In the pioneer Denver newspaper, Baker advertised as follows: "The undersigned keeps a ranch for all descriptions of stock – cattle or horses – on Vasquers Fork [Clear Creek] 4 mi. from Auraria [Denver]. Charges reasonable. James Baker." [14]

In the fall of 1865 Baker went to Middle Park, Colorado, as guide and interpreter for D. C. Oakes, Agent to the Ute Indians.[15] Oakes praised Baker as guide, and a warm friendship developed between the two men that continued throughout life.

In the middle sixties a near-fatal accident befell Baker. The *Colorado Tribune* of June 19, 1867, reported: "Jim Baker, the old Indian interpreter, mountaineer, and trapper, met with a very serious and perhaps fatal accident at the Ute camp on Cherry Creek." Baker was brought to Denver, was treated, and recovered; but an ugly scar thereafter marred the side of his face.

The *Colorado Chieftain* of Pueblo, Colorado, ran this story in its issue of September 5, 1872:

> Jim Baker, an old pioneer hunter and trapper is in town, accompanying as guide a railroad surveying party, that one going through to Salt Lake. He is a Missourian by birth and in company with Capt. Bridger and one or two others came to the Rocky Mountains in 1838, and for 20 years led a roving life, common to trappers and Indian traders, operating from the British possessions as far south as Santa Fe,

13 An old account book gives detailed expenses of operating the toll bridge.
14 *Rocky Mountain News*, June 18, 1859, and subsequent issues.
15 *Ibid.*, Jan. 26, 1866.

but is now settled on a farm situated on Clear Creek four miles from
Denver. An account of his hair breadth escapes from Mexicans and
Indians would fill a large book, and although covered with scars from
wounds received while a trader, yet he is now at an advanced age and
more robust than many men at 25.

Baker began to chafe under the pressure of civilization
and the encroachment of settlers, for he had lived too long
in the open country to be crowded; he wanted "elbow room."
He disposed of his land on Clear Creek to Louis Ramboz
on May 15, 1873, and moved to the valley of the Little
Snake River, on the Colorado-Wyoming border, where he
built a fortified home constructed of logs.[16] Here, at Dixon,
Wyoming, he rehearsed the years and the hardships of his
romantic past.

James Baker was a man of outstanding qualities, loyal and
trustworthy. He had been an excellent guide, scout, and
trapper, and had played an important role in the West.
Frank Hall, early Colorado state official and historian,
called him "kind-hearted, honest, and reliable." [17] Charles
E. Young said his "heart was as large as an American bison
and as tender as a child." [18]

Baker was as rugged as the mountains where he had spent
most of his life. His wrinkled face and forehead contained
lines chiseled by nature; his many adventures were clearly
written on his bronzed features. Truly he was a man of the
mountains.

The career of James Baker came to a peaceful end on
May 15, 1898, and he was laid to rest in a small burial plot

---

[16] This two-story house, 16 by 31 feet in size, was moved to Frontier Park, Cheyenne, Wyoming, in 1917, where it is preserved as a monument to Jim Baker.

[17] Frank Hall, *History of the State of Colorado* (Chicago, 1889), I, p. 150.

[18] Charles E. Young, *Dangers of the Trail in 1865* (Geneva, N.Y., 1912), 103. Baker's son Joseph wrote a very undependable biographical sketch of his father which he ends thus: "I, being a halfbreed Shoshone Indian and my age is 73 years old. From our family of 14 children only three girls and myself remain." This sketch is reproduced in Mumey, *Life of Jim Baker,* 203-24.

about one mile from Savery, Wyoming, across the road from his cabin. A simple board marks the last rendezvous of this great Mountain Man. The light falling on it creates shadows of a pattern that extend toward the rugged mountain peaks where he spent the greater part of his nomadic life.

Henry A. Boller

by RAY H. MATTISON
State Historical Society of North Dakota

Best known for his narrative, *Among the Indians: Eight Years in the Far West, 1858-1866,* originally published in Philadelphia in 1867, Henry A. Boller was a clerk with an "opposition outfit" in the late period of the fur trade. Unlike most of the fur traders, young Boller was reared in an atmosphere of comparative luxury and refinement. The son of a prosperous importer, he was born in Philadelphia on August 17, 1836. As a boy he was an avid reader of stories of adventure. He was particularly fascinated by stories of pioneers and trappers, of which he never tired.[1] At an early age he acquired a book by the artist George Catlin which appears to have influenced greatly his attitude toward Indians.

Young Boller entered the University of Pennsylvania as a member of the graduating class of 1856. Indifferent to college pursuits and a career in his father's business, he longed to travel to distant lands. In the spring of 1857, after quitting college in his senior year, he wrote his father asking permission to go to India or China.[2] In June of that year, instead, he and his father visited St. Louis, presumably with the view of exploring the possibilities of entering the fur trade. (A portrait of Boller, at about this period, appears herein at page 13.)

In the spring of 1858, young Boller, traveling alone, was again in St. Louis. While there he obtained a position as clerk with Frost, Todd and Company, a newly-organized

---

[1] Henry A. Boller, letter to father, March 3, 1857. MS., State Historical Society of North Dakota; hereafter abbreviated SHSND. [2] *Ibid.*

firm that had the financial backing of the wealthy merchant Robert Campbell, and was opposing the monopolistic Upper Missouri Outfit.[3] In May, he began his voyage up the Missouri in the "Twilight," a steamboat leased by Boller's employers. In late June, he arrived at Like-a-Fishook Village, occupied by the Arikara and Gros Ventre (Hidatsa), where the new company was to establish a post, known as Fort Atkinson. This was to oppose the Upper Missouri Outfit's establishment, Fort Berthold, several hundred yards distant. There Boller was to spend two years as clerk, and act at times as *bourgeois* of the post. In the two years while stationed at Fort Atkinson, Boller kept up a prolific correspondence with his well-to-do family in Philadelphia. Literary and very articulate, with a flare for dramatizing events, we wrote letters full of information on the life of the fur traders and Indians at the isolated posts on the Upper Missouri. Unlike most white traders, Boller drank little or none, read his Sunday Services regularly and never "froze" to an Indian woman, although he had "several proposals." [4]

For two years, Frost, Todd and Company stubbornly competed with the Upper Missouri Outfit. In June of 1860, Boller wrote his father: "The two companies have this year consolidated and it is high time, for so hot & reckless has been the competition for the past 4 years, that money has been lost annually." [5] Frost, Todd and Company dissolved by mutual agreement, leaving the business on the Upper Missouri to Clark, Primeau and Company, its subsidiary.[6]

In the summer of 1860, Boller returned to St. Louis with the intention of returning to his eastern home. While in the office of Robert Campbell, he met the well-known Charles

[3] John E. Sunder, *The Fur Trade on the Upper Missouri, 1840-1865* (Norman, Okla., 1965), 200-208.

[4] Ray H. Mattison, ed., "Henry A. Boller: Upper Missouri Fur Trader – Letters, 1857-1860," *North Dakota History*, April, 1966.

[5] Boller, letter to father, June 18, 1860, SHSND.   [6] Sunder, *loc. cit.*

Larpenteur, who, temporarily unemployed, wished to continue in the fur business. Instead of returning to the East, Boller joined a new opposition firm, known as Larpenteur, Smith and Company, which was formed in July, 1860. The partnership was formed of Larpenteur, the veteran trader, Jefferson Smith, and young Boller. For the new company, Boller raised $2,000 from his wealthy father, Smith contributed $4,000, and Larpenteur received financial support from Campbell. Another person who took part in the venture was Robert Lemon, a clerk in Campbell's St. Louis office. Traveling overland, the partners established two posts on the Upper Missouri: one at Poplar River, which was operated by Larpenteur and Lemon; the other, managed by Smith and Boller, near the Upper Missouri Outfit's post of Fort Berthold.[7]

Internal dissension was almost to destroy the new company within less than a year. Larpenteur, a veteran of twenty-five years in the fur trade, apparently took a superior attitude toward Boller, whom he characterized as "a young blatherskite" who "had been but two years in the country," and who "took it on himself to write long letters from Berthold about what I was to do and not to do, and, above all, warned me not to be extravagent in building – as though I had just come into the country." [8] The partnership seems to have been undermined from the start by the suspicions which each partner bore toward the other. In the spring of 1861, after the four had returned to St. Louis with their returns, Smith withdrew from the partnership. Boller was allowed to retain a small share in the newly-organized one, dominated by Larpenteur and Lemon, under the condition that he remain away from the Upper Missouri.[9]

---

[7] Elliott Coues, ed., *Forty Years a Fur Trader: The Personal Narrative of Charles Larpenteur, 1833-1872* (Minneapolis, 1962), II, pp. 309-10.

[8] *Ibid.,* 320, 321-22.

[9] Milo M. Quaife, ed., *Among the Indians: Eight Years in the Far West, 1858-1866,* by Henry A. Boller (Chicago, 1959), xxvi.

Following his fur-trading venture, Boller appears to have returned to Philadelphia. In May, 1863, he set out for the newly-discovered Montana gold field, where he remained less than a year, then returned to Philadelphia. In May, 1864, he again departed for Montana, where he remained for two years, during which period he visited California (in 1866) to obtain horses for the Montana market. In July of that year he returned to the East, and in November he married his fiancee of three years, Mary Parsons.[10]

About this time Boller wrote, perhaps with the help of his wife, *Among the Indians,* its contents closely following the daily "Journals" or diaries which he kept during his stay in the Indian country and the letters which he wrote to his family. The book was apparently published in 1867.[11]

In the following year, the family removed to Junction City, Kansas, where Boller became a cattleman. There they remained for ten years. In June, 1878, Boller removed to Denver, Colorado, where he remained the rest of his days. While there, he was engaged in various occupations which included insurance, real estate, investments and loans, and finally the mining business.[12]

In 1898, Boller was visited by Dr. Elliott Coues, editor of various journals relating to the history of the Upper Missouri. Coues, promising he would secure its publication, urged Boller to revise his *Among the Indians,* to which the former trader agreed. Boller had only begun this revision when Coues died, late in the following year. At the time of his own death, November 1, 1902, Boller had completed most of the revision of his book. Following her husband's death, Mrs. Boller endeavored without success to complete and publish the revised edition. In this connection, Mrs. Boller deposited her husband's letters, together with his

---

10 *Ibid.,* xxvii-xxviii.
11 Quaife, *op. cit.,* xxviii-xxix.   12 *Ibid.,* xxx-xxxi.

journals, with the State Historical Society of North Dakota, with the understanding that Professor O. G. Libby, of the University of North Dakota, would undertake the publication of the revised edition. Unfortunately, the publication of this was never accomplished. It was not until 1959 that a reprint of *Among the Indians,* with Dr. Milo M. Quaife as editor, was published as one of the Lakeside Classics.[13]

[13] Henry A. and Mary Boller Correspondence, MS., SHSND.

Michel Bourdon

by MERLE WELLS
Idaho State Historical Society

Scarcely any information about the early career of Michel Bourdon is available. All the men who knew him are long since gone. Fur trade records referring to him are limited indeed. More than one French Canadian named Bourdon is listed in the North West Company roster of 1804, yet Michel is not among them.[1] Very likely he was too young to have worked for the company then, and any relationship between him and the several Bourdons listed cannot be ascertained. Worse still, variation in the spelling of his name confuses the matter. Even in later years it sometimes came out "Bourdeaux" or something else only generally similar to "Bourdon." David Thompson, moreover, had an interpreter in the service of the North West Company on the upper Columbia whom he called Michel Bourdeaux, or even Michael Beaurdeau.[2] Thompson's Michel Bourdeaux reached the Pacific Northwest at least as early as 1809, and was on hand when Thompson built permanent fur trade posts on Lake Pend d'Oreille (in present Idaho) and on Clark's Fork (in present Montana) that fall.[3]

In July, 1810, Michel Bourdeaux went out with Finnan MacDonald and 150 Flatheads eastward across the continental divide to hunt buffalo on the great plains. There he engaged in a ferocious day-long battle with a slightly larger

[1] L. R. Masson, *Les Bourgeois de la Compagnie du Nord-Ouest* (Quebec, 1889), I, pp. 401, 412.

[2] Thompson Coit Elliott, ed., "Journal of David Thompson," *Oregon Historical Quarterly* (March 1914), xv, p. 43; J. B. Tyrrell, ed., *David Thompson's Narrative of his Expeditions in Western America, 1784-1812* (Toronto, 1916), 424.

[3] M. C. White, ed., *David Thompson's Journals Relating to Montana and Adjacent Regions, 1808-1812* (Missoula, 1950), 75.

Blackfoot band that resented this open Flathead intrusion. With the help of the trappers, the Flatheads resisted the Blackfeet successfully.[4] Later, after going down the Columbia to Astoria in the summer of 1811, Bourdeaux showed up again in the Flathead country.[5] When the Flatheads and the Blackfeet held an impressive, but unproductive, peace conference, February 29, 1812, Michel Bourdeaux served as interpreter for David Thompson, who participated in the conclave.[6] Then, after Thompson departed from the Pacific Northwest for the last time, Bourdeaux set out with MacDonald and the Flatheads on another plains buffalo hunt east of the Rockies, in August, 1812.

Returning from the 1812 buffalo hunt (and another battle with the Blackfeet), Michel Bourdon appears to have spent the next several years as a freeman with his Flathead friends. At least he was engaged, July 27, 1813, for a two-year term as an interpreter for the North West Company's post among the Flatheads.[7] Perhaps he continued there until Donald Mackenzie came back to the Pacific Northwest to reorganize the upper Columbia and Snake country fur trade in 1816.

In any event, by the time of the consolidation of the two great British fur trade rivals – the North West Company

---

[4] Tyrrell, 424-25; White, 210-11.

[5] Lynn M. Barrett, "McKenzie, McDonald, and Ross in the Snake River Country" (M.A. thesis, University of California, 1925), 127.

[6] Tyrrell, 546-47; White, 208.

[7] The way David Thompson remembered the story when he wrote his narrative some thirty or forty years later, Bordeaux had the misfortune not to survive the 1812 battle with the Blackfeet. On this point Thompson is in error. The Michel Bordeau who was hired as Flathead interpreter, July 27, 1813, clearly is Thompson's Flathead interpreter, Michael Bourdeaux. Thompson obviously confused the 1812 engagement with yet another clash with the Blackfeet in 1823, and simply recalled the wrong date for the Bourdeaux calamity. In a short biographical note (*Peter Skene Ogden's Snake Country Journal, 1826-27* [London: Hudson's Bay Record Society, 1961], 92), K. G. Davies and A. M. Johnson quite reasonably identify Michel Bourdon who led the 1822 Snake expedition, with Michel Bordeau, the 1813 Flathead interpreter. The 1822 minutes of the Hudson's Bay Company Northern Department Council which assigned him to the Snake expedition, refer to him as "Michel Bordeau," thus confirming this identification.

and the Hudson's Bay Company – Michel Bourdon had become the most prominent French Canadian trapper in the Pacific Northwest. Identified by his superiors as a young man of unusual success, he came to a position of leadership beyond that ordinarily exercised by French Canadians in those British-led concerns.[8] Joining the Snake brigade which Donald MacKenzie led through the Snake River valley in 1818, Bourdon distinguished himself by exploring Bear River southward into Cache Valley, which he discovered in the 1818-1819 trapping season. There he named Little Bear River. British trappers, moreover, sometimes called Blacksmith River (which they regarded as the middle fork of the Little Bear) Bourdon's River.[9] Continuing to range over the interior Pacific Northwest with Donald Mackenzie's annual Snake expeditions, Bourdon gained experience sufficient that, in 1822 (after Mackenzie had moved on to a new assignment), he took over the Snake brigade and led the annual hunt for beaver that year.

Described by Alexander Ross (who was to lead the Snake expedition of 1824) as a motley crew of castoffs and Indians of dubious competence as trappers,[10] Michel Bourdon's Snake brigade had little hope to accomplish much in 1822. Most of the party – unlike Bourdon, who was employed in the service of the Hudson's Bay Company – were outfitted as freemen. In order to repay the cost of their horses and equipment supplied by the company, they were to bring in furs to settle their accounts at the end of the season. By 1822, regular company factors and traders had no interest in leading the Snake brigade after Mackenzie had left.[11] Having

[8] E. E. Rich, ed., *Peter Skene Ogden's Snake Country Journals, 1824-25 and 1825-26* (London, 1950), 40.   [9] *Ibid.,* 229, 232.

[10] Alexander Ross, *The Fur Hunters of the Far West* (Norman, Okla., 1956), 208-209; T. C. Elliott, ed., "Journal of Alexander Ross: Snake Country Expedition, 1824," *Oregon Historical Quarterly* (December 1913), 370.

[11] W. Kaye Lamb's introduction to *The Letters of John McLoughlin, . . . First Series, 1825-38,* ed. by E. E. Rich (Toronto, 1941), p. xxi.

Bourdon take out the expedition was conceived mainly as a means of keeping the trappers occupied and out of mischief. Accordingly, in a meeting at distant Norway House on Lake Winnipeg, July 8, the company council decided (pending a further reorganization of the Columbia River trade) to empower the management there "to engage in the capacity of a Conductor of Trappers, Michel Bordeau at the lowest rate for which he may agree." [12] So Bourdon set out on a decidedly difficult expedition that regular British officers of the company could not be persuaded to undertake.

From Spokane House he headed across later western Montana and southeastern Idaho. Perhaps he reached his Bear River and Cache Valley haunts again; certainly he got as far as Pierre's Hole. Before he got back, fourteen of his freemen (four of them old Astorians; the rest, Iroquois) deserted, in what proved to be a disastrous effort to take their catch down the Missouri for eventual sale at high Saint Louis prices. Caught short-handed, Bourdon had to cache 700 of his 2200 beaver, pending a return expedition to pick them up the next year.[13] Getting back to Spokane House, September 13, 1822, he had succeeded in preserving most of the leaderless array of otherwise superfluous trappers that Donald Mackenzie had gone to so much effort to organize into the Snake brigade.[14] Without Bourdon's enterprise, Mackenzie's system might have been abandoned.

As matters turned out, the company management, on the strength of "information received from Michel Bourdon

[12] R. Harvey Fleming, ed., *Minutes of Council Northern Department of Rupert Land, 1821-31* (Toronto, 1940), 24.

[13] Frederick Merk, ed., *Fur Trade and Empire: George Simpson's Journal* . . . *1824-25* (Cambridge, 1931), 193-94.

[14] Dale L. Morgan, *Jedediah Smith and the Opening of the West* (Indianapolis, 1953), 144-46. Morgan includes the text of a hitherto unpublished (except for a few phrases in Ogden's journal notes) account of Bourdon's 1822 expedition which is found in the Spokane House post journal, September 13, 1822. This report indicates that during Blackfoot skirmishes Bourdon lost two men.

last fall," was "induced to send a stronger Party along with the Freemen going to that Quarter [the Snake country] this Season [1823], in hopes of being able to get out all the Skins that may be procured there as a freemen when left to themselves become so indolent and careless, that often after they have been to the trouble of procuring Furs at the risk of their Lives, they are too lazy to come in with them and the Consequence is that their furs are either lost or damaged before they reach this place [Spokane House]." [15]

Six regular company servants, led by Finnan MacDonald, returned over Bourdon's 1822 route to recover Bourdon's cache and to trap for another season. This venture, however, proved to be a personal disaster for Michel Bourdon. In a battle with his old enemies, the Blackfeet, on Henry's Fork (in later southeastern Idaho), he was one of several casualties. In his own personal, inimitable presentation, Finnan MacDonald told the unfortunate story:

> We had Saviral Battils with the [Blackfoot] nasion on the other side of the Mountains Poore Meshel Bordoe was kild with 5 more of the Band there dath was revenge as well as we Could revenge it for no less than 68 of them that remane in the Planes as Pray for the wolves and those fue that askape our Shotes they had not a Britch Clout to Cover them selves we Shoe them what war was they will not be so radey to atack People.[16]

---

[15] Merk, 193.

[16] Fleming, 24. MacDonald's statement is part of a letter to J. G. McTavish, April 5, 1824. In his journal for June 7, 1825, Ogden (p. 58) identified the Bourdon battle site of 1823 as Henry's Fork. Of MacDonald's various fights with the Blackfeet in 1823, the major one (in which the Indians lost 68 men, partly by a fire set by MacDonald's forces) was on the Lemhi in a defile just west of Lemhi pass. Ross in his journal for April 29, 1824, describes the Lemhi site (which he passed that day) as "rendered immemorial as being the place where about ten Piegans [Blackfeet], murderers of our people [meaning Bourdon and four or five others in 1823], were burnt to death." This suggests that the Bourdon fiasco was earlier, and is consistent with Ogden's location for the earlier trouble on Henry's Fork. Years later, in *Fur Hunters*, 239, Ross indicated that the Lemhi battleground was the Bourdon site also, and possibly he was right. But Ogden's journal generally is much more reliable than the later recollections of Alexander Ross (as is to be expected anyway), and Ogden's Henry's Fork site is the more likely one.

MacDonald was right in his final observation. In 1824, and after, the Blackfeet showed much greater respect for British trappers. While not free from trouble, the Snake brigade suffered less in the way of losses after that. But the new Blackfoot attitude came too late to be of much help to Michel Bourdon.

John J. Burroughs

by JANET LECOMPTE
Colorado Springs, Colorado

John J. Burroughs was a happy Mountain Man, for he
was able to combine what most American trappers found
mutually exclusive – the freedom of a trapper's life and the
bondage of a wife and children.[1]

Burroughs was from Kentucky, which is the sum of our
knowledge about his early years. He first comes to notice as
a trapper on January 16, 1835, when he and others arrived
at Nathaniel Wyeth's Fort Hall on the Snake River and
were made welcome with a keg of alcohol.[2] According to
Osborne Russell, Burroughs and his friends were deserters
from James Bridger's Rocky Mountain Fur Company brigade wintering at the forks of the Snake River sixty miles
above Fort Hall. They had come to the fort for a job[3] and
were hired as trappers for the spring hunt under Joseph
Gale. In preparation for the hunt, Burroughs and five others
paid $5.85 apiece to the Indians for a lodge.[4]

The party left the fort on March 25, 1835, and waded
through deep snow to Cache Valley of the Bear River. For

---

[1] His name was often spelled "Burris" or "Burrows." He appears to have no
connection with the "E. Bure" or "Burroughs" who was a trapper with Ewing
Young in New Mexico (see T. M. Marshall, "St. Vrain's expedition to the Gila in
1826," *Southwest Historical Quarterly*, XIX, p. 254; J. J. Hill, "Ewing Young in the
Fur Trade of the Far Southwest, 1822-1834," *Oregon Historical Quarterly*, XXIV, pp.
28f) or with the William Burroughs who was in Oregon in 1841 with his Indian
wife ("Journal of William Dunlop Brackenridge," *California Historical Society
Quarterly*, XXIV, p. 321).

[2] Fort Hall account books, ledger no. 1, Library, Oregon Historical Society. Microfilm loaned to author by Richard G. Beidleman of Colorado Springs, whose article,
"Nathaniel Wyeth's Fort Hall," *Oregon Historical Quarterly*, LVIII, pp. 197f, should
be consulted for many names and events of the trappers' west.

[3] Osborne Russell, *Journal of a Trapper* (Boise, 1921), 15.

[4] Fort Hall account books, *loc. cit.*

a month or so they trapped, then camped at the outlet of Bear Lake with a village of Snake Indians at the end of April. In the middle of May, on Gardner's Fork of the Snake, they met James Bridger and his party, who warned them that Blackfeet infested the country. Gale decided to return to the fort, where he and his party arrived May 31.[5]

Because of the swollen streams, the trappers' catch was not impressive. Herring turned in twenty-six beaver, Dempsey twenty-one, Wade nine; Burroughs turned in fewest of all – eight beaver (worth $5 apiece) and one otter (worth $4) which hardly reimbursed him for the sundries he had bought from Joseph Gale's outfit while on the hunt, and for the $10 each trapper had to pay the camp keepers for guarding their horses. Anything left over from the proceeds of the hunt, the trappers spent prodigally at the Fort Hall store on rum, scotch caps, and other luxuries, including a fiddle for which Burroughs and fourteen others paid $1 apiece, stipulating that it was to be kept at Fort Hall until the owners returned from the fall hunt.[6]

If the spring hunt had been unprofitable, the fall hunt was no less than a disaster. John Burroughs was one of fourteen trappers and ten camp keepers who left Fort Hall in the middle of June, 1835, for Yellowstone Lake and the sources of the Missouri under the leadership, again, of Joseph Gale. Their troubles began on June 22, when Abram Patterson drowned in Snake River. On June 28, the trappers had a battle with the Blackfeet at the north end of Pierre's Hole during which Richard Owens and another man were wounded, three horses were killed and six captured. At the Gros Ventres fork of Wind River, their leader became lost and insisted that they were on a branch of the Yellowstone. Disgusted with Gale, seven trappers deserted, taking with them company traps, guns, and horses. At the end of July,

[5] Russell, *op. cit.*, 15-19.   [6] Fort Hall account books.

after floundering under their leader's confused direction for nearly a month, the trappers finally found the Yellowstone country, where they had the misfortune to lose Lewis Boseley, a hunter with thirty years' experience. They camped in Gardner's Hole on the Yellowstone until August 20, when they crossed over the mountains to the Gallatin. Here four more trappers and a camp keeper deserted as a result, according to Osborne Russell, of Joseph Gale's pig-headed tyrannies. The remainder of the party spent several weeks trapping at the sources of the Missouri.

On September 9, they were joined by fourteen trappers from Bridger's camp on Henry's Lake, twenty miles south of them, including Joe Meek and Kit Carson. On the morning of September 10, eight trappers went out to set their traps and were chased back to camp by about eighty Blackfeet. The trappers secured their horses and concealed themselves in the heavy brush around the campsite. For three hours the Indians fired from the top of the river bluffs and even set fire to the brush in which the trappers were hiding, but succeeded only in killing some of the animals.[7] The trappers were fortunate to emerge with their lives from this battle, but the loss of horses and previous death or desertion of their best trappers determined Gale to give up the hunt. He and his party arrived back at Fort Hall on October 15.[8] The most successful trapper of this dismal beaver hunt was John Burroughs, who turned in twenty beaver pelts for which his account was credited with $104. He was forced, however, to give up one of his skins to the company because he and Calvin Briggs had damaged a rifle at Bridger's camp.[9]

John Burroughs and his friends spent the fall of 1835

---

[7] Russell, *op. cit.*, 35-36; *Kit Carson's Own Story of His Life*, ed. Blanche C. Grant (Taos, 1926), 46; F. F. Victor, *The River of the West* (Hartford, 1870), 167f.

[8] Russell, *op. cit.*, 20-42.   [9] Fort Hall account books.

lounging around Fort Hall, waiting for Captain Wyeth to arrive from the Columbia. On October 31, Burroughs bought "¾ doz. gilt buttons," [10] a purchase which may have marked the beginning of his marriage to a Shoshone (Snake) woman whose name, according to George Simpson, was Susan.[11] The marriage was no ordinary one between an American trapper and an Indian woman, for it lasted, as far as we know, for the lifetime of each. Calvin Briggs, a Wyeth trapper from Vermont, married Susan's sister Sarah Ann, and for the next twenty years the two couples and their offspring camped and traveled together throughout the Rocky Mountains, providing a rare picture of familial harmony.[12]

On December 9, 1835, Captain Wyeth returned to Fort Hall and prepared to close out his business, although it was nearly two years before he actually sold the post to the Hudson's Bay Company. Fearing the fort would no longer employ them, on February 20, 1835, John Burroughs, Jonathan Woodman, George Ebberts, Caleb Wilkins, and Lemon Owens formed a partnership, bought $199.08 worth of goods, and went out to trap and trade. They returned on May 25, having lost Jonathan Woodman but gained mightily in peltry. Three horses had to be hired to bring in their beaver and about half of the goods they had originally bought. Their returns consisted of a hundred pounds of beaver at $5 per pound, ten otter at $5, and $32.50 worth of beaver castorum; the net profit to each man amounted to $110.95.

For the remainder of June, Burroughs stayed close to Fort Hall. On June 17 he brought in four beaver for a credit of $30 – but for some reason he decided at this point to give

---

[10] *Ibid.*

[11] Senex, [pseud. of George Simpson], "Pah-U-Tah," *Trinidad Daily News,* undated clipping, probably October or November, 1882, Dawson Scrapbook, I, p. 409, Colorado State Historical Society Library, Denver, Colo.

[12] See quotations from Simpson and Frémont, *infra.*

up his status of free trapper and engage himself again to the company. On June 23, he was credited with the price of a horse ($70), and five beaver traps ($1.30) which he had turned back to the company, and on June 30 he hired out to Fort Hall at a salary of $300 per annum. For the next year or so his purchases at the Fort Hall store were regular, indicating that he went on no more extended trapping trips. His wife lived with him at the post (probably in a lodge nearby), or so his purchase of January 23, 1837, would indicate – "1 hair cord for wife." Burroughs' account with Fort Hall was balanced and closed on August 8, 1837, when the Fort was turned over to the Hudson's Bay Company.[13]

It is probably John J. Burroughs who shows up two years later in the journals of two members of the Peoria party bound for Oregon. On August 2, 1839, while camped on the north fork of Bear River, the Oregonians were joined by two trappers and a squaw. One of the journalists calls the trappers Burns and Ward [14] or Burrows and Ward; [15] the other calls them Burris and Ward.[16] The trappers traveled with the Oregon emigrants for four days, during which they shot an elk, caught two beaver, and presented the emigrants with a pair of moccasins made by the squaw. On August 5th or 6th they parted, the emigrants proceeding to Brown's Hole and the trappers to the south fork of the Platte to meet Philip Thompson with goods brought from St. Louis.[17]

After this, Burroughs' career as a trapper becomes obscure and we see him only in a few vignettes of dubious authenticity but unmistakable purpose – to show him as a courageous man, and as a family man. George Simpson said

---

[13] Fort Hall account books.

[14] "Obadiah Oakley Journal," *To the Rockies and Oregon, 1839-1842,* eds. LeRoy R. and Ann W. Hafen (Glendale, Calif., 1955), 57.

[15] Oakley's original account, entitled "The Oregon Expedition" and published in the *Peoria Register and North-Western Gazetteer* of Nov. 9, 1839.

[16] "Sidney Smith Diary," *To the Rockies and Oregon, 1839-1842,* p. 76.

[17] "Obadiah Oakley Journal," *loc. cit.,* 56.

of Burroughs that his "coolness in danger and difficulties was proverbial." On one occasion, somewhere near Fort Hall, Burroughs, Kit Carson and another man stood off three hundred Blackfeet, killing nineteen including the chief.[18] (Kit Carson, however, mentions several battles with the Blackfeet in his autobiography, but none that fits this exploit.)[19]

Dick Wootton tells another story that bolsters Burroughs' reputation for bravery. One day Burroughs and Dick Owens were out hunting when they unexpectedly came upon a grizzly bear. Both shot, both missed, and the bear charged them. They ran for the nearest tree, a small bushy cedar. Owens managed to climb to the top of the tree, but Burroughs had hardly cleared the ground when the bear caught him by the foot and dragged him back. Being a man "of rare presence of mind," Burroughs dropped to the ground and lay perfectly still until the bear stopped mauling him and left him for dead. The bear then went after Owens in the tree. While Owens fought the brute in hand-to-hand battle, the badly-wounded Burroughs managed to reach his rifle, reload it, and shoot the bear without harming his companion. Both Burroughs and Owens were crippled for life by the encounter, and but for Burroughs' coolness, would have been killed.[20]

George Simpson and Dick Wootton were both impressed by Burroughs' bravery, but they were no less impressed by his pleasant family life, a far rarer thing than bravery in the wilderness. On his way to summer rendezvous with Bill Williams, Calvin Briggs, Lew Anderson and Charles Kinney, Simpson says he met Burroughs and "Frappe" (Henry Fraeb) on the Portneuf River near Fort Hall, where Burroughs had been employed since early in the spring:

[18] Senex [George Simpson], "Pah-U-Tah," *loc. cit.,* 409.
[19] *Kit Carson's Own Story,* cited.
[20] H. L. Conard, *"Uncle Dick" Wootton* (Chicago, 1890), 160-62.

With Briggs, the meeting with his partner was a red letter day, at least he said it was, or something like it, for he was also reunited with his Sarah Ann, who, like Burroughs' Susan, had been having a "high old time" with her people, the Shoshones.

With four women in camp, the labor that would have fallen on two was much lightened, as it was their province to cut up the meat, build the scaffolds upon which it was sun-dried and pack it in *parfleches* for the convenience of transportation and for preservation.[21]

Simpson tells the incident as though he were there, but in fact he was not.[22] The picture of Burroughs, Briggs, and their wives is probably accurate enough, however, for Simpson knew them well in later years at Pueblo and Hardscrabble.

Dick Wootton, another raconteur who, like Simpson, is more noted for the gusto than the accuracy of his stories, describes a trapping party of seventeen men, including Burroughs and Briggs, which left Bent's Fort in June, 1837, trapped the Rio Grande, the Arkansas, and "pretty much all the streams of Colorado and Wyoming," and wintered in Wyoming. Wootton's date, of course, is in error, for Burroughs was then at Fort Hall, but his picture of the Burroughs-Briggs families is undoubtedly a true one:

We had two men in the party, one by the name of Briggs and another named Burris, who were in partnership. These men were brothers-in-law, they having married two Indian women belonging to the "snake" tribe who were sisters.

These two squaws shared the hardships of the trip, traveling along with the party. They did the cooking for their husbands, mended their moccasins and clothes, and took care of themselves quite as well as any of the men. Both Briggs and Burris, with their squaw wives, afterwards went to California, and settled in the neighborhood of Sacramento, where they became very wealthy.[23]

21 Senex [George Simpson] "Pah-U-Tah," *loc. cit.*

22 Simpson testified that he did not come west until 1841, and he accounts for his movements of the summer of 1841 in such a way as to preclude any adventure on the Portneuf (and the last rendezvous was held in 1840). Since Fraeb was killed in August, 1841, the incident had to have occurred before that time.

23 Conard, *op. cit.,* 55.

Another charming picture of a camp of free trappers with their Indian families, which probably included Burroughs and Briggs, is given by J. C. Fremont in July, 1842:

> Seven miles further brought us to a camp of some four or five whites, (New Englanders, I believe,) who had accompanied Captain Wyeth to the Columbia river, and were independent trappers. All had their squaws with them, and I was really surprised at the number of little fat buffalo-fed boys that were tumbling about the camp, all apparently of the same age, about three or four years old. They were encamped on a rich bottom, covered with a profusion of fine grass, and had a large number of fine-looking horses and mules.[24]

At the decline of the fur trade, Burroughs and Briggs turned to farming and stock raising at the Pueblo and Hardscrabble settlements on the Arkansas.[25] In the early summer of 1849 they went with others to California and settled near Sacramento, where Burroughs became a rancher, a very wealthy one according to Wootton.[26] In 1853, Burroughs – ever the family man – decided his children were not being properly educated in this raw new land. Taking his Indian wife and half-breed children, he returned to his old home in Kentucky, and his friends in the West heard of him no more.[27]

---

[24] Brevet Captain J. C. Fremont, *Report of the Exploring Expedition to the Rocky Mountains in the year 1842.* . . . (Washington, D.C., 1845), 30.

[25] See article on Calvin Briggs, this work, for more details of Burroughs' life at these settlements.

[26] Conard, *op. cit.*, 55, 160.

[27] John Brown, *Mediumistic Experiences of John Brown, the Medium of the Rockies* (San Francisco, 1879), 47.

Richard Campbell

by JOHN E. BAUR
Los Angeles, California

Little is known of the early life of Richard Campbell. He was probably born before 1800. By 1827, Campbell was active in Santa Fe. According to M. de Morineau, who was in California in January, 1828, Campbell had led a party of seventeen men from New Orleans to California the previous year. They had arrived in San Francisco to hunt beaver and eventually sold five hundred skins to a Russian ship, bought horses, and returned by their same route.[1]

Alice Bay Maloney, who has made a very careful study of the records, has demonstrated that Campbell was a Catholic, for, according to a document in the probate papers of Ewing Young's estate in Oregon, he is said to have been one, and because he was also a godparent to a Catholic child in New Mexico.[2]

In 1852, Lt. James H. Simpson reported that Campbell in Santa Fe had told him that in 1827 the overland party to California had consisted of thirty-five men and several pack animals and had traveled from New Mexico to San Diego *via* Zuñi and found no difficulties en route.[3] Campbell had been guided by a Mexican named "Carravahal," a native of San Ysidro pueblo. It may be assumed that, west of Zuñi, Campbell descended the Gila and crossed the Colorado at Yuma, perhaps achieving the first arrival of Americans in California from New Mexico by way of Arizona.

---

1 Hubert Howe Bancroft, "Pioneer Register," in *History of California* (San Francisco, 1886), II, p. 740.

2 Alice Bay Maloney, "The Richard Campbell Party of 1827," *California Historical Society Quarterly* (San Francisco), XVIII (December, 1939), 347-54.

3 James H. Simpson, *Journal of a Military Reconnaissance from Santa Fe, New Mexico, to the Navajo Country* (Philadelphia, 1852), 124-25.

About 1832, Albert Pike joined an expedition to trap in the Comanche country at the heads of the Red and Washita rivers. He bought an outfit from a "Mr. Campbell," probably Richard Campbell, and from Taos, Campbell accompanied Pike and his party, of which Campbell and Pike were the only Americans, to the Bosque Redondo region, but on September 20 Campbell turned back to Taos. The trip had been handicapped by a gathering of hostile Comanches and Kiowas in the hunting area.[4]

By the 1850s, Campbell's trapping days were long over. In Doña Ana County, New Mexico, at that time, the first presiding judge of the probate court was one Richard Campbell, probably the same as above. According to Edward D. Tittman, who studied the records of his court, Campbell was an educated man but could not spell well. His handwriting caused Tittman to assume that he was rather elderly, which probably was not the case. Certainly his activities as judge showed that he was a man of courage, who believed in justice, but was forced by the circumstances of that frontier area to become an autocrat. A fee granted him for bringing in an outlaw seems to indicate that he had previously been a sheriff. Richard Campbell died in New Mexico in February of 1860.[5]

[4] Albert Pike, "Narrative of a Journey in the Prairie," *Publications* of the Arkansas Historical Association (Conway) IV (1917), 94-99.

[5] Edward D. Tittman, "By Order of Richard Campbell," *New Mexico Historical Review* (Albuquerque) III (October, 1928), 390-98. Alice B. Maloney gives credence to the claim that this judge was the famous trapper of 1827.

Joseph Dickson

by FRANK H. DICKSON *
Seal Beach, California

The first trappers encountered by the Lewis and Clark Expedition on its return voyage down the Missouri River in 1806 were Joseph Dickson and Forest Hancock. Little has been known or published about these pioneer American traders in the upper Missouri country.

Joseph Dickson, of Scotch ancestry (the name sometimes given the English spelling of Dixon), was born January 13, 1775. His son Col. Joseph Harrison Dickson (who served in the Black Hawk War) writes: "My parents were natives of Pennsylvania, and emigrated to and settled in St. Clair County, Illinois, in the the year 1802." [1] They evidently had stopped for a time in Tennessee, since one of their children was born there. The parents, Joseph and Susan Dickson, with two children, went to Cahokia, on the east bank of the Mississippi, opposite St. Louis. They settled at nearby Turkey Hill with other American families, on what became known as American Bottom.

Joseph Dickson took up trapping and was known as a "free trapper," in that hazardous occupation of the untamed and Indian-infested backwoods of America.

Soon after Dickson's arrival at the American Bottom he found his way up the lower Missouri River to the Gasconade River where he cut timber and trapped until the spring of 1803. He was frequently absent from home on long hunting

---

* Mr. Dickson is a great-great-grandson of Joseph Dickson. – Ed.

[1] Wisconsin *Collections*. Personal Narratives, v, pp. 315-17; C. W. Butterfield, *History of Grant County, Wisconsin* (Madison, 1881), 553.

trips, usually alone, and bagged much peltry which he sold to St. Louis fur houses.[2]

While Joseph Dickson was of that bold and hardy race of Scotch-Irish who were always plunging into the wilderness as the leaders of the white advance, he was also interested in community affairs. Although a trapper all of his days, Joseph wanted land and permanency for his family, which ultimately included nine children who reached adulthood. Trapping was seasonal, and furs had to be taken during the cold months when prime. Cash to purchase a half-section of land was difficult to obtain, even at the low price of $1.25 per acre.

There was talk in St. Louis about the possibilities for enormous profits from furs obtained on the upper Missouri. Canoes loaded with pelts coming downstream destined for St. Louis traders could be seen frequently. When Meriwether Lewis and William Clark arrived in the fall of 1803 and announced their intention to ascend the Missouri and cross over the Rockies, Joseph's mind was made up. He would follow in the wake of Lewis and Clark. He would "make a fortune" and buy land.

Early in the spring of 1804, Dickson interested another free trapper, Forest Hancock, in his plans. Together they worked many weeks gouging out a large cottonwood log into a pirogue. Supplies sufficient for two years were secured. Joseph moved his family to Shiloh, some ten miles inland, for reasons unknown today. The Lewis and Clark Expedition left St. Louis in May, 1804. By the following August, Dickson and Hancock were headed upstream on what has been known in history for more than a century as the fourth expedition of white men to the Yellowstone River.[3]

[2] Brink, McDonough & Co., *History of St. Clair County, Illinois* (Philadelphia, 1881), 242; James Leaton, *History of Methodism in Illinois* (Cincinnati, 1883), I, pp. 168-69.

[3] Burton Harris, *John Colter: His Years in the Rockies* (New York, 1952), 42.

These men from Illinois were experienced canoemen on the lower Missouri. Soon they were crossing the yellow waters of the Osage River and in a few days would enter the upper Missouri at the mouth of Platte River. Some place not far beyond the wind-blown hills where Sergeant Floyd was buried they stopped. Here they prepared their first winter-quarters by digging a cave on the sunny side of a hill. They trapped successfully that first winter, but their furs were stolen. The year 1805 was to bring more disappointment. The fierce Teton Sioux Indians blocked their passage. For safety the two joined a trader named Ceautoin, but still they were ambushed and robbed of their furs. Dickson was wounded by an arrow during the winter. Two or three Indians were killed.[4] The white men were fortunate to escape alive.

In the spring of 1806, both men breathed easier as they continued upstream with the dreaded Sioux left behind. The canoe glided noiselessly past friendly Arikaras. At the Mandan towns they were kindly treated. When far upstream, near the mouth of Yellowstone River, they had a pleasant experience. They met, on August 11, a canoe bearing Captain Clark returning from the Pacific.[5] Clark directed the trappers to the best beaver country and gave them powder and lead. The next day they met Captain Lewis. Until that time neither captain knew whether he was ahead of or behind the other.

Shortly after the meeting with Lewis, two of Clark's lost hunters arrived. One of these was John Colter who, it is believed, recognized Dickson from the winter at Wood River.[6] He was interested in the plans of the trappers but

[4] Peter Cartwright, *The Backwoods Preacher: An Autobiography of Peter Cartwright,* ed. by W. P. Strickland (New York, 1857), 254-57.

[5] Meriwether Lewis, *The Lewis and Clark Expedition* (Philadelphia and New York, 1961), III, p. 772.

[6] Dickson family tradition. Although this narrator has no recollection of John Colter's name being mentioned as the person aided by Dickson, the circumstances

thought their supplies were inadequate. At this time Lewis ordered an advance to overtake Clark. Colter wanted to talk more and suggested the men accompany the party to the Mandans. With Lewis's permission all departed downstream together. During the two-day trip Colter convinced both men of their need for more traps, tools for building canoes, a two-year supply of ammunition, and other items. He thought he could persuade the officers to sell to him the items needed if he could obtain his discharge and join the trappers. Dickson and Hancock must have been amazed at this proposal, because Colter was not a trapper.

The position of these men at the time was a great asset. They were within a few weeks' journey of the richest beaver streams in the Rockies and the fall season was almost upon them. They couldn't afford to turn back now. Colter would be their guide and share equally in the earnings. The combined party arrived at a Minnetarees village on August 14. That evening Colter made his request to the captains,[7] received their permission to join Dickson and Hancock, and the next day the three headed upstream.

Exactly where the trio finally stopped is not known. Family tradition says it was beyond Powder River. Some have suggested the Bighorn River, where Clark said the beaver country begins. Still others, including this narrator, believe the party reached Clark's Fork canyon.

Where these men ultimately halted is not so important as what happened that winter. There has been much speculation about this. Ridiculous assumptions about the acts of the men have appeared in various publications. Some writers have tried to dismiss the matter as an unimportant chance meeting.

point to Colter, since he is known to have been subjected to disciplinary action on account of his frequenting Cahokia taverns. (Received verbally in the fall of 1912).

[7] Lewis, op. cit., III, p. 778.

Theodore Roosevelt, in his *Winning of the West*,[8] apparently sensed that John Colter was unhappy and probably absented himself from the group temporarily during the winter. Actually the men had scarcely arrived when Colter deserted Dickson and persuaded Hancock to do the same. He had precipitated a quarrel with Dickson. In the settlement made between them Dickson got most of the supplies. Colter and Hancock purchased a canoe from the Indians[9] and began their trip downstream, probably in October, but certainly before ice formed in the river. The next summer Colter, traveling downstream alone, was met by Manuel Lisa at the mouth of the Platte. Colter joined Lisa's party and headed back upstream. Hancock may have remained at the Mandan villages for some time. It is said that in 1902 an aged man named Dave Fleming, living in Montana, claimed that Hancock became his stepfather when Fleming was a very young child.[10]

The winter of 1806-07 was extremely long and the snow unusually deep, six to eight feet on the level, where Dickson spent the winter. Continually exposed to the glare of the sun shining on the snow, his eyes became highly inflamed and finally completely blinded. Until that time Joseph had not been particularly religious. Believing himself to be in grave danger of death, he got on his knees and prayed for deliverance. He promised God that if his life was spared he would be a faithful Christian the rest of his life. Immediately he felt a strong impression that if he took the inner bark from a tree that stood near the door of his cave, pounded it up fine, mixed it with water to make a poultice and bathed his eyes in it, he would see again. He did as impressed and went to sleep not knowing whether it was day or night. When he

---

[8] Theodore Roosevelt, *The Winning of the West* (1902, and in Capricorn Books, 1962), 235.

[9] Cartwright, *Autobiography*, 254-57.   [10] Harris, *John Colter*, 54.

awoke his eyes felt easy and the inflammation was subsiding. Ultimately he regained his eyesight. This is what Dickson told Peter Cartwright.[11]

After what Joseph regarded as a miraculous recovery from snow-blindness, he experienced phenomenal success with his traps. In the spring, when the high water had gone out of the streams and Joseph was ready to begin his more than two-thousand-mile journey home, he arranged his canoe into a raft-like craft or lashed two canoes together to transport his many furs. It is believed that there were between fifteen and twenty packs when Joseph arrived in St. Louis. Some furs may have been dug up along the way from caches made while ascending the river.[12]

Dickson traveled downstream mostly under cover of darkness, hiding his cargo during the daytime. Once he relaxed his vigilance and almost lost his life when a burly Indian grabbed his canoe. Another Indian on the bank raised his rifle to fire. Joseph, who was a very strong man, quickly jerked the burly fellow's body in front of his own and the bullet struck the Indian, killing him instantly. This startled the others so much that Dickson got away without injury to himself.

Arriving back in St. Louis in June or early July, 1807, Dickson sold his furs for several thousand dollars[13] and returned home after an absence of almost three years. It was then that he learned he was the father of a fourth child, a boy named Joseph in his honor, who was now two and

---

[11] Cartwright, *Autobiography*, 254-57.

[12] Dale L. Morgan, *The Great Salt Lake* (Indianapolis, 1947), 53; Wisconsin *Collections*, XXII, pp. 388-89 (Sgt. Ordway's notes).

[13] Cartwright, *Autobiography*, 254-57; Leaton, *Methodism*, I, pp. 168-69. Cartwright adds: "he packed up and moved to Horse Creek." It was eleven years later that Dickson moved to Horse Creek. It should be noted, too, that Dickson was probably already in St. Louis when Colter was met by Lisa at the mouth of the Platte. David Lavender, in *Westward Vision* (New York, 1963), 132, suggests that the meeting occurred on July 10, 1807.

one-half years old. Dickson was baptized and joined the Methodist church. Five more children were born to Joseph and Susan while they continued to live on the American Bottom. The first of these was a son whom Joseph named Missouri, in memory of his trip far up the Missouri River. Missouri Dickson was born May 12, 1808.

When Joseph was preparing to move to the Sangamo country he drove his wagon to the ferry-landing in Cahokia, removed the wheels and ferried them across the Mississippi to a blacksmith shop to have the steel rims tightened, or "shrunk." It is supposed that Joseph was assisted that April day in 1818, in delivering the wheels from the water's edge to the blacksmith shop, by the smithy's apprentice, Jim Bridger. Joseph Dickson was the first white trapper in the northern American Rockies, and vanguard of the Mountain Men. Ironically, Bridger was to close that spectacular day of the fur trader when he built his emigrant trading post in Green River Valley just twenty-five years later.

It was in May when Dickson's prairie schooner, drawn by six oxen and followed by two boys on horseback herding livestock, arrived at Horse Creek. This was then the most northern part of Illinois opened for settlement. Less than a dozen families had settled in this remote area, which included the site of the future capital city of Springfield. All had arrived that spring except one family named Pulliam. Kickapoo Indians were all around them. Joseph, like the others, was a squatter. Illinois did not become a state until December. Land was surveyed in 1821 and offered for sale in November, 1823. Col. Joseph H. Dickson says he helped his father build the first white man's cabin in Sangamon County in the summer of 1818, when he was thirteen years old.[14] During the summers Joseph grain-farmed his land but

---

[14] Butterfield, *Grant County,* 553; Inter-State Publishing Co., *History of Sangamon County,* Illinois, 875.

spent the winter months trapping. Illinois still exported
large numbers of deerskins, racoon hides and a few otter
and black bear furs, together with the so-called "small
change" skins (beaver, fox, mink and wildcat).

Even before Joseph had title he donated five acres of his
farm for church and cemetery purposes in 1821. Sangamon
County history credits him with being the prime mover of
Zion Chapel.[15] This chapel has been rebuilt three times and
was still being used in 1952. Peter Cartwright, backwoods
preacher and Methodist circuit-rider to Springfield in 1824-
25, says, "Bro. Dixon [sic] took preaching into his cabin."
He also added that he thought Dickson was one of the best
"stewards of the church" he ever saw.[16] Good citizen that
Joseph was, his interests did not stop with religion. He was
equally concerned about education. Of the school subscription lists inspected in Springfield [17] by this narrator, his
name appeared first on all of them. One teacher remembered
only the name of Joseph Dickson as a subscriber. Moreover, Joseph was active in the political affairs of Cotton Hill
township where he resided. He was judge of elections in
1834 and 1836. A Jeffersonian Democrat until 1835, he
joined the anti-Jackson men called Whigs.

Of the Dickson children who lived to adulthood, six were
sons and three were daughters. Of the six sons, at least four
became early settlers in their own right. Col. Joseph settled
near Platteville, Wisconsin, in 1827; Missouri and Samuel
settled in Delaware County, Iowa, in 1837; and Nathan C.
settled in the Third Black Hawk Purchase in Mahaska
County, Iowa, in 1843. Every male descendant of Joseph
Dickson of which this narrator has knowledge, down to
and including his own father, were farmer-trappers. He

[15] Ibid.; Leaton, Methodism, I, pp. 168-69.

[16] Ibid.; Cartwright, Autobiography, 254-57.

[17] Illinois State Historical Society, Springfield, Illinois. (A personal inspection
made in 1952.)

remembers, as a child, his father's barn-loft filled with pelts turned inside out and stretched on boards each winter.

Joseph's wife Susan died at Horse Creek, but Joseph lingered awhile, according to Cartwright. He died at the home of a daughter in Franklin, Morgan County, Illinois, in 1844, and was buried there. There was not the slightest doubt in Cartwright's mind that Joseph kept faithfully until his death the covenant he made with God far up the Missouri River and its tributaries that awful winter of 1806-07.

William Doughty

by Harvey E. Tobie
Portland, Oregon

William M. Doughty was born in Tennessee in March, 1812.[1] By way of Missouri and the Rocky Mountains, he moved to Oregon when existence as a free trapper became too precarious. As a permanent settler, he assisted his mountain friends and other neighbors to adapt themselves to agricultural living and self government. Then, as far as history is concerned, like the hill on whose lower slopes he resided, he turned his back on colonial commotions and lived in comfortable, industrious retirement.

In mountain conversations, Doughty is revealed as a good hunter, a level-headed adventurer and an agreeable companion. (His portrait appears herein at page 14.) The memorably severe Snake country winter of 1832-33 icily tested those qualities. Just when a snowy blanket confined the game, there were many mouths to feed. Doughty, John Hawkins (sometimes rendered Hawken), Antoine Clement (?) and Joe Meek were the very ones to enjoy doing what had to be done. Initial ill success of the hunting party brought Doughty to the fore as a strategist. If the others would dislodge the bears about to emerge from hibernation, he would shoot them as they ambled into view. Actually, he only wounded the first bear that ran out of the cave. As it re-entered the shelter, converging fire finished it. Doughty

---

[1] Caroline C. Dobbs, *Men of Champoeg* (Portland, 1932), 123; "Genealogical Material in Donation Land Claims," Genealogical Forum of Portland, II, p. 67; tombstone, Gaston Hill Cemetery. Frederick V. Holman, "A Brief History of the Oregon Provisional Government . . . ," in *Oregon Historical Quarterly,* XIII (June 1912), 114, gives the birthplace as North Carolina; so does Mrs. W. E. Warren, *Oregon Biography Pamphlets,* Multnomah County Library, Portland; Fred Lockley in *Oregon Journal,* Feb. 2, 1939, states the birth date as 1810.

killed the next emerging bruin, and the three cave hunters drove out and shot the third. "Hurrah for these Daniels," sang Hawkins, honoring the bear's den survivors.[2]

In December, 1836, in the bend of the Yellowstone, Doughty was the hero of another bear encounter. When Hawkins killed one bear, two others stampeded into the old fort which the trappers were using. Doughty was resting inside. Still panting, from the safety of their perches in cottonwood trees, Meek and Kit Carson taunted their comrade wittily, advising him not to endanger himself by laughing. Ticklish as he was, Doughty restrained himself as the big brutes romped across his prostrate body. "Lazy," his tormentors called him, but we must consider him cool and courageous.[3]

By that time, free trapper Doughty was married to his Shoshone Pigeon, to whom a daughter, Lucy, was born in 1836. Support of a family, native or not, was becoming more and more of a problem. Income from trapping and hunting was disappointing, to say the least. But economic conditions in the States were also very unfavorable, and social welcome for mixed-marriage families could not be expected. Doughty and his friends began to make other plans. Slowly, increasingly, people were making their way across the mountains to the western valleys. Several Mountain Men made a compact. They would go down together and live as neighbors. They would have land and a livelihood, and they would be free to live in any way that they chose. About fifteen Mountain Men went down the Columbia in the fall of 1839. That was the year when Elizabeth Doughty was born. At least by the following spring, the family of four was living in the area west of the Willamette River where they had a cabin near the western slopes of Chehalem Mountain about twelve miles from the city of Newberg.

---

[2] Frances Fuller Victor, *River of the West* (Hartford, 1870), 138-40; Harvey E. Tobie, *No Man Like Joe* (Portland, 1949), 34, 287.

[3] *Ibid.*, 62; Victor, *op. cit.*, 194-95.

Close friends were on the way. When the Newell, Meek and Wilkins families crossed the Willamette near the falls late in 1840, first to welcome them were the Doughtys. Then all moved and camped near Doughty's welcoming cabin. It was an aggravating winter. Worse than the snow which ". . . melted by heavy rains, swelled the mountain streams, the swales, the creeks and the rivers," was the unfamiliar wetness from which the tents, which had served well in the mountains, gave inadequate protection. They were in Ewing Young country where limited supplies could be traded and where there might be employment even though the sawmill had been partially flooded off. In a wet season, there was plenty of water in Wapato Lake by the Doughty home. The wapato, or arrowroot, was a favorite article of Indian diet; and good hunters like Doughty and his friends could supply the families with meat.[4]

Nomadic pursuits, however, would no longer suffice completely to meet the wants of the colonists. Doughty secured seed wheat, farm implements and plow oxen from the Hudson's Bay Co., and, by 1841, planted a spring crop on his favorable hillside. Joe Meek, who was not thus favored, was Doughty's partner in the agricultural enterprise, and the two men, and others, were employed also as guides for Lieutenant George F. Emmons' exploratory expedition. In 1842, the partners put in another crop. On July 25 and 26, 1843, Alvin T. Smith cradled wheat for them.[5]

Safe title to the land that was now home became a matter of importance. With the arrival of the 1842 immigration came news of expected extension of United States laws to Oregon, and of grants to each Oregon immigrant of a section of free land. Would future arrivals contest the ownership of Doughty and others whose holdings were not yet legalized?

[4] Tobie, *op. cit.,* 95; Lewis A. McArthur, *Oregon Geographic Names* (Portland, 1952), 634; Census of 1850, Oregon Historical Society.

[5] Tobie, *op. cit.,* 97, 99; Alvin T. Smith, "Diary," MS., Oregon Historical Society.

Already controversy had begun at Willamette Falls. Would Pigeon be entitled to her share also? To help insure her eligibility, a church wedding was held at their house on October 23, 1842, with Rev. J. S. Griffin officiating to unite Pigeon Shoshone and William Doughty in holy matrimony.[6]

The transplanted mountaineers had even more important actions in mind for protection of their interests. Because the Doughty settlement was adjacent to Ewing Young's estate, the death of that important man in 1841 emphasized to friends and neighbors complications that might arise in an unorganized society. Yet it seems far fetched to assume that, in 1843, mostly abstract considerations such as probate matters or patriotic concern over diplomatic decisions were primary motives for the public acts of Doughty and his friends. Simple self-interest would be sufficient explanation.

A common problem, for instance, was animal depredations, to consider which there was a large turnout on February 2, 1843. At a meeting held March 6, Doughty, along with Charles McKay, Joseph Gervais, Nicholas Montour, Sidney Smith, James O'Neil, Robert Shortess and Etienne Lucier, was appointed to a standing committee, ". . . together with the Treasurer, to receive proofs or evidences of the animals for which a bounty is claimed. . ." A schedule of bounties was drawn up, to be paid by subscription. Bounties were limited to those who had paid their assessment and to whites and their descendants.[7]

The famous meeting at Champoeg May 2, 1843, was held for the stated purpose: ". . . to organize themselves into a civil community, and provide themselves with the protection secured by the enforcement of law and order." When the report of an interim committee regarding the intent of

[6] Dorothy O. Johansen and Charles M. Gates, *Empire of the Columbia* (New York, 1957), 236-37; Dobbs, *op. cit.,* 124, 205; Tobie, *op. cit.,* 293.

[7] Johansen and Gates, *op. cit.,* 239-40; David C. Duniway and Neil R. Riggs, eds., "The Oregon Archives, 1841-1843," in *Oregon Historical Quarterly,* LX (June 1959), 221-27; Dobbs, *op. cit.,* 124, 223, 227.

the meeting was not approved by the first vote, a dramatic reconsideration was arranged through a motion for a "divide." Joe Meek is said to have drawn a line on the ground and invited those in favor of an organization to follow him. This time a "great majority" favored the proposal, and dissenters withdrew. Details of organization were then passed. Joe Meek was made sheriff; and William Doughty, David Hill, Robert Shortess, Robert Newell, Alanson Beers, T. J. Hubbard, W. H. Gray, James O'Neil, and Robert Moore were named as a legislative committee to draft a code of laws and report to a meeting to be held at Champoeg July 5, 1843.

By confusing the representative from Wapato Lake with a better known 1843 immigrant, William P. Dougherty, careless orators who later outlined the history of government beginnings almost succeeded in depriving William Doughty of credit for the excellent achievements of the first Oregon legislature. The important committee met at Willamette Falls (?) on May 16 with Robert Moore as chairman and G. W. LeBreton as secretary. Doughty drew committee assignments as follows: Ways and Means (with Shortess and O'Neil) ; Private Land Claims (with Shortess and Hill) ; and Dividing the Territory (with Gray and Beers).[8]

The Committee on Ways and Means recommended a plan of voluntary subscription, the $1.25 per diem of the legislators to be their share.[9] The Committee on Private Land Claims drew up sensible rules and limitations to legalize

[8] *Oregon Historical Quarterly,* LX, pp. 236-40; Oregon *Spectator,* June 24, 1947; J. Quinn Thornton, "History of the Provisional Government of Oregon," in Oregon Pioneer Assn., *Transactions* (second, 1874), 62; (third, 1875) J. W. Nesmith names W. P. Dougherty as a member of the 1843 emigration which left May 20, 1843; (twenty-eighth, 1900) Gov. T. T. Geer names Dougherty; so does James K. Kelly at the tenth reunion, 1882, p. 18; (thirty-seventh, 1909, p. 338) P. H. D'Arcy names "W. P. Doughty." Even H. W. Scott, "The Formation and Administration of the Provisional Government of Oregon," *Oregon Historical Quarterly,* II (June 1901), 105, names Dougherty; as do others. "Provisional and Territorial Papers," 12186.

[9] *Oregon Historical Quarterly,* LX, pp. 240ff, 244; II, p. 372.

ownership by occupants of maximum 640-acre claims. There
was, however, a startling exclusion:

> No person shall be entitled to hold such a claim upon City or Town
> sites extensive Water Privileges or other situations necessary for the
> transaction of Mercantile or Manufacturing Opperations [sic] and
> to the detriment of the Community.

Thus was the great power controversy reaggravated.[10]
Wisely ignoring the disputed northern boundary, the Dis-
tricting Committee divided the huge area north of California and west of the Rocky Mountains into four districts.[11]

We do not know how much Doughty contributed to the
decisions of the legislative body that adopted the committee
reports. He was absent on the last days of the session, June
27 and 28;[12] and on June 13 he and Philip Thompson and
Henry Black spent half a day rounding up wild horses for
the auction held on the Ewing Young place. Officiating were
George W. LeBreton, clerk, and Joe Meek, auctioneer.
Each of the three wranglers received $1.50 for his services.
For $15 Doughty bought a second-choice horse.[13]

In 1844, with his partner Joe Meek, sheriff of the new
government, as collector, Doughty paid a poll tax and taxes
on 120 horses and 300 cattle – a total of ⅛ of 1% or $1.03.[14]
Then, as today, the Wapato Lake area was a stockman's
paradise. It was, and is, a beautiful countryside where con-
tented cows and horses may be seen grazing on the green
hillsides thrust up by nature in irregular patterns of idyllic
utility. Here was the prized land, ownership of which
Doughty helped to insure for himself as member of Oregon's
first legislature. On September 14, 1847, his claim to 640
acres in Wapato Valley was officially recorded. More accu-

---

[10] *Oregon Historical Quarterly,* LX, p. 267.
  [11] *Ibid.,* 266.   [12] *Ibid.,* 246-47.
  [13] "Ewing Young and His Estate," in *Oregon Historical Quarterly,* XXI (Sept.
1920), 289, 291.
  [14] Leslie M. Scott, "First Taxes in Oregon, 1844," in *Oregon Historical Quarterly,*
XXXI (Mar. 1930), 15.

rate than most claim descriptions of that year, the language reveals the beauty of the homestead through the naming of landmarks used in the survey: white oaks 24 and 28 inches in diameter and a fir grove featuring trees 36 and 42 inches in diameter.[15]

In those first important days in the development of Oregon, one of the unofficial capitals of the new commonwealth was the adequate Doughty dwelling. It was at least the equivalent of the seat of a county about to be bounded and named. It was a church and a community hall. Alvin T. Smith's diary states instances of Doughty's central importance in 1843:

Sab Feb 26th tended meeting at Mr. Doutheys

*   *   *

1843 Sab March 19th went to Mr Doutheys but no meeting   .   .   .

*   *   *

July 24th   .   .   .   went to Doutheys & Meeks in the evening

*   *   *

Sept 2nd tended a temperance meeting at Mr Doutheys   .   .   .[16]

As settlement arranged itself, Doughty's initial centrality was lost. Even today an element of isolation is noticeable in that area. Soon the Doughty family and their neighbors could live to themselves and prosper while oncoming settlers and those more advantageously located attended to the important public matters. Henceforth Doughty's family and his numerous livestock kept him occupied. By 1851 only a stray horse could bring him into public notice through an advertisement.[17]

By 1860 there were seven members of the Doughty family: William, 48; Pigeon, now called Martha, 35; Wallace, 18; Lydia, 7; Mary, 5; Anna, 3; and William, 11 months.[18] Lucy and Elizabeth were no longer with them. The 1870

[15] "Provisional Government Land Claim Records, 1845-1849," Oregon Archives, Oregon State Library, v, p. 76.
[16] Alvin T. Smith, "Diary."   [17] Spectator, Jan. 23 to Feb. 13, 1851.
[18] Census of 1860, Oregon Historical Society.

census credited Doughty with real estate worth $5810 and personal property worth $2420. Mrs. Doughty, who became a Baptist, was this time recorded under the biblically more important name, Mary. Father's right hand man was Wallace, 28; and there were at home: Lydia, Mary, Anna, William, Joseph, Martha and Richard, age 6. Also with the household was a laborer with the royal name, Robert Bruce.[19]

William and Franklin Doughty (Doty) of Maine and Iowa had moved into the neighborhood with their families. They could well have been descendants of that Mayflower pilgrim, Edward Doty, ancestor of James Otis and of the writer of this article. Their presence in Yamhill County suggests a possible relationship with our William Doughty.[20]

Whatever William Doughty's line of descent, his name was not perpetuated by his own four sons, for they did not wed. A century and less ago, boys of Indian parentage were subject to much social discrimination. The six daughters did marry, three of them to Blum brothers. The youngest daughter, Martha, mated in her teens, died young of tuberculosis, leaving an excitingly beautiful enlarged picture. Her son, an alert eighty-five year old, Tom Blum, has no recollection of his grandfather who died May 30, 1872, and was buried on top of one of the beautiful nearby hills. There the Daughters of the American Revolution have placed on his tombstone a plaque honoring the memory of "one of the founders of the Provisional Government," "one of those who on May 2, 1843, at Champoeg saved the Oregon Country to this nation." [21] Whatever his most important acts, he deserved the tribute due a founding father.

[19] Census of 1870, Oregon Historical Society; Horace S. Lyman, *History of Oregon* (Portland, 1903), III, p. 267.

[20] George F. Willison, *Saints and Strangers* (New York, 1945), 418; Frank Dempster Sherman, *Ancestors and Descendants of Harvey Hatch Sherman* (privately printed, 1913), 3.

[21] *Oregon Historical Quarterly,* XXXI (Mar. 1930), 406; photograph of grave in Gaston Hill Cemetery; interview with Mr. and Mrs. Blum, June 13, 1965.

Joe Doyle

by HARVEY L. CARTER
Colorado College, Colorado Springs

This successful frontier trader, whose full name was Joseph Bainbridge Lafayette Doyle, was born in Shenandoah County, Virginia, on July 10, 1817.[1] His parents, Alexander and Anna Doyle, migrated westward before he was grown, settled for a time at Belleville, Illinois, and finally moved on to St. Louis.[2] According to those who were well acquainted with him, Joe Doyle had a better than average education. He first came to the mountains in 1840 and spent two years in roaming around before he settled down as an employee of Bent Brothers and St. Vrain at Bent's Old Fort on the Arkansas River.[3] During his period of roaming around, Doyle was undoubtedly a trapper, but no details of his life during this time have been preserved.

In the spring of 1842, he is said to have joined with George Simpson and Alexander Barclay in building the trading post known as El Pueblo, at the junction of the Fontaine Qui Bouille with the Arkansas River.[4]

---

[1] Doyle's gravestone at Undercliff, Colorado, gives his birthplace as *"en la Ciudad de Lafayette"*; a loose note in the F. W. Cragin Papers, notebook v, gives his birthplace as Mount Pleasant; both sources agree on the county and the date. Mt. Pleasant was Joe Doyle's birthplace, for his father Alexander Doyle was a trustee of the town when, in 1828, the name was changed to Mt. Jackson. Alexander Doyle was a merchant and postmaster in the town and a militia captain in the War of 1812. See John W. Wayland, *A History of Shenandoah County, Virginia* (Strasburg, Va., 1927), 12, 246, 252, 469, 522.

[2] Alexander Doyle's name has not been found in early St. Louis directories. The rest of the family may have followed Joe to St. Louis; his mother and a sister are known to have lived in St. Louis later on.

[3] *The Encyclopedia of the New West* (Marshall, Texas, 1881), 31. The information is contained in a sketch of Alpheus P. Berry, Doyle's son-in-law.

[4] Janet S. Lecompte, "Charles Autobees," in the *Colorado Magazine* (July, 1957), XXXIV, p. 174.

However, Doyle was on the payroll of Bent, St. Vrain and Company from the middle of May to the beginning of August, 1842.[5] Moreover, Mrs. George Simpson stated that the original builders and owners of the Old Pueblo were George Simpson, Robert Fisher, Matthew Kinkead, Francis Conn, and Joseph Mantz.[6] If her statement is correct, Doyle and Barclay must have joined the enterprise in August, 1842, a few months after it was begun but before construction was entirely completed. They may have brought additional capital into the project and have replaced some of the original proprietors. In any case, Joe Doyle began operations as an independent trader with the Indians, using El Pueblo as his base, in the fall of 1842. It was the start of a notably successful career.

Although El Pueblo became the gathering place and trading center for a good many free trappers, and was conveniently located where the Old Trapper's Trail crossed the Arkansas River, it was located on American soil and was subject to restrictions placed on American trade at this time by the Mexican government. Consequently, Barclay, Doyle, and Simpson established, in February, 1844, a new residence and trading post on Mexican soil. This settlement, which was called Hardscrabble, was located about thirty-five miles almost directly west of El Pueblo.[7]

---

[5] Chouteau Papers, Missouri Historical Society, St. Louis. Entries in various ledgers. For this information and several other valuable items, I am indebted to Mrs. Janet S. Lecompte, who generously placed her notes on Doyle at my disposal.

[6] F. W. Cragin Papers, The Pioneers' Museum, Colorado Springs, notebook 1, p. 11. The well-known claim of James P. Beckwourth to have built the Old Pueblo may be dismissed in the face of this and much other testimony. The only question is whether Simpson, Barclay, and Doyle acted together from the beginning or whether Simpson and others acted first and were joined a few months later by Barclay and Doyle, with some needed cash. It is possible, of course, that some sort of agreement had been made between the three, whereby Simpson was to get things started while Doyle and Barclay remained for a time at Bent's Fort in order to earn more capital for the enterprise.

[7] See Janet S. Lecompte, "The Hardscrabble Settlement, 1844-1848," in the *Colorado Magazine* (April, 1954), 86, where the founding of Hardscrabble is definitely

Among those who had come to El Pueblo was a handsome Mexican woman, Teresita Suaso, widow of Manuel Suaso, one of the seventy-six original grantees of the Mora Land Grant of over 827,000 acres. She had with her four children, Tomas, Juana, Maria de la Cruz (always known as Cruz or Crusita), and Rafaela. In October, 1844, Joe Doyle and Cruz, who was thirteen years old, went to Taos and were married by Padre Martinez.[8]

Joe Doyle was an extremely active trader. Although his main business partner was Barclay, he was also in partnership with Will Tharp in 1845.[9] He was also on the road most of the time, either to acquire a stock of goods or to dispose of it to the Indians. His movements may be illustrated from various entries in the brief diary kept by Barclay, beginning in November, 1845. He made his winter trade with the Arapahoes on the South Platte, returning to Hardscrabble in late March, 1846. During the summer of 1846 he went to Missouri, returning with a wagon train of goods early in September, 1846. In 1847, he loaded up and left for the Platte in late January and returned in early March. In late September, he set out upon a trading trip among the Utes. He does not seem to have gone to the States in this year. In mid-February, 1848, we find him returning again from his annual trade with the Arapahoes on the Platte.[10]

In between these major trading trips are references to his

established as mid-February, 1844. The location was between Newlin and Hardscrabble Creeks, about a mile above their confluence and about 6 miles up Hardscrabble Creek from the Arkansas River.

[8] Matrimonial Records, Taos, 1835-1845, p. 270. George Simpson had already married Juana Suaso at El Pueblo and the mother, Teresita, had deserted Matthew Kinkead for Alexander Barclay. This may have been a factor in Kinkead's withdrawal from El Pueblo. Rafaela was not yet nubile, even by Mexican standards; she later married William Kroenig.

[9] John Brown Account Book, 1845-1848, p. 19. Transcript from the Huntington Library, courtesy of Mrs. Janet S. Lecompte.

[10] Barclay Papers, Bancroft Library, Memoranda for March 24, 1846; September 8, 1846; January 26, 1847; March 5, 1847; September 28, 1847; February 12, 1848. Typescript by courtesy of Mrs. Janet S. Lecompte.

trips to El Pueblo, to John Brown's post on the Greenhorn, and to the Big Timbers below Bent's Fort. Occasionally he hunted or fished, but mostly he was concerned with trading or with the maintenance of the wagons or the acquisition of livestock.[11]

The location of Hardscrabble was not as good as that of the Old Pueblo, and on October 19, 1846, Barclay recorded that he "left Hardscrabble for good and aye." [12] It is probable that Doyle and Simpson left also at this time with their families (though Simpson later returned for a while). They constructed a new residence about two miles up the Arkansas from the Old Pueblo, so that a portion of the operations already described were carried on from there.

The Mexican War had changed the outlook in this part of the West, however, so that even this location seemed less desirable than one farther south where money could be made by supplying the military forces in New Mexico Territory. Barclay arrived back from New Mexico on April 14, 1848, where he had acquired a portion of the Scolly Grant at the junction of the Mora and Sapello rivers as a site on which he and Doyle, as equal partners, proposed to build a fort and trading post.[13] He found Doyle and Thomas Fitzpatrick awaiting him, and on April 18 they and others set off by the South Platte route for St. Louis, where Doyle would buy a new stock of goods and transport it to the new location.[14] Meanwhile, Barclay proceeded thither and, in May, began construction of the new post, which was called Fort Barclay. This fort was large and expensive to build. Construction was still going on in October.[15] Altogether, it

---

[11] *Ibid.* Memoranda for December 11, 1845; September 12, 1846; March 25, 1847; April 7, 1847; October 22, 1847.

[12] *Ibid.* Memoranda for October 19, 1846, and succeeding days.

[13] *Ibid.* Memoranda of March 5, 1848, to April 14, 1848. See also F. W. Cragin Papers, Notebook I, p. 1. Mrs. Jacob Beard to Cragin, October 30, 1904.

[14] *Ibid.* Memorandum of April 18, 1848, and that of September 19, 1848, when Doyle arrived at Fort Barclay.

is thought that they spent about $28,000 on the project. It is probable that they expected to be able to sell it to the Federal Government for a military post. Instead of buying it, the government built Fort Union about seven miles away on the Doyle and Barclay land. To add to their troubles, Lucien Maxwell established a store at Rayado which got many of the government supply contracts from Doyle and Barclay.

Doyle, in 1849, spent much time in Santa Fe arranging for licenses for the Indian trade or exemption therefrom and getting business lined up.[16] Barclay's diary ends in January, 1850, so that no detailed picture of Doyle's activities emerges after that date. However, the venture was never prosperous, and Doyle never liked it. He urged Barclay to abandon it and return with him to the Arkansas Valley, where they would start over again.[17] Barclay, an older and less energetic man than Doyle, was unable to bring himself to do this. By July, 1854, the situation was that they had succeeded in getting an annual rental payment from the government on account of Fort Union being on their property, Doyle had returned to Arkansas, where he and Dick Wootton had set up an establishment at the mouth of the Huerfano River, and Barclay remained at Fort Barclay which, at Doyle's insistence, he now advertised for sale.[18] However, the Utes exterminated the Old Pueblo on Christmas day of 1854 and Doyle took his family back to Fort Barclay, as a result.[19] Fort Barclay did not find a buyer, and at the end of 1855 Barclay died. Doyle and Wootton en-

---

15 *Ibid.* Memoranda of April 23, 1848, to October 30, 1848.

16 *Ibid.* Memorandum of June 3, 1849.

17 *Ibid.* Letter of Alexander Barclay, Barclay's Fort, New Mexico to his brother George Barclay, London, England, March 27, 1852.

18 *Ibid.* Undated letter of Alexander Barclay to George Barclay; F. W. Cragin Papers, notebook II, pp. 56-60. Doyle and Simpson brought their families back to El Pueblo in 1853. Doyle built a *placita* at the mouth of the St. Charles River in 1854. It flooded there, so he moved on to the Huerfano.

19 Howard Louis Conard, *Uncle Dick Wootton* (Chicago, 1890), 282-307.

gaged in freighting goods from Kansas City to Albuquerque and later to Salt Lake City. At the end of a trip to the latter place in 1858, Wootton sold out to Doyle.[20]

Meanwhile, Joe Doyle, as the surviving partner of Barclay and Doyle, retained possession of Fort Barclay until he sold it in March, 1856, to William Kroenig and Moritz Beilchowsky for $7,340.68. The Barclay heirs in England were dissatisfied but there seems to be no reason for suspecting Doyle of dishonesty in the matter. He had written off his own loss and was embarking with his usual energy upon a new enterprise.

He established his family on a ranch sixteen miles up the Huerfano River from its confluence with the Arkansas, where in November, 1859, he had acquired, by purchase from the Vigil and St. Vrain Grant, two full miles of the river valley. Here he established one of the first flour mills in Colorado, made irrigation ditches whereby he brought six hundred acres of land under cultivation by 1861, built corrals for sheep and cattle which could be grazed on the uplands, and constructed a large ranch house, known as "Casa Blanca," surrounded by the cabins of the small army of Mexican laborers whom he employed.[21]

The reason for this rapid agricultural expansion, of course, was the influx of people into Colorado Territory, in 1859, in what is called the Pikes Peak Gold Rush. Doyle saw at once that there was money to be made by supplying the people of Denver. In 1858, while bringing a wagon train from Missouri he learned of the gold discovery and divided the train, sending part of it to Denver under Fred Z.

[20] *Ibid.*, 323-63.

[21] *Rocky Mountain News* (weekly) June 13, 1860; June 1, 1861; June 5, 1861. See also Cragin Papers, notebook X, p. 23; notebook VIII, p. 58. It is possible that Doyle did not bring his family from Fort Barclay to the Huerfano ranch until 1862, but his brother-in-law, William Kroenig, was farming on the lower Huerfano in 1859 and both families may have come around that time. .

Salomon, who became his partner in a general store which they opened in Auraria (later a part of Denver).[22] On this same trip, he had engaged O. J. Goldrick to be a tutor for his children, but Goldrick, after a short stay at Fort Barclay, went to Denver and opened the first school there.[23] It was also reported in 1859 that Doyle, together with George Simpson, Dick Wootton, and William Kroenig, owned the Soda Springs on the Fontaine Qui Bouille, which they planned to develop into the "Saratoga of the West." Doyle is given credit for being the one of the four owners who had originally appreciated the value of this property.[24]

Doyle established stores in Cañon City and at the Tarry-all Diggings as well as in Denver.[25] Some idea of the business of J. B. Doyle and Company in Denver may be had from the fact that in one month, August 13 to September 15, 1859, it had receipts of $2,528 in gold dust.[26] From October 1, 1859, to the end of that year, Doyle did $40,000 worth of business.[27] Doyle also continued to supply military posts such as Fort Union and Fort Garland.[28]

Doyle was also becoming active in politics and had been elected a member of the upper house of the territorial legislature.[29] He had previously held other local offices. In the midst of this active and prosperous career, he died suddenly, after an illness of four days on March 4, 1864, in Denver. It was said that he regarded his illness as fatal from the

---

[22] Forbes Parkhill, *The Law Goes West* (Denver, 1957), 110. Also *Rocky Mountain News,* January 1, 1873.

[23] *Rocky Mountain News,* October 6, 1859.

[24] *Missouri Democrat,* November 30, 1859. From Colorado Historical Society, MSS. XXV, p. 66.

[25] *Rocky Mountain News,* December 8, 1859; *Cañon City Times,* September 8, 1860; *Rocky Mountain News,* November 1, 1860.

[26] *Ibid.,* September 22, 1859.

[27] *Ibid.,* November 15, 1860.

[28] *Francisco Papers,* Colorado Historical Society.

[29] *Rocky Mountain News* (weekly), September 17, 1863. His majority was not large and was attributed to the votes of his employees at Doyle's ranch.

outset and refused to take medicine prescribed by his doctors.[30]

Doyle's reputation for integrity was very great and he was held in almost universal esteem. "Honest Joe Doyle" was the way he was commonly referred to by many people. One interesting characterization was this: "He never did a dishonest thing in his life, but he was short-tempered and it didn't do to tread on his toes." He was said to have started many men in business by giving them a stock of goods and ample time to pay. He also furnished land, seed, and teams to many who were without resources but who were willing to work.[31]

Cruz Doyle lived at the ranch but one year after the death of her husband before she too died suddenly on March 1, 1865, of "congestion of the brain." [32] She was said to have been a kind-hearted and hospitable woman. The Doyles had six children of whom three survived, James Quinn Doyle, Mrs. Fannie T. Berry, and Mrs. Florence A. Richards.[33] The Doyle estate was estimated to be worth over $100,000 and was under various administrators and subject to a good bit of litigation.

The career of Joe Doyle is remarkable in that he made a fortune in the declining years of the fur trade, while others of his kind were having a hard time to adjust to changing conditions. It is true that most of his money was made in the last five years of his life by trade with the white mining settlers. But his Indian trade had been profitable enough to

---

[30] *Ibid.,* March 9, 1864. There is some question as to the exact date of his death. It was in early March, possibly as late as March 9. The date is blank on his tombstone.

[31] F. W. Cragin Papers, notebook XI, p. 45. *Rocky Mountain News* (weekly), March 23, 1864.

[32] *Rocky Mountain News,* March 4, 1865.

[33] James Quinn Doyle, of whom much was expected, took to drink and died, very poor, in Trinidad in 1881. Fannie later lived in Chicago, and Florence in Durango, Colorado. See F. W. Cragin Papers, notebook IX, p. 52.

put him in a position to profit further by the advent of the white settlers. Doyle was what is known as a hustler. Most of his time was spent on the road. Another remarkable thing about him is that he was able to build a fortune and at the same time preserve a reputation for honesty and fair dealing.

It is not to be supposed that he helped other people without some profit to himself, but the evidence is clear that he did not take advantage of them. If they prospered, they made money for him. He set A. W. Archibald up in business in Trinidad with $1,800 worth of goods on credit.[34] He persuaded Robert W. Rice, a boy of twelve, who had been taken into White Antelope's Lodge, to leave the Indians. He educated Rice and set him up in the freighting business.[35] He grubstaked men who went to California in 1849, but he never succumbed to the gold fever himself, either in 1849 or in 1859 in Colorado. He maintained himself as a trader in spite of the competition of Bent's Fort, which was overpowering to most other traders. Alexander Barclay often referred in his diary to drinking sprees on the part of many traders, even himself, but never to anything of the sort in connection with Joe Doyle. Doyle worked harder than most of his associates or competitors, he was shrewder than most in knowing operating costs, he knew how to utilize others in his operations. His was a single-minded devotion to business and, in all his dealings, he left an untarnished reputation.[36]

---

[34] De Busk Memorial, 67. Jake Beard's Reminiscences.
[35] Pamphlet 363/15, 207-8, in Colorado Historical Society Collections.
[36] A portrait of Doyle appears herein, at page 14.

John Thomas Evans

by A. P. NASATIR
San Diego State College

The Welsh legend of the discovery of the New World in 1170 by Madoc, son of Oswain Gwynedd, a prince of North Wales, and of the existence in the wilds of America of a tribe of Welsh Indians, was a principal belief of the literary society of the Gwyneddigion, a group among the London Welsh. This London Welsh group was influenced by the appearance of a book by John Williams in 1791 enquiring into the truth of the Madoc tradition and of the existence of a tribe of Welsh Indians living in the interior of America. Their interest was increased by the appearance in London in that same year of William Bowles, who identified the Welsh tribe as the Padoucas. The London group determined to institute a search for those Welsh Indians, after a search of maps gave them a belief that the Padoucas were the lost Welsh tribe of Indians located beyond the Missouri Indians. Funds were raised. John Evans was chosen to accompany Iolo Morganwg in the search. As it turned out, Evans went alone, and Edward Williams furnished Evans with a letter of introduction to the Philadelphia bookseller, William Pritchard, describing the young 22-year-old Welshman as being of a very respectable family and of uncommonly good morals and conduct. Who was this John T. Evans?

Jean, Juan, or John Thomas Evans was a native of Waunfawr, some three or four miles from Caernarvon, in North Wales. He was christened on April 14, 1770, "John the son of Thomas Evan and Annen his wife." His father gained some distinction as a Methodist preacher who died

of tuberculosis in 1788, at the early age of forty-eight. Another of his sons, Evan Evans, was also a preacher and died
of tuberculosis at the age of twenty-four in 1797. It is quite
evident that John Evans was brought up in a pious home,
and perhaps his later journey, at least in part, was a missionary one. One of his childhood associates was the poet
David Thomas, who had written an elegy commemorating
Evans' father and might have been John Evans' school-
master. It probably was the same person who introduced
John Evans to the London Welshmen who profoundly influenced his life. It is certain that John Evans went to
London.

At any event John Evans left England, probably in late
September, arriving at Baltimore on October 10, 1792.

The Celtic dreamer visited Dr. Samuel Jones, the eminent
Baptist preacher who served a few miles outside of Philadelphia, and who attempted to dissuade him from going on
such a perilous journey without companions. But John
Evans was a youth of but twenty-two years of age, impetuous
and self-confident to a fault. Indeed, in letters to his brother,
John Evans speaks of the mission that "God Almighty had
laid on his conscience"; and that he would not fail. After
visiting the old Welsh settlements near Philadelphia, Evans
returned to Baltimore and became a clerk in the counting-
house of two merchants, with whom he spent the winter.
Those merchants as well as others of Evans' friends all tried
to dissuade him from his announced journey, but he was
determined to proceed. For a while he thought of going via
Canada, Montreal, and Detroit, but reverted to his original
plan to go to St. Louis and up the Missouri.[1]

Evans left Baltimore in February, 1793, and spent some

---

[1] The early life of Evans is based upon David Williams, "John Evans' Strange
Journey," in *American Historical Review*, LIV (1949), 277-96; 508-29. See also A. P.
Nasatir, "John Evans, Explorer and Surveyor," in *Missouri Historical Review*, XXV
(1930-31), 219-39, 432-60, 585-608.

time in Philadelphia with Dr. Jones, who failed in another attempt to dissuade the young Welshman. Early in March he left Philadelphia, traveled via Fort Cumberland and Fort Pitt and by boat down the Ohio and up the Mississippi to St. Louis, where he arrived in the spring of 1793. Those were critical times in Spanish Louisiana, when the Missouri Company had sent Truteau up the Missouri and when Jacques D'Eglise had brought information of the presence of British traders among the Mandans and swarming among the Indians of the Upper Missouri, which was territory belonging to His Catholic Majesty. Evans' strange quest, writes David William:

> must have caused surprise to the townsfolk, and the Spanish authorities would no doubt regard with suspicion anyone who might be a British agent. His impulsive nature would tend to lead him into difficulties, for one of his well-wishers feared that he "had not a sufficient knowledge of Mankind to balance his enterprising enthusiasm." What precisely happened it is not possible to say. All that is known definitely is that Don Zenon Trudeau, the commandant at St. Louis, complained that Evans "would not comply with some Spanish etiquette previous to his setting out on his journey," and that Evans was consigned to prison. In prison he remained for an indefinite period (possibly for two years) until he was released on representations being made to the commandant by a Welshman named Jones, said to be a resident of St. Louis.

More influential with Trudeau and as an intercessor for Evans was the United States judge in the Northwest Territory at Kaskaskia, George Turner. Zenon Trudeau visited Judge Turner[2] in Kaskaskia and in a conversation with him mentioned John Evans, stating that he had detained Evans until he could get further account of him and his design. Turner, who had previously heard of Evans, requested that he should be allowed to proceed on his projected journey,

---

[2] George Turner was appointed to the bench of Judges of Western Territory in 1789. He was appointed from South Carolina, where he had served as an officer in the Revolutionary army. He resigned his judgeship in 1797. C. E. Carter, *Territorial Papers of the United States,* II, pp. 217-18; 222.

for even if his search for Welsh Indians proved fruitless, his journey might still lead to valuable discoveries. Turner got an introduction to Trudeau for Evans and wrote Evans giving him advice relating to dealing with Indians; and he asked Evans to bring him the skin of a strange animal which he described to him. Turner's talks and aid proved profitable to Evans, for Evans was released from prison and Trudeau provided him with passports in Spanish, French and English. Trudeau told the judge he would keep him informed of any news he received of Evans' movements. Turner had also told Trudeau about Evans' desire to take a companion. Thus Evans was in St. Louis just when preparations were being made by the Missouri Company for a large third voyage up the Missouri under the direction of James Mackay. And by fortuitous circumstances Mackay had already heard of Evans.

Morgan John Rhees had gone to America in search of a location for a Welsh settlement. He went into the Northwest Territory and met Judge Turner who had given the Welshman an account of what had happened to John Evans up to that time. At Cincinnati, Rhees met James Mackay and, when Mackay told him of his plans to remain on the Missouri for three or four years to trade with the Indians, Rhees begged him to give "all the assistance he could to John Evans should he meet him." Rhees discussed the question of the Welsh Indians and the Padoucas with Mackay and gave the latter a small vocabulary of the Welsh language. "Having arrived in Louisiana and got ready for my voyage," wrote Mackay, "I sent for and engaged for my assistant Mr. Evans, who spoke and wrote the Welch language with facility." [3]

Evans set out on his trip with Mackay in August, 1795.[4]

---

[3] Thus began the association between Mackay and Evans which developed into one of mutual respect and friendship.

[4] See account of James Mackay in this Series. From this point on, most of the

It is not necessary to enter into the details of Mackay's journey here, except to say briefly that the expedition was made up of four pirogues of merchandise and thirty-three men. They followed Mackay's instructions and plans. They proceeded slowly up the Missouri, and after forty-four days' journey they reached the mouth of the Platte River. Mackay remained eleven days with the Oto Indians and then proceeded to the Omaha villages. As winter was about to set in he decided, as had been provided for in his plans, to winter in that area, and hence he constructed Fort Charles. As food was scarce, Mackay sent a party of his men to join an Indian hunting party which set out in November and returned twenty-five days later. On November 24, Mackay decided that since he had no information of what was happening among the Arikara, and since he was not able to send a party there by water, he would send a well-accompanied detachment by land to obtain information. This party, however, met up with a considerable party of Sioux hunting buffalo and, taking advantage of the cover of night, they retreated successfully to Fort Charles where they arrived on January 6. Evans was in charge of one of those parties. Mackay placated the Sioux with abundant presents, held a council with them, and succeeded in opening communication with them.

Meanwhile Mackay's goods were being pillaged, in part by the Poncas. The Scotsman sent reports of British intrigues and incursions among the Indians of the upper country, especially via the San Pedro and Des Moines rivers. Since one of the objects of Mackay's expedition was to drive out the British from among the Mandan, where they had established a fort, and since Mackay feared that he might not arrive among the Mandan until late in the summer, he decided to dispatch Evans and a company of men with in-

documents have been printed in Nasatir, "John Evans," *op. cit.,* and in A. P. Nasatir, *Before Lewis and Clark* (2 vols. St. Louis, 1952).

structions to ascend the Missouri in 1796, meet Truteau, and then proceed to cross the mountains in an attempt to reach the Pacific Ocean.

On January 28, 1796, Mackay issued his lengthy set of instructions to Evans for discovering a passage from the sources of the Missouri to the Pacific Ocean. The instructions required Evans to keep a journal recording latitude, longitude, weather and winds, and a second journal recording the extent and location of minerals, vegetables, plants and animals, Indian tribes and remarks descriptive thereof. "You will take care to mark down your route and distance each day, whether by land or water; in case you will be short of ink, use the powder, and for want of powder, in the summer you will surely find some fruit whose juice can replace both." He was instructed to consult Truteau, who was supposed to be either among the Arikara or Mandan; and detailed directions concerning the accuracy of his records, meeting with parties of Indians, and rules of conduct were prescribed. He was equipped with a supply of merchandise for placating the natives (but was warned to distribute the merchandise sparingly as presents among the new nations of Indians), who were to be informed that other parties of whites would follow him.

Evans was directed to keep within the bounds of 40 degrees of north latitude until he arrived within the area between 111 and 112 degrees longitude, west; then he was to travel north to the 42nd parallel and thence due west. The distance from the Rocky Mountains to the Pacific Ocean, Mackay estimated at not more than 290 leagues. Evans was told not to incur the jealousy of the Russians on the coast, but on his way thither he was to take possession of all the territories traversed in the name of King Charles IV, King of Spain, and the Missouri Company, inscriptions embodying both names to be carved on stones or trees as he passed from river to river. These were to serve as "unques-

tionable proof of the journey that you are going to make."
Finally, Evans was instructed not to deliver or show anything regarding his discoveries to any person save Mackay,
Clamorgan, or another representative of the company in the
presence of the Lieutenant Governor.[5]

Evans set out shortly thereafter, probably early in February. On February 19, Mackay wrote Evans a letter telling
him of his loneliness since Evans had left, despite his em-
ploying himself constantly on some trip. He told him of
some other possible variations of his route, based upon information from Jacques D'Eglise, and enclosed a sketch of
the Yellowstone River given D'Eglise by the Indians. Mackay told Evans to reveal his plans and projects to no one,
not even to Truteau, except what is necessary "to forward
your expedition and for your information you will at all
events try to see the white people on the Coast if it should
answer no other purpose than that of corresponding by letters it will be of great service as it will open the way for a
further discovery."

Mackay also instructed Evans to tell Truteau to make an
inventory of what goods he might have on hand in the spring
and to have it forwarded to him. Truteau was to inform the
Indian nations that Mackay was on his way up the Missouri
River.[6] However, Evans did not succeed in getting very far,
Evans estimating about three hundred miles, when they met
up with a war party of Sioux. Evans and his men were
forced to make a hasty retreat, and they were successful in
reaching Fort Charles unharmed.[7]

[5] Mackay's instructions together with a map of the conjectured route are given in
Nasatir, *Before Lewis and Clark,* II, pp. 410-15.

[6] Mackay to Evans, Fort Charles, February 19, 1796, Nasatir, *Before Lewis and
Clark,* II, pp. 415-17. Mackay of course was to replace Truteau as agent of the
Missouri Company.

[7] Nasatir, *Before Lewis and Clark,* II, p. 540; Williams, *op. cit.,* 519. Evans
ascended the Missouri as high as the White River, about 80 leagues above the
Mahas, where he met a war party of Sioux Indians who pursued Evans' group and,

Before setting out again Mackay gave other instructions to Evans and also a manifesto dated Fort Charles, May 27, 1796:

To All British Subjects Trading to the interior parts of N[orth] America, and all other persons of whatever description who may frequent the said Country:

His Catholic Majesty having granted to his subjects (the Missurie Company) that part of his dominions siteuated on both sides of the Missurie to its Westernmost source and from its source to the coast of the Pacific Ocean, and North to the hight of land, that divides the waters that empties into the Missurie from those that falls into Hudson's Bay.

I am therefor commanded to forbid and prevent all forigners whatever (especiely all British subjects) who are or may be in the neighbourhood of his Majestys dominions to enter any part of the said Chartered dominions on pain of confiscation of all such offenders property and such punishment as the law of the land may inflict on the conveyers of such property.[8]

_____

had it not been for the weather and the approach of nightfall, would probably have stopped him. Fortunately Evans was able to escape and retreated to Fort Charles. After Evans reported, Mackay sent to the Sioux asking for a conference, which was held about a month later, and communication was obtained. Mackay now sent Evans out again. Mackay's "Journal" in Nasatir, *Before Lewis and Clark*, II, pp. 494-95.

[8] Hudson's Bay Company archives, printed in Nasatir, *Before Lewis and Clark*, II, pp. 461-62. Perhaps somewhat jumping the gun, Clamorgan wrote to Carondelet on April 10, 1796, presumably after he had heard from Mackay that the latter had sent Evans on his journey, that the Maha and Ricara forts had been established and that "next June we hope to receive word of the construction of the forts of the Mandans and Poncas," the latter having promised also a fort among the Otoctatas for the fall. Therefore, Clamorgan asked the Governor-General for a commission as Commandant of the forts that the company was building in the Missouri for Mackay. Nasatir, *Before Lewis and Clark*, II, p. 418. Carondelet issued such a commission to Mackay on May 11, 1796. *Ibid.*, II, pp. 427-29. And on April 30, 1796, Clamorgan wrote Carondelet: "It seems very likely that a year from next June I shall be able to announce to you the discovery of the Pacific Ocean by crossing this vast continent and to offer to you an exact map of the course of the Missouri which hitherto I have been able to obtain only from vague reports of several voyageurs." *Ibid.*, II, pp. 424-25; see also 423-24.

Evans "took a chart" of his journey, and marked down with care and accuracy his route. His chart or map possibly was made later and based on Evans' sketches and information which he gathered from the Indians. Evans says that he had explored and taken a chart of the Missouri for 1800 miles. His map was sent to

Evans left again on his second try on June 8 and followed the route he had taken in February.[9] He proceeded from the Ponca territory by river. After a long and fatiguing voyage he reached the Arikara village on August 8. Evans had some trouble with the Arikara; they wanted all his goods and would not let him pass. While tarrying with the Arikaras for a number of weeks, he met several chiefs of tribes living to the west, particularly the Cheyenne, who expressed their attachment to the Spanish standard. "Judging it necessary for the better insuring the success of my enterprise to take Possession of the fort built at the Mandaine Village by the English Traders of Canada," said Evans, "I succeeded in persuading the *Rickaras* to let me go so far as there with a few Goods."

Evans reached the Mandan village on September 23. After he had distributed medals, flags, and other presents to the natives and delivered a harangue in favor of Spain, to which they readily gave their assent, Evans took possession of the fort belonging to the British traders, hoisted the Spanish flag, and christened it Fort Mackay. He undoubtedly found some British traders including René Jusseaume, and he evidently gave them copies of James Mackay's proclamation and told them to return to their posts on Rivière Tremblante, and Brandon House, and other forts (notably La Souris) in Canada from which both the North West and

President Jefferson and used by Lewis and Clark. A. H. Abel, "A New Lewis and Clark Map," in *Geographical Review,* I (1916), 329-45. R. N. Hamilton, "Early Cartography of the Missouri Valley," in *American Historical Review,* XXIX (1934), 645-62; A. Diller, "Maps of the Missouri River Before Lewis and Clark, in *Studies and Essays . . . in Homage to George Sarton* (New York, 1946), 509 *et. seq.;* D. Jackson, "A New Lewis and Clark Map," in *Bulletin* of Missouri Historical Society, XVII (1961), 117-32. See maps numbers 1-6 in *Atlas,* which is vol. VIII of the Thwaites edition of *Original Journals of the Lewis and Clark Expedition* (Cleveland, 1904); and also Williams, *op. cit.,* 520.

9 From this point on the documents are printed in Nasatir, *Before Lewis and Clark;* in Nasatir, "John Evans," *op. cit.;* and in narrative form in the introduction to volume I of Nasatir, *Before Lewis and Clark.*

Hudson's Bay companies sent traders to the Mandan villages.

On October 8, 1796, Cuthbert Grant, a "nor'wester interior leader," addressed a letter to Evans at the Mandan Village, Missouri, from his favorite residence, Rivière Tremblante Fort, stating that as he had found "by Mr. James Mackay's letter that the Missisourie [sic] is chartered by a Company I wish to withdraw what little the N.W. Co. [?] has their [sic]." Grant complained that the company's business with the Mandan had been a losing proposition and that for some time he had wished to withdraw, and he entreated Evans to deliver "to the bearer" all the goods belonging to Jusseaume that might be in his possession. Evidently Grant knew about, or at least suspected, the capture and confiscation by Evans of the British post, together with its contents. Grant further informed the Welshman that Jusseaume would return to the Missouri during the ensuing month in order to settle his affairs. Grant thanked Evans for his kindness in "lending a man to Mr. [Neil or Donald] Mackay" and requested Evans' assistance in the efforts of his company to find and apprehend deserters from their brigades, promising to reciprocate the favor should opportunity arise; he also requested Evans to make an account of everything belonging to Jusseaume that he might deliver to the men.

Evans tells us that on the same date as the date of Cuthbert Grant's letter, October 8, several British traders arrived at the Mandan villages. Not having a sufficiency of men, Evans made no attempt to oppose their entry or object to their introducing the merchandise which they brought with them; but, using other means, the Welshman outwitted his fellow Britishers, causing a hindrance to their trade and, some days after, forcing them to take their departure. As these traders would necessarily return to Canada, Evans sent with them James Mackay's proclamation forbidding

all foreigners from entering "any part of his Catholic
Majesty's Dominions in this Quarter under any pretext
whatever." James Sutherland at Brandon House received
that message and proclamation on October 25, and on the
next day talked with the returning British traders who told
him that Evans had permitted Mr. Mackay [Neil or Don-
ald] "to return for this time without confiscation of his
property, but on the promise of not returning again with any
more goods."

On November 23, Sutherland replied from Brandon
House (on the Assiniboine six miles above [west] the mouth
of the Souris): "Your written declaration dated Fort
Charles the 27th of May last, prohibiting all British Subjects from trading at the Missourie, has come to our hands.
This may effect the traders from Canada a little but nothing
those from Hudson's Bay." Nevertheless Sutherland inquired as to whether he could be permitted to visit the Missouri in order to trade horses, Indian corn, and buffalo robes
"which articles we suppose not to be connected with the Fur
Trade and consequently expect you will have no objections."
But Evans replied on December 20, 1796 (received at
Brandon House January 16, 1797) that the trade from the
North to this place (Mandan villages) was strictly prohibited and he did not have the power to authorize his
request. He expressed doubt that permission would be
granted, since those articles were the staple trade of the
country, and said that Sutherland would be informed when
the Agent of the Company, Mackay, would arrive at the
Mandan post.

However, the Northwesters were more aggressive. From
the North West Company's post near or at the mouth of La
Souris River, in close proximity to Brandon House, John
McDonnell addressed a letter to Evans which bears the same
date, November 23, as Sutherland's letter. McDonnell informed the trader at the Missouri that he was sorry his

company was obliged to trouble him (Evans) with *another*
visit "much against our wills" – its purpose ostensibly "to
fetch the dearly acquired debt of Mr. Jusseaume." Jean
Baptist Desmarais was sent with some goods in order to
bring back Jusseaume's furs. As winter was setting in,
McDonnell found it difficult to get any of the "turbulent"
French-Canadians to undertake the journey to the Mandan.
He succeeded, however, after having been forced to advance
some goods on credit to the men – a risky thing to do.

McDonnell had warned the *voyageurs* that their goods
were likely to be confiscated, but "they replied that they
heard that Mr. Evans was a *bon garcon* and hoped upon
asking leave to trade what little they brought that you
[Evans] would not refuse them as they [had] so little that
it would not injure your interest in the least." McDonnell
entreated Evans to aid Desmarais "in apprehending Chayé
[?] and conveying him back to his duty as he has three years
of his time to serve the Company." He also asked Evans'
assistance in collecting something from Garreau, who was
indebted to several members of the Company, and he forwarded a liberal present, including "two European mag-
azines and a Guthrie's Geographical Grammar for your
amusement." Before concluding, McDonnell informed
Evans that La Grave had run away three years before at the
Rivière Qu'Appelle, heavily indebted to him; he enclosed,
also, Jusseaume's "will and power to have his Peltries and
little slave girl" delivered to the bearer, and thanked him
for allowing one of his men to "accompany Mackay in his
distress."

Desmarais reached the Mandan and delivered the letters
addressed to Evans by Sutherland and McDonnell before
December 20, for on the latter date Evans wrote his reply
to Sutherland's letter. Desmarais' party returned to La
Souris post on January 16, but on the first or second night
out on their return journey they had lost their horses, which

had fallen into the hands of the Pawnee. Consequently, they had been obliged to leave their property behind, and it was now determined to send another party to the Missouri to recover it. Sutherland allowed two of his men to accompany this expedition (which was composed of Northwesters), "out of curiosity – to see the Mandan villages" and to attempt to purchase a slave girl. He also sent a gift to Evans and invited the latter to inform him of such news as when he expected "the gentleman from below at your post, what your Intentions are with regard to exploring further up the River, if your agent general be the same Mr. James Mackay who was formerly a Trader here in Red River. These perhaps you will say are tedious inquiries, but I suppose a gentleman of your ability's can have no objection to any communication which does not immediately concern the Company's affairs in so remote a country."

The party arrived at the Mandan villages on or before February 6 and returned to the Souris and Brandon House at 3 p.m. on the 25th of the same month. The two men that Sutherland had sent on Desmarais' expedition reported that Evans had been as "cival to them as his wretched condition would admit," but that he had not permitted them to trade with the natives. Instead Evans himself traded all the goods they had and gave them furs for it; they returned with four sleds well loaded with furs. They reported that they could have done better if they had been allowed to trade with the Indians themselves; that the Indians were displeased with Evans on that account and would endanger his (Evans') situation; that many Indians were fond of the English and Mr. Evans hoisted his Spanish flag.

On February 26, 1797, just a few hours after the return of the expedition from the Missouri, both McDonnell and Sutherland addressed replies to the missives it had brought them from Evans. These two letters show, more than ever, the intense rivalry between the North West and Hudson's

Bay Companies, and also afford us an insight into Evans' activities among the Mandan. Writing in a pleasant mood, Sutherland thanked Evans for the kindness to the "two English lads" that he allowed to accompany the expedition. He heard that Evans had some complaints to make against the "Northwesterners" and remarked that it was "not without reason." Could he have had the opportunity of talking personally with Evans, he would have told the Spanish Subject much more on that score. (Even before the end of 1796 the H.B.C. men had been noting that the Northwesterners were at least contemplating the idea of taking possession of the upper Missouri.) "There is no harm in your being on your guard against designing people," said Sutherland, "a word to the wise is sufficient." The H.B.C. leader told the Welshman that he need have no more fears of any further visitations on the part of members of his company, for the Hudson's Bay Company "never as yet has been known to violate any law either foreign or domestic." He thanked Evans for the information he had imparted to him, and said that his letters would be sent to the Governor and Council. Sutherland also said that he wished he might have an opportunity of meeting and speaking with Evans personally and of exchanging adventures, "for as well as you I have been appointed by providence to traverse the wild regions of America for several years past."

John McDonnell, however, spoke in another tone. He wrote angrily, even sarcastically. Since Evans had apparently suspected (and even perhaps threatened to arrest) La France, and evidently did not like him or his cohort Jusseaume, McDonnell decided to send those two men to the Missouri where they might vindicate themselves from Evans' aspersions. Let their conduct

> be what it will you would expose yourself in acting agreeable to your letter. British subjects are not to be tried by Spanish laws, nor do I look upon you as an officer commissioned to aprehend oth[er] people's

servants, if you serve a chartered Comy. why not show the Spanish Governors Orders, declarations, denunciations or manifestoes, prohibiting others from frequenting that country. Then shall we leave you in peace: Be at bottom of it who will most certain I am that there is most complicated vilainy carried on this year at the Missouri in many respects witness the debauching of Chaye last fall, and the offering 200 dollars to the English men arrived yesterday if we were nearer neighbors than we are we could easily come to an understanding It must give any sensible person no grand Idea of your Missouri Company making use of such Canaille as I have reason to think many of your Engages are by judging of the remainder by La Grave Garreau Chaye etc. Such as are not runaways from here are Deserters from La prairie du Chien & other places in the Mississippi. La France goes with Jusseaume to help the latter in bringing his family.

Jusseaume, accompanied by Baptiste La France, set out from the North West Company's post at the mouth of La Souris River shortly after February 26 and arrived at the Mandan village on March 13. Difficulties arose. Evans tells us that Jusseaume brought merchandise to distribute as presents among the Mandan and the neighboring tribes, to win them from their fidelity to His Catholic Majesty. Jusseaume and his cohorts attempted to induce the chiefs to enter Evans' house under the guise of friendship in order to murder him and pillage his property, but their loyalty defeated the dastardly project. Instead, the chiefs informed Evans of it and promised to guard him against any attack. Jusseaume even attempted to take Evans' life, but was frustrated through the alertness of the latter's interpreter. The Indians dragged Jusseaume away and would have killed him had not Evans intervened. A few days later Jusseaume left. According to Evans, it was the intention and purpose of the Canadian traders to spare " – no trouble or Expense to maintain a Fort at the Mandaine Village Not that they see the least appearance of a Benefit with the Mandanes but carry their views further, they wish to open a trade by the Missouri with the Nations who inhabit the Rocky Mountains, a Trade, that at this Moment is Supposed to be the best on the Continent of America."

But the Brandon House Journal entry for Good Friday, April 14, 1797 records:

> News from the Mandans, Mr. Evans and the Canadians was almost at fisticuffs in atempting to prevent them from Trading with the natives, and not having goods himself set all the Indians out against him, he was obliged to set off with himself and all his men down the River for Fort Charles, the Indians threatning to kill them if they refused being greatly exasperated against them for preventing the Subjects of G. Britain from coming to Trade with them; The Indians has plenty of Furs still among them particularly the Grovanders (or bigg bellys) and are determined to visit this place nixt fall or at least to meet Traders halfway, what a pitey there is not men and goods to encourage this Trade.

Evans left the Mandans, probably on May 9, and descended to St. Louis where he arrived on July 15, 1797. He left promising to return and furnish them with arms and ammunition. Mackay had returned earlier, possibly in May. Upon his return Evans communicated with Dr. Samuel Jones, and Morgan Jon Rhees extracted the substance of his reports for American newspapers, *New York Daily Gazette* and *Philadelphia Gazette and Aurora,* and together with a letter of Rhees', it appeared in the *Monthly Magazine* for March, 1798. He reported on the non-existence of Welsh Indians in the Missouri River between latitude 35 and 49 and stated he now thought they did not exist anywhere.

Whether or not Evans wanted to do otherwise, he was offered a position in the Spanish service.[10] On November 9, 1797, Antonio Soulard, the government surveyor for the Illinois country issued instructions relative to "Mr. J. Evans' Voyage to Cape Girardeau to Survey the lands of the inhabitants of the said post and dependencies." Zenon

[10] From this point on see Nasatir, "John Evans," *op. cit.*

Trudeau asked Evans to look around for a piece of land which he would grant to him. He did choose a place on the upper parts of Zenon River (now called Hubbell Creek), and he flattered himself that he, together with a partner, could provide a comfortable living. Although Evans was but twenty-eight years old, he mused on the "shortness of life and the frowns of delusive fortune." He asked the Lieutenant Governor to grant that land to him. He would explore the back country of Cape Girardeau.

> My arduous Desire to Present a Plan for my future happiness and the particular pleasure which observed you [Trudeau] to have in alleviating the distresses of the Unfortunate – Has thus encouraged me to be so earnest in my Petition for the spot where I promise myself – while I gratifie a natural inclination to mechanism like wise to be of some public use.

Evans spent some time as a surveyor in the Cape Girardeau area, especially around Cape La Cruz. Lorimier remonstrated with him to please measure the lands according to the instructions of Mr. Soulard. The names of many land grants that were surveyed by Evans are still extant.

On December 23, 1797, James Mackay wrote to Evans, telling him that the severity of the winter and the want of opportunity had prevented his being able to descend to New Orleans. He had taken, or rather had been granted, some land and wished that Evans had been there to survey it for him. Mackay had all along intended to descend the river to New Orleans and had contemplated taking Evans with him. The ice in the river prevented his leaving and he probably would not be able to leave until "some time in the new year." Sometime before February 5, 1798, Evans had requested a grant of land from Lorimier which the latter denied. On May 18, 1798, Soulard wrote Evans about the latter's *malheur* [misfortune] and told Evans that he could work at his surveying in the area as long as there would be work, but admonished him to follow the instructions that he had given him. Evans corresponded with a number of men from Cape Girardeau. Probably on June 18, Evans replied to Soulard's letter from Cape La Cruz. Here he complained about payments for surveys made and said that he would pay attention to the matters mentioned in Soulard's letter to him. "I do not survey anymore – on acct. of the woods being too thick. I intend to begin in Octr. again." He mentioned that he had written to His Excellency, presumably Zenon Trudeau, "Pettitioning for a tract of Land and I humbly beg of you to draw the Petition and speak a few words for me. In all probably I shall become an Inhabitant of this post and have a family perhaps before long." Evans would have liked to visit St. Louis then, but "circumstances will not allow of it now."

Sometime before July 18, 1798, Evans left the Cape Girardeau area and perhaps went to live in St. Louis. Weston addressed a letter on that date to "Mr. John Evans to be left at Mr Glenmorgan [Clamorgan] Merchs. St Louis." Presumably sometime in 1798, Evans descended to New Orleans. Mackay descended the river earlier in that year. Trudeau reported on March 5, 1798, that Mackay was going to leave or had left [11] and used Evans' work as part of his in his petitions for appointments and favors from the Spanish governor. Gayoso de Lemos was impressed with both Mackay and Evans, knew of their usefulness to the Spanish service and wanted to keep them both in that service. He wrote to the Minister Francisco de Saavedra on November 22, 1798, of the paramount importance to Spain to protect the northern border of the territory of New Spain and to prevent the English from penetrating New Mexico and ousting the Spanish from the Missouri.[12]

---

[11] Nasatir, *Before Lewis and Clark,* II, p. 545.

[12] This letter of Nov. 22, 1798, is quoted in the biographical sketch of James Mackay, footnote 22, elsewhere in volume four of this Series.

The letter cited indicates that Evans was living in New Orleans at the time. There he presumably remained. On May 20, 1799, Gayoso wrote to Mackay,

> Poor Evans is very ill; between us I have perceived that he deranged himself when out of my sight, but I have perceived it too late; the strength of liquor has deranged his head; he has been out of his senses for several days, but, with care, he is doing better; and I hope he will get well enough to be able to send him to his country.

But such was not the case, and before the end of the month Evans was dead. Thus came to an end the short life of a Welsh Methodist who performed service for the Roman Catholic government of Spain, played an important part in the exploration of the wilderness of North America, and contributed to the work of Lewis and Clark, of whose great exploits John Evans was truly a precursor.[13]

---

[13] The last part of this discussion is based upon the documents in Nasatir, "John Evans: Explorer and Surveyor," in *Missouri Hist. Rev.*, xxv (July 1931), 591-608.

Jacob Fowler

by RAYMOND W. SETTLE
Monte Vista, Colorado

Jacob Fowler (1764-1849), government contractor, surveyor, trapper, hunter, Indian trader, merchant, traveler, and diarist, was born in Winchester (Westminster?), Maryland, March 1, 1764.[1] His parents, with their four sons, Jacob, Edward, Matthew, and Robert, removed from that place to Ligonier Valley, Pennsylvania, in 1768, and after three more moves settled in the neighborhood of Fort Vanmeter, ten miles inland from Wheeling, Virginia, in 1778.[2] These numerous removals westward were caused by Indian hostility. This situation compelled the people to live in forts during much of the year.

In 1782, when the notorious Simon Girty led a body of Indians against Fort Henry at Wheeling, Virginia, and neighboring posts Jacob, then only eighteen years of age, bore a man's part in the defense of Fort Vanmeter. Many acts of heroism were performed in those flaming days, such as that of Elizabeth Zane, at Fort Henry in November of that year, who dashed from the safety of the fort under heavy fire by the Indians to bring in a keg of powder which had been inadvertently left in the cabin belonging to her brother Ebenezer, some rods from the gate.[3] In November, 1782, Fowler piloted 1,050 mounted men under Colonels Benjamin Logan and one of the Bowman brothers, John or Joseph, from Bryant's Station (Lexington) to the mouth of the Licking River, where they joined General George

---

[1] Charles Cist, "Biography of Jacob Fowler," in Cincinnati *Western Advertiser,* Oct. 31, Nov. 7, 1849.

[2] Cist, *op. cit.,* 4.

[3] Cist, *op. cit.,* 6; John Frost, *Pioneer Mothers of the West* (Boston, 1859), 37-46.

Rogers Clark in his successful raid upon the Indian towns along the Miami River.[4]

In the latter part of the Revolutionary War the Fowler family left the Fort Vanmeter settlement and moved to Wheeling, where Jacob formed a personal acquaintance with the famous quartet of Indian fighters – Martin, Lewis, Jacob, and John Wetzel, who lived on Wheeling Creek twelve or fourteen miles from its mouth.[5]

After the close of the war, Fowler, in partnership with Abraham Creigh and Robert McConnell, hunted on the Muskingum and its tributaries to supply the various posts and settlements in that area with meat.[6] In 1789 he, with Benjamin Hulin, loaded a flatboat with whisky, cider, and merchandise and floated down the Ohio River to the settlements of Marietta, Ohio, and Kanawha, Virginia. This was his first venture in the trading business. After the goods were all sold he went down to Cincinnati, which had been laid out a few months before, to visit his brother Matthew, with whom he took a contract to supply new Fort Washington and the town of Cincinnati with meat. Their hunting was usually ten to fifteen miles into Kentucky. That same year Fowler bought lots in the village of Cincinnati.[7]

In the spring of 1790 he went back up the Ohio River to Point Pleasant where he met his former partner Hulin, who had just had a narrow escape from Indians, and Lewis Wetzel. In the summer of 1791, Fowler returned to Cincinnati where he met General Arthur St. Clair,[8] who, upon

---

[4] Mary K. Jones, "History of Campbell County," read at Centennial Celebration, July 4, 1876, Newport, Ky., p. 3. See also Theodore Roosevelt, *Winning of the West* (New York, 1905), III, pp. 63, 70, 72, 77, 84.

[5] Charles Cist, "Obituary of Jacob Fowler," in Cincinnati *Western Advertiser*, Oct. 24, 1849.

[6] Cist, "Biography," *loc. cit.*

[7] Cist, *op. cit.*, 10-12; Benjamin Van Cleve, "Memoirs," in *Quarterly Bulletin, Historical and Philosophical Society of Ohio*, XVII, p. 18.

[8] Cist, *op. cit.*, 13, 16-17. Gen. Arthur St. Clair, governor of Northwest Territory and commander of the army.

orders from President Washington, was making preparations to lead an army of 2,400 frontiersmen against the
Indians. Fowler accepted the appointment of Assistant Surveyor under John S. Gano,[9] afterward General, marched
away with it, and served as scout and hunter. While on this
campaign he heard that his brother Matthew had been
killed near Fort Hamilton, not far from Cincinnati, by the
Indians.[10] His brother Robert escaped unhurt.

St. Clair's disastrous campaign is well known.[11] Fowler
was in the thickest of the battle until he saw the day was
hopelessly lost; then he joined his terror-stricken comrades
in their flight from the awful scene. Beyond Fort Jefferson
they met Colonel Hamtramck with 500 to 600 reinforcements and provisions for the stricken army.[12]

About 1792 Fowler sued General James Wilkinson for
scouting pay, which had been withheld on the grounds that
all he did while in service was loaf around Indian camps
with an Indian wife. The case came to trial, the jury returned a verdict in favor of Fowler, and the judge ordered
that the General be held in jail until the debt was paid.[13]

Fowler married the widow Esther Sanders, *nee* de Vie, of
Newport, Kentucky, probably not long after St. Clair's
defeat. They had at least three children – Edward, Benjamin, and Adelaide – and possibly more.[14] He built a cabin
on the site of Newport, Kentucky, and in 1793 assisted Gen-

9 Roosevelt, *op. cit.*, 146, 151, 154; Cist, *op. cit.*, 17.

10 Cist, *op. cit.*, 17, 20.

11 Cist, *op. cit.*, 21-29; Van Cleve, *op. cit.*, 28; James McBride, *Pioneer Biography: sketches of lives of some early settlers of Butler County, Ohio* (2 vols.,
Cincinnati, 1869), I, pp. 148-49, 154, 156-59.

12 Roosevelt, *op. cit.*, v, pp. 169-70. This was one of the most crushing defeats in
the history of Indian warfare, exceeding in losses those of Gen. Braddock in 1755.
Van Cleve, *op. cit.*, 28.

13 Charles T. Greve, *Centennial History of Cincinnati* (2 vols., Cincinnati, 1904),
I, pp. 301, 308, 371.

14 Jacob Fowler, *Journal of* (New York, 1898), xi-xii; Mrs. James Joyce Arthur,
Annals of the Fowler Family (Austin, Texas, 1901), 313-17; Lewis Collins, *History
of Kentucky* (Louisville, 1877), 424.

eral James Taylor from Virginia, one of the main promoters
of the town, in surveying a road from that place toward
Lexington, Kentucky.[15] In 1795 he was keeping a tavern in
Newport, and the first meeting of the trustees of Newport
Academy was held in his home September 21, 1799.[16]

Like all frontiersmen of the day, Fowler was possessed
of a craving for a huge amount of land. He crossed the
Licking River to Covington, Kentucky, and bought two
thousand acres of what became the site for the city.[17]

Records concerning Fowler's activities during the ten or
twelve years following the turn of the century seem non-
existent. With the outbreak of the War of 1812 he made the
acquaintance of 26-year-old Hugh Glenn, who came to Cincinnati from Mason County, Kentucky, prior to 1811. On
October 12 of that year, Glenn and other prominent men of
Cincinnati organized the Farmers and Mechanics Bank.[18]
With the outbreak of the war Fowler became a contractor
in the Quartermaster's Department of the United States
Army with the rank of assistant quartermaster. His responsibility was to furnish the army with whiskey, beef, bread,
biscuits, bacon and other commissary supplies. General
William Henry Harrison also called upon John H. Piatt,
merchant of Cincinnati and a relative of Fowler, for rations
to sustain the volunteers and regular troops. At that time
Fowler was serving around Detroit and the Maumee
Rapids, furnishing supplies for the garrison at Fort Wayne
and British prisoners of war. In this work he frequently
came in contact with Hugh Glenn. In 1814, Fowler, Glenn,

---

[15] James A. Padgett, "Letters of James Taylor to the Presidents of the United
States," in *Register of Kentucky State Historical Society*, xxxiv (1936), 104.

[16] Jones, *op. cit.*, 7-8.

[17] Fowler, *op. cit.*, x.

[18] Cincinnati *Western Spy*, Oct. 26, 1811; Gorham Worth, *Recollections of Cincinnati, 1817-1821* (Albany, 1851), reprinted in *Quarterly Publications of Historical
and Philosophical Society of Ohio*, xi, p. 42. [For further information concerning
Hugh Glenn and his varied activities, see sketch by Harry R. Stevens in this
Mountain Men series, ii, p. 161.]

and Robert Piatt, cousin of John H., formed a partnership, called Jacob Fowler & Company, to supply rations for British prisoners of war at Long Point, Ontario, and Fort Wayne. In the summer of 1816 he established a small factory in Newport and manufactured hemp bagging for dry beans and tobacco.

In 1817, Fowler signed Glenn's bond to guarantee the faithful discharge of a contract with the United States War Department. In 1818 he became Glenn's agent at Fort Crawford, in which capacity he drove cattle from Prairie du Chien in Wisconsin to St. Louis, Missouri, looking after Glenn's business as contractor to furnish supplies to various posts in the west, including Fort Osage on the Missouri River and Fort Smith at Belle Pointe on the lower Arkansas River. In November-December, 1817, Glenn accompanied Majors Stephen H. Long and William Bradford to that area.

When Glenn's contract with the government expired, he and Fowler busied themselves for the next two or three years buying large tracts of land in Illinois and elsewhere.[19]

In July or August, 1820, Glenn went to the lower Verdigris River and, with Charles Dennis as partner, opened an Osage trading post sixty miles northeast of Fort Smith on the Verdigris River, a mile above its confluence with the Arkansas. In the spring of 1821 he went back to Cincinnati for a short visit. While there, he and Jacob Fowler made plans for an expedition to the headwaters of the Arkansas River to trade with the Indians and trap beaver. Having wound up his business affairs as best he could, Glenn left Cincinnati early in June and went to St. Louis. There he employed some of the men, especially French-Canadians, for the proposed expedition. Traveling on, he reached Fort Smith on August 5 and secured a license from the Com-

---

19 The number of acres in Glenn's name is not known but it was very great. That Fowler was also interested is certified by records in several Missouri River counties.

mandant, Major William Bradford, to trade with the Indians along the Arkansas River and its tributaries.

Fowler arrived at Fort Smith late in August, possibly with more men. On September 6 they left the fort and marched to Glenn's trading post on the Verdigris, where they remained until September 25, making final arrangements for their undertaking. Among other items Fowler carried in his personal baggage was a supply of note paper, pens, and a bottle of ink, for he meant to record such events of the journey as he thought worthy of remembrance. Every night while his companions loafed about the campfire, he sat apart writing down, in a fascinating, sometimes mystifying scrawl resembling Egyptian hieroglyphics, the events of the past day. At first glance the average reader would find it hopelessly illegible, but by close, persevering study of his sometimes weird handwriting it may be read.

One of the most charming features of the document is his unique phonetic spelling ."Where" becomes "wheare," "proceed" is written "purceed," the name of his partner Glenn becomes "glann," "bed" is spelled "beed," "here" appears as "heare," "made" is written down as "maid," "pleasant" is "pleesent," "horse," as "hors," "delighted" as "delited," and so on. His capitalization follows no pattern whatever, and to him punctuation was an unknown art. One is, however, impressed by his fidelity to his self-imposed task, for he never missed a single day's entry. When he returned home he placed the manuscript in the family archives, where it remained totally unknown for seventy-six years, until 1898, when Francis P. Harper brought out an edition of 950 copies edited by Elliot Coues. The original is now in the library of the University of Chicago.

As the cavalcade moved up the Arkansas River, it presented an interesting spectacle. There were twenty men, thirty horses, and seventeen pack mules loaded with beaver traps and Indian trade goods.²⁰ Day by day they trudged along the east leg of the great bend of the Arkansas, with little to break the monotony except an occasional rainstorm, the loss of a few horses to the Osage Indians, and a couple of hunters getting themselves lost in the vast prairie. Thus the first fur brigade to penetrate the Southwest got under way.

On October 26, near present Cimarron, Kansas, they camped at an old Indian fort where they discovered the tracks of shod horses – proof that white men had recently passed that way, though they had no idea who they might be. They were made by William Becknell's party ²¹ from Franklin, Missouri, on its way to Santa Fe. On November 14, while in camp at the mouth of the Purgatory River, the first and only casualty of the expedition occurred. Lewis Dawson was so severely mauled by a grizzly bear that he died the following day.²²

Five days later, on November 19, they met a Kiowa chief and thirty to fifty warriors who gave evidence of a friendly disposition. The chief and two warriors remained with the expedition that night, while the others returned to the tribe to spread the news that white traders were in the country. The following day the chief traveled upstream with them. During the day the remainder of the tribe came in and set up some two hundred lodges, each containing from twelve to twenty persons.

Although Glenn and Fowler did not know it, they had

---

20 It should be borne in mind that in planning this expedition, Glenn and Fowler intended only to trade with the Indians along the Arkansas River and trap beaver on its headwaters on American soil. On September 27, 1821, twenty-two days after they set out from Glenn's trading house, Mexico gained her independence from Spain and rescinded the restrictions on foreign traders entering the country. Our traders did not learn of this until some three months later. Fowler, *op. cit.,* 72, 74, 94, 95.

21 Becknell's career will be narrated later in this series.

22 Dawson made the fatal mistake of attacking single-handed and wounding a grizzly bear. No experienced hunter, white or red, would have done such a thing.

stumbled upon the spot where an Indian fair or rendezvous, as the Mountain Men called such occasions a few years later,[23] was in progress. They had finished their fall hunt and were ready to go home for the winter. They had come from as far north as the upper Missouri River and the Red River on the south. Hostilities, if any existed, were temporarily adjourned, everyone had a good time, tribes that were poor in horses bought all they could afford, and stole any they could get away with.

The following day 350 lodges of Comanches came in and also camped near the white men. Next came the Arapahoes and Cheyennes. When all had arrived, Fowler estimated they numbered from ten to eighteen thousand, of all ages and both sexes. The expedition was now in a perilous situation. The Comanches openly declared they would kill the traders and take their goods.[24] The Cheyennes were willing to help, but the Kiowas and Arapahoes, who outnumbered all the others combined, claimed the white men as their friends and property.[25] In spite of the critical, perilous situation, a party of six men led by Isaac Slover was sent into the mountains upstream on December 3 to trap beaver. On

[23] The first of these was held by William H. Ashley in the Green River Valley in 1825.

[24] "friday 23 nov 1821 – this morning a Councel was hild amongst the Cheefs of both the nations (Kiowas and Ietans, or Highatans or Comanches), and Conl Glann . . . was told by the Ietan Cheef that the Ware Ready to Receive the goods in his possession that His father the Presedent had sent them – But When He was told that there Was no Such goods He Became in a great Pashion and told the Conl that he was a lyer and a theef and that He Head Stolen the goods from his father and that He the Cheef Wold take the goods and Segnefyed that He Wold kill the Conl and His men too. . ." Fowler, op. cit., 53-54. In 1820 Major Stephen H. Long had come through Comanche territory along the Arkansas and Canadian rivers and met this identical chief and told him that President Monroe would send him "plenty of goods and that the goods We Head Ware Sent to him and that We head no Wright to traid them." Fowler, op. cit., 58.

[25] The Cheyennes joined the Comanches, but at the critical moment a large number of Arapahoes joined the Kiowas in declaring their friendship for the white man. Being outnumbered, the Comanches abandoned their warlike intentions and a battle to the death was avoided. Fowler, op. cit., 54.

December 28 the remainder moved camp to a spot on the south side of the Arkansas River, opposite the site of future Pueblo, Colorado.

Two days later a party of sixty Spanish traders from Taos and Santa Fe [26] came to camp with the information that Mexico had achieved independence from Spain and that the law prohibiting foreigners, especially Americans, from trading or trapping in the country had been abolished. Consequently, Glenn decided to accompany them on their return and secure permission to enter Mexico. He set out on January 2, 1822, leaving Fowler in charge of the expedition and taking four men with him.

Glenn promised to come back or send word in fifteen days, but if he did neither they were to conclude that he had been thrown into prison. In that event they would make their way back to Missouri as best they could. The following morning five of the men mutinied because they did not expect that the Spaniards would allow Glenn, to whom they looked for payment of their wages, to return. Fowler, with the help of his brother Robert, succeeded in putting down the rebellion.

On January 20, 1822, Fowler crossed the Arkansas River to the site of future Pueblo on American soil and built a strong stockade and horse pen. On January 28 all fears concerning Glenn's safety were set at rest by the arrival of Baptiste Peno with the news that Glenn's trip to Santa Fe was successful. He had secured the desired permission, gotten a license to trap in New Mexico, and would meet Fowler and the other members of the expedition at Taos.

Fowler led the now jubilant party along the old Taos Trail [27] toward the south, following the eastern base of the

---

[26] Comancheros.

[27] The old Indian-Spanish route from Santa Fe through Taos and across the Sangre de Cristo mountains by way of Sangre de Cristo Pass to the Arkansas River, which Pierre and Paul Mallet followed on their historic journey from St. Louis to

Sangre de Cristo Mountains. They crossed the range through Sangre de Cristo Pass, skirted the southeast edge of the San Luis Valley, passed the site of future Fort Garland, and reached Taos on February 8, 1822, where they found Glenn awaiting them. Two days later two trapping parties were sent back up the Rio Grande to the San Luis Valley, to remain out until May 1.

On February 10, Fowler himself set out for the same area, and Glenn returned to Santa Fe. In the following weeks the three parties set their traps upstream on the Rio Grande as far as Wagon Wheel Gap, with only meager success, because the streams were all frozen over and the animals remained in their houses. The three parties returned to Taos where all had arrived by May 1. Here they remained until June 1, making preparations for their return to Missouri. On that date they went out, crossed the Taos Mountains through Taos Pass and bore east toward the Arkansas River, which they reached at the site of present Coolidge, Kansas, on June 11.

The journey eastward along that stream was without significant incident except that on June 28, in present Franklin County, Kansas, they saw the tracks of William Becknell's three wagons on their way to Santa Fe. The significance of those tracks, made by the first wagons to cross the Great Plains, seems to have been entirely lost upon Fowler.

On July 5, 1822, they rode into Fort Osage on the Missouri River. There they bought two canoes (pirogues), built a platform upon them, piled their furs and baggage upon it, and floated down to St. Louis, where they arrived about July 15. Four men were detailed to bring on their horses. After two days in the city, Fowler set out for Cincinnati by

Santa Fe, New Mexico, in 1739-1740. They were the first white men to enter New Mexico from the Mississippi and Missouri rivers. Folmer, "The Mallet Expedition of 1739 through Nebraska, Kansas and Colorado to Santa Fe," in *Colorado Magazine*, XVI, pp. 161-73.

water, where he arrived on July 17, 1822, having been absent over thirteen months. He crossed the Ohio River to Covington, Kentucky, and was at home with his family.

Glenn remained in St. Louis, paid off the members of the expedition, settled accounts for supplies, etc., and sold the furs they had laboriously transported on packhorses across the plains, to the American Fur Company for $4,499.64.[28] Just what Fowler's financial interest in the expedition was is rather obscure, but he undoubtedly had a stake in it. When Glenn paid his men and bills for supplies and equipment he had $2,624.85 left.

Although limited to a considerable degree, the expedition achieved certain definite results. The fact that it successfully made the round trip to New Mexico, sustained itself on the Great Plains and in the mountains for almost a year with the loss of only one man, and encountered no difficulty with the Indians or Mexicans, may be certainly regarded as notable achievements.

Furthermore, although Fowler's journal lay unnoticed for seventy-six years, and the information it contained was not available to later travelers to New Mexico, and neither Glenn nor Fowler ever made another trip, the rank and file of the members of the expedition returned to their homes on the Missouri River, St. Louis and the Illinois country. Certainly they made no secret of their great adventure. What they said encouraged others to take the long trail leading westward. In addition, some of the members, such as Isaac Slover, Nathaniel Miguel Pryor, and perhaps others returned to the southwest as hunters and trappers.

On Monday, October 15, 1849, Jacob Fowler died at his home in Covington, Kentucky, leaving a daughter, Abigail; two sons, Benjamin and Edward; one brother, Robert;

---

[28] Contract between Lieutenant Charles Ward and Jacob Fowler, June 20, 1823. National Archives, Record Group no. 94.

probably his wife; a number of grandchildren, among whom was Frances Scott; and a great-granddaughter, Mrs. Ida Symmes, who became the custodian of Fowler's journal. She was a granddaughter of Captain John Cleve Symmes, author of *The Theory of Concentric Circles* (Cincinnati, 1826), and a great granddaughter of Hon. John Cleve Symmes, member of Congress from New Jersey, who, on the north bank of the Ohio River, bought a great body of land on which the city of Cincinnati was founded.[29]

---

[29] Fowler, *op. cit.,* x.

Henry Fraeb

by LeRoy R. Hafen
Brigham Young University

Henry Fraeb, partner in the famous Rocky Mountain Fur Company and subsequently a proprietor of Fort Jackson on the South Platte River, was a leader of Mountain Men during the most active days of the fur trade in the central Rockies. Fraeb, whose name was usually rendered "Frapp" by his trapper companions, was a German from St. Louis, Missouri. Of his early life nothing has yet come to light, nor can we tell the year of his first entry into the fur trade. By 1829 he was already sufficiently seasoned to be a leader of trappers.

Following the rendezvous of 1829 on the Popo Agie branch of Wind River, he was associated with Milton Sublette and Jean B. Gervais in conducting a party down the Bighorn to trap that stream and other affluents of the Yellowstone.[1] His experiences are not reported. But at the rendezvous of 1830 Fraeb comes clearly into the picture. He is one of the five partners that buy out Smith, Jackson, and Sublette and become the founders and proprietors of the Rocky Mountain Fur Company.[2] His partners were experienced fur men – Thomas Fitzpatrick, James Bridger, Milton Sublette, and Jean B. Gervais.

After the breakup of the 1830 rendezvous on Wind River, Fraeb and Gervais led a party of thirty-three men to the Snake River region.[3] Near the mouth of Salt River they ran

---

[1] F. F. Victor, *The River of the West* (Hartford, Conn., 1870), 57.

[2] Documents exhibiting this transfer are in the papers of the Missouri Historical Society, St. Louis.

[3] *Robert Newell's Memoranda,* edited by Dorothy O. Johansen (Portland, 1959), 31.

into a party of American Fur Company men, and lower down the Snake met John Work and a brigade of the Hudson's Bay Company. Fraeb's party finally made its way back to Bear River and to Cache Valley, Utah. Here they were holed in by three-foot snow.[4] Of their spring movements we have no record.

Fitzpatrick, who went down to Missouri in the spring of 1831, arrived there too late to get supplies as planned. Instead, he went with the Smith, Jackson, and Sublette caravan to Santa Fe, where he obtained his supplies and headed north to meet his partners. The roundabout route made it impossible for him to arrive as expected. Fraeb, on Green River in July,[5] waited impatiently for the company goods. Finally he turned to a Crow medicine man to learn what had happened to his partner. After much dancing the seer uttered his findings: Fitzpatrick was not dead, but was on the wrong road.[6]

So Fraeb set out to find him. On the North Platte, below the Sweetwater, he met the belated supply train. While Fitzpatrick turned back to Missouri to assure supplies in time for the next year's rendezvous, Fraeb returned to his trapper band. After supplying these men he pushed on westward to find and supply the other R.M.F. men. This party, under Milton Sublette and Bridger, after giving up hope of receiving supplies, had turned north from Cache Valley and begun their fall trapping. Finally, on Salmon River of northwestern Idaho, Fraeb caught up with his partners and gave them provisions. Ferris says the ensuing debauchery lasted for several days, after which all settled down into winter quarters.[7]

---

[4] W. A. Ferris, *Life in the Rocky Mountains,* edited by P. C. Phillips (Denver, 1940), 58-60, 64, 69.

[5] Victor, *op. cit.,* 98. At Green River on July 9, 1831, Fraeb signed for the Rocky Mountain Fur Company a promissory note to William Gordon for $30; the original is in the Sublette Papers, Missouri Historical Society.

[6] Victor, 99.   [7] Ferris, *op. cit.,* 126.

For the spring of 1832 the R.M.F. men, presumably includ-
ing Fraeb, trapped Henry's Fork, Snake River, and Salt
River before coming in to the appointed rendezvous at
Pierre's Hole.[8]

Fraeb was at this large and well-known meeting of 1832,
and in the ensuing famous battle. At the initial breakup of
the bands, Fraeb, heading about thirty men who were mostly
Canadian half-breeds,[9] started for Snake River in company
with Milton Sublette's and Wyeth's parties. Not many miles
out they met a band of Gros Ventres, and the battle was soon
on. During the fight, one of Fraeb's men crawled close to
the rear of the Indian fort, rolling a log in front of him.
Shots hit the log but not the man. Another of his men, a
Canadian half-breed, rashly crawled up to the wall of the
fort and peeped over the top, only to receive two bullets in
his forehead. Nidever says he "was half drunk at the time,
liquor having been distributed among the men during the
early part of the fight.[10] When it was reported that Indian
reenforcements were on the way and had attacked the main
white camp, Fraeb withdrew his men.[11]

On July 24 Fraeb, Gervais, and Milton Sublette, with
Wyeth in tow, again set out for fall trapping fields.[12] Early
in this trip an incident occurred which John Ball describes:

> Mr. Frapp had an Indian wife who traveled along with him, and
> the Indians of the party, some of them, had their wives, these women
> as good horsemen as the men, always riding astride. One day we de-
> layed our march, we knew not why, till after a time we heard an out-
> cry for a few minutes from Frapp's wife, out to one side in some
> bushes. And we soon learned the cause of our laying over, was to give
> her the opportunity to lay in, give birth to a child in camp and not on

8 Newell, *op. cit.,* 32.
9 George Nidever, *Life and Adventures,* edited by W. H. Ellison (Berkeley, 1937),
25, 26. See also John Ball, *Autobiography of* (Grand Rapids, Mich., 1925), 77-79;
and F. G. Young (ed.), *The Correspondence and Journals of Captain Nathaniel J.
Wyeth* (Eugene, Ore., 1899), 159 [hereafter cited as Wyeth].
10 Nidever, 28.   11 *Ibid.,* 29.   12 Wyeth, 160.

our day's march. But the very next day, she sat her newborn baby, feet down, into a deep basket that she hung to the pummel of her saddle, mounted her horse and rode on in the band as usual. And she had another child of two or three, who had his own horse. He was sat on the saddle and blankets brought around him so as to keep him erect, and his gentle pony went loose with the other pack horses, which kept along with those riding and never strayed from the common band.[13]

After laying in some buffalo meat provisions on the Snake River, Sublette and Wyeth continued down that stream. Fraeb left them and led his party south towards the Great Salt Lake.[14] He worked his way to the head of the North Platte and into the mountain parks of present Colorado. His whereabouts is learned from the report that a trapper named Guthrie was killed by lightning. Fitzpatrick reports it as occurring in the fall of 1832.[15] Joe Meek gives interesting details, though misdating the incident:

A number of persons were collected in the lodge of the Booshway, Frapp [Fraeb], to avoid the rising tempest, when Gutherie, who was leaning against the lodge pole, was struck by a flash of the electric current, and fell dead instantly. Frapp rushed out of the lodge, partly bewildered himself by the shock, and under the impression that Guthrie had been shot. Frapp was a German, and spoke English somewhat imperfectly. In the excitement of the moment he shouted out, "Py Gott, who did shoot Guttery"!

"G — a'Mighty, I expect; He's a firing into camp," drawled out Hawkins, whose ready wit was very disregardful of sacred names and subjects.[16]

By early June, 1833, Fraeb was with Fitzpatrick on the upper North Platte, where it was arranged that the former should go east for supplies.[17] He had gone but a little way when he met Robert Campbell, westbound with a supply

[13] John Ball, 80.   [14] Nidever, 30.
[15] Fitzpatrick's letter of Nov. 13, 1833, in the Sublette Collection, Missouri Historical Society.   [16] Victor, 157-58.
[17] Fitzpatrick's letter of June 4, 1833, to Robert Campbell, Missouri Historical Society.

train. Fraeb took over most of the goods and transported them to rendezvous on Green River.[18]

For the fall 1833 trapping Fraeb took a party of twenty men down the Green River and the Colorado, with Bill Williams as guide.[19] Early next spring, according to Joe Meek, they were visited on Bill Williams Fork of the Colorado in Arizona by some of Joe Walker's men returning from California.[20] The combined parties, says Meek, visited the Moquis, Grand River and New Park (Colorado), and finally went to the rendezvous of 1834 on Ham's Fork of Green River.

At this meeting the R.M.F. Company was dissolved. The financially-inept partners could not compete successfully with the powerful opposition. Fraeb was the first to withdraw; in the settlement he received forty head of horses, forty beaver traps, eight guns, and $1000 worth of merchandise, William Sublette buying his share in the company.[21] Gervais next sold out, receiving about half as much as Fraeb. The company was then reorganized as Fitzpatrick, Sublette, and Bridger.

Fraeb probably carried on independent trade during the winter. He and Gervais went down to Missouri with Fontenelle in 1835 and spent the ensuing winter in Missouri.[22]

In the spring of 1837 Fraeb and Peter Sarpy, another experienced fur man, formed a partnership, backed by Pratte, Chouteau & Co. of St. Louis. Trade merchandise to the amount of $10,909.75 was billed to Sarpy & Fraeb on April 10, 1837, and, in addition, cash and goods totaling

18 Elliott Coues (ed.), *Forty Years a Fur Trader. . . Narrative of Charles Larpenteur* (New York, 1899), 25.

19 Fitzpatrick's letter of Nov. 13, 1833, to Milton Sublette; Sublette Collection, Missouri Historical Society.

20 Victor, 152.

21 Dissolution papers in the Sublette Collection, Missouri Historical Society.

22 See William Sublette's letters to Robert Campbell of Nov. 2, 1835, and Jan. 12, 1836, Robert Campbell Papers, Missouri Historical Society.

$564.57 were furnished from the retail store of Pratte, Chouteau & Co.[23] This retail store account gives the names of many of the company employees. A wage of $200 per year was the amount promised most of the men. Wagons were employed for transportation of the goods to the South Platte River. The adobe trading post, built on the South Platte River for receiving and dispensing the goods, was called Fort Jackson.[24]

In September an inventory at the fort was taken and on December 2, 1837, part of the goods were sent down to the Arkansas River for trade with the Indians during the winter.[25] The Fort Jackson proprietors entered into trade competition with the men at neighboring forts Lupton and St. Vrain, and also sent goods up to the North Platte to compete with Fort Laramie. Sarpy, in a letter from the North Platte to partner Fraeb on Feb. 18, 1838, wrote: "My object is to do all the harm possible to the opposition and yet without harming ourselves." [26] The results of the winter's trade amounted to $10,046.93; the principal item being 2761 buffalo robes at $3.37½ each. Only fifty-three beaver skins were included; these listed at $3.25 per pound.

The competition was too keen, forts too numerous on the South Platte; so in the autumn of 1838 Sarpy and Fraeb sold their Fort Jackson and its contents to Bent & St. Vrain. The inventory of the goods fills nine pages.[27]

Fraeb appears to have gone to St. Louis, and in the spring of 1840 he and Bridger came out with goods to the last

---

[23] Choteau-Maffitt Collection, Missouri Historical Society.

[24] The location of the fort was determined and its ruins found by this writer in 1924, near Ione, Colorado. Its name was not then known. Later I found at the Missouri Historical Society documents that identified it as Fort Jackson. See my article, "Fort Jackson and the Early Fur Trade on the South Platte," in the *Colorado Magazine,* v (1928), 9-17.

[25] Calendars 722 and 729 in the Chouteau-Maffitt Collection, Missouri Historical Society.   [26] *Ibid.,* Calendar 720.

[27] A photostat of the list is in the library of the State Historical Society of Colorado.

rendezvous.[28] The two men formed a trading partnership.[29] That fall Fraeb and Joseph R. Walker took beaver pelts out to southern California and traded them to Abel Stearns, Los Angeles merchant. They sold him 417 pounds of beaver for $1147. In exchange they received sugar, coffee, tobacco, beans, soap, and *aguardiente;* and 100 mares at $2 each, 17 mules at $12, and 2 stallions at $10 each.[30]

By July, 1841, Fraeb and his men were back on Green River, in time to meet the first covered wagon caravan bound for Oregon and California, guided by his old partner, Fitzpatrick. Rev. Joseph Williams of the emigrant party says Fraeb's company "was mostly composed of half breeds, French, and Dutch, and all sorts of people collected together in the mountains, and were a wicked, swearing company of men." [31] John Bidwell of the emigrants, says Fraeb's party purchased a supply of whiskey from the emigrants.[32]

While Bridger was at the partners' fort on Green River, Fraeb led a party southeast to make meat. In the valley of the Little Snake, a branch of Yampa River, they met up with a large party of Cheyennes, Arapahoes, and Sioux. A pitched battle occurred in late August, 1841. A number of contemporaries reported the engagement.[33] Two participants

---

28 Newell, 39.

29 See the letter of W. L. Sublette to W. D. Stewart, Sept. 1842, in the Sublette Collection, Missouri Historical Society.

30 See the accounts in Stearns Papers, Box 73, Huntington Library, San Marino, Calif. Included are orders and a letter signed by Fraeb.

31 Williams' *Narrative,* reprinted in LeRoy R. and Ann W. Hafen, *Far West and Rockies Series,* III (Glendale, 1955), p. 230. Father De Smet in his *Life, Letters,* etc., edited by Chittenden and Richardson, says that Fraeb had just returned from California.

32 The *Century Illustrated Monthly Magazine,* XLI (New Series, XIX), 119.

33 Rufus B. Sage was told by Mountain Men in September, 1841, that Fraeb and four of his men were killed. Two years later he visited the site of the engagement. See his reports in Hafen and Hafen, *Far West and Rockies Series,* IV, p. 149; and v, p. 184. Sage says the enemy lost fifteen or twenty killed but drove off eighty head of horses. J. C. Frémont was told of the fight by Bridger and others in 1842. He reports that the enemy "Indians lost eight or ten warriors, and the whites had their leader and four men killed." – *Report of an Exploring Expedition,* etc. (Wash-

later gave detailed reminiscent accounts.

Jim Baker, picturesque Colorado pioneer, who had come out with the Bartleson party of emigrants in 1841 and joined Fraeb at Green River, gave an interesting account to an interviewer in 1886:

> Shortly after I came out here the second time we were camped on the very creek where I live now – Snake River we called it then – and there we had a lively fight with a party of about 500 Sioux, Cheyennes, and Arapahoes. The Arapahoes didn't do much fighting, but they urged the others on. There were twenty-three in our party, and I can give you the names of every one of them. Old Frappe was in command. The Indians made about forty charges on us, coming up to within ten or fifteen paces of us every time. Their object was to draw our fire, but old Frappe kept shouting "Don't shoot till you're sure. One at a time." And so some of us kept loaded all the time. We made breastworks of our horses and hid behind stumps. Old Frappe was killed, and he was the ugliest looking dead man I ever saw, and I have seen a good many. His face was all covered with blood, and he had rotten front teeth and a horrible grin. When he was killed he never fell, but sat braced up against the stump, a sight to behold. Well, when the fight was over there were about a hundred dead Injuns. There were three of our party killed.[34]

Basil Clement also gave a reminiscent account:

> We had a fight with the Sioux and Cheyennes there [on Little Snake River]. Old Frapp (Henry Fraeb) was killed there, he was one of the three partners. We went there (from Black's Creek) on a

---

ington, 1845), 40. Frémont passed the site of the battle on his return from California in 1844. W. L. Sublette in his letter of September, 1842, to W. D. Stewart, *op. cit.,* says Fraeb and three others were killed.

Capt. Howard Stansbury, guided near the site of the battle by Jim Bridger in 1850, was told of the fight by Fraeb's partner. Stansbury reports in his *Exploration and Survey of the Valley of the Great Salt Lake,* etc. (Washington, 1853), 239, a preliminary fight and then the main attack about ten days later. Fraeb "had but forty men; but they instantly 'forted' in the corral attached to the trading post and stood on their defence. The assault lasted from noon until sundown, the Indians charging the picket several times with great bravery; but they were finally repulsed with the loss of forty men. Frappe himself was killed, with seven or eight of his people."

[34] *Denver Tribune-Republican,* July 10, 1886.

buffalo hunt to make jerked meat. We got meat of the Sioux and
Cheyennes, with 47 men. After we had plenty of meat they made a
dash for us. We defended ourselves. That was in the morning about
8 o'clock. This was about July, some time early in July. We fought
them from the morning about 8 o'clock till dark. They killed ten of
our men, and killed 110 head of horses that belonged to us; and of the
45 head of horses alive, there was only five not wounded. All that we
had to protect us was dead horses. We made a fort of them. The next
morning we fired guns and showed fight, for them to come out, but
they wouldn't come.[35]

The site of the battle, according to Jim Baker, was at the
mouth of Battle Creek, in Routt County, Colorado, about a
half mile from the Wyoming line. Battle Creek and Battle
Mountain take their name from Henry Fraeb's last fight.

---

[35] *South Dakota Historical Collections,* XI, p. 291.

Isaac Graham

by DOYCE B. NUNIS, JR.
University of Southern California

Relatively little is known about Isaac Graham's life prior to his debut as a fur trapper in the Southwest. His father, reputedly a descendant of the famous Stuart sympathizer, Sir James Graham of Claverhouse, the Viscount Dundee, and Jane Cock, daughter of a renowned British admiral, immigrated to colonial America on the eve of the Revolutionary War with his wife. He settled in Fincastle, Botetourt County, Virginia, not long after the battle of Yorktown. There on September 1, 1800, Isaac Graham was born.[1]

By 1803, Jesse Graham heeded the call westward and moved his family to Crab Orchard, Lincoln County, Kentucky. Several years later he died, leaving his widow with twelve children to rear — two girls and ten boys, Isaac being the youngest — and in dire economic straights. Isaac, probably like most of his brothers, received no formal schooling; he learned neither to read nor write, other than being able to sign his name.[2]

---

[1] The data for Graham's family and pre-trade background has been drawn from Dorothy A. Hertzog, "Isaac Graham: California Pioneer," (unpublished M.A. thesis, University of California, Berkeley, 1942), 2-7. (Mrs. Hertzog relied on a family account written by Graham's daughter, Mrs. Matilda Jane Graham Rice, a statement which must be weighed with care.) Additional data has been drawn from newspaper obituaries: San Francisco *Bulletin* and *Alta California,* November 9, 1863, p. 5, col. 5, and p. 1, col. 2, respectively; Watsonville *Pajaro Times,* November 14, 1863, p. 2, col. 4; Santa Cruz *Riptide,* October 19, 1950, p. 35, col. 1.

Unfortunately, Graham's personal papers were destroyed. A letter in the "Pioneer File," California State Library, Sacramento, from Mrs. Rice to Mr. M. J. Ferguson, December 9, 1918, records: "I have not many of Father's papers left as they were all destroyed after Father died by my husband as of no good to anybody. . ." In the same library's "Pioneer Index," however, Mrs. Rice attests to the essential biographical facts pertaining to her father in respect to his birth, parents, and death.

[2] Henry J. Bee, "Recollections of the History of California," MS., 7, Bancroft

While seven of his older brothers served with Andrew Jackson's troops during the War of 1812, the young lad found employment as a jockey, training that was to stand him in good stead in later years.[3] This apprenticeship was his only known "education." However, life at Crab Orchard might well have included sharing youthful experiences with the soon-to-be-famous fur trade Sublette brothers, William and Milton, when they settled there in 1812.[4]

Like many uneducated frontiersmen, restless but hopeful, Graham joined a party of young men who traveled westward to Missouri in 1818 in search of fortune and adventure. He wintered at Fort Hudson on the Missouri River, and in the spring moved on to Marthasville where he contacted Daniel Boone, "a cousin on his mother's side of the family."[5] There he spent the following three years, and reputedly was at Boone's bedside when the famed old man died in 1820.[6]

A few years after Boone's death, Graham decided to return to Kentucky. However, he got only as far as Jonesville, Tennessee, where he stopped to work. Soon after, in 1823, he married a Miss Jones and fathered four children: two sons, Isaac Wayne and Jesse Jones, and two daughters.[7]

Library, University of California, Berkeley. The fact that all of Graham's correspondence, what little survives, was written by others but signed by him, is further proof of his illiteracy.

[3] Graham to Abel Stearns, writing from Natividad, California, February 16, March 23, 1840. Stearns Collection, Henry E. Huntington Library. These two letters relate to Graham's offer to ride for Stearns in an impending horse race. Also, see Thomas J. Farnham, *The Early Days of California* (Philadelphia, 1859), 66-67, for supporting details on Graham's experience as a jockey.

[4] John E. Sunder, *Bill Sublette* (Norman, Okla., 1959), 14.

[5] Hertzog, "Graham," 4; Watsonville *Pajaro Times*, November 14, 1863.

[6] San Francisco *Bulletin*, November 9, 1863. The Watsonville *Pajaro Times*, November 14, 1863, relates: "In 1821 he [Graham] was again a traveler – this time to the Rocky Mountains; however, on reaching Fort Smith [Arkansas], and there meeting Billy Ware, another [California] pioneer, he stayed for some time, and then retraced his steps to Tennessee, where he married, and became the father of four children."

Although ensconced with home and hearth, Graham surrendered his placid Tennessee life for the more exciting
beckoning frontier. Perhaps his decision was involuntary.
One account relates that because of "some offence that he
committed he had to leave the State and found his way into
New Mexico." [8] Whatever the actual circumstances, by 1830
Graham began to earn his livelihood as a trapper. He
launched that career at Fort Smith, Arkansas.[9]

In early May, 1830, three dozen or so young men, who
were deft in handling a rifle and at hunting small game,
formed a trapping party at Fort Smith under the command
of an elderly gunsmith from Crawford County, Tennessee,
Colonel Robert Bean. Though none of the recruits, including the leader, had any experience as trappers – only three
had ever fought Indians – the brigade of novices boldly set
out for their projected hunt on or about May 7. Although
it is impossible to fix with certainty the number of the initial
party, Graham commenced his trapping activities along side
Job F. Dye, Isaac Williams, Henry Naile, George Frazer,
George Nidever, T. Ambrose Tomlinson, and Jacob P.
Leese, all eventually destined to spend the remainder of
their lives as California residents.[10] Until late summer the
company moved ever westward with little inconvenience.

[7] Hertzog, "Graham," 5; Santa Cruz *Riptide,* October 19, 1950, p. 35, col. 1.
Marriage date given in *Report of Cases Argued and Determined in the Supreme
Court in the Year 1852* (Philadelphia, 1854), II, p. 504.

[8] B[enjamin] D. Wilson, "Reminiscences," MS., Shorb Collection, box 17, Huntington Library. (Another copy in the Bancroft Library.)

[9] Graham's fur trade activities before his removal to California are recorded,
although not consistently, in Job F. Dye, *Recollections of a Pioneer, 1830-1852* (Los
Angeles, 1951), and *The Life and Adventures of George Nidever [1802-1883],*
edited by William H. Ellison (Berkeley, 1937), memoirs which were written in their
later years. (Hereinafter cited *Dye Recoll.* and *Nidever Adventures.*)

[10] *Dye Recoll.,* 2-5; *Nidever Adventures,* 4-7; Mrs. F. H. Day, "Sketches of the
Early Settlers of California: Jacob P. Leese," *The Hesperian,* II (June, 1859), 146.
LeRoy R. Hafen, "The Bean-Sinclair Party of Rocky Mountain Trappers, 1830-32,"
Colorado Magazine, XXXI (July, 1954), 161-71, presents a summary of the company's
initial organization and activities.

One September day, however, while traveling along the north bank of the Arkansas' north fork, the party met a band of eighty Pawnee. The next afternoon, having left the Indians behind, Graham set out on a buffalo hunt with George Nidever. Four miles from their camp, the pair were trapped by a large party of seemingly belligerent Arapahoes. Caught in open country, "the nearest timber being that of the river belt, fully a mile and a half away, and a pack of fleet footed redskins close upon" them, the two realized their only hope lay in reaching that defensive, but distant cover.

Although Graham was "a good runner," in fact the best in the ranks, he stayed with the slower moving Nidever because "it was not his character to desert a comrade in danger." After a mile of running pursuit, the Indians closed in. "Graham, although naturally a brave man, was not a little frightened and was almost exhausted." Fearful of capture, he turned to fire, failing to "see the foremost Indians throw down their guns." Fortunately, Nidever had and prevented him from shooting. "Had he shot, he would have fought to the last," only to be overpowered in the end. Nidever's quick action and the subsequent successful parley with the Arapahoes saved their lives.[11]

Thereafter, the party was plagued by Indian hostility, death, and misfortune. The company's "poor success in catching beaver and killing game," and awareness of the threat of impending wintertime, led the brigade, "after holding a grand council," to start for the warmer clime of New Mexico. It was then late November.

Through good fortune, the party discovered a buffalo trail which took them, in spite of snow, across the mountains which lie between the Arkansas and the "Rio del Norte." A week's passage on a difficult trail brought them to the banks of the Rio Grande and a hunting ground plentiful with buffalo and deer. Without further impediment, the

---

[11] *Nidever Adventures*, 10-14, 37. *Dye Recoll.*, 5-6, is garbled on this event.

party arrived at Arroyo Seco, situated ten miles from the Rio Grande on the Arroyo Hondo, a river which flows into the Rio Grande about forty miles from the northern boundary line of New Mexico. Twelve miles south lay Taos.[12]

Having reached a safe but disputed sanctuary, the party split.[13] A number returned to Fort Smith, while others elected to seek local employment. Some chose to join the second expedition of Ewing Young to California, which set out from Taos in September, 1831.[14] But not Graham. He decided to stay with Alexander Sinclair. Some fourteen or fifteen of the original band decided likewise.[15]

Several weeks after their December, 1830, arrival in Arroyo Seco, and apparently assured of a winter haven, with or without the government's endorsement, Graham, George Nidever, and Alexander Sinclair endeavored to retrieve the party's traps, which had been cached on the Arkansas. But their rescue effort was thwarted by heavy snow and continuing Indian hostility. Quickly the three men returned to their New Mexican refuge empty-handed.[16]

12 *Ibid.*, 8-13; *Nidever Adventures*, 14-19, who puts the beaver catch at forty to fifty skins (p. 17). Day, "Leese," 147, states that in the month of November the party established a "rendezvous on the north fork of the Arkansas, about one hundred miles above Pikes Peak. On the 27th of the month, "Mark Nidever and Frederick Crist (or Christ) were slain," while Graham and three others (Dye, Naile, and Price) "barely escaped with their lives." After this unhappy occurrence the company headed for New Mexico.

13 Letter of Dr. James S. Craig, Santa Fe, January 2, 1831, printed in the *Arkansas Gazette*, June 8, 1831. *Dye Recoll.*, 16-17, notes that three men were sent to "report to the authorities [in Taos], which we did by informing them that we had no general passport, but was forced by privations and distress to come into the settlements, and asked for the favor to pass the winter under the protection of Mexico." Ten days later, told to leave, they ignored the order.

14 For those who returned to Fort Smith and/or joined Ewing Young, see the Little Rock *Advocate*, October 13, 1830; *Arkansas Gazette*, November 2, 1831; *Nidever Adventures*, 19-20; *Dye Recoll.*, 18; Hubert H. Bancroft, *History of California* (7 vols., San Francisco, 1884-1890), III, pp. 388-89, and notes.

15 Among those remaining were probably at least the following: Bidler (?), Bowen, Carmichael, Frazer, Graham, Naile, G. Nidever, Pollum, Price, the two Sinclairs.

16 *Nidever Adventures*, 21, gives March, 1831, as the erroneous date when the

Early spring found the frustrated trappers ready to move. Selling what few skins they had caught during their initial hunt for supplies to stake them in a second attempt, in March, 1831, under Alexander Sinclair's command, the small band headed for the Platte River. Without incident or injury they reached the north fork and stumbled into a valley rich in beaver. When they returned to Arroyo Seco, July 4, 1831, each hunter had "about two packs of skins of 60 each." To avoid the heavy Mexican duties levied on pelts, the catch was smuggled in and profitably disposed of in Taos. Each skin netted the hunters ten dollars on the clandestine market.[17]

Endowed now with sufficient capital and enriched with greater confidence, the party refitted and set out in September, 1831, for the headwaters of the Arkansas for another assault on the beaver. Sinclair and his men decided on the Green River to spend the winter. In November they selected "a large deep valley . . . about 10 miles wide and 20 in length, and opening into a valley on the north and into another on the south," possibly the upper valley of the Green River under the Wind River Mountains, for their winter quarters. When they settled down, they had already trapped nearly a hundred beaver en route.[18]

In March, 1832, when the thaw came, the camp-bored men left the valley and followed the Green to its head, "with the intention of trapping that season on the headwaters of the Columbia." Leisurely they hunted along the Green until May when they rudely learned that their intended destination "was already being trapped by other companies"

---

party reached Arroyo Seco. (The letter written by Dr. Craig from Santa Fe, January 2, 1831, as cited in the preceding note 13, indicates December, 1830, as the more appropriate date.)   [17] *Ibid.*, 22.

[18] *Ibid.*, 22-23. In April, 1832, Kit Carson recorded that his party, commanded by Thomas Fitzpatrick, met Sinclair's band on the Green River and that they had wintered on the "Little Bear River, a branch of [the] Green." Milo M. Quaife (ed.), *Kit Carson's Autobiography* (Chicago, 1935), 23.

– the Rocky Mountain Fur Company, the American Fur Company and Hudson's Bay Company were all actively competing for the fur harvests in that region.[19]

This intelligence provoked the temporary dissolution of the brigade. As free trappers, mutual interest and personal loyalty had been their only bonds of union. Now, faced with organized and formidable competition, dissension split them asunder, "some going in one direction and some another." However, the majority decided to continue their association and struck out towards the Platte to hunt. The paucity of records does not disclose Graham's decision. Little matter, since the company was reunited in early July at the Pierre's Hole rendezvous. But not all: a member of the Platte-bound group was slain by Indians.[20]

The 1832 rendezvous proved memorable. Present were such longtime Mountain Men as James O'Fallon, Moses Harris, James Bridger, Henry Fraeb, Thomas Fitzpatrick, Milton and William Sublette, as well as newcomers who would leave their names large in fur trade annals: Nathaniel Wyeth, Captain Benjamin Bonneville, Zenas Leonard, Joseph Reddeford Walker. Also present were Alexander Sinclair's free trappers, "some 14 or 15," including Graham.[21]

On July 17, Wyeth and eleven of his original party, the others having decided to return to St. Louis with William Sublette, joined a band of trappers under Milton Sublette and Henry Fraeb, whose intention was a hunting foray to the Columbia. The first evening they encamped eight miles southwest of the rendezvous site. Sinclair's trappers, having "decided to trap that season on the Marys River [Hum-

[19] *Nidever Adventures,* 23-24; Hiram M. Chittenden, *The American Fur Trade of the Far West* (2 vols., New York, 1902), I, pp. 247-48, 299. (Perhaps this intelligence came from Fitzpatrick's party.)

[20] *Nidever Adventures,* 24-25.

[21] *Ibid.,* 25. Since the party was reunited, it probably can be safely assumed that Graham was among them.

boldt], a small stream about South West of Salt Lake," left
Pierre's Hole with them and that night camped "a short
distance in their rear."

The following morning Sinclair's men packed and rode
over to the neighboring camp. Soon after their arrival, two
groups of Blackfeet, numbering 250 to 300, were spotted
near at hand. Immediately Milton Sublette dispatched a
call for help to his brother William, still in residence at
Pierre's Hole. With alacrity, he arrived accompanied by
his most experienced hands. The scene was set for the battle
of Pierre's Hole. That ensuing fight need not be described
here other than noting that it did affect Isaac Graham and
his associates: Alexander Sinclair perished in the brief
struggle. As a precaution, the leaderless band returned to
Pierre's Hole with the Wyeth-Sublette-Fraeb party.

July 24 found the two groups on the move once again. At
the Raft River, Sinclair's former crew, now under the probable command of George Nidever, parted with Wyeth, but
continued on with Fraeb's splinter group. "Just north of
Salt Lake," they took leave of them. The remainder of the
season, one which was marked "with fair success," was spent
trapping along the Humboldt in Nevada.[22]

As the trapping season drew to a close, in October the
company started north, anticipating spending the winter in
their previous quarters in the Green River valley. During
the course of that severe winter, they visited the headwaters
of the Colorado and Yellowstone and "trapped a few beaver
between the Green and Platte rivers." Other than suffering
from the extreme cold and the loss of a few horses from
Indian thievery, the winter proved monotonous.[23]

The following year, 1833, found the small band by April
hunting in their familiar haunt along the north fork of the

---

[22] The aforementioned details have been drawn from *Nidever Adventures,* 24-30;
Sunder, *Bill Sublette,* 108-10; J. Cecil Alter, *Jim Bridger* (Norman, Okla., 1962),
122-23.   [23] *Nidever Adventures,* 30-32.

Platte. As time for the appointed rendezvous approached, they headed for the prearranged site on the Green River. There an assembly of some three hundred trappers convened in July for the annual trading event.[24]

Graham's subsequent movements after the Green River rendezvous in July, 1833, until his registered appearance in California in 1836, are an enigma. In a protest filed in 1841 and another affidavit prepared ten years later, Graham testified that he came to California in "1835 or 1836 – bringing with him a regular passport which he presented to the Alcalde [of Los Angeles] on or about the 16th January 1836." [25] Assuming his testimony to be correct, one can only surmise as to how and exactly when Graham actually did come to California. The unravelling of his "lost years" hinges upon his arrival date in California. Examining existing facts may cast some light on that problem.

It is quite clear that the 1833 rendezvous was a major turning point for the fifteen or sixteen men who had been constant comrades since leaving Fort Smith in early May, 1830.[26] Other than a brief disagreement in 1832, they had been steadfast in their association: those three years testify to their mutual affection and interest. One authority opines that when the rendezvous concluded, the remaining band hired themselves out variously to Captain Benjamin L. E. Bonneville.[27] It will be remembered that Bonneville organized his company into three parties, dispatching Joseph R. Walker to explore and trap in the Great Salt Lake region.

24 Chittenden, *Fur Trade,* I, p. 300.

25 Records of Boundary Claims Commissions and Arbitrations. Claims vs. Mexico, November term 1848, Case no. 250. Record Group 76, National Archives.

26 Alter, *Jim Bridger,* 123, states that there were sixteen members remaining in Sinclair's party after his death. Ellison, editor of *Nidever Adventures,* 103, note 73, gives the figure fourteen. These two estimates would seem to agree with the previous ones given by Nidever – fourteen or fifteen men. However, since Nidever reports the death of two of the party, this would lower the figure accordingly.

27 Ellison in *Nidever Adventures,* 103, note 73.

That party proceeded on to California and the shores of the Pacific.[28]

When Walker's party commenced its epochal journey, July 24, George Nidever recorded, *We joined him,* making a party in all of 36." [29] Most authorities agree that Walker's personnel totaled at least forty men.[30] If Nidever's testimony is taken at face value, it is possible that the remaining members of the original 1830 Bean party, who had continued as a free-trapper brigade, joined Walker's ranks. If this was the case, Graham arrived in California with that party in November, 1833.

It would appear, then, that 1833 should be accepted as the date of Graham's California arrival, even in spite of his later testimony. Evidence on this point is scattered and contradictory, but nevertheless indicative of the fact that Graham did settle in the state prior to his listing in the Los Angeles census of 1836.[31]

Bancroft suggests that William Ware probably came to California with Walker in 1833. Ware later became one of Graham's partners, as did Joseph L. Majors. Majors reported that he left Nashville, Tennessee, with Ware and Graham and reached California in 1834. Bancroft supposes that Majors probably came from New Mexico with Graham in that year. But on another occasion he lists Graham as a pioneer of 1833. He even hedges this by noting in his "Pioneer Register" that Graham, although generally said

---

[28] For a resume of that journey, see Robert G. Cleland, *This Reckless Breed* (New York, 1950), chap. VIII.

[29] *Nidever Adventures,* 32. (Italics supplied.)

[30] Alter, *Jim Bridger,* 138; Cleland, *This Reckless Breed,* 285; Washington Irving, *The Adventures of Captain Bonneville,* edited by Edgeley W. Todd (Norman, Okla., 1961), 281.

[31] The 1836 Los Angeles census was required when the pueblo moved to form its local government. Graham was listed as a transient from the United States, age 34. The listing of "Henrique Hale," age 26, "Transient," is unquestionably Henry Naile. *Los Angeles City Archives,* III, p. 466, City Clerk's Office, Los Angeles City Hall.

to have "come to Cal[ifornia] in [18]33 . . . I have found no details of his arrival, which was very likely in [18]34 or [18]35." [32]

There are, however, several pieces of evidence which support the contention that Graham was a member of Walker's 1833 party and arrived in California that year. In 1837, Graham and his longtime friend and business partner, Henry Naile, brought legal action against the estate of John Price, deceased, one of the original Bean party recruits – and a man, interestingly enough, whom Bancroft lists as being with Walker in 1833. The alcalde of San Jose, Juan Alvires, appointed William Gulnac and Dr. John Marsh as the estate's receivers and referees. A decision in the case was rendered on the basis of the receipt:

> Recd. Decr. 20, 1833. Sixty dollars in full of my part of a note contracted by A. St Clair [Alexander Sinclair] to Isaac Graham, which note now is in the hands Gh. Labie, Taos, New Mexico.
>
> for Alexr. St Clair   F. P. St Clair [Pruett Sinclair] [33]

Pruett Sinclair was undoubtedly a member of Walker's expedition and this receipt, a replacement, was executed in California in 1833: the original was in the possession of Labie in New Mexico.

But more. Graham told his best publicist, Thomas J. Farnham, in a personal interview, that he had been in Cal-

---

[32] Bancroft is extremely contradictory in his treatment of Graham's California arrival date. He mentions dates ranging from 1833 to 1836. *California,* III, pp. 388, 391, 408-409, 412, 763; IV, p. 18, note, 728; V, p. 767. Theodore H. Hittell, *History of California* (4 vols., San Francisco, 1898), II, p. 279, accepts the year 1833, but does not indicate how Graham reached the coast. *History of Monterey County* . . . (San Francisco, 1881), 32, also accepts 1833 as Graham's year of arrival.

[33] County of Monterey Archives, VII, pp. 1470-71. Printed, but mistranscribed, in Leon Rowland, "Isaac Graham, Swash Buckling Soldier of Fortune, Swaggered Through Pioneer Days of Santa Cruz," in Santa Cruz *Evening News,* August 1, 1936, p. 7, col. 4. Ezekiel Merritt testified he was present at the settlement in December 1833. Bancroft, *California,* III, p. 391, mentions Merritt as a member of Walker's 1833 expedition.

ifornia "seven years." [34] That statement was made in May, 1840, which would place his arrival in California, 1833. If Graham did arrive in that year, he came as a member of Walker's company, as did most of the remaining Sinclair brigade who had been recruits in Colonel Bean's 1830 trapping party.[35]

Assuming, then, that Graham came overland to California with Walker in 1833, his activities until 1835 are a complete mystery. One thing is probably certain: he continued to ply his skill as a hunter.[36] Perhaps he engaged in trapping sea otter along the coast as a free trapper, as did his former trapper-friends, George Nidever and Job F. Dye, for otter skins commanded a respectable profit.[37] Working his way south along the coast might well explain his appearance in Los Angeles and the inclusion of his name in the 1836 census, which described him as a "transient," along with his old friends, Isaac Williams, Jonas Bidler, and Henry Naile.[38]

[34] *Early Days of California,* 115. Farnham, p. 62, writes that Graham "had forced his way over the Rocky Mountains and located himself in Upper California." Alfred Robinson, *Life in California* (Philadelphia, 1891), 181, agrees, writing, "He had pioneered his way across the Rocky Mountains, in company with several others, who, like him, preferred the hunter's fare to a life of ease and comfort in their own country." It is important to note that both Farnham and Robinson knew Graham personally. Also, Graham's obituary notice in the Watsonville *Pajaro Times,* November 14, 1863, gives his arrival in California as 1833, and the San Francisco *Alta California,* November 9, 1863, states Graham had been a resident of California "for over thirty years." Graham's daughter, Mrs. Rice, testifies in the "Pioneer Index," California State Library, to 1833 as Graham's California arrival date, but erroneously adds that he came overland with Kit Carson — an impossibility.

[35] When Jacob P. Leese reached Los Angeles with Ewing Young, December 24, 1833, "Here he had the good fortune to meet with one of his old associates, Isaac Williams, and also *heard of several others in the country.*" Day, "Leese," 148. (Italics supplied.)

[36] In November, 1836, he was still being referred to as a "hunter." Doyce B. Nunis, Jr. (ed.), *The California Diary of Faxon Dean Atherton, 1836-1839* (San Francisco, 1964), 32.

[37] *Nidever Adventures,* 34-38; *Dye Recoll.,* 28-30.

[38] All listed under variant spellings in Los Angeles City Archives, III, p. 466.

By 1836, the sea otter trade was well on the wane as a profitable enterprise; the unrestricted hunting of the mammals had by that date almost exterminated the species. Turning from that dying occupation and aware that successful fur-trapper days were over, Graham, in association with Henry Naile and William Dickey, leased a site from Manuel Butron, grantee of the Rancho Natividad, where they constructed a crude whiskey distillery. Situated in the Pajaro Valley, about twenty-five miles east of Monterey, the partners built a rude tule hut which quickly became a "noisy and disreputable" rendezvous for "runaway drunken sailors" and "ruffians." [39] No doubt Graham had acquired his distillery skill in his Kentucky-Tennessee days. This new-found career was to lead to notoriety for Graham, a fame he never would have achieved as a lowly trapper. It all began in 1836.

Following the death of Governor José Figueroa, September 28, 1835, Alta California entered upon a period of political instability. Within a span of sixteen months, four governors came and went. The last of these, Nicolás Gutiérrez, was deposed by a native revolution. That revolt, spearheaded by the 27-year-old secretary of the Territorial Deputación, Juan Bautista Alvarado, easily succeeded, because Graham recruited sufficient *rifleros,* all "dead shots," who rallied to his leadership. In exchange for their active support, Alvarado promised to reward these fighters with citizenship and land.[40]

---

[39] Wilson, "Recollections," MS., Shorb Collection, Huntington Library; Robinson, *Life in California,* 181-82; Rowland, "Graham," Santa Cruz *Evening News,* August 1, 1936. B. D. Wilson states that Graham lived in New Mexico "on the still-houses where he managed to eke out a subsistence, till he departed for California," and labels him "a drunkard."

[40] Robinson, *Life in California,* 132-84; Alfred F. Morris, "The Journal of a 'Crazy Man,'" edited by Charles L. Camp, *California Historical Society Quarterly,* XV (June, 1936), 115; Farnham, *Early Days of California,* 62-65.

Joined by Graham's volunteer company of fifty or sixty riflemen,[41] Alvarado marched with his native forces to Monterey on the night of November 3, 1836. The following morning Graham launched the attack. Impatient with the progress of negotiations between the contending leaders under a flag of truce, he "touched off one of the guns just by way of giving them a hint that they must bear in hand." Gutiérrez capitulated without a shot, and the victorious Alvarado assumed the governorship. Graham's *Los Rifleros Americanos* were the decisive ingredient.[42]

In the four years which followed the 1836 revolution, the political climate of Alta California continued to seethe with recurring unrest. Not long after Alvarado assumed the governorship, he marched to southern California to quell defiant opponents. Graham and his riflemen accompanied him.[43] Again, the opposition collapsed in the face of the governor's crack shots, and a period of modest, though short-lived, stability ensued.

Gradually, however, Alvarado discontinued calling on Graham for military support. In the bargain, he failed to honor his pledges of citizenship and land grants. In short order, the two men became estranged – an estrangement that never healed. When news of the Texans' revolt reached Alvarado's ears, he posted a close watch on Graham and his Natividad cronies.[44] Suspicion and fear replaced alliance and confidence.

---

[41] Alfred Robinson wrote to Bryant & Sturgis, December 18, 1836, that the riflemen were "Wood sawyers and Hunters to the number of 50 or 60." Robinson Papers, California Historical Society Library. *Nidever Adventures,* 46, gives the figure as forty.

[42] Nunis (ed.), *Atherton Diary,* 31-35, for an eyewitness report. Also, see "Journal of Captain John Paty, 1807-1868," *California Historical Society Quarterly,* xiv (December, 1935), 318-19. Full details of this affair can be found in George Tays (ed.), "The Surrender of Monterey by Governor Nicolas Gutierrez, November 5, 1836," *ibid.,* xv (December, 1936), 338-63.

[43] Morris, "The Journal of a 'Crazy Man,'" 115-16.

[44] Hertzog, "Graham," 31-32; Robinson, *Life in California,* 191.

Accused of killing six head of cattle belonging to a neighbor, José Joaquin Gómez, Graham was sentenced, July 30,
1838, to eight months' penal service.[45] Disgusted with the
harassment foisted on him and his associates, Graham and
Henry Naile sought to form a party to return to the United
States, but few came forward and the project withered.[46]
Had the proposed venture been realized, Graham's name
might well be lost in the dust of history. The occasion of his
claim to fame soon came.

Eighteen-forty was Isaac Graham's year of destiny. In the
early morning hours of April 7, he and his Natividad
friends were placed under arrest by Governor Alvarado.
That action signaled what historians have called the "Graham Affair." It is a complicated and contradictory story,
like much of Graham's life, and presents, as Bancroft said,
"unusual difficulties to the historian." [47] To present the incident fully would require separate treatment, but it was this
incident that Thomas Jefferson Farnham, as eyewitness,
seized upon to create the romanticized image of Graham,

> . . . a stout, sturdy backwoodsman, of a stamp which exists only
> on the frontiers of the American States – men with the blood of the
> ancient Normans and Saxons in their veins – with hearts as large as
> their bodies can hold, breathing nothing but kindness till injustice
> shows its fangs, and then, lion-like, striking for vengeance. This trait
> of natural character had been fostered in Graham by the life he had
> led. Early trained to the use of the rifle, he had learned to regard it as
> his friend and protector; and when the season of manhood arrived, he
> threw it upon his shoulder and sought the wilderness, where he could
> enjoy its protection and be fed by its faithful aim. He became a beaver
> hunter – a cavalier of the wilderness – that noble specimen of brave
> men who have muscles for riding wild horses and warring with wild
> beasts, a steady brain and foot for climbing the icy precipice, a strong

---

[45] *Archives of Monterey County,* III, p. 3, MS., Bancroft Library.

[46] *Nidever Adventures,* 55.

[47] Bancroft, *California,* IV, p. 2. Bancroft concluded, "It is now, and probably will
ever be, impossible to give a version that can be regarded as accurate in every particular." His treatment of the affair is still the most judicious.

breast for the mountain torrent, an unrelenting trap for the beaver, a keen eye and a deadly shot for a foe. A man was this Graham, who stood up boldly before his kind, conscious of possessing physical and mental powers adequate to any emergency.[48]

As for Graham's protagonists, Farnham dubbed Alvarado "a pompous coward" and his military commander, José Castro, "a villain with . . . flabby cheeks, uneasy eyes, and hands and heart so foul as instinctively to require a Spanish cloak, in all sorts of weather, to cover them. . ."[49]

Without detailing the incident, suffice it to state that Graham was canonized as the heroic frontiersman. He was perfectly described as the prototype, dressed in "hunting shirt of buckskin and pants of the same material, [which] covered his giant frame; a slouched broad brimmed hat hung around his head, and half covered his large, quite, determined face."[50] But more.

Arrested by the governor's orders, along with a large number of other aliens, Graham was brought to trial and adjudged guilty of high treason. Forty-six prisoners, twenty-three Englishmen and twenty-three Americans, were sentenced to permanent exile, Graham amongst them. Packed aboard the bark "Joven Guipuzcoana," they suffered much during the dreadful passage to Tepic. In transit, they touched at Santa Barbara to pick up five additional prisoners, and disembarked at San Blas for a brief, but hungry and thirsty stay. Among the prisoners were Graham's old trapping comrades Bowen, Dye, Frazer, and Tomlinson.

While at Santa Barbara, Graham told Farnham:

---

[48] *Early Days of California*, 61. Farnham arrived in Monterey on April 18, 1840. Bancroft, *California*, IV, p. 25. Also, see Morris, "The Journal of a 'Crazy Man,'" 118-31, and "Statement of James Meadows Respecting the Graham Affair of 1840," *Noticas del Puerto de Monterey*, IV (December, 1960), 3-6; V (March, 1961), 4-7; V (September, 1961), 2-5.

[49] Farnham, *Early Days of California*, 54, 67.

[50] *Ibid.*, 63. The use of an etching, reputedly of Graham, as a frontispiece in later editions is significant, but misleading. The original edition, published in 1844, had no such illustration.

. . . I reckon these villains will see me die like a man. And if I do die, I wish you to go to Tennessee and Kentucky and tell the boys of our suffering. My bones on the stake, their rifles will make spots on their vile carcasses. Two hundred Tennessee riflemen could take the country; and its a mighty pity it should be held by a set of vagabonds who don't regard the honor of God or the rights of men. I have been here now seven years; have always been a peaceful man, except when I took part with the Californians against tyranny of Government officers sent up from Mexico. And now I am lassooed like a bear for slaughter or bondage, by the very man whose lives and property myself and friends saved. Well, Graham may live to prime a rifle again! If he does, it will be in California! [51]

This was a blatant appeal to the rising spirit of Manifest Destiny which was beginning to sweep the United States. Farnham, self-appointed publicist and propagandist, used the "Graham Affair" to fan the sparks of that spirit. The "Graham Affair" became a kind of rallying cry, comparable to "Remember the Alamo," as a justification for American penetration and eventual conquest of California. To this end, Graham became the symbol – he personified in his glamorized heroism a means which would amply justify the end.[52]

After a year of confinement and a lengthy retrial in Mexico, in June, 1841, the remaining exiles, Graham among them, were cleared as "entirely innocent of the offences alleged against them," and as entitled to compensation for their losses.[53] The British Consul in Tepic, Eustace Barron,

---

[51] *Ibid.,* 115. Henry Naile was also arrested, but because of severe wounds was not sent to Mexico.

[52] Robert G. Cleland, *The Early Sentiment for the Annexation of California* . . . (reprint; Austin, [1915]), 21-23. The "Graham Affair" figures large in the later correspondence of U.S. Consul Thomas O. Larkin with Washington, D.C. George P. Hammond (ed.), *The Larkin Papers* (10 vols., Berkeley and Los Angeles, 1951-1964), II-III, *passim.* Also, see Frank Knapp, Jr., "Mexican Fear of Manifest Destiny in California," in *Essays in Mexican History: The Charles Wilson Hackett Memorial Volume,* edited by Thomas E. Cotner and Carlos E. Castañeda (Austin, 1958), 192-208.

[53] Eustace Barron to Larkin, June 3, 1841. Hammond (ed.), *Larkin Papers,* I, pp. 87-88. Graham was compensated, but the amount is still open to question. The

arranged for passage back to California on the schooner
"Bolina." On July 20, 1841, Graham and his fellow exiles
triumphantly landed at Monterey.[54] Francis Mellus confided
to his diary "of the return of some of the foreigners who
were sent from here in April of last year to Mexico. They
returned in a Mexican vessel (schooner) at the expense of
the Mexican Government. Mr. Graham, who before was a
raw Kentucky man, has returned quite polished; he was the
principal sufferer." [55]

Graham had had his great moment of glory. His place
in history was secured. He had given his name to a *cause
célèbre* that would be more remembered than anything that
happened in his life before or after.

Because his Natividad property had been confiscated,
Graham commenced a new occupation, lumberman. Commonly called "sawyers" at that time, he began his new
career in the hills above Santa Cruz Mission, a region rich
in timber with an excellent harbor which accommodated
shipment of the cut lumber. To insure the success of the new
venture, Graham became a partner with several others,
including his constant friend, Henry Naile, in acquiring
interest in the Zayante Rancho, situated nine miles north of
Santa Cruz on the west side of Zayante Creek near the confluence with the San Lorenzo River. There Graham and his
partners constructed California's "first water power sawmill." [56]

documents relating to his claim are in Record Group 76: Records of Boundary
Claims Commissions and Arbitrations. Claims vs. Mexico, November Term, 1848,
Case no. 250, National Archives. Graham's petition listed his claim at $35,094. The
statement was sworn to before John A. Sutter and was prepared by Thomas ap
Catesby Jones in Monterey, December 8, 1842. Hertzog, "Graham," 71, states that
Graham's daughter recalled her father received $38,000 in 1851 as a settlement.

[54] Full particulars of the "Graham Affair" can be found in Bancroft, *California*,
IV, pp. 2-33.

[55] Entry for July 21, 1841, MS., 35. Huntington Library.

[56] Hertzog, "Graham," 73-75. Graham's interest in Zayante Rancho was confirmed in 1870. Bancroft, *California*, IV, p. 656.

Wisely, Graham sustained his connection with lumbering and reaped considerable benefit during the heyday of the Gold Rush. In 1851-1852, he received $200 per thousand feet of lumber. To facilitate the exploitation of the region, he constructed a road to the beach which still bears his name. Not content with harvesting the timber on his land, by 1842 Graham and his partner, Naile, put cattle on their Zayante property. On Naile's death in 1846, Graham continued his business pursuits alone.[57]

But Graham's reputation, whether real or imagined, as a man of little principle continued to haunt him during the waning days of Mexican suzerainty over California. Charges of harboring deserted sailors, theft of hides, rumors of plots and counterplots, swirled around Graham, his situation made more precarious by the abortive "conquest" of California by Commodore Thomas ap Catesby Jones in October, 1842. And there was some truth to the charges! As for Graham, behind the threats and harassment, he saw only the stealthy hand of his arch enemy, Alvarado. With revenge uppermost in his thoughts, he bided his time. A "legal" opportunity soon matured.

In 1842, Alvarado in disgust resigned the governorship and was succeeded in August by a Mexican-appointed successor, General Manuel Micheltorena. At first well received by the populace, his administration quickly turned sour. Personally esteemed by the inhabitants, the fault was not with Micheltorena: unrest was fomented by the behavior of his troops who had been recruited from the streets and prisons of Mexico. Theft and vice became rampant. Even though the governor often compensated theft victims from his private purse, as the reputed infamies of the *cholo* army

<hr>

[57] E[dward] S. Harrison, *History of Santa Cruz County* (San Francisco, 1892), 60; Samuel H. Willey, *History of Santa Cruz County* (San Francisco, 1879), 11; Bayard Taylor, *Eldorado* (2 vols., New York, 1850), I, p. 195; Hertzog, "Graham," 77-78.

mounted, Micheltorena's popularity declined proportion-
ately. Revolt spread throughout the land, aided and abetted
by Alvarado and José Castro.[58]

Most of the Americans and other aliens living in northern
California, at the instigation of Graham and John A. Sutter,
rallied to Micheltorena's cause – primarily to protect land
grants obtained from him and with the hope that their
"loyal" action might quiet the growing governmental fear
of aliens and immigrants. Graham's motives were all too
obvious: he despised Alvarado and no doubt sought to
avenge himself. Graham and Sutter jointly raised a company of over a hundred riflemen. This body of men became
Micheltorena's mainstay. But not for long.[59]

Although initially successful in suppressing the revolting
Californios in the north, the contingent of foreign riflemen
quickly grew tired of the General and his disreputable army
and began to desert in increasing numbers as the troops
moved on southern California which was aflame in open
revolt. But not Graham. He stuck with Micheltorena until
the opposing forces engaged on February 20, 1845, at the
farcical "Battle of Cahuenga," near Los Angeles. Not long
after firing commenced, under a flag of truce the American
supporters of the revolutionaries parleyed with Micheltorena's foreign supporters and persuaded them to remain
neutral. Only then did Graham withdraw. The loss of the
rifleros sealed Micheltorena's fate.[60]

Micheltorena's defeat and exile mark the end of Graham's
participation in shaping the political life of California.

[58] Bancroft, *California,* IV, pp. 484-502.

[59] Larkin to Parrot & Co. and to Secretary of State John C. Calhoun, January
21, 25, 1845. Hammond (ed.), *Larkin Papers,* III, pp. 20-21, 23-24.

[60] *Ibid.,* 50-51, 79-83, 95-96; Arthur Woodward (ed.), "Benjamin David Wilson's Observations on Early Days in California and New Mexico," *Annual Publication* of the Historical Society of Southern California, XVI (1934), 97-101; Bancroft,
California, IV, pp. 502-513.

From 1845 until his death, November 8, 1863, Graham never again would command the popular attention which was lavished on him by Farnham in the "Graham Affair," nor would he recover from having associated himself with Micheltorena in 1844-1845.[61] Although celebrated for having "alone, by his firmness and courage" deposed a governor,[62] Graham faded from the larger stage of history to lead a rather humdrum, but not untroubled private life.[63]

An 1844 California visitor described him, at the height of his popular reputation, as "a stout, heavy set, stalwart looking man about forty-five year of age. . . His countenance expressed shrewdness, firmness, and rough intelligence, with something of quiet, dry humor." [64] (A portrait of Graham appears herein at page 15.) Although visitors praised Graham, those who knew him had only harsh words. Alvarado labeled him an assassin and bully. A onetime southwestern trapper and longtime California resident, B. D. Wilson, branded him "a bummer, a blowhard, and a notorious liar, without an atom of honesty in his composi-

---

[61] For example, when elections were held for the office of Clerk to the State Supreme Court, April, 1850, Graham, a candidate, received *one vote!* Harrison, *History of Santa Cruz County,* 81. Graham was buried in the Evergreen Cemetery, Potrero, California. Obituaries were published in San Francisco *Bulletin* and *Alta California,* November 9, 1863, and in the Watsonville *Pajaro Times,* November 14, 1863.

[62] W[illia]m M. Wood, *Wandering Sketches of People and Things in South America, Polynesia, California . . . During a Cruise on Board the U.S. Ships Levant, Portsmouth, and Savannah* (Philadelphia, 1849), 229.

[63] Graham's subsequent life is distinguished only by two events worthy of mention. First, he was a party to the first jury trial in California, September 4, 1846. Details on this can be found in Walter S. Colton, *Three Years in California* (New York, 1850), 47-49. Second, Graham took a second wife, Catherine Bennett, in 1845, apparently unaware that his first wife was still alive. As a result, Graham had a marital maelstrom on his hands when his earlier marriage was confirmed. The end result was a decision from the State Supreme Court which established a number of legal precedents for California. Descriptive details are in Hertzog, "Graham," 96-105, while the court's decision is found in *Reports of Cases Argued and Determined in the Supreme Court in the Year 1852,* II, pp. 503-505.

[64] Woods, *Wandering Sketches . . . ,* 228-29.

tion. Mr. Farnham, and others who have 'written up' that man, have done injustice to the public." [65]

When Hubert Howe Bancroft completed his sketch of Graham for the "Pioneer Register" in his *History of California,* he candidly stated:

> But for the unmerited praise that has been so profusely accorded him, and his own never-ending abuse of better men, it might be in doubtful taste to dwell on the man's true character. In N[ew] Mex[ico] and on the plains, where he was well known . . . he had the worst of reputations, amply justified by his career in Cal[ifornia]. At the best, he was a loud-mouthed, unprincipled, profligate, and reckless man, whose only good qualities seem to have been the personal bravery and prodigal hospitality of his class, with undoubted skill as a hunter, and a degree of industry.[66]

There is little evidence to dispute that judgment. Graham was all those things. But because he was all those things, he left an indelible imprint on the history of California. No historical treatment of the state can fail to take due notice of Isaac Graham – trapper, hunter, rifleman.

---

[65] Juan Bautista Alvarado, *Historia de California,* MS., III, p. 160, Bancroft Library; Wilson, "Recollections," MS., Shorb Collection, Huntington Library.

[66] Bancroft, *California,* III, p. 763. Hittell, *History of California,* II, p. 266, believed that Graham had "enterprise and intelligence" and "a considerable degree of personal magnetism."

James A. Hamilton (Palmer)

by RAY H. MATTISON
State Historical Society of North Dakota

One of the more obscure members of the trading fraternity, James Archdale Hamilton (Palmer) was a noteworthy person at Fort Union during the 1830s. Little is known about him before he came to the United States and became a bookkeeper for the Upper Missouri Outfit. He apparently spent several months in the late summer and early fall of 1830 where at Fort Tecumseh, he was described as "an English gentleman traveling for curiousity." [1] He later was frequently in charge of Fort Union during the absences of Kenneth McKenzie, the longest period being from June 26, 1834 to November 17, 1835. [2]

Known in the fur trade as James A. Hamilton, his real name according to Charles Larpenteur who knew him in the middle 1830s at Fort Union, was Archibald Palmer. Larpenteur described him as "an English nobleman who, from some cause or other unknown to many, had been obliged to leave England and come to America." A "man of fifty, who had habitually lived high," Hamilton was afflicted with the gout. This disease, according to the critical Larpenteur, kept Hamilton "either very pleasant or very crabbed, but, upon the whole, kept him crabbed; so he was not liked, though much respected." [3]

During his visit to Fort Union in 1832, George Catlin

---

[1] *South Dakota Historical Collections,* IX (1918), 135.

[2] Hiram M. Chittenden, *The American Fur Trade of the Far West* (New York, 1936), I, p. 387.

[3] Elliott Coues, ed., *Forty Years a Fur Trader on the Upper Missouri: The Personal Narrative of Charles Larpenteur, 1833-1872* (Minneapolis, 1962), I, pp. 85-86.

was entertained by Hamilton "whose intellectual and polished society" added to the artist's pleasure while at that isolated post. He found the trader's mind "a complete storehouse of ancient and modern literature and art," and Hamilton's "free and familiar acquaintance with the manners and men of his country" gave "him the stamp of a gentleman." [4]

When Maximilian, Prince of Wied, and Charles Bodmer, the artist, visited Fort Union in 1833, they were received by Hamilton, whom the prince described as "an Englishman, who, during the absence of Mr. Mc Kenzie, had performed the functions of director." [5] After voyaging up the Missouri to Fort McKenzie, the two Germans returned to Fort Union in October. There they spent four enjoyable weeks before embarking to Fort Clark, at which place they remained during the winter. Hamilton, who was in charge of Union, regally entertained the prince and artist and gave them every assistance possible. Maximilian and Bodmer "enjoyed the evening[s] in conversation with Mr. Hamilton, by the fireside, over a glass of punch," which beverage the prince stated was "our daily refreshment during our four weeks' stay at Fort Union." [6] Every evening, in company with the trader, whom they found "a well-informed Englishman," they "formed a circle round the fire," where their "conversation turned as well on" their "distant native land as on the wilderness of America." [7] Hamilton provided them with much information about the Upper Missouri. He showed the prince a manuscript he had written on the legendary Hugh Glass, which he intended to publish. [8] The Englishman tried to persuade Maximilian and Bodmer to remain

[4] George Catlin, *Letters and Notes on the Manners, Customs, and Condition of the North American Indians* (London, 1841) I, p. 21.

[5] Reuben G. Thwaites, ed., *Travels in the Interior of North America, by Maximilian, Prince of Weid* (Cleveland, 1905), I, p. 374.

[6] *Ibid.*, II, p. 197.   [7] *Ibid.*, II, p. 205.   [8] *Ibid.*, II, p. 197.

at Fort Union for the winter. However, the two Germans wanted to procure information about the Mandans and Hidatsa so they instead spent the winter at Fort Clark.[9]

Dr. Washington Matthews knew Hamilton only by reputation. According to Dr. Matthews, Hamilton, because of his dissimilarity to the other members of the trading fraternity, was an object of gossip and wonder to the other white inhabitants of the Upper Missouri at that time. Unlike his contemporaries, he had neither an Indian mistress nor Indian family. He had a repugnance to Indians, whom he called "beasts." On one occasion, he is said to have angrily thrown a beautiful silk colored handkerchief into the fire because an admiring Indian had picked it up to examine it. Hamilton wore only the finest clothes and always dressed in the latest London fashions. Every year boxes were sent from London to St. Louis and then forwarded to him at the mouth of the Yellowstone. The trader wore ruffled shirt fronts, a great gold chain about his neck, and was always polished, well-scented, and oiled. He was reputed by the French *voyageurs,* who held him in awe, to have taken a bath and put on a clean shirt every day.[10]

Despite Hamilton's background, he appears to have grasped the practical aspects of the Indian trade. When a half-breed family, while on a drunken spree, threatened the life of the storekeeper if he would not continue to give them whiskey, Hamilton told him to put laudanum in their drinks. Following Hamilton's advice, the storekeeper soon had the trouble-makers in deep slumber.[11] On another occasion, fearing that a war party which had during the night been admitted to the fort, would cause trouble, the traders on the advice of Hamilton made a great show of turning the

[9] Annie Heloise Abel, ed., *Chardon's Journal at Fort Clark, 1834-1839* (Pierre, 1932), 357.
[10] *Forty Years a Fur Trader,* I, pp. 84-85, fn. 11; Abel, *op. cit.,* 215, fn. 60.
[11] *Ibid.,* I, pp. 77-78.

artillery and other arms of the fort on the visitors. As a result, the frightened Indians became suddenly quiet and at daybreak made a peaceable departure.[12]

According to Larpenteur, after leaving Fort Union in the mid or late 1830s Hamilton went to St. Louis, where he served as cashier for the American Fur Company.[13] In April, 1839, he resumed his full baptismal name, J. A. Hamilton Palmer.[14] He died in St. Louis about February, 1840, and was buried in the "Episcopal Burial Ground." He left considerable property, for which Pierre Chouteau, Jr. and Kenneth McKenzie were appointed administrators, which included an interest in "Half-Breed Sac and Fox-lands" in Iowa, and capital stock in the Missouri Insurance Company.[15]

---

[12] *Ibid.,* I, pp. 82-84.

[13] *Ibid.,* I, p. 86.

[14] Abel, *op. cit.,* 233, fn. 93.

[15] *Ibid.,* 232, fn. 92.

William Laidlaw

by RAY H. MATTISON
State Historical Society of North Dakota

William Laidlaw is described by Hiram M. Chittenden, recognized authority on the fur trade, as "next to Kenneth McKenzie," as "the ablest of the fur traders who came to the Missouri with the Columbia Fur Company." [1] Together with the other two members of the trio with whom he was prominently identified, Daniel Lamont and McKenzie, Laidlaw made his way to St. Louis by way of the St. Peters and Mississippi rivers in February, 1822, and in June of that year filed his intent to become an American citizen. [2]

Unlike both McKenzie and Lamont, of whom little is known before they entered the United States, there is no uncertainty about the prior residence of Laidlaw. Born in 1798 or 1799, he was the son of Robert Laidlaw of Kingledoors and Elizabeth Williamson, both of whom came from prominent Scotch families. William made his way to Canada prior to 1820 and was put in charge of a model farm in the Selkirk settlement on the Red River. While in that capacity he failed to give satisfactory service. He earned a reputation for being "thoughtless . . . dissipated and extravagent," and preferred "marching around the country to superintending his agricultural operations." [3]

The new company which he joined in the United States, to become known as the Columbia Fur Company, of which

---

[1] Hiram M. Chittenden, *The American Fur Trade of the Far West* (New York, 1936), I, p. 385.

[2] Dale L. Morgan, ed., *The West of William H. Ashley* (Denver, 1964), 59.

[3] Annie H. Abel, ed., *Chardon's Journal at Fort Clark 1834-1838* (Pierre, 1932), 218, fn. 66; Mrs. Margaret L. Laidlaw, letter to Ray H. Mattison, February 24, 1965.

McKenzie, Laidlaw, and Lamont were soon to be the dominating members, began operations in 1822. Establishing Fort Tecumseh, near present Pierre, South Dakota, as its base of operations on the Missouri, the company soon established trading houses down the river as far as the mouth of the Platte, in the region where John Jacob Astor's Western Department of the American Fur Company was attempting to build up a trade monopoly. To the northwest on the Yellowstone and upper Missouri, the Columbia Fur Company, through independent traders and trappers, pushed its business into the country of the Crows and Blackfeet. Although McKenzie, as president, had general superintendence of the company, Laidlaw and Lamont, at Fort Tecumseh, were in charge of the trading operations below that post.[4]

After the merger of the Columbia Fur Company with the Western Department of the American Fur Company in 1827, in which the Upper Missouri Outfit became a sub-department of the Astor-dominated firm, Laidlaw occupied much the same position as formerly.[5] From Fort Tecumseh (to be supplanted by Fort Pierre in 1833) he and Lamont directed the posts extending below that establishment to the mouth of the Big Sioux River. Laidlaw's character as a supervisor may be judged in part by the many carping letters which he wrote to the traders working under him.[6] Below is an example:

. . . I am much surprised and disappointed at the same time to learn from Charles that Emillien Primeau has opposed you so successfully, he has now got a much greater portion of the trade than I ever

---

[4] Paul C. Phillips, *The Fur Trade* (Norman, Okla., 1961), II, pp. 412-17; Chittenden, *op. cit.,* I, pp. 327, 385.

[5] The Fort Pierre Letter Book indicates Laidlaw spent the winter of 1829-1830 at the Yanktonnais post and the following winter at the Company's post on the Cheyenne. *South Dakota Historical Collections* IX [1918], pp. 103, 139, 141, 146, 148, 149.

[6] See Fort Pierre Letter Book, MS, Chouteau-Maffitt Collection, Missouri Historical Society, St. Louis.

expected he would; considering the advantage you had over him in
every respect, and after the instructions you had to push the trade so
that what Furs or Robes he might get would be a loosing concern for
him. . . (Letter from William Laidlaw to William Dickson, June
12, 1835. Chouteau-Maffitt Collection, Missouri Historical Society).

One of Laidlaw's chief responsibilities was to keep the company supplied with "pork eaters" and horses, so he appears
to have spent much of his energies in that direction.[7]

Laidlaw was in charge of Fort Tecumseh when the famous Indian artist, George Catlin, visited that post in 1832.
Laidlaw helped Catlin in obtaining Indian subjects, who
had been warned by their medicine men that the artist was
"strong medicine" and sudden death would result if they
permitted themselves to be sketched.[8]

When Maximilian, Prince of Wied, and Charles Bodmer,
the artist, visited Fort Pierre in the following year, Laidlaw was in charge of the establishment. At that time, this
post was, next to Fort Union, the largest fur trading house
on the Missouri. Laidlaw lived in a one-story dwelling,
"conveniently arranged, with large rooms, fire-places, and
glass windows." [9]

In the spring of 1834, after spending the winter at Fort
Clark, the German prince and the artist stopped at Fort
Pierre enroute to St. Louis. Maximilian, recovering from
scurvy as the result of the inadequate diet at Clark, was
again the guest of Laidlaw. Although Fort Pierre was in
want of fresh provisions, the prince again enjoyed the lux-
uries of "wheaten bread," "potatoes, cabbages, carrots, several kinds of preserves and pickles, as well as coffee, sugar,
tea &c.," [10] which he had been without for so long a time.

---

[7] Abel, *op. cit.*, 219, fn. 66; *South Dakota Historical Collections,* IX, pp. 157, 159.

[8] George Catlin, *Letters and Notes on the Manners, Customs and Condition of
the North American Indians* (London, 1841), I, pp. 220-21, 224.

[9] Reuben G. Thwaites, ed., *Travels in the Interior of North America by Maximilian, Prince of Wied* (Cleveland, 1905), I, p. 317.

[10] *Travels in the Interior of North America,* III, p. 89.

The prince, upon departing from the fort, received from
Laidlaw "many fresh provisions of different kinds," which
he stated "greatly contributed to the perfect re-establish-
ment of my health." [11]

Following the reorganization of the company in 1834,
Laidlaw still served the Upper Missouri Outfit, first as an
employee and later as a partner.[12] According to Charles
Larpenteur, Laidlaw was in charge of Fort Union during
the winter of 1839-1840,[13] and also in 1844.[14]

When the two naturalists, John Audubon and Edward
Harris, went up the Missouri in 1843, they both met Laidlaw who was at that time in charge of Fort Pierre. Audubon
described the trader as "a true Scot and apparently a clean
one." [15] He again met Laidlaw on his return trip down the
river that year.[16]

In the late 1840s, Laidlaw "drops out of sight" in the
Upper Missouri fur trade.[17] When the firm of Pierre Chouteau, Jr., and Company was reorganized in 1848, one of the
twelve shares of the company went to William Laidlaw.[18]
Because of a $6,000 note given to Francis Chardon in 1844,

[11] *Ibid.*, III, p. 92.

[12] John Audubon described Laidlaw as "one of the partners" in 1843. (Maria
Audubon, ed., *Audubon and His Journals* [London, 1898] I, p. 499). However, this
writer has found no evidence that he was made a partner until 1848.

[13] Elliott Coues, ed., *Forty Years a Fur Trader on the Upper Missouri* (Minneapolis, 1952) I, p. 160. Audubon makes a similar statement. (*Audubon and His Journals,* II, p. 132).

[14] *Forty Years a Fur Trader,* I, p. 211.

[15] *Audubon and His Journals,* I, p. 500.   [16] *Ibid.,* II, pp. 164, 165.

[17] He is not mentioned by John Palliser, Thaddeus Culbertson, or Rudolph
Friederich Kurz who made journeys up the Missouri in 1847-1848, 1850, and 1851-
1852 respectively, and kept journals of their travels. (John Palliser, *The Solitary
Hunter;* or, *Sporting Adventures in the Prairies* [London, 1856]; John F. McDer-
mott, ed., *Journal of an Expedition to the Mauvaises Terres and the Upper Missouri
in 1850 by Thaddeus A. Culbertson,* BAE Bulletin 147 [Washington, 1952]; J. N. B.
Hewitt, ed., *Journal of Rudolph Friederich Kurz,* BAE Bulletin 115 [Washington,
1937]).

[18] LeRoy R. Hafen and Francis M. Young, *Fort Laramie and the Pageant of the
West, 1834-1890* (Glendale, 1938), 131; See also Abel, *op. cit.,* 263.

Laidlaw was insolvent when he died in October, 1851, following Chardon's death three years earlier.[19] According to
Chittenden, Laidlaw, at his Missouri home, "kept an open
door to his friends as long as his money lasted" but the
trader "died a poor man." [20]

Laidlaw was a severe taskmaster to his subordinates.
According to Abel, there "are indications among the many
records of the Upper Missouri Outfit of positive hostility
to him." [21] Larpenteur described him as "an old tyrant" [22]
and "a fiery, quick-tempered old Scotchman." [23] The tee-
totaler Larpenteur characterized the combination of Laidlaw, Edwin T. Denig, and James Kipp's nephew, Jacquies
Bruguiere, as the "Trinity at [Fort] Union" and "a trio of
greater drunkards could not have been got together." [24] Indians would trade for robes, he claimed, with Laidlaw in
the office, steal them back and trade them with Brugiere at
the regular shop. "The reason why Mr. Laidlaw opened
trade in the office was, he said, Brugiere got too drunk to
hold out; but Laidlaw was the greater drunkard of the
two." [25] Laidlaw's reputation for dissipation while at Fort
Pierre is general knowledge.[26]

Despite his shortcomings, Laidlaw apparently had a less-
publicized warmth of character which he exhibited only to
his close friends and his family. After Jacob Halsey, while
on a drunken spree, was killed near Laidlaw's Liberty,
Missouri, home, Laidlaw assumed the responsibility for
Halsey's fatherless children as well as his own. He sent both
Halsey's and his own sons, one of whom died in February,

---

[19] Abel, *op. cit.,* 269; *Weekly Tribune,* Liberty, Missouri, Oct. 17, 1851.

[20] Chittenden, *op. cit.,* I, p. 386. This is substantiated by Mrs. Margaret L. Laidlaw, who is preparing a 3-volume history of "Laidlaws in America," from materials
obtained from Missouri Historical Society, St. Louis.

[21] Abel, *op. cit.,* 219.

[22] *Forty Years a Fur Trader,* I, p. 160.

[23] *Ibid.,* I, p. 212.

[24] *Forty Years a Fur Trader,* I, p. 162.

[25] *Ibid.*

[26] Abel, *op. cit.,* 211.

1859, to Kemper Academy. Laidlaw educated his five half-breed daughters by his wife Mary Ann, the daughter of a Sioux chief, at Menard Academy at Kaskaskia, Illinois. When he retired in Missouri in the mid 1840s, following his years on the Upper Missouri, he took his Indian wife with him. His daughters grew to womanhood in Missouri, where they married.[27]

Laidlaw was very fond of hunting and racing ponies. While at Fort Pierre he kept a horse, which he sometimes raced against Indian ponies and other traders' horses.[28]

[27] Abel, *op. cit.,* 211-413; 215, fn. 60; Mrs. Margaret L. Laidlaw, *loc. cit.*
[28] *South Dakota Historical Collections,* IX (1918), 111, 113, 114, 150; Abel, *op. cit.,* 73.

Antoine and Abraham Ledoux

by Janet Lecompte
Colorado Springs, Colorado

Antoine and Abraham Ledoux were among the early
trappers and traders at the headwaters of the Platte and
Arkansas rivers, Pawnee traders and interpreters, and
finally, farmers in New Mexico. The brothers Ledoux were
born in central Canada,[1] sons of Antoine and Magdalena
Lucie Ledoux.[2] Antoine was born in 1779, Abraham in
1786.[3] By 1812 they had come to St. Louis, for in that year
they enlisted in the Missouri Fur Company brigade under
Manuel Lisa which left St. Louis in May and in August
began the building of Fort Manuel on the Missouri.[4] They
were included in a list of engagés as "Ant. & Abraham
Leroux [or Ledoux]," the editor's brackets giving an early
example of the frequent confusion between Antoine Ledoux
and the later and more famous frontiersman, Antoine
Leroux.[5] While the fort was being built, Antoine and Abraham bought trade goods from the company and left, apparently in a party of twenty-six men under Lisa, to trade with
the Gros Ventres up the river.[6] On August 26, the Ledoux
brothers returned with sixty-three pounds of beaver.[7] In

[1] F. W. Cragin's notes of an interview with Felipe Ledoux, Las Vegas, N.M., Feb.
13, 1908, Cragin Collection, Pioneers' Museum, Colorado Springs, Colo.
[2] Fray Angélico Chávez, "New Names in New Mexico, 1820-1850," *El Palacio,*
vol. 64, nos. 9-10 (Sept., Oct., 1957), 314.
[3] Grant Foreman, "Antoine Leroux, New Mexico Guide," *New Mexico Historical
Review,* XVI, no. 4 (Oct., 1941), 367; "Mexico – Naturalization, 1829-1831," Ritch
Papers, Henry E. Huntington Library, San Marino, Calif.
[4] John C. Luttig, *Journal of a Fur-Trading Expedition on the Upper Missouri,
1812-1813,* ed. Stella Drumm, (N.Y., 1964).
[5] *Ibid.,* 157.   [6] *Ibid.,* 69, 73.
[7] "Missouri Fur Company Ledger Book, 1812-1813, 1817," William Clark papers,
XXX, p. 32, Kansas State Historical Society, Topeka, Kan.

January, they were credited with eighty-seven beaver and a horse, but after they bought goods in March and April they were able to trade only six robes,[8] for now the Indians with whom Lisa traded had been incited to hostility by the British, and the trade was ruined. By June, 1813, Lisa had abandoned his fort and returned to St. Louis, having had fifteen of his men killed by Indians.[9]

During the next decade, the Ledoux brothers spent much of their time at the headwaters of the Platte and Arkansas rivers, trapping the streams and trading with the Arapahoes and other tribes, and making their home with the Pawnees who lived on the Platte River in east central Nebraska. One or both of them may have engaged with Joseph Philibert, whose party of eighteen Frenchmen left St. Louis for the mountains in May, 1814. A year later, in the summer of 1815, Philibert left his men on the Huerfano River and went to St. Louis for supplies. When he failed to return at the appointed time, his men crossed the mountains to Taos where they were kindly received and spent the winter. In January, 1816, Julius DeMun, who with his partner A. P. Chouteau had bought out Philibert's goods and the time of his men, found Philibert's trappers in Taos and brought them back to the mountains. In May, 1816, twenty-four of them were camped on the Greenhorn, south of the Arkansas, where they were arrested by Spaniards and brought to Santa Fé. After a brief imprisonment they were released and allowed to return to St. Louis.[10]

A suspicion that one or both of the Ledoux were a part of the Philibert or Chouteau-DeMun parties is based on a tradition among their New Mexican friends that they were

---

[8] *Ibid.*   [9] Luttig, *op. cit.,* 15.

[10] Letter of Julius Demun, St. Louis, Nov. 25, 1817, to William Clark, *American State Papers,* Foreign Relations, IV, p. 211f; Ezekiel Williams, Boonslick, Aug. 7, 1816, to Joseph Charless, ed. of the *Missouri Gazette,* quoted in F. E. Voelker, "Ezekiel Williams of Boon's Lick," *Bulletin,* Missouri Historical Society, VIII, no. 1 (Oct., 1951), 26f.

of a very early party of trappers who wandered into lands claimed by Spain, where they were sighted by Spaniards, disarmed, and brought into Taos. The same story is recited by three independent sources, but each is so many times removed from authority that the story cannot be given full credit.[11]

By 1820 the Ledoux brothers had been living for some years among the Pawnees at one of three Pawnee villages on the Loup Fork of the Platte. In the middle of June, 1820, Major Stephen H. Long's expedition reached the villages and, at the most westerly of them, hired Joseph Bissonnette *dit* Bijou as guide and interpreter, and Abraham Ledoux as hunter and farrier, both at a wage of a dollar a day.[12] Dr. James, journalist of the expedition, said of them, "Both were Frenchmen, residing permanently among the Pawnees, and had been repeatedly on the head waters of the Platte and Arkansa, for the purpose of hunting and trapping beaver." [13] They guided the party up the Platte to the foot of the mountains, then south to the Arkansas along the front range, and east to the mouth of the Purgatory. Here their contract expired, but although eager to get home in time for the fall hunt, the two Frenchmen feared the Indians and remained with the party until August 7, near the great bend of the Arkansas. Then they set out, the two of them alone, to travel three hundred miles to their village. Leaders of the expedition were well pleased with their services, especially those of Bijou, but Ledoux was also mentioned favorably as having provided a copious vocabulary of Pawnee

11 F. W. Cragin's notes of an interview with Jacob Beard, El Paso, Tex., Oct. 31, 1904, Cragin Collection; Cragin's notes of an interview with Octave Geoffrion, Las Vegas, N.M., Feb. 29, 1908, Cragin Collection; Joseph Tassé, *Les Canadiens de l'Ouest,* II (Montreal, 1878), 186.

12 LeRoy R. Hafen and Ann W. Hafen, "The Journal of Captain John R. Bell," *Far West and Rockies Series,* VI (Glendale, Calif., 1957), 104.

13 "James's Account of S. H. Long's Expedition 1819-1820," R. G. Thwaites, ed., *Early Western Travels, 1748-1846* (Cleveland, 1905), XV, p. 220.

words and an account of their manners and customs (which was later lost).[14]

Both Antoine and Abraham Ledoux had Pawnee wives. Antoine's wife bore him a son in 1818 [15] who was later baptized in New Mexico. Abraham's wife bore him a daughter in 1819, who was baptized "Maria Pierre" in the Cathedral of St. Louis on July 2, 1823, and that is the last we hear of her.[16]

In 1824, Antoine Ledoux left the Pawnees after being attacked by one of them and nearly killed. While he was crossing a ravine near his village, he was ambushed by an "enemy" and shot in the abdomen with an arrow. He fell into the ravine and would have died there had his wife not become alarmed and gone out with several other squaws to search for him. When they found him, the squaws tried to pull out the arrow, but the shaft came off leaving the arrow-head in his abdomen. There it remained, a large and hard protuberance, for the rest of his life.[17]

The incident received some recognition, and, in fact, nearly caused a war with the Pawnees. On July 9, 1824, Benjamin O'Fallon, Upper Missouri Indian Agent, wrote, "I have now to inform you of a circumstance which from the friendly disposition of the Grand Panis when I left here, I could not have Anticipated. About 15 days previous to my arrival a young man of that Tribe, waylaid an Interpreter, who was returning to the Panis villages in company with a Chief and other from a visit to me at this place, and shot him with them, which inflicted three wounds one of which is supposed to be mortal. . ." O'Fallon demanded that the tribe surrender the young man, but the Indians angrily

---

[14] *Ibid.*, 227. [15] Chavez, *op. cit.*, 314.

[16] St. Louis Cathedral records, microfilm in Missouri Historical Society Library, St. Louis.

[17] Cragin's notes of an interview with Octave Geoffrion, *loc. cit.*

refused.[18] By October the Pawnees were angrier still at O'Fallon's demand, and William Ashley, about to take out an expedition to the mountains through Pawnee country, reported to William Carr Lane that twenty-nine warriors and their chiefs had arrived at Fort Atkinson "to settle the difference without delivering the offender." [19] By November the affair had been settled to the Pawnees' satisfaction by General Atkinson, who was represented as "more flexible and more humane than the Major O'Fallon." [20]

Ledoux was not expected to live, but he recovered after one or two months,[21] and decided to leave the village. He went to New Mexico, leaving his Pawnee wife but taking with him his seven year old son, Antoine, who was baptized at Taos on January 21, 1825.[22] Shortly after his arrival at Taos he took a wife, Polonia Lucero, and their first son, Pedro Celestino, was baptized May 25, 1825. The couple had many more children in the years to come.[23]

Abraham also left the Pawnee villages, probably at the same time as his brother, and came to Taos, bringing his Pawnee wife with him.[24] By 1826 he had divested himself of the Indian woman and married Guadalupe Trujillo, of a rich Taos family,[25] by whom he had a son, José Julián, baptized April 21, 1827, and a succession of children there-

18 Benjamin O'Fallon, Council Bluffs, July 9, 1824, to William Clark, Superintendent of Indian Affairs, St. Louis, quoted by Dale L. Morgan, *The West of William H. Ashley* (Denver, 1964), 82.

19 William H. Ashley, Fort Atkinson, Oct. 29, 1824, to William Carr Lane, quoted in Morgan, *op. cit.,* 99.

20 J. P. Cabanne, Establishment at the Bluffs, Nov. 8, 1824, to Pierre Chouteau, in Morgan, *op. cit.,* 99.

21 Lucien Fontenelle, Council Bluffs, Feb. 26, 1829, to John Dougherty, *Letters Received by the Office of Indian Affairs, Upper Missouri Agency, 1825-1835,* National Archives Microfilm Publication (Washington, D.C.). Fontenelle says it was Abraham who was wounded, but Octave Geoffrion heard Antoine tell the story himself in Mora, N.M.

22 Chávez, *op. cit.,* 314.

23 *Ibid.*

24 Octave Geoffrion, *loc. cit.*

25 Felipe Ledoux, *loc. cit.*

after.[26] He was granted Mexican citizenship on February 12, 1830.[27]

The Ledoux brothers lived out their lives quietly in New Mexico. In 1841 they were both living at Taos, both married, both farmers.[28] Abraham died at Taos in about 1842, leaving, among other children, a son José for whom the town of Ledoux, N.M., was named, and a son Felipe who was a guide for Marcy in 1858.[29]

By the early part of 1846, Antoine had moved east over the mountains to land he owned lying on the south side of the main road through the Mora valley near the town of Mora.[30] In April, 1846, he visited the Arkansas Valley settlements of Hardscrabble and Pueblo, and at Bent's Fort he helped Alexander Barclay load up some furs onto wagons bound for the States.[31] During the 1847 uprising against foreigners in New Mexico, he escaped death at the hands of the Mexicans by fleeing to the mountains with another Frenchman and subsisting on game until the danger was past.[32]

Antoine died in November, 1859 [33] and was buried in the yard of the Catholic church at Mora.[34] His Pawnee half-breed son Antoine, who claimed that he had been captured at the forks of the Platte by the Sioux as a child and raised

[26] Chávez, op. cit., 314.

[27] "Mexico – Naturalization, 1829-1831," Ritch papers, op. cit.

[28] "List of American Citisens Residing in the vally of Taos New Mexico," with letter of Charles Bent to Manuel Alvarez, January 30, 1841, Alvarez papers, Benjamin Read Collection, Museum of New Mexico, Santa Fe. Bent adds that the Canadians here named are those who were in Missouri when the transfer was made by France to the U.S. in 1803 and are considered U.S. citizens.

[29] Felipe Ledoux, loc. cit.; and History of the Arkansas Valley, Colorado (Chicago, 1881), 865.

[30] Book A-1, Taos (N.M.) county records, p. 157.

[31] Barclay Diary, Barclay papers, microfilm copy in Colorado State Historical Society, Denver, Colo.

[32] Geoffrion, loc. cit.   [33] Grant Foreman, loc. cit.

[34] F. W. Cragin's notes of an interview with Rafael Romero, Mora, N.M., March 7, 1907, Cragin Collection.

among them, lived at Fort Laramie for many years and was "a perfect encyclopaedia of all events that had happened on the Platte in the early days."[35] He served as a guide for troops at Fort Laramie until his death in 1881.[36]

[35] C. G. Coutant, *History of Wyoming* (Laramie, 1899), 301.

[36] *Ibid.;* LeRoy R. Hafen and Ann W. Hafen, "Powder River Campaigns," *Far West and Rockies Series,* XII (Glendale, 1961), 110, 368; *John Hunton's Diary,* ed. L. G. Flannery, I, II, III (1956, 1958, 1960), *passim.;* "Address of L. C. Bishop, Fort Laramie, July 7, 1947," *Annals of Wyoming,* XX, p. 90.

Stephen Louis Lee

by DAVID J. WEBER
University of New Mexico

The name of Stephen Louis Lee is most often associated with that of Charles Bent, for on that awful winter day in 1847 when Bent was butchered in Taos, Lee, then sheriff, was also killed. Yet, Lee had been a trapper and trader in New Mexico long before the Bent brothers had come to the area and his story, so little known to historians, seems worth the telling.

The American ancestry of Stephen Lee dates back to one Richard Lee, who settled in Virginia in 1640.[1] Stephen was one of six known children of John Lee of Kentucky, the first bricklayer in St. Louis, and his wife, Mary Ann.[2]

Stephen Louis Lee claimed to have first entered New Mexico in 1824, traveling there with a group of merchants. He was then about sixteen years of age and, although his trade was that of printer, he came to the area as a *"casador,"* or trapper.[3] For reasons unknown to this writer, Lee became known in New Mexico as both Esteban Luis Lee, and Francisco Antonio Luis Lee.[4]

Shortly after Lee's arrival, trapping in Mexican territory

---

[1] Letter to this writer from Mrs. Virginia Lee Mullen, Tampa, Florida, June, 1965.

[2] J. Thomas Scharf, *History of St. Louis City and County* (Philadelphia, 1883), II, p. 1286. Will of Mary Ann Lee, 1848, St. Louis County Records, U4-437. This information was most graciously provided by Mrs. Janet Lecompte of Colorado Springs, Colorado.

[3] Request for naturalization to the Ayuntamiento of Taos, January, 1830, Mexican Archives in New Mexico, State Records Center, Santa Fe, New Mexico. Hereinafter cited as MANM.

[4] There is no doubt that these names apply to the same person, for I have found them used interchangeably in four documents.

was prohibited to foreigners. We would probably know nothing of his activity in this clandestine trade except that, on one occasion, he was apprehended by Mexican authorities. In December of 1829 it was suspected that Lee, José de Jesús (Alexander) Branch, Juan Jeantet and José Manuel Alen had smuggled contraband beaver fur into New Mexico. The first Alcalde of Santa Fe, Juan Rafael Ortiz, discovered that these men, along with three Mexicans, had been trapping on the headwaters of the Platte. Ortiz found them innocent of any crime, however, for he believed their story that they had not actually brought the furs into New Mexico, but had left them with companions who transported them to the Missouri River.[5] The men who spirited the furs to the Missouri have not yet been identified – if, indeed, they existed at all.

In 1830 Lee placed his trapping activities within the pale of Mexican law. On February 12 of that year he, along with his Canadian trapping companion of 1829, José Manuel Alen,[6] became a Mexican citizen. In doing so he was following the example of such other notable Taos trappers as Carlos Beaubien, John Rowland, Antoine Robidoux, Mathew Kinkead, Richard Campbell and his other trapping companions of 1829, José de Jesús Branch and Juan Jeantet.[7] It would be unfair to suggest that Lee's change of citizenship was motivated solely by a desire to trap in Mexican territory, but he could hardly have been unaware of the advantage of his new status. Lee may have been considering this step as early as 1826, when he and Richard Campbell, both Presbyterians, requested baptism in the

[5] Statement of Juan Rafael Ortiz, first Alcalde of Santa Fe, December 28, 1829, MANM.

[6] Fray Angelico Chávez, "New Names in New Mexico, 1820-1850," El Palacio, vol. 64 (1957), 293.

[7] List of persons naturalized in New Mexico in 1829, 1830 and 1831, Ritch Collection, no. 113, Huntington Library, San Marino, Calif.

Roman Catholic Church.[8] Lee probably received the sacrament in that same year.[9] His adaptation to Mexican culture was not hampered by his marriage, on January 23, 1829, to a Taos woman, María Luz Tafoya. José Manuel Alen served as the best man.[10] A daughter, María Benigna, was born in Taos on April 15, 1830.[11] Stephen Lee also had a son, John Lee, born on April 28, 1842.[12]

There is little record of Lee's activities in the decade following his naturalization, but he probably continued trapping and trading from his base in Taos. In 1835, for instance, he was involved in the Chihuahua trade and in selling supplies to the presidio troops at Santa Fe.[13] In 1838, if not earlier, Lee formed a business partnership with his trapping companion of 1829, Alexander Branch.[14] The "Companía de Branch y Lee," imported goods from St. Louis over the Trail in 1838, 1839, and 1840,[15] but the

---

[8] The response to their request was delayed in order that Church authorities might determine the sincerity of their motives for conversion. Rough draft of a letter from Vicar General and Visitador, Agustín Fernandez de San Vicente, to the priest at Taos, Mariano José Sanchez, Santa Fe, June 15, 1826. Accounts, LXVII, p. 13, Archives of the Archdiocese of Santa Fe, Santa Fe, New Mexico.

[9] Lee's request for naturalization, January, 1830, MANM. Taos baptism records are missing between July 30 and October 15, 1826, so the date cannot be confirmed.

[10] Marriage Book, Taos – 39, box 36, p. 40. Archives of the Archdiocese of Santa Fe.

[11] Chávez, "New Names in New Mexico, 1820-1850," p. 314.

[12] Will of Mary Ann Lee, St. Louis County Records, U4-437. I do not know where John was born or who his mother was. There is no record of his baptism in Taos. We have found no evidence that María Luz Tafoya was, or was not, his mother.

[13] Francisco Antonio Lee vs. Manuel Cisneros, Santa Fe, August 10, 1835, MANM. List of debts owed by the Sub-comisaria of Santa Fe to Louis Lee, June 20, 1835, MANM. Lee was still living in Taos in 1836. In that year his name appears on a "Lista de los Ciudadanos de la Jurisdicción de Taos que deben marchar ala Campaña a Navajo el dose de Septiembre," MANM.

[14] The first record of this partnership appears in MANM in 1838. This does not, however, preclude an earlier union.

[15] The value of their merchandise is noted in the "Libro Manual de Cargo y Data," for each of these years in MANM. The company's name is written in Lee's hand each year; he either accompanied the goods over the Trail or else received them in Santa Fe.

partnership was dissolved by the death of Branch in late 1840. The firm had dealt in furs, as well as the other commodities of the prairie trade, for, in early 1841, Lee sold Charles Bent 382 pounds of beaver pelts. No inexperienced trader, Bent had the furs dried and beaten until they weighed 365 pounds.[16]

After the death of Branch the firm found itself with several unpaid creditors.[17] Charles Bent explained to Manuel Alvarez, United States Consul at Santa Fe, that he was trying to help, but Lee was in the hands of an unscrupulous Mexican lawyer: "Lee is a mear sypher in the business. He is even more ignorant of his one [own] interest than I suposed him. . . ."[18] But Bent's opinion of Lee was mild in comparison to that of Dr. J. H. Lyman. Convinced that Lee had conspired to rob him, Lyman thought that he was "a scoundrel of the worst grade. . .   He is a villain and now all honorable men can but scorn and detest him.[19]

Lyman's and Bent's observations notwithstanding, it would appear that Esteban Luis Lee, from the late 1830s until the time of his death, was one of the leading members of the tiny foreign-born community which made Taos its home. Lee was active in local politics and, even after the death of Branch, operated a store and a still in Taos.[20] His business operations apparently extended to Santa Fe, for, between 1840 and 1842, Lee owned a four-room house on the principal street of that city.[21]

---

[16] Charles Bent to Manuel Alvarez, Taos, March 22, 1841, in "The Charles Bent Papers," *New Mexico Historical Review*, xxx (1955), 157. Hereinafter cited as "Bent Papers."

[17] See, for example, the case before José Simón Apodaca, Regidor of Santa Fe, March 30, 1841, MANM.

[18] C. Bent to Alvarez, Taos, January 16, 1841, "Bent Papers," xxix (1954), 311.

[19] J. H. Lyman to Manuel Alvarez, Angostura, November 29, 1840 and December 7, 1840. Read Collection, nos. 173 and 174, State Records Center, Santa Fe, New Mexico. This story is also told in Josiah Gregg, *Commerce of the Prairies* (Norman, 1954), 161.

[20] C. Bent to Alvarez, Taos, February 26, 1846, and May 3, 1846, "Bent Papers," xxx (1955), 346 and xxxi (1956), 161.

Lee was an ardent protector of the property rights of foreign-born residents, such as himself,[22] and he seems to have earned the respect of his former countrymen, the St. Louis traders and trappers. He was, for example, one of the godparents at the baptism of Kit Carson in 1842.[23] It was Stephen Lee who delivered Charles Bent's fine to Taos when, in February of 1843, the latter was imprisoned there, in the midst of strong anti-American feeling.[24] That summer, Lee was instrumental in relaying Bent's warning to Governor Manuel Armijo that Texans under Jacob Snively intended to attack the west-bound caravan.[25]

Lee also appears to have remained on good terms with his new countrymen and their government. In an 1844 election for electors to choose two Taos officials, Lee received the largest number of votes, even exceeding those of the powerful padre, Antonio José Martínez.[26] Lee's good standing in the Mexican community was also demonstrated when he received the Sangre de Cristo grant. On December 20, 1843, only three days after Lee, with Charles Beaubien's thirteen year old son, Narciso, presented a request, Governor Armijo ordered that they be put in possession of over a million acres of land on the present New Mexico-Colorado border. While there is no evidence that Lee merited the award for any

---

[21] Year of 1847, First Book (A), Record of Land Established by Law, Federal Bureau of Land Management, Santa Fe, New Mexico.

[22] See Read Collection, nos. 8b and 9, State Records Center, Santa Fe, New Mexico. Also, Petition to the governor from Lee, C. Beaubien, H. Gold and G. Long, asking for greater protection from Indians in Taos, Santa Fe, June 8, 1844, MANM.

[23] A photograph of the baptismal record appears in Brother Claudius Anthony, "Kit Carson, Catholic," *New Mexico Historical Review*, x (1935), facing p. 324.

[24] David Lavender, *Bent's Fort* (Garden City, 1954), 219. C. Bent to Alvarez, Rio Arriba, February 28, 1843, "Bent Papers," xxx (1955), 166.

[25] Lavender tells the story of Bent's involvement in this incident in *Bent's Fort*, 223-24. I link Lee with Bent's message on the basis of two letters: Juan Andres Archuleta to the governor, Santa Fe, June 30, 1843, and Archuleta to Pascual Martínez, July 1, 1843, MANM.

[26] C. Bent to Alvarez, Taos, February 28, 1846, "Bent Papers," xxx (1955), 347.

outstanding service to the Mexican nation or Governor Armijo, there is no reason to believe that Lee was merely the puppet of Charles Beaubien. Claims that Lee was the brother-in-law of Charles Beaubien, the brother-in-law of Narciso, or an employee of Charles, seem to be without foundation.[27]

In April of 1846, Lee made his last trip to the United States,[28] possibly to buy merchandise for his store in Taos. Upon his return in the fall of that year, perhaps in November with his brother General Elliott Lee,[29] the flag of the United States flew over New Mexico's towns. In early December Stephen Lee was appointed sheriff of Taos,[30] but mutiny would soon be in the air. On the morning of January 19, 1847, Pueblo Indians stormed the jail to demand that Lee release three prisoners. Lee was willing to comply, but the prefect, Cornelio Vigil, intervened. Vigil was immediately killed in this incident, which is often seen as the spark that ignited the Taos conflagration. Lee was killed then or soon after, on, in, or near his house at the southwest corner of the plaza.[31]

[27] These various claims appear in Lavender, *Bent's Fort,* 228; Jim Berry Pearson, *The Maxwell Land Grant* (Norman, 1961), 5, 7, and Herbert O. Brayer, *William Blackmore: The Spanish-Mexican Land Grants of New Mexico and Colorado 1863-1878* (Denver, 1949), 61. The main facts concerning the Sangre de Cristo Grant are summarized in LeRoy R. Hafen, "Mexican Land Grants in Colorado," *The Colorado Magazine,* IV (1927), 83-86.

[28] C. Bent to Alvarez, Taos, April 1, 1846, "Bent Papers," XXXI (1956), 76.

[29] Elliot Lee was sheltered by Padre Martínez and thus escaped death in the Taos revolt, LeRoy R. Hafen (ed.), *Ruxton of the Rockies* (Norman, 1950), 191. Three days after Stephen was killed Elliot was baptized by the Padre. The baptismal record indicates that Elliot came to New Mexico in November. Baptismal Book, Taos – 52, box 75, Archives of the Archdiocese of Santa Fe, Santa Fe, New Mexico.

[30] Letter from New Mexico, December 14, 1846, in *St. Louis Daily Reveille,* February 25, 1847.

[31] This incident appears in many sources. For a contemporary account see *St. Louis Daily Reveille,* April 9, 1847. The location of Lee's house appears in *St. Louis Weekly Reveille,* November 29, 1847.

George Frederick Ruxton, who visited Lee shortly before his death, remembered being

> hospitably entertained in the house of an American named Lee, who had for many years traded and trapped in the mountains, but who now, having married a Mexican woman, had set up a distillery and was amassing a considerable fortune.[32]

Yet, when Lee died, his share of the Sangre de Cristo Grant was sold by his son-in-law, Joseph Pley,[33] to Charles Beaubien for one hundred dollars, in order to pay Lee's debts.[34]

Stephen Louis Lee came to New Mexico as a youthful Mountain Man, became a successful merchant and, like Ceran St. Vrain and Manuel Alvarez, might have become an important figure in territorial New Mexico had his years not been shortened by the Taos revolt.[35]

---

[32] Hafen (ed.), *Ruxton of the Rockies,* 191.

[33] Pley had married Lee's daughter, María Benigna, on June 10, 1844; Chávez, "New Names in New Mexico, 1820-1850," 314.

[34] New Mexico Land Grant Papers, microfilm in the University of New Mexico Library, reel 12, file 14, report 4, Albuquerque, New Mexico. Pley hardly seems to have complied with the wishes of the court that he sell only as much land as was needed to pay Lee's debts, and at a price no less than the appraised value of the land.

[35] A portrait of Lee appears herein, at page 15.

Jacob Primer Leese

by GLORIA GRIFFEN CLINE
Sacramento State College

Jacob Primer Leese, like so many western settlers, had a multifarious career which gained him prominence in several fields of endeavor. Leese, who so often is associated with the settlement of Yerba Buena (San Francisco) and the Bear Flag Revolt, is seldom remembered as a Mountain Man; yet it was the beaver trade that brought him to California in 1833.*

Jacob Primer Leese was the son of Jacob Leese and Joanna Primer Leese and was born to this union on August 19, 1809. His middle name was given to him not only because it was his mother's maiden name but to honor her father, Adam Primer, who had rescued the elder Leese, a fellow German countryman, from the field at the Battle of Brandywine during the Revolutionary War.

After his marriage to Joanna Primer in 1800, Jacob Leese and his wife emigrated from Philadelphia to St. Clairsville, Ohio, then called Newelstown, where they kept a public house. It was here that Jacob P., his brother, and four sisters were born. His early years under twenty were spent in the mercantile business in Ohio; in 1829 he forsook this area to accept an offer from a Mr. Cobb to take charge of his business at Baton Rouge. During the course of his trip southward, his boat became damaged and stopped at Memphis for repairs. While in this Tennessee city, Leese happened to read a newspaper which advertised an expedition being outfitted by John Rogers and Calvin Coffee at Fort Smith, for the purpose of trapping in the Rocky Mountains for a period of three years.[1]

---

* A portrait of Leese appears at page 16 of this volume.

Leese felt that the opportunities for wealth would be greater in the West than in Baton Rouge, since he believed that he had the ability to do well on the frontier. He considered himself an excellent shot and calculated that he could shoot an average of one beaver a day, which would earn him $5 – a substantial day's wages. Therefore, he left Memphis for Fort Smith, the expedition's organizational site, about the first of February, 1830, and traveled via Montgomery's Landing to Little Rock, where he fell in with a group of Creek Indians with whom he traveled to the Arkansas post.

Upon his arrival, Leese presented himself to Captain Rogers, who informed him that "All the outfit will be furnished in advance, as well as such merchandise as is required for the three years' expedition, payable in beaver-fur at three dollars per pound, on the return of the expedition." [2] After acceding to this agreement, Leese and the forty-odd other men [3] who composed the expedition, prepared to leave for the West. The date of departure from Fort Smith is somewhat obscure, for Leese states that it was April 1, 1830,[4] but an article which appeared in the *Arkansas Gazette,* April 6, 1830, indicates that the departure was planned for April 15.[5] The party must have met with further delay, for

---

[1] At least two separate articles appeared in midwestern newspapers regarding this subject. The first is dated Fort Smith, July 20, 1829, and indicates that the departure date from the Arkansas fort was scheduled for September 15, 1829. Apparently, difficulty developed, for an article which appeared in the *Missouri Gazette,* September 2, 1829, stated that the date of departure had been postponed until the following spring. See: LeRoy R. Hafen, "The Bean-Sinclair Party of Trappers," *The Colorado Magazine,* XXXI (July 1954), 161-71.

[2] F. H. Day, "Sketches of the Early Settlers of California: Jacob P. Leese," *The Hesperian,* II, no. 4 (June 1859), 146.

[3] Leese states that the expedition was composed of forty-two men, and he lists thirty-five of them. *Ibid.,* 2. However, Job Dye, a member of the group, states that the number was forty-three. Job Francis Dye, *Recollections of a Pioneer, 1830-1852* (Los Angeles, 1951), 2.

[4] "The Leese Scrap Book," *Quarterly of the Society of California Pioneers,* VIII (March 1931), 9.

[5] LeRoy R. Hafen, "The Bean-Sinclair Party, *op. cit.,* 164.

it evidently did not make its departure until sometime during the first week of May.[6]

It took the party approximately three months to cross the plains via the south and north forks of the Canadian River. By the latter part of August, they struck the Arkansas and proceeded up the river to the vicinity of Pike's Peak. With prospects of a severe winter approaching, Captain Bean, the expedition's leader, decided to establish winter quarters on the upper Arkansas, west of Pikes Peak.[7] On November 27, when only six men were in the vicinity of the camp, Indians attacked, and killed Nidever and Frederick Christ; Isaac Graham, Henry Naile, John Price, and Job Dye narrowly escaped. Owing to this calamity, a great reduction of provisions, and the dubious trapping success of these inexperienced men,[8] the group decided to proceed southward in order to spend the winter in New Mexico.

Leese had apparently lost his enthusiasm for hunting by the time he reached the Mexican settlements, for a few days after his arrival he returned to his early career of merchandising and took employment with Ceran St. Vrain. Leese seemed to enjoy his work at St. Vrain's posts of Taos and Abiquiu, for when in October, 1831, many of his friends who had been members of the Bean-Sinclair Party chose to join Ewing Young in an expedition to California, Leese elected to remain. It was not until two years later, when Leese received "flattering information"[9] about California from several of Young's 1831 party, that he decided to change his abode.

It is not particularly clear with whom Leese made the trek to California, but in his interview with Mrs. Day he

6 Job Dye sets the date as May 7, 1830. Dye, *Recollections*, 2.

7 Leese states that the camp was approximately one hundred miles from Pikes Peak (Day, "Leese," *The Hesperian*, 147), while Job Dye indicates that the distance was sixty miles. Dye, *Recollections*, 7.

8 George Nidever indicates that only forty or fifty beaver had been taken by that date. W. H. Ellison (ed.), *The Life and Adventures of George Nidever* (Berkeley, 1937), 7.   9 Day, "Leese," *The Hesperian*, 148.

indicated that he set out from New Mexico with a "Spanish" trading caravan. The distance to Los Angeles was covered in slightly less than two months, the party arriving at its destination on the day before Christmas.[10] Here he met one of his old associates, Isaac Williams, and heard about others in the country, with several of whom he later renewed his friendship.

Shortly after his arrival in California, Leese became interested in the mule trade. In February, 1834, he was part of a group of 125 New Mexicans, with some of whom he undoubtedly had come over the Old Spanish Trail, who were seeking horses from Robert Elwell, an early Santa Barbara settler. June 1, 1834, found him in Monterey where he became acquainted with Governor Figueroa, who gave him letters to the padres of the missions and a passport for travel through the province. He had apparently decided to attempt to control the mule trade between California and New Mexico, and thus began his plan of operation by first visiting San Miguel Mission, where he obtained one hundred mules at fourteen dollars each, one half to be paid down and the other half on his return. He made a similar arrangement with the padres at San Luis Obispo and was able to return to Los Angeles by September with 450 mules and horses.

By October, Leese, with nine companions, was ready to drive his herd from southern California to New Mexico, with the intention of joining a returning Mexican party on the banks of the Mojave River. Upon arrival, Leese learned that the Mexicans had gone on before, leaving Leese and his men alone to make their way across the barren stretches. Several days later Leese and his party were attacked by Indians and their animals driven off or slaughtered; of the 450 horses and mules which had left Los Angeles, only twenty-seven could be rounded up after the onslaught. News

---

[10] *Ibid.*

then reached Leese that of the nineteen Mexicans that he was pursuing, five had been massacred in a similar attack nearby. Therefore, Leese returned to Los Angeles by his outgoing route, ready to forsake the mule trade as he had the fur trade and to return to the type of enterprise that he knew best – merchandising.[11]

After several years in business in that southern California community, Leese decided that perhaps commercial prospects were greater on the upper coast,[12] so in the spring of 1836 he began his trek northward. From the home of Carlos Carrillo in Santa Barbara, he accompanied the newly arrived Mexican governor, Colonel Mariano Chico, and his eighteen soldiers to Monterey, where the group arrived on May 1. During the course of the next few days, Leese was able to gain from his new-found friend, Governor Chico, a letter authorizing him to travel to and settle at Yerba Buena.[13] At about the same time he formed a partnership with Nathan Spear and William S. Hinckley, Monterey merchants, with the plan to establish a branch store at Yerba Buena with Leese in charge.

The house or store built by Leese on the one-hundred-vara lot granted him by Governor Chico, on the block now bounded by Grant, Stockton, Sacramento, and Clay streets, has been considered by many the first building to be erected in present San Francisco. However, this honor seems to belong to Captain William A. Richardson, who established a place of habitation at Yerba Buena in June of 1835, one full year before Leese's arrival. Richardson in a deposition made in 1853 stated: "Jacob P. Leese was the first settler,

11 LeRoy R. and Ann W. Hafen, *Old Spanish Trail, Santa Fe to Los Angeles* (Glendale, Calif., 1954), 178-81.

12 Zoeth Skinner Eldredge, *Beginnings of San Francisco from the Expedition of Anza, 1774 to the City Charter of April 15, 1850* (N.Y., 1912), 508, suggests that Leese was advised by some "shipowners trading on the coast" to settle at Yerba Buena.

13 Hubert Howe Bancroft, *History of California* (San Francisco, 1886), IV, pp. 421-22.

who came after me. He built his house on July 3, 1836." [14]

Leese's house was built miraculously fast, if the reports are to be believed, for it was begun on July 1 and finished in time for an American Independence Day celebration, which is considered the first to be held in that port city. As J. M. Guinn stated: "Mr. Leese was an energetic person. He built a house in three days, gave a Fourth of July celebration that lasted two days, and inside of a week had a store opened and was doing a thriving business with his late guests." [15]

Leese must have been as energetic in affairs of the heart as he was in business, for shortly after the July festivities he began courting Rosalía Vallejo, sister of the prominent Sonoma resident, General Mariano Guadalupe Vallejo. In April of 1837 he proposed to her and seven days later, on April 7, they were married, against her brother's wishes. In the following year, to this union was born Rosalía, who was the first white child to have been born at Yerba Buena.

Undoubtedly through his advantageous marriage, Leese was able to gain permission to occupy land closer to the waterfront, a privilege hitherto withheld from everyone. For the sum of twenty-five dollars Leese received, on November 4, 1837, a one-hundred-vara lot at a location later to become known as Montgomery Street, between Sacramento and Commercial streets. Here, in May, 1838, Leese erected a frame building ". . . about Thirty by Eighty feet. . . It was just one house, about half of it a store and the other half a dwelling house." [16] Shortly after the completion of this establishment, Leese became involved in

---

[14] "Deposition of William A. Richardson, August 20, 1853 in Case No. 280 Before the U.S. Land Commission." Copy in the files of the California Historical Society. See: "Report on the First House in Yerba Buena," *California Historical Quarterly,* XI (March 1932), 75.

[15] J. M. Guinn, *History of the State of California and Biographical Record of Santa Cruz, San Benito, Monterey and San Luis Obispo Counties* (Chicago, 1903), 176.

a quarrel with Spear and Hinckley, apparently over the division of $13,000 in profits, which resulted in the dissolution of the partnership.[17] Leese continued the business alone until September 9, 1841, when he sold his Montgomery Street holdings to the Hudson's Bay Company for $4,600 in goods at fifty percent advance on Fort Vancouver prices.[18]

After the transaction Leese transferred his residence and place of business to Sonoma, where he was the owner of the Rancho Huichica. However, he retained ownership in the Cañada de Guadalupe, Visitación, y Rodeo Viejo near Yerba Buena, which he had been granted the same year, and traveled to that side of the bay on numerous occasions — once when he witnessed John Sutter's purchase of Fort Ross on December 13, 1841.[19]

During the next few years Leese was extremely active. In 1843 he drove a herd of cattle to Oregon. His vigorous participation in local politics is described by Thomas O. Larkin in his usual phlegmatic terms: "fair standing and respectability; influential among his countrymen, and has some influence among the natives; bold, active, and enterprising; is at times alcalde for the year; has nothing to do with politics out of his own district." [20] When Larkin was appointed President Polk's "secret agent" in October, 1845, he considered Leese to be the most influential American in the northern California area, and enlisted his support in the scheme of American annexation of this Mexican province.

---

16 Eloisa (McLoughlin Rae) Harvey, "Life of John McLoughlin, Governor of the Hudson's Bay Company's Possessions on the Pacific Slope at Fort Vancouver," MS., Bancroft Library, p. 23. Also see: Thomas P. Burns, "The History of a Montgomery Street Lot in Yerba Buena from November 4, 1837 to June 14, 1850," *California Historical Quarterly*, XI, no. 1 (March 1932), p. 69.

17 Bancroft, *History of California*, IV, p. 110.

18 William Glen Rae to John McLoughlin, Yerba Buena, October 14, 1841, B.223/c/1, Hudson's Bay Company Archives.

19 Bancroft, *History of California*, IV, p. 179.

20 Thomas O. Larkin, "The Prominent Men of California in 1846," *Pacific Monthly*, X (August 1863), 156.

When war came the following year, the "Bear Flaggers" took the Vallejos and Victor Prudon into custody while Leese, who had agreed to accompany the group to Sutter's Fort as interpreter was ironically incarcerated as well.

With the discovery of gold, Leese is said to have made considerable money in the mines during 1848-49. However, in February, 1849, he sailed for China on the "Eveline," under an arrangement with his old friend Larkin, and returned ten months later with "the richest and most valuable cargo of Chinese goods ever brought to this market."[21] It appears that upon his return he moved to Monterey, where he became involved in many speculations which were "marked by boldness rather than ability; and his wife's large property with that of his, all disappeared." In 1863 he attempted a colonizing venture in Lower California, which was doomed to failure; after this he "left for the east." Little is known about his activities for the next twenty years, but a newspaper in 1885 reported that Mrs. Leese, the mother of seven grown children, was living in Monterey, while her husband Jacob was residing in San Antonio, Texas, in good health but extreme poverty.[22]

Leese apparently returned to San Francisco in 1890, for on August 4th of that year, while crossing Fourth Street, he was struck and run over by a wagon. He was taken to St. Luke's Hospital where he was cared for by the Society of California Pioneers, the organization of which he had been vice-president in 1855. He never recovered from this accident and died on February 1, 1892, with the funeral arrangements being made by his Society benefactors,[23] a rather ignominious conclusion to the life of one of California's best-known pioneers.

21 "Leese Scrap Book, "Society of California Pioneers, 26-33.

22 Bancroft, History of California, IV, pp. 710-11.

23 "Leese Scrap Book," Society of California Pioneers, 37. "Daggett Scrapbook," I, p. 18, California State Library; Obituaries: San Francisco Chronicle, February 2, 1892; San Francisco Call, Feb. 2, 3, 4; Sacramento Union, Feb. 2, 1892.

William Morrison

by RICHARD E. OGLESBY
University of California, Santa Barbara

One of the first American businessmen in Illinois to become involved in the fur trade west of the Mississippi River was the Kaskaskia merchant, William Morrison. Born in Bucks County, Pennsylvania, March 14, 1763,[1] the eldest son of John and Rebecca Bryan Morrison received his mercantile training at the hands of an uncle, Guy Bryan, a wholesale dry goods dealer in Philadelphia. In 1790, Bryan took his nephew into partnership, forming the firm of Bryan and Morrison,[2] and the pair decided to extend their enterprise into the promising markets of the West. Morrison was to be the company's field agent, with headquarters at Kaskaskia, Illinois, while Bryan was to remain in Philadelphia to import necessary merchandise and to sell the various furs, skins, and pelts sent in by his partner. It was an ideal combination, with Bryan's well-established contacts in the East complimenting Morrison's youthful vigor on the frontier.

William Morrison arrived in Kaskaskia with a load of merchandise sometime during the summer of 1790,[3] and quickly established himself among the predominantly French inhabitants of the small community. In 1792, he constructed a large warehouse-store-office combination which became and remained the center of his far-flung business operations stretching out to Prairie du Chien, the

---

[1] Family Chronicle, Morrison Papers, Missouri Historical Society, St. Louis, Missouri.

[2] John L. Tevebaugh, "Merchant on the Western Frontier: William Morrison of Kaskaskia, 1790-1837," PH.D thesis, University of Illinois, 1962, p. 4.

[3] *Combined History of Randolph, Monroe, and Perry Counties, Illinois* (Philadelphia, 1883), 67.

Rocky Mountains, Santa Fe, New Orleans, and, of course, Philadelphia.[4] In addition to dry goods, Morrison handled hardware, groceries, general merchandise, Indian trade goods, and trader and trapper supplies. By 1805, his business was reputed to gross $100,000 annually.[5]

A typical frontiersman, Morrison involved himself in a number of activities besides storekeeping. He speculated in land, joining other Americans in spreading the rumor among the inhabitants that the United States was going to force all Frenchmen to give up Catholicism and forfeit their slaves under the Northwest Ordinance. In their haste to move across the Mississippi and into Spanish Louisiana, the French sold out for almost nothing. Apparently the procedure was quite successful, for Morrison eventually claimed nearly fifty thousand acres, not all obtained by means so savory, and later had almost twenty thousand acres confirmed.[6] When Illinois achieved statehood in 1818, there was much competition among speculators with regard to the location of the new state capital, and Morrison, hoping to have his site designated, laid out the town of Donaldson along the banks of the Kaskaskia River. He had been shrewd in locating along the Kaskaskia, but Vandalia won the prize.[7]

Morrison, and his several brothers who followed him west, dabbled in politics as well as land speculation. William became a member of the first board of trustees for the town of Kaskaskia, brother Robert a clerk of the court of common pleas (which court judged the validity of William's land claims), and the brothers became leaders in the anti-Harrison, Illinois faction in Indiana territorial politics.

---

[4] Tevebaugh, "Morrison," 34.   [5] Ibid., 79.

[6] Francis S. Philbrick, ed., The Laws of Indiana Territory, 1801-1809 (Springfield, 1930), lxxxv, indicates that Morrison had over 26,500 acres disapproved for such reasons as forgery and perjury. Most of the claims are in American State Papers, Public Lands, II.

[7] Solon J. Buck, Illinois in 1818 (Springfield, 1917), 308.

In the latter capacity, William Morrison supported slavery, and the division of Indiana Territory into Indiana and Illinois. The heat engendered by this movement was so great that duels were fought, and even murder was committed.[8] But William Morrison never held elective office. His main concern was with business, and from that he received the majority of the wealth he accumulated.

Soon after his arrival in Illinois, the young easterner sought to break into the closed society of St. Louis as an outlet for some of his merchandise. Although Mound City merchants operated under monopolistic grants from the Spanish government, Morrison was able to supply Jacques Clamorgan in 1794, and, through Charles Gratiot, developed a connection with the influential Chouteau family.[9] St. Louis was the gateway to the Indian trade of the West, a trade in which Morrison became interested. As soon as the United States purchased Louisiana, he established a direct trade with the Osage Indians of western Missouri.[10] From there it was but a step to the vast lands beyond.

In 1804, Morrison, hoping, perhaps, to reopen the historic connection between Kaskaskia and Santa Fe, equipped Baptiste La Lande with about $2,000 in merchandise and sent him across the plains to the Spanish outpost. The venture was unsuccessful, as La Lande, "Finding that he had sold the goods high, had land offered him, and the women kind, he concluded to expatriate himself and convert the property of Morrison to his own benefit." Morrison saw neither his merchandise nor his agent again.[11]

---

8 A brief resume of the complicated story of Indiana Territory politics is contained in *ibid.,* and Clarence W. Alvord, *The Illinois Country, 1763-1818* (Springfield, Illinois Centennial Commission, 1920). Duels and murders are described in Philbrick, ed., *Laws,* cclxvi; and W. A. B. Jones, "John Rice Jones," Chicago Historical Society *Collections,* IV (Chicago, 1890), 230-70.

9 Tevebaugh, "Morrison," 48.   10 *Ibid.,* 84.

11 Zebulon M. Pike, *The Expedition of Zebulon M. Pike,* Elliott Coues, ed., 3 vols. (New York, 1895), II, pp. 501-502. Hiram M. Chittenden, *The American Fur Trade of the Far West,* 2 vols. (Stanford, 1954), II, p. 491.

The Northwest, glowingly described by the men of Lewis and Clark in 1806, seemed to offer prospects at least as promising as Santa Fe. To tap the fabulous wealth of furs on either slope of the Rocky Mountains, William Morrison, together with his fellow Kaskaskian, Pierre Menard, joined with the St. Louis merchant and adventurer, Manuel Lisa, to send an organized and equipped band of hunters and traders up the Missouri River in the spring of 1807.[12] It was the first of a long procession of companies seeking a fortune in fur. Morrison was one of the suppliers of merchandise to the organization, and it was expected that most of the furs brought down would be marketed through Guy Bryan in Philadelphia. The value of their initial outfit was about $16,000 – not particularly large, but enough to provide a substantial beginning should conditions prove favorable. Neither Morrison nor Menard accompanied the party up the Missouri, but they designated George Drouillard, recently discharged from the Lewis and Clark expedition, as their personal representative, while Lisa assumed field command. Their two keelboats proceeded to the junction of the Yellowstone and Big Horn Rivers, where Fort Raymond was constructed and trading commenced.

Lisa remained at the post long enough to see the men off on the spring hunt before packing up the collected pelts and returning to St. Louis. The modest profit earned, in less than a full hunting season, encouraged the partners to expand their agreement, Drouillard becoming a full member, and to prepare to continue their assault on the mountains.[13] This success also had stirred the St. Louis traders from their somnolence, and, led by Pierre Chouteau, they suggested a much expanded organization, a co-partnership of ten mem-

[12] Richard E. Oglesby, *Manuel Lisa and the Opening of the Missouri Fur Trade* (Norman, 1963), 39f.

[13] Bryan and Morrison Store, Kaskaskia Ledger D, 438, William Morrison Records, reel 1, microfilm, Illinois Historical Survey, Lincoln Hall, Urbana, Illinois.

bers to be capitalized at about $40,000. An agreement was reached over that winter, and, on March 3, 1809, the formal organization of the St. Louis Missouri Fur Company was completed.[14] Lisa, Morrison, and Menard retained full partner status, but Drouillard was not included. The new organization purchased all the assets of its predecessor, so the original trio did quite well indeed.

William Morrison did not accompany the rest of his partners upstream in the spring of 1809, his multifarious interests keeping him tied to Kaskaskia, but he sent his brother Samuel in his stead.[15] Although guaranteed an income during the first year's operations by a contract signed with Governor Meriwether Lewis for the return of the Mandan chief Shahaka to his village, the St. Louis Missouri Fur Company was beset by constant difficulties. The Blackfeet Indians proved intractable foes, preventing the trappers from utilizing the rich Three Forks area; the Embargo Act of 1807, and its various successors prior to the War of 1812, stopped the importation of trade goods; and, finally, the war itself depressed the fur market for some years, all of which kept the company from reaching its full potential.

The lack of immediate success caused some internal strife among the partners, including a dispute between Morrison and Lisa over Morrison's alleged misuse of company furs. The argument spilled over into an acrimonious exchange of letters in the *Missouri Gazette* in November of 1810.[16] Shortly thereafter, Morrison had a falling out with the Chouteaus, perhaps over the same matter, and, while he remained a nominal partner in the Missouri Fur Company when it was created out of its forerunner in 1812, he took no part in the organization's activities, and, in fact, withdrew

---

[14] Oglesby, *Lisa*, 70.

[15] Frederic Billon, *Annals of St. Louis in Its Territorial Days from 1804 to 1821* (St. Louis, 1888), 220.

[16] *Missouri Gazette*, November 14 and 21, 1810.

completely from St. Louis and the western fur trade to concentrate on other things.

The advent of the War of 1812 provided William Morrison with many new opportunities, and his departure from the fur trade did not much concern him. He now concentrated on general merchandising and government contracting. He made agreements with the military to supply posts from Vincennes to Fort Osage, and from Fort Massac to Prairie du Chien. In addition, he was awarded a contract to deliver mail between specified points in the Illinois Territory, and, through William Clark and Auguste Chouteau, Morrison supplied Indian presents at the various treaty convocations called by the Indian commissioners.[17] The Missouri lead mines were booming, and Morrison became closely associated with Moses Austin and others, marketing their lead products in the East. The economic future looked bright. Unfortunately, the wartime expansion of business proved only temporary.

The close of hostilities brought with it a great change in the Illinois country, and marked the beginning of Morrison's troubles. Army contracts for supplies were cancelled, and the government began delivering its own mail, but, worse than that, a great flood of new people moved into the area bringing with them a much more complex social order. Suddenly Illinois was no longer a raw frontier. The Indians were pushed west of the river and took their trade with them. The wild and wooly days of no-holds-barred competition gave way to more orderly and disciplined commerce, and Morrison was unable to make the adjustment. Most damaging of all, however, was Guy Bryan's retirement from the partnership in 1815.[18] With Bryan's departure, Morrison lost his valuable eastern connection. The Panic of 1819 further depressed the business community, and the shortage

---

[17] Tevebaugh, "Morrison," 147f.   [18] Ibid., 225.

of money continued to limit enterprise for some years afterward. Dating from Bryan's withdrawal, Morrison's business interests declined and his influence waned to the time of his own retirement in 1830. He died at his home in Kaskaskia April 9, 1837.[19]

During his long and hectic lifetime, William Morrison was married three times: to Marie Catherine La Source in 1794, who died in 1798; to Euphrasie Hubardeau in 1799, who died in 1812; and finally to Eliza Bissell in 1813. He was described by Governor John Reynolds as "kind and benevolent," "honest and upright," and a "self-made man."[20] His fine residence was used to fete the Marquis de Lafayette during his 1825 visit to Kaskaskia, and long remained a showplace in Illinois. Instrumental in activating the frontier in Illinois and the West, Morrison was unable to keep abreast of the rapid march of events, but his early successes enabled him to settle down to a life of relative ease in his later years. Such a privilege was granted to few of the pioneers of the fur trade.

[19] *Ibid.*, 304.
[20] John Reynolds, *Pioneer History of Illinois* . . . , Second Edition (Chicago, 1887), 160-65.

Henry Naile

by DOYCE B. NUNIS, JR.
University of Southern California

The first Los Angeles census, taken in 1836, enrolled the name of "Henrique Hale," American, age twenty-six, "Transcient." [1] That same census also carried the names of Isaac Graham, Jonas Bidler, Isaac Williams, Jacob P. Leese, William Wolfskill, J. J. Warner, and William Chard – all one-time trappers in the American Southwest.[2] Indeed, "Henrique Hale," Henry Naile, had been a constant companion of Isaac Graham since 1830, when the two launched their fur trade adventures as recruits in Colonel Robert Bean's party. From that initial association, the two formed a lifetime friendship which later matured into a ten-year business partnership after they settled in Santa Cruz County, California, in late 1836.

Henry Naile's life prior to 1836 is only sparsely recorded. Born in Alabama in 1810 or 1811,[3] he first appears on the roster of Bean's party when the company assembled at Fort Smith, Arkansas, in early May, 1830.[4] During the ensuing three years, Naile and his comrade, Graham, trapped the

---

1 *Los Angeles City Archives,* III, p. 466, City Clerk's Office, Los Angeles City Hall.

2 *Ibid.,* 465-66.

3 Deposition by Henry Naile to Thomas ap Catesby Jones, Monterey, December 3, 1842. Records of Boundary Claims Commissions and Arbitrations. Claims vs. Mexico, Claim no. 59. Record Group 76, National Archives. The year of birth is derived from the 1836 Los Angeles census age of "26 years" and a similar census at Branciforte in 1845 where his age is given as 36 years old. Hubert H. Bancroft, *History of California* (7 vols., San Francisco, 1884-1890), IV, pp. 118 note, 751.

4 William H. Ellison (ed.), *The Life and Adventures of George Nidever* [*1802-1883*] (Berkeley, 1937), 20, although the name is spelled Nale (hereinafter cited as *Nidever Adventures*) ; Job F. Dye, *Recollections of a Pioneer, 1830-1852* (Los Angeles, 1951), 5, but spelled Nail. The correct spelling of Naile is taken from the deposition cited in note 3, *ante.*

region from the Rio Grande to the Yellowstone, from the Platte to the Humboldt.[5] In November, 1833, probably with Joseph R. Walker's brigade, Naile and Graham arrived in California. Like most trappers who found their way to the Pacific coast, they might well have spent the following two years in hunting sea otter.[6] But by 1836, aware that profitable fur-trade days were over, Naile turned to more solid pursuits. With Graham and William Dickey as partners, the three leased a site from Manuel Burton, grantee of the Rancho Natividad, situated about twenty-five miles east of Monterey in the Pajaro Valley.[7] There they constructed a crude whiskey distillery, built a rude tule hut, and soon gained for themselves an unsavory reputation.[8]

Not content with running a primitive tavern, Naile followed the lead of Graham in supporting the revolutionary cause of Juan Bautista Alvarado. When Alvarado laid siege to Monterey in early November, 1836, Naile was a member of Graham's *Los Rifleros Americanos,* a contingent of crack shots whose presence helped bring down the government of Governor Nicolás Gutiérrez. After that initial success, the *Los Rifleros* moved south to bring southern California under the new governor's control.[9]

---

[5] For details, see LeRoy R. Hafen, "The Bean-Sinclair Party of Rocky Mountain Trappers, 1830-32," *Colorado Magazine,* XXXI (July 1954), 161-71, and volume one in this Series, pp. 116-19.

[6] For evidence surmising the California arrival year as 1833, see this author's sketch on "Isaac Graham" in this volume. Since Graham and Naile were devoted friends, I am of the opinion that the two were inseparable companions from 1830 until Naile's death in 1846. Bancroft, *California,* IV, p. 751, lists Naile as arriving from New Mexico in 1836. Apparently he relies exclusively on the 1836 Los Angeles census for that surmise.

[7] Leon Rowland, "Isaac Graham, Swash Buckling Soldier of Fortune, Swaggered Through Pioneer Days of Santa Cruz," Santa Cruz *Evening News,* August 1, 1936, p. 7, cl. 4.

[8] B[enjamin] D. Wilson, "Recollections," MS., Shorb Coll., Box 17, Henry E. Huntington Library; Alfred Robinson, *Life in California* (Philadelphia, 1891), 181-182.

[9] *Ibid.,* 132-184; Thomas J. Farnham, *Early Days of California* (Philadelphia,

Once secure as governor, Alvarado quickly became estranged from Graham and his riflemen. Aware of the
governor's hostility and suspecting that he had launched a
campaign of designed harassment against them, Graham
and Naile tried to recruit a party in 1839 for return to the
United States, but without success.[10]

By 1840, Alvarado's dark suspicions that Graham and
his friend Naile were plotting a revolt against his regime at
Natividad produced the notorious "Graham Affair." [11] In
the early morning hours of April 7, government forces
burst in on the sleeping partners and placed them under
arrest. The charge was treason. In the ensuing, confused
struggle, Naile was severely wounded. A "lance was thrust
through his thigh, and a deep wound in his leg, which
nearly separated the cord of the heel" was inflicted upon
him. Clapped in double irons with Graham, Naile, "pale
from the loss of blood and vomiting terribly," [12] was rudely
handled by the arresting party who aimed "most deadly
blows" at the prisoners.[13]

Brought to trial along with the other accused, Naile,
because of his wounds, was not packed aboard the "Joven
Guipuzoana" on April 24 for exile and imprisonment in
Mexico. Instead, he was given two months in which to dispose of the property jointly held by him, Graham, and
William Dickey. At the end of that time he was ordered to
leave California forthwith.[14] The partners' losses were later

---

1859), 62-65; George Tays (ed.), "The Surrender of Monterey by Governor
Nicolas Gutiérrez, November 5, 1836," *California Historical Society Quarterly,* xv
(December, 1936), 338-363.

10 *Nidever Adventures,* 53.

11 Full details can be found in Bancroft, *California,* iv, pp. 2-33, and a decidedly
biased account in Farnham, *Early Days of California,* 70, *et seq.*

12 *Ibid.,* 72, although the name is spelled Niel. A similar account is found in
Alfred F. Morris, "The Journal of a 'Crazy Man,'" edited by Charles L. Camp,
California Historical Society Quarterly, xv (June, 1936), 122.

13 Farnham, *Early Days of California,* 74.

14 Bancroft, *California,* iv, p. 14 note.

to become the subject of claims against Mexico, Naile asking $20,000 for damages.[15]

On June 13, several weeks before Naile was under sentence to leave California, the United States sloop "St. Louis," commanded by French Forrest, dropped anchor at Monterey to investigate the treatment of American citizens by the local California authorities. Although no punitive measures were taken, Captain Forrest appointed Ethan Esterbrook to act as United States consul.[16] This show of direct United States interest in the "Graham Affair" undoubtedly stayed the execution of Naile's sentence of banishment. When Graham and a number of other exiles returned triumphantly to Monterey on July 20, 1841, Naile probably greeted his year-absent comrade warmly.[17]

Shortly after Graham's return, the two men acquired the Rancho Zayante, situated nine miles north of Santa Cruz, from Joseph L. Majors.[18] In partnership with Peter Lassen, a Dane, and Frederick Hoegel, a German, the first water power sawmill in California was constructed on the property to exploit the fine stand of timber. By 1843, Graham and Naile were the exclusive owners of the mill, and lumbering became one of their major enterprises.[19]

Not content with lumbering, Graham and Naile decided to run cattle on their ranch. In 1842, the partners applied for their brand, GN (Gram-Neil).[20] The profit from hides

[15] Claims vs. Mexico, Claim no. 59. Record Group 76, National Archives. Naile's claim was never paid, due to his death before settlement. Related claims are found for Dickey in Claim no. 59 and for Graham in Claim no. 250.

[16] Robert G. Cleland, *Early Sentiment for the Annexation of California* . . . (reprint; Austin, [1915]), 22-23.

[17] Diary of Francis Mellus, July 21, 1841, MS., 35, Huntington Library.

[18] Bancroft, *California,* IV, pp. 656 note, 728. In the latter reference Bancroft suggests that Majors may have come to California with Graham.

[19] Dorothy A. Hertzog, "Isaac Graham: California Pioneer," (unpublished M.A. thesis, University of California, Berkeley, 1942), 74-75.

[20] Document 442, Cattle Brands, 1842, and Document 313, June 8, 1843, in Santa Cruz County Recorder's Office, Santa Cruz.

was still an attractive lure. However, lumbering and raising cattle were further augmented by opening another distillery.[21]

Life as a *ranchero* was far from peaceful for Naile and Graham. The governmental authorities still viewed all their activities with deep distrust and suspicion. Accusations and harassments continued, fomented by their arch enemy, Alvarado, or at least so Naile and Graham believed.[22] When Don Manuel Micheltorena, the new governor from Mexico, arrived, the two partners cast their lot in support of his regime. To protect their ranch title, Naile became a Mexican citizen in 1844, although Graham did not.[23] And when Micheltorena was confronted by a revolt led by Alvarado and José Castro, Graham and Naile rallied to Micheltorena's side, only to taste defeat at the hands of the insurgents when battle was joined near Los Angeles at Cahuenga Pass, February 20, 1845.[24]

Returning to their ranch, the two partners resumed their occupations. Graham's marriage some months after to Catherine Bennett undoubtedly brought about a rearrangement in his association with Naile.[25] But tragedy soon struck: Henry Naile was killed.

Naile died a violent death, a result of a dispute which arose with James Williams over property rights to the Zayante Creek sawmill. An effort to solve the matter through negotiations failed. The circumstances leading up to Naile's death were graphically reported by Thomas O. Larkin, April 13, 1846:

> For some weeks the Williams and Graham & Naile have had a dispute respecting the mill. On Saturday the 11, Williams & Naile met

21 Hertzog, "Isaac Graham," 79.
22 Morris, "The Journal of a 'Crazy Man,'" 227.
23 Bancroft, *California*, IV, p. 751.   24 *Ibid.*, 485-515.
25 Graham was married in a civil ceremony, September 26, 1845. Rowland, "Isaac Graham," Santa Cruz *Evening News*, p. 7, col. 1.

at St. Cruz with Arbitrators binding themselfs under a Bond of 2000$ each to abide by the decision. During the day (so said) Naile often drew his Pistol on James W. and was prevented from firing. On the Ws. leaving the place on Horse back, Naile followed, stopt him, pulled off his coat & drew on W. a six Barreled pistol. Mr. Martin prevented his using it. Naile then and at the Mission told Jas. Williams, that if he came that tomorrow he would take his life, calling Witnesses to hear his words, adding that he was not drunk, but cool and sober. Told W. accordingly to bring his Rifle. Yesterday all the parties again met at the mission. Williams was there before Naile. When the latter rode up he jump'd off his horse, and under the horse's neck presented his gun, or Rifle. Jas. Williams at the moment presented his Rifle and fired. His Ball went thro' Naile breast who immediately fell. Not one word before or afterwards past between them. In 15 minutes W. & his Brother John left for Mont. They tell the story as you now have it and say Naile laid dieing where he fell. At 5 or 6 this morning W. gave himself up to me, requesting a trial for murder. I called at the moment on the Alcalde and took W. to the prison, where he is now confined. Should the case prove as he represented it, he will have but little trouble. They say on Saturday the Alcalde at Sta. Cruz tried to curb Naile, and from the bad Language of the latter, had to let him alone.[26]

News of Naile's death provoked a strong remonstration from Dr. John Marsh and several other American residents. Writing to Larkin on April 15, "as the representative of our Country here," he stated: "We have just learned with feeling of the deepest regret that Mr Henry Nale, a respectable American citizen was yesterday murdered at Sta Cruz by another American. In consequence of the well known laxity & want of energy in the laws of the country we are aprehensive that the murderer will go unpunished without your intervention in this affair; we therefore respectfully request you take such steps as you may deem most likely to ensure the due execution of justice." Above all, the irate petitioners wantèd Larkin to use his "authority &

---

[26] George P. Hammond (ed.), *The Larkin Papers* (10 vols., Berkeley and Los Angeles, 1951-1964), IV, pp. 284-85.

influence to prevent the repetion of such horrible crimes." [27]

For slaying Henry Naile on April 12, 1846, James Williams was brought to trial, but was acquitted. Perhaps anticipating his death, on the eve of the fatal shooting, Naile signed over his rights to the Rancho Zayante to his long-time friend, Graham, his last gesture of friendship. [28]

In death, there were few testimonials to Henry Naile. Dr. Marsh called him "a respectable American citizen," when actually he was a Mexican citizen at the time of his death. More to the point, one who knew him well later recalled that "Henry had a good heart but was altogether governed by Graham's selfish motive which was the cause of his death." [29] Perhaps true, but there is nobility in dying for a friend. If nothing more, Henry Naile should be accorded the laurel, Isaac Graham's most devoted friend in life and in death. That bond of friendship was forged in the tradition of the Mountain Men whose personal code included the dictum of undying loyalty.

---

[27] *Ibid.,* 288.

[28] Rowland, "Isaac Graham," Santa Cruz *Evening News,* p. 9, col. 7; Hertzog, "Isaac Graham," 88; Bancroft, *California,* v, p. 41 note.

[29] James W. Weeks, "Reminiscences," 107-108, MS., Bancroft Library, University of California, Berkeley.

Peter Skene Ogden*

by TED J. WARNER
Brigham Young University

Peter Skene Ogden was a leading character in the Anglo-American struggle for fur trade and empire in the great Pacific Northwest. As a brigade leader for the Hudson's Bay Company he conducted an annual expedition into the Snake River country, seeking to create a "fur desert" between United States territory and the southern approaches to the Columbia River. The British implemented this policy to discourage American trapper penetration and the consequent entry of the pioneer farmer.[1]

Ogden was described by a contemporary as "humorous, honest, eccentric, law-defying, short, dark and exceedingly tough, the terror of the Indians and the delight of all gay fellows." [2] He was born in Quebec City in 1794, the son of Tory parents who had fled New York to England during the American War for Independence. His father, a judge in the royal service, after several years' residence in England accepted appointment to a Canadian judgeship in 1788. The year Peter was born his father was transferred to Montreal, and it was in this place that he spent his boyhood. His family hoped that he would enter the ministry or the legal profession in his father's and grandfather's footsteps, and he appears to have received some legal training. This type of life, however, did not appeal to him and at an early age he

---

* This sketch is based on the writer's master's thesis, "Peter Skene Ogden and the Fur Trade of the Great Northwest," Brigham Young University, 1958. A portrait of Ogden appears herein at page 16.

[1] Frederick Merk (ed.), *Fur Trade and Empire, George Simpson's Journal, 1824-1825* (Cambridge, 1931), 252.

[2] Ross Cox, *The Columbia* (Norman, 1957), 249-50.

abandoned his studies and sought employment as a clerk with Astor's American Fur Company, at that time operating in the Great Lakes region.[3] At the age of fifteen or sixteen he joined the North West Company, a Canadian concern operating in direct violation of the Crown monopoly granted to the Hudson's Bay Company.[4]

From 1810 to 1817 Ogden served as a clerk at several North West Company posts in the Hudson Bay region and in the latter year received appointment to command the company trading post at Ile-a-la-Crosse.[5] In 1818 the company officials found it expedient to transfer him from the Athabasca region to the then all-but-inaccessable Columbia, or Northern Department, in the Pacific Northwest.[6] From Fort George on the Columbia River he led trapping parties into the country between that river and Puget Sound and around the harbors north of the Columbia.[7] The company was sufficiently impressed with his ability to reward him with promotion to the rank of brigade leader on July 12, 1820. He conducted trapping expeditions out of Spokane House and Thompson's River Post between 1819 and 1821.[8]

The year 1821 was a turning point in Ogden's career. In that year a "voluntary" merger of the North West with the Hudson's Bay Company, ordered by the Crown, was effected. Ogden had been an outspoken opponent of the Hudson's Bay Company and had alienated its officials. In 1818 they had been instrumental in persuading the Crown to issue an indictment against him for murder.[9] In the West he likewise proved a severe irritant to the Company, so in the 1821 merger his name, along with those of other out-

[3] E. E. Rich (ed.), *Peter Skene Ogden, Snake Country Journal 1824-25 and 1825-26* (London, 1950), p. xvi.

[4] *Ibid.*   [5] *Ibid.*, p. xvii.

[6] T. C. Elliott, "Peter Skene Ogden, Fur Trapper," *The Quarterly of the Oregon Historical Society*, XI (September, 1910), 236.

[7] *Ibid.*, 240.   [8] Rich, *Peter Skene Ogden*, p. xx.

[9] Elliott, "Peter Skene Ogden, Fur Trader," 236.

spoken foes of the Company, was excluded from the list of Nor'westers who were to be retained in service. Ogden thus found himself, after devoting more than eleven years to the fur trade, without a position. He decided to journey to London and discuss his future with high officials of the Company.[10] Apparently he favorably impressed certain "gentlemen" and upon the recommendation of Sir George Simpson, the newly appointed governor of the Northern Department, Ogden was reinstated as Clerk of the First Class in the Northern Factory, with a salary equivalent to the amount of a Chief Trader's share.[11]

Ogden returned to the Oregon Country and was placed in charge of the Spokane House District. From this post he dispatched Alexander Ross on an expedition into the Snake Country. Governor Simpson, however, was not impressed with Ross. According to the governor:

> The Snake Country Expedition has hitherto been considered a forlorn hope the management of it the most hazardous and disagreeable office in the Indian Country. . . This important duty should not in my opinion be left to a self-sufficient empty-headed man like Ross who feels no further interest therein than as it secures to him a Saly of L 120 p Annum and whose reports are so full of bombast and marvellous nonsense that it is impossible to get at any information that can be depended on from him.[12]

Accordingly when Ross returned to Spokane House on November 25, 1824 he was handed a letter appointing Ogden to command of the Snake Country expeditions and Ross to take charge of Spokane Post.[13]

Between 1824 and 1830 Ogden was to make six so-called "Snake Country expeditions." On his first, he was ordered to proceed "directly for the heart of the Snake Country

---

[10] Rich, *Peter Skene Ogden*, p. xx.   [11] *Ibid.*, p. xxiii.

[12] Merk, *Fur Trade and Empire*, 45-46.

[13] T. C. Elliott (ed.), "Journal of Alexander Ross; Snake Country, 1824," *The Quarterly of the Oregon Historical Society*," XIV (December, 1913), 371.

towards the Banks of the Spanish Rio Colorado, pass the Winter & Spring there and hunt his way out by the Umpqua and Wilhamet Rivers to Fort George." [14] The brigade, consisting of Ogden, his clerk, two interpreters, seventy-one men and boys, together with wives and children of the trappers, and equipped with 372 horses, 364 beaver traps, and eighty guns, departed Flathead Post on December 20, 1824. According to Alexander Ross this was "the most formidable party that has ever set out for the Snakes." [15] Accompanying the brigade were seven unwelcome American trappers, brought by Ross to that post from his expedition to the Snake Country, who were now on their way back to the Green River for a rendezvous with their compatriots of the Ashley organization. [16]

For five weeks the party proceeded in a southeasterly direction. They crossed the continental divide via Gibbon Pass to the sources of the Missouri River. This region was very rich in both beaver and buffalo, but the hunting was exceedingly hazardous, as the region was infested with the treacherous Blackfeet Indians. In addition, the British were now trespassing on American soil and doubtless Ogden realized this, but no mention of it was made in his journals. The brigade turned back to the Oregon Country and reached the Salmon River waters. Delayed by heavy snows in the passes of the Salmon River Mountains, they were at a standstill for twenty days, but on March 20 the mountains were finally breached and on April 2, 1825, they reached the Snake River. Trapping operations began at once, and though of "tolerable success" were of "short duration" due to the murder of a trapper who was scalped by the Blackfeet. This death caused Peter considerable difficulty with his men,

---

[14] Merk, *Fur Trade and Empire*, 46.

[15] Elliott, "Journal of Alexander Ross," 385.

[16] Frederick Merk, "Snake Country Expedition, 1824-25. An Episode of Fur Trade and Empire," *The Quarterly of the Oregon Historical Society*, xxxv (June, 1934), 112-13. The leader of this group was Jedediah Strong Smith.

who were reluctant to continue farther into the Snake Country; but with cajolery and threats he persuaded them to proceed. When the expedition reached Bear River on April 26, 1825, the Americans separated from the British brigade, "they in ascending Bear River, and we in descending." [17]

Difficulties continued with the trappers, especially after Piegan Indians stole twenty horses, but again promises and threats induced the trappers to continue.

On Cub River, a tributary of the Bear, near present Franklin, Idaho, Ogden encountered a party of forty Snake Indians who informed him that a large party of Americans had wintered there and had left early in the spring but without many beaver.[18] Inasmuch as the Americans had worked the lower portions of the various streams, Ogden found it necessary to work higher up in the foothills and canyons. As a result, he pushed southward along the face of the Wasatch Mountains, through the present sites of Smithfield, Logan, and Hyrum, Utah; and entered Ogden Valley (the present Huntsville area, and not present Ogden City) by the way of Paradise Canyon.[19]

[17] Basic to any understanding of Ogden's movements in the Utah region are the carefully edited portions of Ogden's journal and his clerk, William Kittson's journal, by Dr. David E. Miller of the University of Utah. According to Dr. Miller the fact that the Americans headed upstream while Ogden and his brigade turned downstream is of significance in view of the fact that it virtually excludes Jedediah Smith from any claim he may have to the honor of having discovered Great Salt Lake. Several men saw it before he could have arrived at its shores. David E. Miller, "William Kittson's Journal Covering Peter Skene Ogden's 1824-25 Snake Country Expedition," *Utah Historical Quarterly*, XXII (April, 1954), 125-42 and the same writer's "Peter Skene Ogden's Journal of His Expedition to Utah, 1825," *ibid.*, XX (April, 1952), 159-86.

[18] According to Professor Miller, this is a highly important entry in the Ogden-Kittson journals because it definitely locates for the first time the camp of John Weber's Rocky Mountain trappers, known to have been in the region that winter. It was probably from this American camp near present Franklin, Idaho, that Jim Bridger made his famous "bull boat voyage" down Bear River to discover Great Salt Lake either in the fall of 1824 or winter of 1825. Either date would antedate Ogden's arrival anywhere near the lake.

[19] Miller, "Kittson's Journal," 135-36. Ogden did not see nor visit the site of the present city which bears his name.

After trapping more than six hundred beaver in Ogden Valley, the British pushed southward "over a rugged hill" (near present Snow Basin) and were soon on the Weber River, just west of the present location of Mountain Green. This river was also described as "falling into the Large Bear Lake already mentioned." [20]

Ogden was now approaching events which were to cause him much humiliation, the Hudson's Bay Company much concern, and historians considerable debate. On May 23, the British encampment was visited by two Hudson's Bay Company deserters accompanied by three Canadians, a Russian and an old Spaniard, "this party under the command of one Provost." [21] Shortly after the arrival of this group another one of twenty-five to thirty Americans commanded by Johnson Gardner camped nearby. Gardner visited Ogden in his tent and an exchange between the rival leaders concerning the ownership of the territory they were in ensued. Gardner claimed it was American territory and that the British were trespassers; Ogden asserted that they were in territory jointly owned by the British and American governments.[22] In reality, since they had passed the forty-second parallel, they were both trespassing deep into Mexican territory.

In the region of joint occupation, two theories of trading were in operation: one the monopoly, the other unrestricted competition. The HBC represented the monopoly and, as such, worked under the handicap of being an English corporation and having to exercise full diplomatic restraint in order to prevent conflict; the free-wheeling Americans, under no restraint, had the advantage of thinking they were on home grounds. Gardner ordered Ogden to "return from whence they came without delay" and Ogden replied that when he received orders from the British government to

---

[20] *Ibid.*, 137.

[21] This was Etienne Provost who was operating from a Santa Fe base and had wintered on the Green River.

[22] Merk, "Snake Country Expedition, 1824-25," 109-10.

abandon the country he would, but not until then. Gardner then warned the British that they remained at their peril.[23]

A general sense of oppression was felt by the British trappers that year. They were paid low prices for their furs and charged exceedingly high prices for their provisions and equipment at the Hudson's Bay Company stores. Consequently they remained year after year heavily in debt – a sort of debt peonage. They had long looked for an opportunity to desert and, now believing they were in American territory, many of Ogden's trappers crossed over to the side of the high-paying Americans. Eventually twenty-three trappers, carrying with them about seven hundred furs, defected to the American side.[24]

When the Hudson's Bay officials reviewed this situation they came to the conclusion that:

> We can afford to pay as good a price as the Americans and where there is risk of meeting their parties it is necessary to pay as much or something more to avoid the risk of a result similar to that of Mr. Ogden. By attempting to make such expeditions too profitable the whole may be lost.[25]

Consequently, prices to be paid for furs were increased and prices for provisions were lowered. These changes were to have a salutary effect upon the morale of the trappers and were to assist the British mightily in their objectives in the Snake Country.

Ogden arrived back at Fort Nez Perces on November 2, 1825, with only four hundred skins, which was "certainly far from what we had a right to expect." [26]

He had written to Governor Simpson on June 27, 1825:

> You need not anticipate another expedition ensuing Year to this Country, for not a freeman will return, and should they, it would be to join the Americans.[27]

[23] Ibid.   [24] Ibid., 112.
[25] Merk, Fur Trade and Empire, 286-87.
[26] Merk, "Snake Country Expedition, 1824-25," 118-19.   [27] Ibid., 115-16.

However, the British reappraisal of their operations and the reforms instituted resulted in Ogden's dispatch into the Snake Country on his second expedition to that region, only twelve days subsequent to his return.

Ogden's orders were to proceed straightaway to the "River discovered by Silvaille (supposed to be a Branch of the River said to Fall in the Ocean South of the Umqua) thence towards Lac Sale make a Circuit West and come Out about the Clamet river." [28] The brigade, thirty-seven strong, proceeded down the Columbia from Fort Nez Perces to the Deschutes River, up that stream to near its sources, and thence eastward in the direction of the Snake Country. This part of Oregon had never been trapped by white men, but as it lay to the south of the Columbia it was included in the area to be trapped thoroughly. A Snake Indian who had spent many years among the Cayuse was secured as a guide, but he gave Ogden considerable difficulty. Great hardships were suffered from cold and hunger. Many horses were consigned to the pot and for ten days they had only one meal every two days. [29]

On February 2, 1826, they crossed the Blue Mountains and arrived on the South Branch (Snake River) of the Columbia. The men had been on short rations so long that they resembled "so many skeletons." They reached the Malade, or Sickly River, on March 3. On the twelfth, after five days without food, the hunters returned to camp with thirteen elk. "Never did men eat with a better appetite; many did not stop to go to bed till midnight."

On Raft River many of his trappers became sick from eating beaver meat. Ogden submitted himself as a guinea pig and ate some of the meat. Although he did not imme-

[28] E. E. Rich (ed.), *The Letters of John McLoughlin from Fort Vancouver to the Governor and Committee, First Series, 1825-38.* (London, 1941), 33.

[29] The information concerning this expedition is taken from T. C. Elliott (ed.), "Journal of Peter Skene Ogden; Snake Expedition, 1825-26," *The Quarterly of the Oregon Historical Society,* x (December, 1909), 331-65.

diately become sick, four days later he was seriously ill.
The British were surprised at this illness. They knew that
Sickly River got its name because of illness induced by
trappers' eating beaver of that river. That was due to the
beavers' eating certain roots which tainted the meat; the
beaver on the Raft ate wild hemlock which caused a similar
illness.

By the last day of March the brigade had trapped a
thousand beaver. Three thousand skins were considered
necessary for a successful expedition, and Ogden hoped to
secure this number in spite of the many hardships and difficulties encountered. On April 2, they reached the Portneuf
Fork and encamped. This was excellent beaver country, and
Ogden speculated that if the Indians would leave them
alone, they would do well there. A week later, however, the
situation which Ogden dreaded most developed. His brigade had another encounter with an American trapping
party. This group of twenty-eight men, which included
some of his deserters of the previous year, entered the British camp and displayed some surprise at seeing the crusty
Ogden again in the Snake Country. They believed, evidently, that the results of the first expedition and the
threats made at the first meeting would keep the British out
of the area. But they underrated Ogden. His fear of a second
general defection was allayed when he learned that his
deserters were already tired of their new masters. Several
of them, indeed, made payments in beaver to be credited to
their old company accounts. The next day the two groups
separated. None of the British trappers appeared the least
inclined to desert.

On July 17, 1826, Ogden reached Fort Vancouver, thus
ending his second Snake Country expedition. Despite the
severity of the winter and obstacles encountered, which left
them only three of the eight months for actual trapping, his
returns exceeded all expectations. He had collected 3,800

beaver and otter skins, yielding a profit of 2500 pounds. More important than this, however, was the knowledge Ogden gleaned of the region:

> From the Country we explored this year we obtained only 100 Beaver . . . however, we have the satisfaction to know that the Southside of the South Branch of the Columbia has been examined and now ascertained to be destitute of Beaver.

With this knowledge the British could now concentrate greater efforts on the rivers and streams facing St. Louis.

Two months elapsed before Ogden returned to the Snake Country.[30] He departed on September 12 and by November 1, 1826, the expedition was at Malheur and Harney Lakes in Southeastern Oregon. They reached Pauline Mountain, crossed it and arrived at East and Pauline lakes. West from Pauline Lake was the Des Chutes River which they reached on November 18. For two months the brigade had wandered through unexplored terrain and had secured only five hundred beaver, not due to lack of exertions of the trappers but because of the poverty of the country. From the Des Chutes the British proceeded southward to streams which drained into Klamath Lake. Southwestern Oregon also was not rich in beaver. Early in December they reached Lower Klamath Lake. On February 10, 1827, the brigade was in northern California, probably on the Pit River. On February 12, trapping operations were commenced on the Klamath River. There were many beaver along this stream, although extremely shy, because the Indians hunted them for food. On February 14, Ogden named a mountain in the vicinity "Mt. Sastise" (Mount Shasta) from the tribe of Indians in that locality.

By the end of February conditions were again bad, due to scarcity of food. Ogden complained:

---

[30] The information for this expedition is taken from T. C. Elliott (ed.), "Journal of Peter Skene Ogden; Snake Expedition, 1826-27," *ibid.*, XI (June 1910), 201-22.

This life makes a young man sixty in a few years. Wading in cold water all day they earn 10 shillings P. beaver. A convict at Botony Bay is a gentleman at ease compared to my trappers.

Over two thousand beaver had been taken by April 22. From May 14 to 24, Ogden traveled eastward and proceeded to the main stream of "Salt Lake River" (Malheur River). This second crossing of Oregon was attended likewise by severe hardships. They suffered greatly from lack of water, and thieving Indians stole fifty-six horses, although all but seven were later recovered. Their camp of the previous November, on Malheur and Harney lakes, was reached on June 6. For the past six months they had been wandering in heretofore unexplored country. The Snake Indians lurked constantly around the camp, waiting for opportunities to steal horses. According to Ogden, the natives in this region had destroyed upwards of sixty thousand beaver, not one of which had reached a Hudson's Bay Company factory.

The brigade reached the Snake River just below the Malheur on July 16, 1827. Ogden left the trappers and, with four men, made his way to Fort Nez Perces to make preparations for the arrival of the main body. After accomplishing this at Nez Perces he journeyed to Fort Vancouver, where he arrived on August 5. The fur returns amounted to almost 2500 skins – short of what was considered a successful expedition, but certainly far in excess of what might have been expected in such barren country as they had operated in that season.[31]

This expedition, although not a financial success, was still important, for it proved this region to be unprofitable for trapping operations, and future effort could be expended in other directions.

On September 5, 1827, Ogden and his brigade departed

---

[31] Rich, *The Letters of John McLoughlin*, 49-50.

Fort Nez Perces, once again bound for the Snake Country.[32] They crossed over to the Powder River, and on September 18 "encamped on River Brule" (Burnt River). On the Weiser River, Ogden's trappers reported many American traps. The presence of a large body of Americans blasted Ogden's hopes of taking many animals there. He advanced southward on the Snake River until he reached Reed's River (Boise River) on October 6; American trappers were already there. Ogden trapped this stream for two days and produced only eight beaver. He then decided to abandon that quarter. On the Weiser, Payette, and Boise he had expected big returns; as it turned out these streams yielded only 140 skins.

On Christmas Eve, at Snake River, an American party of six men, commanded by Samuel Tullock, joined the British. That night around the campfire the Gardner-Ogden affair of 1825 was discussed. Tullock said his company would readily enter into an agreement regarding the deserters because Gardner's conduct had not been approved by his superiors. "I shd. certainly be shocked if any man of principle approved of such conduct as Gardner's," was Ogden's indignant notation in his journal that night.

Snowshoes were the key to mobility in the deep snow, and the Americans were highly desirous of obtaining them from the British. Ogden issued orders that none should be sold or traded to the Americans. Ogden had good reason for trying to prevent the Americans from reaching their rendezvous.

> I dread their return with liquor. A small quantity would be most advantageous to them but the reverse to me. I know not their intentions but had I the same chance they have, long since I would have had a good stock of liquor here, & every beaver in the camp would be mine.

[32] The information concerning this expedition is taken from T. C. Elliott (ed.), "Journal of Peter Skene Ogden; Snake Expedition, 1827-1828," *The Quarterly of the Oregon Historical Society,* XI (December, 1910), 361-79.

Ogden evidently held a different idea of trafficking in liquor with the Indians than did the Company. By January 27, 1828, the Americans succeeded in making their own snow-shoes, which Ogden felt they should have done in the first place, yet these were "poor make-shifts & will give them trouble." Ogden figured it would be at least a month before the Americans could cross the mountains and return with reinforcements and then, he gloated, "there will be no beaver skins left among the Snakes."

When a group of deserters from the American firm of Smith, Jackson and Sublette, to whom they were heavily in debt, joined the British brigade, Ogden was considerably worried lest the American leaders indiscriminately seize British furs to apply to the defectors' accounts. Ogden stated that he knew nothing of their indebtedness, but that it was clearly the American leader's duty to secure both his men and the debts they owed. Ogden reminded the Americans that his present conduct was "far different from theirs . . . four years since." The Americans remarked that the episode was to be regretted, but that at that time there was no regular American company, otherwise he should have received compensation for the losses he sustained. To this Ogden recorded in his journal: "It may be so. At all events, dependent on me, they cannot acknowledge less. I have acted honorably and shall continue so."

From the Portneuf River Ogden proceeded to the Snake, which he reached on April 1. By April 24 his men had trapped two thousand beaver. On April 27 they crossed the Blackfoot Hills and on May 6 began the trip home. They reached Fort Nez Perces on July 19. Ogden's fourth Snake expedition fur returns far exceeded his expectations.

Ogden's fifth Snake Country expedition should have brought to him the honor of having one of the West's important rivers named after him. He was the first to arrive on the banks of the Humboldt River and the first to follow it from its source to its sink. The river has been known by various names – Mary's River, Unknown River, Swampy River, and Ogden's River. It remained for the ubiquitous John C. Frémont in 1843 to attach to it the name of the great German geographer and scientist, Baron Alexander von Humboldt. The Baron never saw the river which now bears his name and, according to Thomas Ambrose Cramer, "it does him little credit here. He was filled with wisdom and goodness; it only with mineral and vegetable poisons." [33]

Ogden remained at Fort Vancouver two months before departing on his fifth Snake expedition. On September 22 he left Fort Nez Perces, following his track of the previous year.[34] By November 9, he was on the Humboldt River and his trappers were out in all directions. The beaver were extremely shy because the Indians trapped them. These natives were the most "miserable looking wretches" Ogden had yet encountered. "A race of animals less entitled to the name of man" would be impossible to find, he said.

The weather was mild until November 25, when snow fell. The party followed the stream eastward until the frozen "Unknown River" dwindled into a small streamlet, then struck east across country. On December 18 they were in the Utas country and on the 26th Ogden wrote in his journal:

> Had a distant view of Salt Lake. Heavy fogs around it. Country is covered with cedars. From the tracks, buffalo must be abundant. At present none. On the eve of camping we were surprised to see our guide come in with a cheerful countenance. He informed us he had seen an Indian who reported buffalo, not far off. I trust this is true, as we are wretched reduced to skin & bone. Hunters killed 3 antelope.

[33] Dale Morgan, *The Humboldt* (New York, 1943), 6.
[34] The information for this expedition is taken from T. C. Elliott (ed.), "Journal of Peter Skene Ogden: Snake Expedition, 1828-1829," *The Quarterly of the Oregon Historical Society,* XI (December, 1910), 381-99. See also Gloria Griffen Cline, *Exploring the Great Basin* (Norman, 1963), 112-25. Dr. Cline had the benefit of the original Ogden journal to trace his course on this expedition.

This will assist, tho' poor food at this season, but far preferable to horse flesh that die of disease.

On December 30, they reached the plain of the Malade River, a tributary of the Bear. For two months they trapped the Malade, the Portneuf, and Bear in southern Idaho and northern Utah.

Silent partners in the fur trade were the trappers' Indian wives, who usually accompanied the trapping expeditions and endured all the hardships, fatigue, famine, and drudgery of the journey, but who are rarely mentioned in the journals or official records. Mountain Man Joe Meek in his reminiscences relates an incident concerning the "wife of Ogden" which illustrates the character of these women. Meek writes that the American trapping party to which he was attached had trapped the Blackfoot and Snake Rivers and had then proceeded south to Ogden's Hole. Here they encountered Peter Skene Ogden's brigade. Immediately the Americans began bartering with the Indian employees of the British for furs. They made no progress until they opened a keg of whisky and under its influence extracted most of the furs from Ogden's Indians. Naturally this was disagreeable to Ogden as well as unprofitable, and a hostile feeling prevailed between the rival camps.

While matters were in this stage a stampede occurred one day among the British horses. Two or three of the animals ran into the American camp. Among them was the horse of Ogden's wife, with her baby hanging to the saddle. The mother followed the horse into the hostile camp and retrieved it. At this moment she saw one of the Hudson's Bay Company pack horses loaded with beaver which had also run into the American camp. The Americans had already begun to exult over this circumstance, as they considered this chance load of beaver as theirs according to the laws of war. Ogden's wife disagreed. She mounted her horse, seized

the pack horse by the halter, and led it out of the camp. At
this action some of the trappers cried out, "Shoot her, shoot
her!" but a majority interferred, exclaiming: "Let her go,
let her alone; she's a brave woman; I glory in her pluck."
While the clamor continued Ogden's wife galloped away
with her baby and the pack horse.[35]

In late March Ogden divided his party and sent one division to Fort Nez Perces through the Snake Valley, in his
track of 1826. With fourteen men he retraced his steps to
Unknown River. Reaching the river and following it, by
May 27 they encamped within a mile of a large lake called
by Ogden "Unknown Lake." From here the brigade journeyed to the Pit River in northern California. Since this
region was now considered to be McLeod's territory, Ogden
decided to return to Fort Nez Perces. He left the brigade
on July 6 and with two men proceeded for Nez Perces to
make arrangements for arrival of the brigade. From the
standpoint of fur returns this expedition was considered
highly successful, with over four thousand furs taken.

Ogden's sixth and last "Snake Country" expedition (1829-
30) carried him from Fort Vancouver on the Columbia
River to the "Gulph of California," hence up the entire
length of California's San Joaquin and Sacramento valleys
and across Oregon back to the Hudson's Bay Headquarters.

On August 10, 1828, Jedediah Smith, fresh from the
Umpqua Massacre, had arrived at Fort Vancouver. His
arrival made the British increasingly aware that they had
neglected a potential threat on their southern flank.[36] Chief
factor John McLoughlin, ever on the search for new trapping grounds, was at that moment outfitting a reconnais-

---

[35] Francis F. Victor, *The River of the West; Life and Adventure in the Rocky
Mountains and Oregon* (Hartford, 1870), 95-96. Meek said this episode occurred in
1830 at Ogden's Hole. Inasmuch as Ogden was not in this vicinity that year it
probably occurred during the Fifth Snake Expedition, in 1829.

[36] Dale Morgan, *Jedediah Smith and the Opening of the West* (Indianapolis,
1953). This is the best study of Smith and his peregrinations in the West.

sance expedition for the California region. That this was
Mexican territory did not bother him. In the pursuit of
furs "the operations of its Expeditions, may be considered
as extending as far in a Southerly & Westerly direction as
Beaver can be found." [37] And Governor Simpson wrote:

> In regard to the Territorial rights of the Mexican Republic, we
> follow the example of the Spanish functionaries on the Coast, and
> opponents from the United States, by making no enquiries about
> them.[38]

While Ogden was at Fort Vancouver recuperating from
his fourth Snake expedition and preparing for his fifth, he
had renewed his acquaintance with Jedediah Smith. The
two had met previously in the autumn of 1824 when Smith
and his six companions attached themselves to the Alexander
Ross Snake brigade and accompanied him back to Flathead
Post to spend the winter. In the spring of 1825, taking the
benefit of Ogden's protection from that post to the Snake
Country, Smith had separated from the British brigade on
March 19, 1825, on Bear River. The seven Americans had
been unwelcome travelers with Ogden, who attributed the
misadventures which later befell him on the trip to the
knowledge the Americans had of his movements.[39]

During the two weeks prior to Ogden's departure for the
Humboldt he became "intimately acquainted with poor
Smith," and it was from this association that Ogden became
interested in a southwestern and California expedition.
When he returned on July 24, 1829, he was immediately
outfitted for an excursion to the California waters, since the
British were eager to reach and trap these streams before
American trappers were informed of Smith's explorations.

So in September, 1829, with thirty men, Ogden departed

[37] E. E. Rich (ed.), *Part of Dispatch from George Simpson Esqr., Governor of Rupert's Land to the Governor & Committee of the Hudson's Bay Company, London* (London, 1947), 52.　　[38] *Ibid.*
[39] Merk, "Snake Country Expedition, 1824-1825," 112.

on an expedition that was to carry him to southern California.[40] After leaving the Columbia the brigade journeyed a month through sterile country, on a march accompanied by days-on-end without food, water, or wood for fuel. Many horses starved to death and the men were "compelled to eat the emaciated carcasses and as a last resort, to quench their thirst with their blood." When they reached Unknown River they found it choked with ice and snow, a situation which "blasted all hopes of a fall hunt." [41]

The Brigade reached the "Great Sandy desert of Great Salt Lake "in January, 1830.[42] The desert was traversed after much suffering, and then they "had a range of rocky Mountains to cross." They struck the Sevier River, which they followed to its discharge into a salt lake. This country they found destitute of beaver. From this point they probably followed Smith's track, possibly guided by one of the survivors of Smith's party. At any rate they at least had the advantage of an account of the region written by Smith.

Following a southwestern course in February, 1830, the British party reached the "South Branch of the Rio Collarado." Then "after three days' further traveling, over a country as barren as ever Christians traversed" they arrived among a tribe of Indians living on the Colorado and which Ogden "strongly suspected" to be the Indians who had

---

[40] The journals of this expedition were lost on July 3, 1830, at the Dalles when Ogden's boat was upset and his papers, five hundred skins and the lives of nine men were lost. To piece together the course of this expedition it has been necessary to rely upon John Scaglione, "Ogden's Report of His 1829-1830 Expedition," *California Historical Society Quarterly,* xxviii (June, 1949), 117-24 and the book written by A Fur Trader (Peter Skene Ogden) *Traits of American Life and Character* (London, 1833). There is some question as to Ogden's authorship of this book but the incidents related do correspond closely with portions of his career. Alice Bay Maloney, "Peter Skene Ogden's Trapping Expedition to the Gulf of California, 1829-30," *California Historical Quarterly,* xix (December, 1940), 308-16, is also helpful. Gloria Cline's *Exploring the Great Basin,* 125-27 has additional new material.

[41] Scaglione, "Ogden's Report of His 1829-1830 Expedition," 121.

[42] *Ibid.* Gloria Cline, *Exploring the Great Basin,* does not believe that this was in Utah. See pp. 126-27.

treacherously attacked Smith in 1828. Ogden placed his
men on the alert to guard the horses, and ordered them to be
ready with guns and spears. He allowed some Indians into
his camp in order to keep an eye on them and perhaps dissuade them from attacking. His strategy did not work,
however, because presently one of the guards was wounded
and the alarm given that the Indians were securing the
horses. Ogden ordered a general discharge, to be followed
by a charge with the spears, but the first was sufficient. The
rest of the Indians fled the field when they observed that
twenty-six of their fellows "in a single moment were made
to lick the dust."

From the Mojave Indian villages the British continued
down the Colorado "till nigh the Gulph of California." [43]
From the Gulf, Ogden turned northward, but since he had
no desire to encounter Mexican authorities and to answer
embarrassing questions, he kept well to the east of the Mexican missions and settlements. He followed the "South
Branch of the Bonaventura" (San Joaquin River) and
trapped that stream from its source to San Francisco Bay,
collecting a thousand skins along the way. An American
brigade from Santa Fe, under Ewing Young, caught up
with Ogden at San Francisco. Since Ogden had preceded
the Americans, their returns were meager. The Yankees
traveled with the British for ten days and separated when
they reached Pit River. From this point the British followed
the trail back to Fort Nez Perces, where they arrived on
June 30, 1830.

The results of this expedition, as far as the net returns of
fur were concerned, were very disappointing, being "one
third less than last year." [44] McLoughlin described the California waters as the "poorest in Furs" that Ogden had thus
far explored, "but as it was a new country we could not

[43] Rich, *The Letters of John McLoughlin,* 86.
[44] Scaglione, "Ogden's Report of His 1829-1830 Expedition," 122.

know it was Stocked in Beaver till he had explored it." [45]
From a geographical standpoint, however, considerable
knowledge concerning the California hinterland was gained.

Upon Ogden's return from his California expedition he
found at Fort Vancouver a letter which relieved him of his
Snake Country command and appointed him to establish a
fur trading post at the mouth of the Nass River, some ten
degrees north of Fort Vancouver.[46] That Ogden was not
enchanted by such an assignment may be noted in the following:

> I have been a wanderer far and near, my perverse fate never permit-
> ting me to sojourn long in the same spot; but driving me about with-
> out cessation, like a ball on a tennis-court. While in the heyday of
> youth, this vagrant kind of life was not without its charms to one of
> my unsettled disposition; with advancing years, however, soberer
> tastes, and less adventurous desires have crept over me, until I could
> heartily wish for a life of greater tranquillity. The potentates who
> rule my destiny seem, however, otherwise inclined, and I now discover,
> to my overpowering chagrin and discomfort, that what I began will-
> ingly, and regarded as amusement, I must continue in earnest and
> against the grain, like physic administered to one who might with it
> "to the dogs" – "le flux, m'amena le reflux m'meme." When, oh,
> when, will this life of involuntary peregrination cease? [47]

In April, 1831, Ogden's party departed Fort Vancouver
and arrived at their destination on May 11. A new post was
erected and christened "Fort Simpson." For three years
Ogden conducted trading and trapping operations in this
Nass River region.[48]

In 1834 another British expedition, with Ogden in command, was organized to establish a trading post on the Stikine River. At the mouth of this stream the British found a

[45] Rich, *The Letters of John McLoughlin,* 86.

[46] T. C. Elliott, "Peter Skene Ogden, Fur Trapper," 251.

[47] Ogden, *Traits of American Life and Character,* 34.

[48] Hubert Howe Bancroft, *History of the North West Coast, 1800-1848,* (San
Francisco, 1884), 629.

Russian blockhouse and a Russian corvette and two fourteen-oared boats which forbade entrance into the river. A considerable controversy ensued. Ogden and his men could not legally settle the matter, nor did they have the physical means to force their entry into the Stikine. He therefore retired from the scene.[49]

Ogden was later chagrined to learn that it was insinuated he had acted with "too much caution or in other words with cowardice." He demanded that Governor Simpson clear his name of the "foul stigma" of these charges by asserting that he had acted to the "ultimate interest of the Concern." [50] When the British government received word of the Russian violation of the spirit of the Convention of 1825, they vigorously protested. The result was that the Russian government eventually paid damages amounting to 20,000 pounds sterling, ceded Fort Wrangel, leased to the British the shore strip which was the basis of the controversy, surrendered the Stikine post, and also gave permission to build an establishment still farther to the north on the Tako River. In view of the concessions ultimately made by the Russians it is evident that Ogden's caution was vindicated and that the restraint he exercised resulted in far greater gains for the Company and the Empire than would have been realized had he provoked the Russians into a shooting war.

Peter Skene Ogden was promoted to chief factor, the highest field grade in the fur business, on January 1, 1835. This promotion was accompanied by his assignment to the command of the New Caledonia District at Fort St. James on Lake Stuart. For nine years (1835-1844) Ogden remained in charge of this district [51] and enjoyed a career here comparable to Chief Factor John McLoughlin's career in the Columbia Department.

---

49 *Ibid.,* 630-33.
50 Elliott, "Peter Skene Ogden, Fur Trapper," 253-54.   51 *Ibid.,* 255-56.

In the spring of 1844, Ogden took a year's leave of absence, his first vacation in twenty-two years. He attended to business matters conected with the estate of his mother, who had recently died, and also visited relatives and friends in Canada, New York, and in Europe. He returned to Canada in the spring of 1845 and was at the Red River encampment on his way back to Oregon when Governor Simpson assigned him to take charge of the Warre-Vavasour expedition to the Columbia Country.[52]

The Warre-Vavasour expedition had its origin at a critical point in the Anglo-American controversy over Oregon. The British Cabinet was alarmed over the situation, especially with American expansionists proclaiming Manifest Destiny, and with the election in 1844 of James K. Polk, who had campaigned on slogans of "Fifty-four Forty or Fight" and "The Reannexation of Oregon," and who had proclaimed that American title to Oregon was "clear and unquestionable." The British felt that they too had clear title to Oregon and decided to dispatch a reconnaissance mission to obtain "a general knowledge of the capabilities of the Oregon territory in a military point of view, in order that we may be enabled to act immediately and with effect in defense of our rights in that quarter, should those rights be infringed by any hostile aggression or encroachment on the part of the United States." Ogden convoyed Lt. Henry J. Warre and Lt. M. Vavasour to Oregon, Governor Simpson noting that his knowledge and experience would "guard against privation, inconvenience or danger along that route." Ogden greatly assisted the lieutenants in their reconnaissance, but the reports of Warre and Vavasour reached the British government too late to influence the negotiations. The 49th parallel was accepted as the boundary in June, 1846.

---

[52] See Joseph Shafer (ed.), "Documents Relative to Warre and Vavasour's Military Reconnaissance in Oregon, 1845-6," *The Quarterly of the Oregon Historical Society*, x (March, 1909), 1-99.

Ogden did not return to Fort St. James and the command of the New Caledonia District upon completion of his assignment with the Warre-Vavasour expedition. He was, instead, assigned to Fort Vancouver, where he shared the management of the Columbia District with Chief Factor James Douglas until 1849. From 1849 to 1852 he was the only chief factor on the Columbia. In the latter year, Dugald MacTavish was sent to assist him.[53]

In June, 1846, with the establishment of the Anglo-American boundary, a perplexing problem arose concerning the properties of the Hudson's Bay Company within United States territory. By that treaty the Company was given certain rights south of the boundary line, including permission to navigate the Columbia River south of the 49th parallel. Fort Vancouver continued to be the supply point for the Company's forts along the coast and for the Sandwich Islands, and trade with Oregon settlers and the Indians of the interior continued to be large. As manager of this largest business concern in the country, the responsibilities of Ogden were varied and great. While some American settlers were rather hostile to the Company, and this hostility helped to form the Oregon Provisional Government at Champoeg on May 2, 1843, Ogden's tact and diplomacy held him in high esteem with the majority of Americans in Oregon. He came to be called "Governor Ogden" by the settlers and was described as "a short man, dark complexioned, witty and lively in conversation and distinguished in appearance."[54]

The Whitman Mission massacre of November 29, 1847, gave Peter Skene Ogden the opportunity of performing his greatest service to the pioneer settlers of Oregon. In addition to the sixteen people murdered by the Cayuse Indians at Waillatpu (six miles west of the present city of Walla

[53] Elliott, "Peter Skene Ogden, Fur Trapper," 262.   [54] *Ibid.*, 263.

Walla), the natives took prisoner forty-seven others – five men, eight women and thirty-four children.[55] The murder of Marcus Whitman, his wife, and the others, posed a complicated problem for Ogden, who was among the first to learn of the disaster. He represented a foreign corporation located in United States territory. Should he take the initiative and attempt a rescue, or simply report it to the Americans then meeting in their provisional legislature in Oregon City, twenty-five miles away?

Although the legislature was the recognized American authority in the territory, it was practically powerless to begin and prosecute a war with the Indians. On the other hand, the Hudson's Bay Company had the necessary forces. Ogden was a skilled and forceful negotiator among the natives, but for him to attempt the rescue and fail could incur the wrath of both the people of Oregon and the American government toward him, his company, and the British government. But the situation was desperate. Early on the morning of December 7, Ogden set off en route to the scene of the massacre. He traveled with his usual complement of men, without display of arms, and at normal speed, in order not to arouse the suspicions of the natives. It required twelve days to reach his destination. On December 24, he assembled the chiefs of the Walla Walla, Cayuse, and Nez Perces tribes for a conference. He made no promises to them, but pointed out that if the Americans were aroused they would wage war which would not end until "every man of you is cut off from the face of the earth." He appealed for the release of the captives, offering to pay a small ransom. Chief Tiloukaikt of the Cayuse replied:

> Chief, your words are weighty, your hairs are gray. We have known you a long time. You have had an unpleasant journey to this place. I cannot therefore keep the families back. I make them over to you, which I would not do to another younger than yourself.

---

[55] *Ibid.*, 276-77.

Seven days of anxious waiting followed before the captives being held at Lapwai were turned over to Ogden. The Americans were conducted to Fort Vancouver and thence to Oregon City, and none too soon. Word was received that some of the Oregon Volunteers had arrived at the Dalles, and the Cayuse War had begun.

In December, 1851, Ogden left Fort Vancouver for Montreal for a leave of absence. There is some indication that he considered retirement from the fur trade at that time. Had he followed the inclinations of others and the desires of his eastern relatives he would have settled down to a life of ease in the society of congenial and well-to-do people in Montreal. But his first love was the great Pacific Northwest, and he determined to spend his last days there. He remained in the East for almost a year and then returned to Oregon, where he again undertook the management of the Hudson's Bay Company business which still flourished. The constant exposurse during his career in the field had whitened his hair and brought on some of the infirmities of age. Still, he was active in the fur business until a few months before his death. When poor health finally forced him to retire, he went to Oregon City, where at the homestead of a son-in-law, Archibald McKinley, he spent his last few months, an invalid, but fondly cared for by his wife and a daughter. Although the best of medical treatment and attention were available to him at Fort Vancouver, he preferred to die in the companionship of his family, and in this public manner gave confirmation of his affection and loyalty to his Indian wife of many years.[56]

During this illness Dr. McLoughlin was a regular visitor and he urged Ogden to permit a formal marriage ceremony with his wife. Ogden refused, stating that if his many years

[56] T. C. Elliott, "Remarks at Unveiling of Memorial Stone to Peter Skene Ogden At Mountain View Cemetery, Oregon City, October 23, 1923," *The Quarterly of the Oregon Historical Society,* XXIV (December, 1923), 382.

of open recognition of their relationship and of their many children were not proof enough, then the empty words of man would not add anything of value. Unfortunately, this refusal caused delay and trouble in the settlement of his estate, because members of his family in Canada and England instituted proceedings to break his will on the ground that there was no legal proof that he ever married. A compromise was finally arranged by Sir George Simpson, who was the executor of the estate, which amounted to at least fifty-thousand dollars.[57]

Peter Skene Ogden died on September 27, 1854, in his sixtieth year. He had been baptized into the English Episcopal Church, and the funeral service was read by the Reverend St. Michael Fackler, the first resident Episcopal rector of Oregon. The body was laid to rest in Mountain View Cemetery at Oregon City.

For nearly seventy years the last resting place of this man who had served so long and well in Oregon was largely forgotten. It was not even marked by a tombstone.[58] Finally, on October 23, 1923, as a result of the combined efforts of three organizations, the Oregon Historical Society, the Oregon Pioneer Association, and the Sons and Daughters of Oregon Pioneers, a fitting granite marker was erected over his grave.

---

[57] Elliott, "Peter Skene Ogden, Fur Trapper," 273-74.

[58] Frederick V. Holman, "Address at Unveiling of Memorial Stone to Peter Skene Ogden at Mountain View Cemetery, Oregon City, October 23, 1923," *ibid.*, 378.

Pierre Chrysologue Pambrun

by KENNETH L. HOLMES
Linfield College, McMinnville, Oregon

On October 1, 1839, Thomas Jefferson Farnham, a traveler over the Oregon Trail from Peoria, Illinois, wrote in his diary, "At ten o'clock today, I was kindly received by Mr. Pambrun at Fort Walla Walla. This gentleman is a half-pay officer in the British army. His rank in the Hudson Bay Company, is that of a 'clerk in charge' of this post. He is of French extraction, a native of Canada. I breakfasted with him and his family. His wife, a half breed of the country, has a numerous and beautiful family. The breakfast being over, Mr. Pambrun invited me to view the premises." Then follows a description of the famous fur-trading post: "The fort is a plank stockade, with a number of buildings within, appropriated to the several uses of a store, blacksmith-shop, dwellings, &c. It has a bastion in the northeast corner, mounted with cannon." [1]

Farnham stayed for two hours with the hospitable French Canadian, "But as if determined that I should remember that I would have been a welcome guest a much longer time, he put some tea and sugar and bread into my packs, and kindly expressed regrets that our mutual admiration of Napoleon should be thus crowded into the chit-chat of hours instead of weeks. A fine companionable fellow; I hope he will command Walla Walla as long as Britons occupy it, and live a hundred years afterwards."

Although the language is more colorful than that of most observers, Farnham's description of Pierre Pambrun is

---

[1] Thomas Jefferson Farnham, *Travels in the Great Western Prairies, the Anahuac and Rocky Mountains, and in the Oregon Territory* (London, 1843), 151-52.

typical in praising the Frenchman's friendliness to American travelers and his sheer openheartedness in giving them aid along their way, at least up to the point where they would become serious economic competitors against the Hudson's Bay Company.

Pierre Chrysologue Pambrun was born near Vondreuil, Province of Quebec, Canada, on December 17, 1792, the son of Andrew Dominique Pambrun and Angelique Hyracque.[2] The father was a man of some education, and he saw to it that his son received a better-than-average education for that time and place.[3] During the War of 1812 Pierre joined a French Canadian *Voltigeur* regiment and rose rapidly through the lower ranks of the British army to become a corporal in January, 1813, a sergeant in February of the same year, a second lieutenant in 1814, and an ensign in 1815.[4] The *Voltigeurs* under Colonels George Macdonnel and Charles de Salaberry, the latter a French Canadian trained in the British army, were instrumental in repelling the United States forces under General Wade Hampton on the Chateauguay River, southwest of Montreal, during the fall of 1813.[5] Pierre Pambrun served in the army until the

[2] Marie Leona Nichols, *The Mantle of Elias* (Portland, Oregon, 1941), 262. The records of the Roman Catholic missions in the Oregon Country are translated in the back of this book as a kind of appendix. This constitutes an invaluable record of the vital statistics of the French Canadians in the employ of the Hudson's Bay Company. There is a short biography of Pambrun in Joseph Tassé, *Les Canadiens de L'Ouest,* 2 vols. (Montreal, 1882).

[3] There is in the Public Archives of Canada, Ottawa, a letter from Andrew Dominique Pambrun, agent of Hon. De Lotbiniere, to his son, Pierre Chrisologue Pambrun, a *Voltigeur,* dated Oct. 28, 1812, giving Pierre advice on how to succeed in a military career. Manuscript Group 24, L 8, vol. M-1, pp. 280-85. In the early records of Pambrun's career in the Canadian archives his middle name is spelled "Chrisologue," but in later life every reference, private and public, uses the "Chrysologue" spelling, which has been followed here.

[4] The above letter tells of promotions to corporal and sergeant. Other documents in the Public Archives of Canada reveal the further promotions: Record Group 8, C797, p. 227 tells of advancement to second lieutenant, and Record Group 9, A-7, vol. I, pp. 16-17, of listing as ensign.

[5] Duncan A. McArthur, "The War of 1812," *Cambridge History of the British Empire: VI, Canada and Newfoundland* (Cambridge, England, 1930), 230.

spring of 1815, when he entered the services of the Hudson's Bay Company in April.[6] His educational background qualified him to become a clerk, and in the years following he served the Great Company well enough to be advanced to chief trader in 1839.[7] The French Canadians usually served as trappers and voyageurs and carried out the more menial tasks in the company service, few of them achieving the distinction and position attained by Pambrun.

A month after joining the Hudson's Bay Company he left with Colin Robertson, an ex-employee of the North West Company, who was leading one hundred French Canadians to the Red River Colony, at the site of present Winnepeg, to protect Scottish settlers in that remote spot from attacks by cohorts of the North West Company.[8] On June 19, 1815, Pambrun was with Governor Robert Semple's force, which attempted to defend the Red River settlement from a party of mounted half-breeds dressed as Indians and led by a *Metis* named Cuthbert Grant. Of the small Hudson's Bay Company force of some thirty men, twenty-one were killed, including Robert Semple himself. Several were captured, and a few escaped by swimming across the Red River in the gloom of nightfall. Pambrun was one of those who escaped.[9]

In the long months of litigation by the North West Company against Lord Selkirk, Pambrun was arrested once by the Northwesters in May, 1816, but released soon afterwards.[10] Among the many charges and counter-charges that passed back and forth between the two companies were two by the North West Company against Pambrun: In the Quebec *Gazette* for March 19, 1818, he was charged with a

---

[6] E. E. Rich, ed., *The Letters of John McLoughlin*, First Series, 1825-1838, *Publications of the Hudson's Bay Record Society*, IV (London, 1941), 351, referred to hereafter as Rich, *McLoughlin Letters*.

[7] *Ibid.*, 352.   [8] *Ibid.*, 351.

[9] *Narratives of John Pritchard, Pierre Chrysologue Pambrun, and Frederick Damien Heurter Respecting the Aggressions of the North-West Company* (London, 1819), 43-45.

[10] Rich, *McLoughlin Letters*, 351.

robbery of persons unknown in the Fond du Lac country back in 1816, and also with allegedly stealing property in February, 1817, at Red River, from one Bazil Belanger.[11] Soon after this he was on his way to England, where he was a witness at the trial in London of Paul Brown and Francois Firmin Boucher, the half-breeds accused of killing Governor Robert Semple.[12] Pambrun stayed in England through 1819, when he returned to Canada.[13]

There followed a westward movement all of his own, as year after year Pambrun approached closer to the Pacific shore. He was clerk at Cumberland House, and was with an expedition to the Bow River in what is now Alberta, near present Calgary, in the summer of 1822.[14] In a report from Edmunton House covering 1822-23 Colin Robertson wrote of Pambrun that he was "high spirited and ambitious" and "highly capable of conducting any enterprise where courage and perseverance is required." [15] In 1823-24 he was stationed on the Smoky River, a branch of the Peace River, in present-day northwestern Alberta Province. The next year he and William Connolly opened Fort Kilmaurs on Babine Lake, a long finger lake in present northern British Columbia.[16] This was in the Hudson's Bay Company's massive Columbia District of the Oregon Country. Then in 1826 Pierre Pambrun traveled into the southern Oregon Country, along with James Douglas and Francis Ermatinger, to Fort Vancouver, the new Hudson's Bay Company post across from the mouth of the Willamette River on the northern bank of the Columbia. On this journey he met David Douglas, the English botanist, at Fort Okanogan. The scientist noted the meeting in his journal on Tuesday, June 6, 1826.[17]

[11] "Bills of the Court of King's Bench," *Quebec Gazette,* March 19, 1818.

[12] Rich, *McLoughlin Letters,* 351. Also Amos, I., *Report of Trials in the Courts of Canada* (London, 1820), 70-81.

[13] Rich, *McLoughlin Letters,* 351.   [14] *Ibid.*

[15] *Ibid.*   [16] *Ibid.*

When Pambrun arrived at Fort Vancouver in the summer
of 1826, he brought with him his wife, Catherine (Kitty),
daughter of Thomas Humperville. An Indian woman of the
Cree tribe was her mother. Pierre and Kitty had met at the
Red River settlement in 1820. There were two small sons
along – Andre Dominique, five, and Pierre Chrysoloque Jr.,
three years old.[18]

Pierre Pambrun was a mainstay on the staff at Fort Vancouver for a number of years, gaining the respect of Chief
Factor John McLoughlin during that time. In March, 1832,
McLoughlin assigned Pambrun to Fort Walla Walla as
chief clerk in charge of the post.[19] Walla Walla was a
particularly significant situation to the company, for it was
an important stopping place for all parties east and west
across the continent, and besides this the inland post was the
jumping off place for the Snake River country farther east
and a center of trade for the Cayuse, the Nez Perce, the
Walla Walla, and other high country tribes of Indians.

It was during the same year, 1832, that Governor George
Simpson of the Hudson's Bay Company wrote a trenchant
word picture of Pierre Pambrun in his "Book of Servants'
Characters," which may be examined in the archives of the
Hudson's Bay Company at Beaver House in London. The
"Character Book," a classic of the fur trade, was evidently
kept privately for the governor's own use and not intended
for other eyes. The word sketches of company employees
were originally numbered, but not labeled by name. The
clue to the names was not made available until long after
Simpson's death, when a single sheet was discovered among

---

[17] David Douglas, "Sketch of a Journey to Northwestern Parts of the Continent
of North America During the Years 1824-'25-'26-'27," *Quarterly of the Oregon Historical Society*, v (December, 1904), 345.

[18] Nichols, *op. cit.*, 261-62.

[19] Letter from John McLoughlin to George Simpson, March 15, 1832, Burt Brown
Barker, *Letters of Dr. John McLoughlin* (Portland, 1948), 259.

his papers, and the mystery of the identities solved.[20] Here is what the "Character Book" records of Simpson's opinion of Pambrun, who was number 70:

> A Canadian about 45 years of age – 17 years in the Service. – An active, steady dapper little fellow, is anxious to be useful but is wanting in judgment and deficient in Education: – full of "pluck", has a very good opinion of himself and is quite a "Petit Maitre". Does not manage the business of his Post well, owing more to a want of discretion & foresight than to indifference or inattention: would drink I am of opinion if not under restraint. – Cannot look to an interest in the business. – Stationed in the Columbia.

John McLoughlin's opinion of Pambrun seems to have been more favorable than Simpson's. Five years after this, McLoughlin wrote of the French Canadian that he had "managed the affairs of Walla Walla, one of the most troublesome posts (if not the most troublesome) in the Country, with the utmost skill and judgment." [21]

Pambrun, a Roman Catholic, is credited with stimulating the interest of the Indians in the white man's religion. This was especially true of the Nez Perce, to whom he is supposed to have given elementary instruction in morals when they came to trade.[22] When Dr. Marcus Whitman and Rev. Henry Spalding and their wives traveled west in 1836 and established missions, one at Waiilatpu, not far from Walla Walla, the other at Lapwai, on a creek of that name upstream from the juncture of the Snake and Clearwater Rivers in the present Idaho panhandle, Pierre Pambrun gave them indispensible help and encouragement. Spalding wrote to his mission board on October 2, 1836,

---

[20] The author used the "Book of Servants' Characters" (A34/2) at the Hudson's Bay Company Archives in London. It is quoted here with the kind permission of the Governor and Committee of the Hudson's Bay Company. The history of the "Character Book" is told in Douglas MacKay, *The Honourable Company* (New York, 1938), 198-202.

[21] Rich, *McLoughlin Letters,* letter of October 31, 1837, p. 196.

[22] Francis Haines, *The Nez Percés* (Norman, Okla., 1955), 54.

You will hardly believe when I tell you, that Mr. Pambra [sic] who has done so much to forward our object, spending more than a month in travelling with us, and has been with us to look at a location, and says he will do everything in his power to help us, and wishes us to take his children to bring up, is a Roman Catholic.[23]

A delightful description of Fort Walla Walla and its superintendent was written by Mrs. Marcus Whitman in her diary on September 1, 1836, just after the missionary party had arrived from the tedious journey. They had come in early in the morning and been treated to breakfast.

After breakfast we were shown the novelties of the place, they are so to us. While at breakfast, however, a young cock placed himself upon the cell [sill] of the door and crowed. Now whether it was the sight of the first white females or out of compliment to the company I know not, this much for him. I was pleased with his appearance. You may think me simple for speaking of such a small circumstance as this. . . The dooryard was filled with hens turkeys pigeons & in another place we saw cows hogs & goats in abundance, & I think the largest & fattest cattle & swine I ever saw. We were soon shown a room, which Mr Pambran said he had prepared for us by making two bedsteads . . . bunks, on hearing of our approach. . . Having arranged our things, we were soon called to a feast of mellons, the finest I think I ever saw or tasted. The mushmelon was the largest measuring eighteen inches in length, fifteen arround the small end and nineteen around the largest end. You may be assured we were not any of us satisfied or willing to leave the table untill we had filled our plates with chips.[24]

On September 2 Narcissa Whitman added a note about Mrs. Pambrun: "I have not yet introduced you to the Lady of the House. She is a native. From a tribe east of the mountains. She appears well, does not speak English but her native language & French." [25]

[23] "Letter of Reverend H. H. Spalding and Mrs. Spalding, Written Shortly After Completing Their Trip Across the Continent," *Quarterly of the Oregon Historical Society*, XIII (December, 1912), 377.

[24] Clifford Merrill Drury, *First White Women over the Rockies*, I (Glendale, Calif., 1963), 94-95.   [25] *Ibid.*, 95.

The two women continued as staunch friends. Kitty
Pambrun was with Mrs. Whitman for two weeks before the
birth of Alice Clarissa Whitman on March 14, 1837. Narcissa wrote, "She with my Husband dressed the babe. It
would have made you smile to see them work over the little
creature. Mrs P never saw one dressed before as we dress
them having been accostomed to dress her own in the native
stile." [26]

In his capacity as chief clerk (advanced to chief trader
on November 27, 1839)[27] at Fort Walla, Pambrun welcomed many of the American travelers over the Oregon
Trail. Among these were Nathaniel Wyeth, Benjamin
Bonneville, John K. Townsend (the naturalist), Joe Meek,
Robert Newell, William Craig, and numerous others. They
often made comments in letters, diaries, or reminiscences
about the hospitality of the French Canadian. It is obvious,
however, that Pambrun would go only so far as considerations for the welfare of the company would allow. Washington Irving commented, in regard to the treatment of
Benjamin Bonneville, that the latter applied to purchase
supplies of Pambrun "but soon found the difference between
being treated as a guest, or as a rival trader. The worthy
superintendent, who had extended to him all the genial rites
of hospitality, now suddenly assumed a withered-up aspect
and demeanor, and observed that, however he might feel
disposed to serve him, personally, he felt bound by his duty
to the Hudson's Bay Company, to do nothing which should
facilitate or encourage the visits of other traders among the
Indians in that part of the country." [28]

Pierre Pambrun is usually credited with the leadership of
a Hudson's Bay party in 1839 that traveled from Fort Walla

[26] *Ibid.*, 126.   [27] Rich, *McLoughlin Letters,* 352.
[28] Washington Irving, *The Adventures of Captain Bonneville* (Norman, Okla.,
1961), 261.

Walla to Fort Nisqually, just south of present Tacoma, Washington, thus being the first to explore Nisqually Pass, which crosses the Cascade Range just south of Mount Rainier.[29]

He lived only a fraction of the years that Thomas Farnham wished for him, for on May 15, 1841, Pambrun died from a fall from his horse. John McLoughlin wrote a report of this incident to the London headquarters of the company on May 24, saying that he had received word from Dr. Marcus Whitman of Pambrun's death.[30] The beneficiaries under his will, particulars of which are in the Hudson's Bay Company Archives in London, were his wife, Kitty, five sons and four daughters.[31] Pambrun's body was buried for a time at Fort Walla Walla. Later it was moved to the Roman Catholic cemetery at Fort Vancouver, where it was reburied on March 9, 1844.[32]

In the same letter in which he reported Pambrun's death, John McLoughlin wrote, "In losing him, the Company loses an excellent officer and a most able manager of the place under his charge, one of the most difficult places to manage in the Indian Country, and a man most anxious to do his utmost to forward the Interest of the concern." [33]

---

[29] Oregon City, *Oregon Spectator,* May 13, 1847.
[30] Rich, *McLoughlin Letters,* 34.   [31] *Ibid.,* 352.
[32] Nichols, *op. cit.,* 277.   [33] Rich, *McLoughlin Letters,* 34.

Daniel T. Potts

by GERALD C. BAGLEY
Jackson, Wyoming

The popular and romantic conception of Mountain Men consists of a stereotyped image of hardy, adventuresome, freedom-loving, reckless, even violent wayfarers of the trackless savage-infested West. This author takes issue with the stereotype. My thesis, based on the primary sources furnished by Daniel T. Potts, suggests that fur traders were a diverse lot who entered the mountains for widely varying reasons – some of which are far removed from the romantic tradition.[1] The personnel ranged from innocent youths, who were enlisted along with their fathers, to rogues seeking asylum from society. Moreover, a good number probably signed the roster under misconceptions; they were "enterprising young men" seeking easy wealth and romantic adventure.[2] Though the men received full measure of adventure, only a few realized wealth.

True, some of the men came to appreciate western life and remained to give real substance to the image of the

---

[1] The original sources of the fur trade clearly show that trappers were of varying types. Of particular interest in this respect are: John C. Ewers (ed.), *The Adventures of Zenas Leonard, Fur Trader* (Norman, 1959); Warren A. Ferris, *Life in the Rocky Mountains*, Paul C. Phillips, ed. (Denver, 1940); Aubrey L. Haines (ed.), *Osborne Russell's Journal of a Trapper* (Portland, 1955); Thomas James, *Three Years Among the Indians and Mexicans* (New York, 1962). Narratives written long after the authors left the mountains tend to romanticize and embellish the trapper life. The prime example is: T. D. Bonner (ed.), *The Life and Adventures of James P. Beckwourth* (New York, 1931).

[2] Presumably, many of William Ashley's and Andrew Henry's "Enterprising Young men" were in this category. The headnote of one of Potts' letters published in a Philadelphia newspaper declares: "It [the letter] comes from a native of Pennsylvania who, actuated by a spirit of romantic adventure has left a good mill . . . to wander the wilds of the West." Donald M. Frost, *Notes on General Ashley, the Overland Trail and South Pass* (Barre, Mass., 1960), 62.

Mountain Men, but others remained under compulsion, for society held more threatening possibilities for them.[3] The majority of the men stayed only for a few years; when the opportunity of a settlement-bound caravan permitted it, they returned to less dangerous regions.

A prime reason for the stereotyped picture of the Mountain Men is the lack of authentic records of their exploits. The image of brave, independent, and violent men is largely fashioned from second and third hand tales told *after* these men left the mountains. One mountain-written chronicle, in obvious contrast, not only testifies to the diversity of the western fur traders, but was written by a trapper who bears little resemblance to the traditional image. He was Daniel T. Potts, a young man of twenty-six, who went to the Rocky Mountains with the William Ashley and Andrew Henry expedition in 1822 and remained there until 1828. Because of several long letters he penned from famous summer rendezvous, Potts has become the prime chronicler of the Rocky Mountain fur trade during this early source-starved period.[4] His letters reveal that bravery and an appreciation of western beauty, as well as cowardice and nagging fear of western danger, were features of the trapper mentality.

Daniel Potts, a native of Pennsylvania, appears to have had a fair education and some experience as a miller before – as family tradition has it – "anxious to see life and the country, he went West." [5] As with many others of his generation, his father, Zebulon Potts, fought in the Revolutionary

---

[3] Ewers, *op. cit.,* 160-61.

[4] Daniel T. Potts wrote five letters dated from 1824 to 1828, and several were published in early newspapers. Representative accounts of these have been collected in Donald Frost, *op. cit.* Long extracts of the letters were published in, Dale L. Morgan, *The West of William H. Ashley* (Denver, 1963). The complete texts of all known letters are in the unpublished master's thesis of the present author at Brigham Young University. The known manuscripts are in the Yellowstone Park Museum at Mammoth, Wyoming. Throughout the remaining narrative these letters will be referred to as *Potts Letter* and the year of its date.

[5] Frost, *op. cit.,* p. ix.

War. Evidently father, like son, was an astute observer of dramatic events, for in an engraving showing George Washington praying at Valley Forge, another man, peering from behind a tree (evidently unnoticed by Washington), is supposedly Zebulon Potts.[6] Daniel Potts also did his observing and chronicling in an uncommissioned style. He entered the western fur trade for adventure and possible wealth; his chronicling of trapper life and western discovery was pure "happenstance." He was simply one of the few trappers who could write, and luckily, some letters were preserved.

From information in one of these letters, historians place the date of departure for the Ashley-Henry expedition as April 3, 1822, when the heavy-laden keelboats were forced into the current of the river for the long voyage upstream.[7] Potts and his enterprising companions were immediately appalled at the rigor of their new occupation. They were forced to employ every imaginable method in struggling up the turbulent Missouri. Poles, oars, sails, and a long cordelle were all utilized in the bone-bending work of moving the cumbersome keelboat against the current. Hard work, however, the men could put up with, but as the distance back to the settlements was steadily increased, a new and more vexing discomfort arose. Either from lack of preparation or from a deliberate attempt by the company to live off the land, rations became scarce. By the time the boat reached Cedar Fort (about five hundred miles above Council Bluffs) the situation was desperate. The genteel Potts, who was used to better fare, declares that:

> . . . we where reduced to the sad necessity of eating aneything we could cetch as our provision where exausted and no game to be had . . . we were glad to get a Dog to eat and I have seen some geather she skins of Dogs up through the Camp sing [singe] and roast them and eat heartyly.[8]

[6] From the Potts family tradition.   [7] Potts Letter, 1824.
[8] Ibid.

These trying conditions were more than the men had signed up for. Many of them no doubt contemplated desertion, and some carried it out, hoping to return to more civilized regions. Potts was included among a party of nine deserters, but strangely, for only a short time. He soon lost his clothes, gun, and companions, then stumbled from one merciful tribe of Indians to another, and wandered approximately 450 miles down the Missouri River before happening onto another of Ashley's boats which was struggling upstream. Potts, by now in an emaciated condition, gratefully rejoined the mountain-bound party and resigned himself to the fact that surviving on any fare with the group was preferable to starving alone.[9]

In deserting, he participated in what seems to have been typical behavior among early fur trade personnel. Thomas James, who accompanied Manuel Lisa up-river in 1809, relates that of 175 Americans who enlisted with the expedition, only ten remained by the time the boats reached the Mandan Villages.[10]

Potts' long and lonely wilderness hike was probably his most protracted mountain ordeal, but not his most painful — this was to come the following spring. He spent the winter high on the Missouri, on a smaller branch called the Musselshell, with an unlikely set of cabin-mates. They included the later-famed and God-fearing trader, Jedediah Smith, along with the notorious trio, Mike Fink, Talbot, and Carpenter. These last three were killed in a violent and sensational manner later in the spring.[11] It was then that Potts also had a second streak of ill luck. While one of his companions was cleaning his loaded rifle, the piece accidently discharged and shot the ram-rod through both of Potts' knees. In a classic understatement Potts relates that the incident

---

[9] *Ibid.*   [10] Thomas James, *op. cit.,* 5.
[11] The death of Mike Fink is well narrated in Dale L. Morgan, *Jedediah Smith and the Opening of the West* (New York, 1953), 46-49.

"brought me to the ground." It also laid the young trapper up for "the spring hunt, and almost forever."[12]

During the summer of 1823, while in convalescence at Henry's Fort at the mouth of the Yellowstone River, Potts missed participating in two celebrated fur trade sagas. The first occurred when Ashley, struggling up the Missouri with additional recruits and supplies, had a set-to with the Arikara Indians. These savages killed or wounded some thirty men before the whites escaped.[13] A formidable combination of trappers, Sioux Indians, and United States Dragoons returned with cannon and reduced the village to a shamble of mud-covered huts. The bulk of the population, however, abandoned the settlement under the cover of night and escaped. At this juncture, the army of retribution immediately dispersed, with a contingent of trappers under Andrew Henry returning by land to the mouth of the Yellowstone. While on this march the second sensational incident occurred: the mauling of Hugh Glass by a grizzly bear.[14] This classic adventure has been frequently recounted.[15]

The story, due to its incredible report of human tenacity, has had some embellishment with legend. In recent years Bridger's biographer has discounted the tale as a product of frontier story-telling.[16] In a little-known letter, however, the first he wrote as a Mountain Man, Daniel Potts corroborates the main features of the original story. In precisely the proper context of time and place Potts relates that:

one man was allso tore nearly all to peases by a White Bear and was left by the way without any gun who afterwards recover'd.[17]

Potts thus begins his mountain chronicling by giving credence to what is perhaps the most famous of western tales.

12 Potts Letter, 1824.   13 *Ibid.,* See also Potts Letter, 1826.
14 Charles L. Camp (ed.), *James Clyman Frontiersman* (Portland, 1960), 15.
15 See Morgan, *Jedediah Smith,* 96-108, for one of many accounts.
16 J. Cecil Alter, *Jim Bridger* (Norman, 1962), 38-43.
17 Potts Letter, 1824.

Daniel did not learn of the Hugh Glass story until several months after it happened, for he was ahead of the main party. After recovering from his painful knee wounds he had, along with his leader Andrew Henry, proceeded up the Yellowstone to the mouth of the Big Horn. Here Potts and seven others were dispatched "a traping accross the Rocky Mountains," while Henry and the remaining men commenced building a fur post. Potts and his fellows were to proceed towards the Wind River Valley (in Wyoming) to winter with the Crow Indians. Before reaching that place, however, Potts fell heir to another typical mountain misfortune. He became lost while traversing the Owl Creek range, and in the course of struggling through waist-deep snow, severely froze his feet. Two toes were completely lost and two others in part, greatly impeding his spring hunt.[18]

After some benevolent care by a Snake Indian Chief, Potts eventually reached the Crow encampment in the late fall of 1823. Here, he and his seven companions were joined by another contingent of Ashley-Henry men under the direction of Jedediah Smith. Early the following spring, Smith and his band attempted a passage over the continental divide and finally succeeded in making a torturously cold and windy crossing near, and perhaps through, the later-famed South Pass.[19]

Potts and his friends remained in Wind River Valley, conducting a successful spring hunt on the eastern slope of the Rockies. As summer approached these men made contact with Henry and arranged with him to rendezvous and exchange their peltries for trade goods and additional supplies to carry them over the mountains. At some point, probably between the bend of Wind River and the mouth of the Big Horn, the detachment held a meeting that may

---

[18] *Ibid.*   [19] Morgan, *Jedediah Smith,* 78-95.

have been the prototype of the famous rendezvous system. Upwards of forty-five whites were present, exchanging goods and information.[20] Here Potts' contingent informed Henry of South Pass: "a passage by which loaded waggons can at this time reach the navigable waters of the Columbia River."[21] Daniel and his companions had no doubt become familiar with the terrain of the pass on their spring hunt. News of the discovery was taken by Henry to the settlements and published in several newspapers, thus making it the effective discovery of the famous gateway to the West.[22]

Led by John H. Weber, an ex-sea-captain, Potts and a large party of hunters went through the South Pass during the summer months and proceeded across the Green River drainage into the Great Basin. The region encompassing present northern Utah became a favorite to Daniel, who penned the earliest descriptions of many of its principal features. Potts was particularly impressed with the beautiful Bear Lake and sent the following description to his brother:

> [In] The first valley as you approach from the head of the river, is a small sweet lake, about 120 miles in circumference, with beautiful clear water, and when the wind blows has a splendid appearance.[23]

A particular quality evident in Potts' letters is his appreciation for western beauty. His descriptions of "large snowy mountains," "transparent streams," "crystal lakes," and "fathomless hot pools" have a lyrical quality that is perhaps the most pleasing feature of his letters.

Potts' contingent spent the winter of 1824-25 on Cub Creek, a tributary of Bear River. Sometime before the

---

[20] It is conceivable that a considerable rendezvous was held when Henry traded goods for furs with his trapping contingents in the summer of 1824, making it much more the prototype of the rendezvous system than the small meeting of Smith's men the same year. Gerald Bagley, unpublished thesis, 35-39. Hereafter cited as Bagley thesis.   [21] Frost, *op. cit.,* 126.

[22] Bagley thesis, 45-47.   [23] Potts Letter, 1826.

spring hunt, young Jim Bridger tramped down the latter stream to determine its course. Following the river to where it fed a large body of salt water, Bridger thought he had arrived on the shores of the Pacific Ocean. It turned out to be the Great Salt Lake, and Jim probably was its first white discoverer. Potts no doubt saw it the same spring; he later penned the first good description of the briny lake:

> The G.S. Lake lies in a circular form from N.E. to N.W. the larger circle being to [the] S. It is about 400 miles in circumference, and has no discharge or outlet, it is generally shallow near the beach, and has several islands, which rise like pyramyds from its surface. The western part of the lake is so saturvated with salt, as not to desolve any more when thrown into it.[24]

Potts apparently deserves credit for naming the lake. At any rate, he is the first to call it by its present designation. The name Great Salt Lake is used three times in his letter of 1826 – a year before this title had general use in frontier newspapers.

Following the spring hunt conducted in the northern Great Basin, Potts and his trapping companions rendezvoused on Henry's Fork of the Green River to exchange their furs for supplies. From this time an annual rendezvous in some form became a feature of the mountain life.

Mountain rendezvous, however, like Mountain Men, have undergone an embellishment under the pens of some writers. Supposedly, rendezvous were wild saturnalias of drunken debauchery – grand meetings and violent mixings of trappers, Indians, and straight-grain alcohol, the latter somewhat questionably diluted with hot pepper, molasses, tobacco, and water. The drama has obviously been over-played. For though some of the later summer fairs attended by truant army officers and English sportsmen may have been wild affairs, the first few fail to fit the romantic pat-

---

[24] *Ibid.*

tern. In 1825, the summer trading seems to have occurred without two of the supposedly necessary ingredients: Ashley forgot to bring any whiskey, and no one seems to have invited the Indians.[25] The rendezvous of 1826 was no grand meeting at all. Trading and other business were carried on intermittently by various participants in different parts of northern Utah.[26] Both rendezvous seem to have resembled sober business dealings rather than reckless regalias of mountain frivolity. Potts, the most trustworthy of chroniclers, depicts the social joviality of 1826 in formal and orderly tones:

> We celebrated the 4th of July, by firing three rounds of small arms, and partook of a most excellent dinner, after which a number of political toasts were drunk.[27]

In no instance does Daniel give credence to the popular notion of the summer trade fairs.

---

[25] Dale Morgan breaks down the 120 men present at this rendezvous in his, *William Ashley,* 288.

[26] With the varying and secondary sources, the site of the Rendezvous of 1826 has been subject to considerable difference of opinion. The present author hopes to have settled the matter in Bagley, thesis, 77-78. The general argument is as follows: Newspaper accounts credited to Ashley indicate that at least some of his caravan reached Great Salt Lake. These accounts say Ashley "went to the station of the party which he had left beyond the mountains . . . thence descended a river, believed to be the Buenaventura (actually Bear River) about one hundred and fifty miles to the Great Lake." The same source speaks of "The Lake which terminated the expedition westward," *Alexandria Gazette,* December 28, 1826. See Frost, *op. cit.,* 137-38. Also in Morgan, *William Ashley,* 153. The caravan evidently arrived in Cache Valley around May 25, and according to Robert Campbell the trading lasted two weeks; *ibid.,* 145. This would presumably end the rendezvous at the early date of June 8. Yet, the change of partnership occurred on July 18; *ibid.,* 150. Also, Daniel Potts' letter was dated July 16, 1826. With about a month and a half in northern Utah, Ashley and his men could have held the initial trading in Cache Valley and then descended to Great Salt Lake. Any celebrating was also carried on intermittently and in varying spots. James Beckwourth indicates frivolity when the goods were opened; T. D. Bonner, *op. cit.,* 70. Daniel Potts tells of some good eating, political toasts, and gun salutes on the 4th of July; Potts Letter, 1826. There was, perhaps, another celebration on July 18 when the change in partnership was signed and Ashley prepared to leave. Beckwourth indicates this on pp. 73-74. These three occasions of mountain joviality occurred in different areas of northern Utah.

[27] Potts Letter, 1826.

Between 1824 and 1826 Daniel Potts doubtless carried on
a fairly typical trapping career: hard work during the
spring and fall hunts, a trade rendezvous in the summer,
and cozy inactivity (possibly in company with friendly
Indians) during the winter. By now inured to mountain life,
Potts pursued his career motivated by the prospects for gain
and the opportunity to see new country. He did, however,
miss civilized life. At the rendezvous of 1826, he was on the
eve of returning to St. Louis with the home-bound caravan,
but was dissuaded by the promise of exploring a route to
California with Jedediah Smith.[28] For reasons unknown, he
was not included in Smith's "South West Expedition," but
instead made a foray to the North, into a region of perhaps
more geographic interest, and undoubtedly more danger. A
year later he recounted his ill luck: "I took my departure
for Black-foot Country much against my will as I could not
make a party for any other rout." [29] At the time, Daniel little
realized that there were more unusual sights in Blackfoot
Country than in any other part of the West: the region
encompassed what is presently known as Yellowstone National Park.

The party left northern Utah (the site of the Rendezvous
of 1826) and soon reached Snake River in Idaho, where
they were daily harassed by Blackfeet Indians.[30] Despite
these skirmishes they continued north into unknown country,
proceeding up Henry's Fork from where it joins the larger
branch of Snake River. Thirty miles up-river they angled
to the right and crossed the Teton Range (aptly described
as a "large ruged Mountain" by Potts), possibly over Con-
nent Pass. Descending the other side of the mountain, the
men once again struck Snake River and followed the stream

---

[28] *Ibid.*

[29] Potts Letter to Robert Potts, 1827. There are two known letters written by Potts
in 1827. This one contains the account of his foray into Yellowstone Park.

[30] *Ibid.*

"to its source which heads on the top of the great chain of Rocky Mountains which separates the water of the Atlantic from that of the Pacific." [31] Potts, though aware that he was advancing into the key to the western river systems, was nonetheless unprepared for the other phenomena of the region. Continuing over the continental divide he came into view of the beautiful Yellowstone Lake, a sheet of clear water bounded by evergreen shores. No doubt enthralled by the high, mountain lake, Potts wrote that:

> . . . the Yellow-Stone [River] has a large fresh water Lake near its head on the verry top of the Mountain which is . . . as clear as Crystal.[32]

Once down on the lake shore, Potts and his party were again awe-struck by the unusual thermal activity. Hot pots and geysers played, some steadily and others intermittently, as they had, unobserved by white men, for centuries. In a passage that became the most important he ever wrote, Potts described the area:

> . . . on the South borders of this Lake is a number of hot and boiling springs some of water and others of most beautiful fine clay and resembles that of a mush pot and Throws its particles to the immense height of from twenty to thirty feet. . . The Clay is white and of a Pink and water appears fathomless as it appears to be entirely hollow under neith. There is also a number of places where the pure su[l]phor is sent forth in abundance. One of our men Visited one of those whilst taking his recreation there at an instant the earth began a tremindious trembling and he with dificulty made his escape when an explosion took place resembling that of Thunder. During our stay in that quarter I heard it every day.[33]

This account establishes Potts as the first describer and the first confirmed visitor to Yellowstone Park. He evidently hunted in this region during the fall months and no doubt viewed many of the wonders of the area. No other members of his party are presently known.

---

[31] *Ibid.*   [32] *Ibid.*   [33] *Ibid.*

Following his trapping foray into Blackfoot country, Potts returned to the northern Utah region to winter. Since the weather remained warm, he and several others made a journey of exploration south and west of Great Salt Lake. They evidently made their spring hunt in this region before returning to Bear Lake for the rendezvous of 1827.

At the rendezvous, inflation under the new traders (Ashley had sold out to three of his subordinates) greatly vexed Daniel. He lamented the high prices of trade goods in a letter to a friend in Pennsylvania.

> There is a poor prospect of making much here, owing to the evil disposition of the Indians, and the exorbitant price of goods. For example,
>
> | | |
> |---|---|
> | Powder . . . . | 2.50 per lb. |
> | Lead . . . . | 1.50 |
> | Coffee . . . . | 2.00 |
> | Sugar . . . . | 2.00 [34] |

Potts continues the above list to include the important staples of the fur trade, thus making one of the few economic accounts of the period.

A desire "to see life and the country" while improving his economic condition had motivated Daniel Potts to become a trapper and trader in the West. By 1827 he had satisfied the first desire, but Indians, adversity, and opportunistic traders had thwarted his second objective. Potts thus became convinced that he must seek his fortune elsewhere. He had managed, however, to accumulate a small sum and was determined to enlarge it by violent effort during a final year in the mountains. His efforts were of no avail. Again stymied by adversity in the form of the most severe winter in living memory, Potts was forced to leave for the frontiers with less capital than he had hoped. He departed with the settlement-bound fur caravan around August 1, 1828, and arrived some seventy days later in St. Louis.[35]

---

[34] Potts Letter to "Dr. Lukens," 1827.   [35] Potts Letter, 1828.

Potts was overjoyed to be free of the forebodings of violent death that pervaded the mountains. Earlier he had written, "A man in this Country is not safe neither day nor night, and [I] hardly ever expect to get back." [36] In a letter to his brother in Philadelphia he expressed his new-found feelings of safety:

> with congratulation and a heart overflowed with joy to think that I can write to you from a place incompassed within the bounds of civilition I arrived at this place about a week since after a long and fatigueing journey of about seventy days after which my mind has become more tranquil.[37]

Civilization, however, proved to be even less kind to Potts than had the mountains. For he soon became engaged in a venture shipping horses and cattle from Texas to New Orleans, and while thus employed he passes from the record. According to family tradition, he went down with a ship that sank with all hands in the Gulf of Mexico.[38]

This last entry on Potts seems most anticlimactic. Perhaps this is so due to the preeminencc of the West over the sea in American folklore. Somehow, death at the hands of fierce Indians would have been a more heroic departure than drowning at sea. Moreover, Potts *was* out of his element, for by most measures he was a Mountain Man. Though at times a disillusioned, luckless, and consequently a reluctant one, he had nonetheless become skilled in western life, inured to its hardships, appreciative of its beauty, and probably more successful than average in extricating its wealth. His letters also prove that not all Mountain Men remained in the West primarily for the life of "wild freedom" possible there. They often enlisted in the fur trade under misconceptions, then were temporarily trapped by

---

36 Potts Letter, 1824.   37 Potts Letter, 1828.

38 From a short biography of Daniel T. Potts in *The Potts Family,* published in Cannonsburg, Pennsylvania, 1901. It appears also in Frost, *op. cit.,* p. ix. See also Bagley thesis, appendix, 140.

their environment. After a fair trial, a good many quit the business with satisfaction. Their places were subsequently filled by other diverse and sometimes misguided recruits who repeated the pattern – sojourning for a time in the West and in their turn giving substance to the romantic and heroic image of the Mountain Men.

Rufus B. Sage

by ANN W. HAFEN
Provo, Utah

Of the four hundred Mountain Men to appear in this *Series,* Rufus B. Sage is perhaps the only one who wrote and published a contemporary book based on his experiences in the Far West. His *Scenes in the Rocky Mountains* appeared in 1846, in a paperback and a hard cover edition. Carey & Hart of Philadelphia was his publisher. The author was not content until a map was included in the hard cover edition, which retailed at one dollar per copy. The paperback sold for fifty cents, without a map.

Sage's 303-page book on the West went through many printings during the next twenty years. The first edition included 3000 paper bound and 500 hard cover copies. In this edition the author was merely listed as "A New Englander." Within a year – 1847 – the Second Edition Revised appeared; thereafter his name was inserted as author. Still later, under Sage's name on the title page was the added line, "The Western Adventurer."

In 1854 the book was re-issued with eleven woodcut illustrations. In 1855 it was printed as the Third Edition Revised. The 1857 publication included twenty-five illustrations and the volume was bound with decorated and stamped cloth over boards, but no map was included. Editions are reported for the years 1858, 1859, and 1860. Other undated cheap reprints were issued later, but none of the editions carried an index.

In later years Sage's book was nearly forgotten. Then in 1956, a two-volume edition, edited by the Hafens, was published with an introduction, a biographical sketch of the author, footnotes, several family letters, and an index. The publishers, The Arthur H. Clark Company, used their customary fine format and good materials to produce handsome volumes.[1]

Rufus B. Sage was born in Cromwell, Connecticut, on March 17, 1817. He was the youngest of seven children born to Deacon Rufus Sage and Jerusha Butler Sage. Left fatherless at the age of nine, Rufus was early thrown upon his own resources. By attendance at the common school and an academy he obtained the basics of an education. Upon this he built through his own efforts.

He was reared in a religious home. At fourteen he joined the Congregational Church. He signed the pledge-roll of the first Temperance Society in Connecticut and continued as a life-long abstainer from spirituous drinks. He refused tobacco, drank coffee seldom, and tea never. A report says: "He has never been laid by from sickness for a single day during his whole life."

At the newspaper office in Middletown he learned the printer's trade. This skill was to provide him employment and give him important contacts and opportunities. In 1836, when he was nineteen years old, he set forth to experience ten years of adventuring that would carry him over most of the American nation of his day, through the western frontier territory and across the border to Mexican soil. Happily, he was equipped by training and temperament to record those experiences and observations for the benefit of others.

Rufus left his Connecticut home – that "world of steady habits" – to make his first visit, in 1836, to the great city of New York. He soon wrote his mother saying:

---

[1] The materials for this sketch are taken from the publication: LeRoy R. and Ann W. Hafen, *Rufus B. Sage, his Letters and Papers, etc.* (Glendale, Calif., 1956), 2 vols. The portrait which appeared as the frontispiece in the 1956 edition, also appears herein at page 17.

New York is certainly a large city but somehow or other not the city
I thought it was . . . its splendor falls far below what I had
anticipated. Instead of viewing it with wonder and astonishment as I
expected that I being a raw Yankee should, . . . I seemed as
much at home as though I had always lived there. . . Finding
nobody I knew, I thought I would go around and take a squint at
the city. . . Brooklyn is a fine place, not quite such a sink of
polution as N.Y. But by the by, N.Y. is not near so bad a place as I
thought for, yet it is bad enough. . . But, dear Mother, there is
one thing I find . . . that he who was the God of my fathers
is still my God, and watches continually over my path. . .[2]

Rufus soon found, with his printer's training, that he
could pick up a newspaper job in almost any city he visited.
Two months of work in New York were sufficient. He did
not like the cooking there. "Good conscience! What Yankee
ever saw such cooking? It needs a stomach made of India
Rubber to render it palatable. . . I cannot make it very
profitable to stay here, everything bears such an enormous
price. I can pay my way it is true and save a little but yet I
think I can make more in some place where I can live
cheaper."

He had his sights set for western Ohio. His sister Jerusha,
who was married to a Presbyterian minister, lived there.
With his mother's blessing on this her youngest child,
Rufus sailed down the Connecticut River, along the Sound
to New York City, and up the Hudson River to Albany.
A six-day trip along the Erie Canal – part of the time walk-
ing the towpath and part of the way riding the horse-drawn
boat. From Buffalo he tramped along the shore of Lake
Erie to Ashtabula, Ohio, and then worked his way southward to Marietta, where his sister welcomed him into the
family circle. He was soon asked to teach the school there,
but one month was enough of that for this nineteen year old
Yankee, despite the "16 dol. per month and board."

[2] *Ibid.*, 31-34. All subsequent quotations are from this same work.

He soon turned to the newspaper business, where he got a job as compositor at the *Marietta Gazette*. In his letters to his mother he sang the praises of this, his new world.

> Now for the beauties of Ohio . . . which language fails me to describe. . . Words are but wind. . . The very land is poetry and the atmosphere is song. Old Connecticut! tis now that I forget thee! tis now that I substitute the far West in thy place. . . The West is free and willing to receive the needy! Let him but once plow the ground, and but once sow his seed and then behold the harvest. Who searches after comfort, and who would gain enjoyment?
>
> To such we would say – No longer stay away
> If here you chance to roam, There'll dawn a brighter day.

Rufus' restless spirit took him to West Virginia, where he served as foreman on a newspaper in Parkersburg, and was proud to report that he received $364 for the year.

In the early spring of 1838, Rufus Sage and a partner bought a boat, loaded it with a cargo of ice, and set sail down the Ohio. From there they proceeded to the lower Mississippi where he expected to make a fortune – at least $2000. Something went wrong – he never explained what – and all he got out of the venture was experience. What he saw there, however, made of him an unrelenting foe of the institution of slavery. While in Mississippi he visited some ancient Indian mounds and wrote stories about them.

By August 1st he was back in Marietta, Ohio. Again he turned to a newspaper job. At Circleville, Ohio, where he was employed, he organized a debating society that held weekly meetings. For the Fourth of July celebration he wrote a song which was sung and was published in the local newspaper.

In 1839 he moved to Columbus, Ohio, and worked as a compositor on the *Ohio State Bulletin*. Unhampered by family ties or responsibilities, he studied in the State Library and attended sessions of the state legislature to improve his knowledge of government.

By 1840 he found himself engaged in the political struggle to put General William Henry Harrison in the presidential seat. He published a weekly and then a daily campaign paper to help the Whig battle. "When Harrison takes his seat as President," Rufus wrote in a letter to his mother, dated Nov. 23, 1840, "I have good reason to believe that he will give some appointment under government, which will ensure me, if not a competency, at least a living."

The untimely death of President Harrison seems to have caused Sage to turn from politics and to throw his energies into travel – westward, perhaps to Oregon. In this new world he would find something worthwhile to write about, perhaps something he could do to help his country. He induced a number of young men to join in planning an expedition into the West, but none of the number really advanced farther than the planning stage.

At Independence, Missouri, he found himself alone, ready to test his fortunes in the West. He penned a letter to his Mother.

INDEPENDENCE, JACKSON COUNTY, MISSOURI
Sunday, May 30th, 1841

MY VERY DEAR MOTHER: Little did I think while penning my last letter to you, that my next would date from this place; yet so it is. . . For a long time I had a wish to explore the Territory of Oregon. . . We started from St. Louis, expecting to join the American Fur Company and proceed with them. We arrived in St. Louis too late, for the Company had left; and now we are waiting in this place the departure of an independent Company which is to leave here about the 20th of July, with whom we are to go. The journey is a safe one; no danger is to be apprehended from the Indians. We are to get from $20 to $25 per month – every thing found.

My design is to collect materials for a *book,* which I intend publishing upon my return. How long I shall be gone I know not, possibly two years. I shall be able to communicate meanwhile, with my friends once in six months. Immediately upon my return, should Providence permit it, I will hie to the land of my fathers, – to the friends I left behind me. I anticipate that the intended expedition will add to my health, as it has that effect upon all those engaged in the Fur Trade.

On August 21, 1841, Rufus wrote another letter to his mother, announcing that

> I leave in three or four days for the Rocky Mountains, where I expect to winter. . . Give yourself no uneasiness about me. That great and good Being who has from my childhood watched over and guarded me in all my wanderings, will still protect me, in the Rocky Mountains as well as otherwheres. . . In Him I trust – and trusting fear not. . . I may visit Oregon before coming back – possibly not. If I return east next spring, it will be for the purpose of visiting Washington. My health is good. . . I leave on Monday – day after tomorrow. . .
>
> Your affectionate Son, RUFUS B. SAGE

As planned, on September 2, 1841, Rufus left Independence, Missouri, with Lancaster P. Lupton's trading party. It was destined for the Indian trade at Fort Platte, near Fort Laramie. Rufus was unaware that the trade goods, so carefully guarded en route, was liquor, "which brought furs from the Indians when nothing else could."

During the winter, Rufus went on two trading expeditions, north to the White River and west to the upper Platte. He did much exploring of the region, making careful notes for his intended book. In 1842 he tried boating furs down the Platte River, but had to give up the venture. Back at Independence, where he expected to draw his wages and return home for a visit, he found that his employer, Mr. Lupton, had gone bankrupt, which left Rufus in the same deplorable condition.

Once again he wrote a letter to his mother:

> July 20, 1842
> I have just arrived in this town from my trip to the Rocky Mountains, much improved in health and increased in flesh. . . I spent the winter in the mountains on the headwaters of the Platte River, and as pleasantly as could be expected in a place so remote from

civilized society and its enjoyments. . . The whites in that country are worse than the Indians. In hospitality the Indians excell all others. . . The chastity of the Sioux women surpasses that of their fairer sisters. Indeed, it is seldom you see a prostitute among them. Since I left the States, I have been among the following nations — Shawnees, Delawares, Kickapoos, Iowas, Sacs, Pottowotomies, Mohaws, Osages, Otows, Pawnees, Shians and Sioux, by all of whom I have been treated with great friendliness. . . I have collected the materials for a work upon that country, which when time permits, I shall write out. I have collected specimens of *gold* and *mineral coal* which can be procured in that neighborhood in almost any quantity. It is a country rich in minerals. The climate is most delightful — soil fertile. . . Our only subsistence during the past winter was buffalo meat, which, by the by, is the *best meat I ever tasted.* . . My intention has been to return home this summer, but the times are so hard and money so scarce, that I am afraid I shall have to defer it, much against my will. Possibly I may return to the Mountains and spend the ensuing winter there. . . I am pained at not having heard a word from home for nearly two years. *Do please to write me as soon as you get this.*

In less than a month, on August 10th, Rufus wrote a hurried note from Westport.

DEAR MOTHER: I start this morning for the Mountains. I am well. . . Dangers beset my path it is true, but my trust is in God. . .   Good bye, RUFUS B. SAGE

Still intent in his plan to write a western book, Rufus chose to return to the mountains as a "Free Trapper" and traveler. Pursuing the Oregon Trail, he visited posts in the Colorado region. He traveled from Fort Lupton south to Pueblo and on to New Mexico. Visiting Fort Uinta in eastern Utah, he later traveled on to Fort Hall, a British fur trade post on the Snake River in Idaho. A short stay here gave him an insight into the Hudson's Bay Company and its operations. From other travelers he learned also much about the West Coast. Further travel took him to Texas, after which he spent a memorable winter in the Estes Park area of Colorado. In the spring of 1844 he joined a company of traders returning to the States. By July, 1844, he was back in Ohio, dabbling in the newspaper game. At Columbus, on August 17, he wrote to his mother:

> . . . It seems like old times again to hear from you. It has been now, nearly 4 years since my ears were blessed with such news. I have been away beyond the Rocky Mountains, and in New Mexico and Northwestern Texas. Since I left the United States I have spent most of the time in travelling. I suppose I must have travelled during the last 3 years, 15 or 16,000 miles. God has blessed me with improved health, and has returned me safe from all dangers.

In 1845 he returned to his old home in Connecticut after an absence of ten years. In this quiet retreat he prepared his book of travels. The following year the work was published.

Many topical treatments in the volume might be quoted if space permitted – such as: advice to travelers (I, p. 219), description of Fort Platt (220), Christmas on White River (244), Chief Bull Eagle (252-53), moccasin making (309), Bighorn sheep (319-21), the carcague (wolverine) (332), bear stories (310-14), Hudson's Bay Company (V, p. 171), eagle catching (283), and winter camp (284-85).

A few such descriptions are quoted here as samples:

> A genuine mountaineer is a problem hard to solve. He seems a kind of *sui genus,* an oddity, both in dress, language, and appearance, from the rest of mankind. Associated with nature in her most simple forms by habit and manner of life, he gradually learns to despise the restraints of civilization, and assimilates himself to the rude and unpolished character of the scenes with which he is most conversant. Frank and open in his manners and generous in his disposition, he is, at the same time, cautious and reserved. In his frankness he will allow no one to acquire an undue advantage of him, though in his generosity, he will oftentimes expend the last cent to assist a fellow in need. Implacable in his hatred, he is also steadfast in his friendship, and knows no sacrifice too great for the benefit of those he esteems. Free as the pure air he breathes, and proudly conscious of his own independence, he will neither tyrannize over others, nor submit to be trampled upon. . .

His dress and appearance are equally singular. His skin, from constant exposure, assumes a hue almost as dark as that of the Aborigine, and his features and physical structure attain a rough and hardy cast. His hair, through inattention, becomes long, coarse, and bushy, and loosely dangles upon his shoulders. His head is surmounted by a low crowned wool-hat, or a rude substitute of his own manufacture. His clothes are of buckskin, gaily fringed at the seams with strings of the same material, cut and made in a fashion peculiar to himself and associates. The deer and buffalo furnish him the required covering for his feet, which he fabricates at the impulse of want. His waist is encircled with a belt of leather, holding encased his butcherknife and pistols – while from his neck is suspended a bullet-pouch securely fastened to the belt in front, and beneath the right arm hangs a powder-horn transversely from his shoulder, behind which, upon the strap attached to it, are affixed his bullet-mould, ballscrew, wiper, awl, &c. With a gun-stick made of some hard wood, and a good rifle placed in his hands, carrying from thirty to thirty-five balls to the pound, the reader will have before him a correct likeness of a genuine mountaineer, when fully equipped (IV, pp. 127-28).

At our noon encampment we commenced the process of "making meat," . . . It consists simply in cutting into thin slices the boneless parts of buffalo, or other meat, and drying them in the wind or sun. Meat thus cured may be preserved for years without salt. . . It is astonishing how long a time fresh meat may be kept without injury, upon the grand prairies, in dry weather, when it receives the free access of air. . . I have known it to be preserved, in this way, for ten or twelve days in the heart of summer (IV, p. 196).

The usual mode of dressing skins, prevalent in this country among both Indians and whites, is very simple in its details and is easily practiced.

It consists in removing all the fleshy particles from the pelt, and divesting it of a thin viscid substance upon the exterior, known as the "grain"; then, after permitting it to dry, it is thoroughly soaked in a liquid decoction formed from the brains of the animal and water, when it is stoutly rubbed with the hands in order to open its pores and admit the mollient properties of the fluid, – this done, the task is completed by alternate rubbings and distensions until it is completely dry and soft.

In this manner a skin may be dressed in a very short time, and, on application of smoke, will not become hardened from any subsequent contact with water (v, pp. 283-84).

Next to horses, women constitute an Indian's chief wealth. This circumstance not unfrequently results in one individual appropriating to himself six or eight.

The squaw is compelled to dress robes and skins, make moccasins, cure and take care of meat, attend to the horses, procure fire-wood, and perform sundry other little drudgeries that an Indian will not do. Through her he becomes possessed of the means of procuring from the whites such articles as his necessities or fancy may require. A plurality of wives with him, therefore, is more a matter of economy than otherwise (IV, pp. 262-63).

The sales of Sage's book went rather well and he decided to marry. He and a "charming brunette," Marietta Miller, announced their marriage for December 1, 1847. Rufus was thirty years old; his bride was twenty. They were to become the parents of five children.

Rufus Sage lived his remaining years as a farmer in the little Connecticut town where he was born. He died at seventy-six, on December 23, 1893; his wife followed him on March 22, 1900. A tall red sandstone shaft in the village cemetery marks their graves.

Marcellin St. Vrain

by HARVEY L. CARTER
Colorado College, Colorado Springs

A younger brother of the better known Ceran St. Vrain, Marcellin St. Vrain was born at Spanish Lake, Missouri, on October 17, 1815. He was the tenth and last child of Jacques Marcellin Ceran de Hault de Lassus de St. Vrain and Marie Felicité Dubreuil.[1] He was given a good education and was graduated from a college in St. Louis. Immediately after his graduation, he came to Bent's Old Fort on the Arkansas with one of the wagon trains of Bent Brothers and St. Vrain. In all probability the year was 1835.[2]

At Bent's Old Fort, he served his apprenticeship in the ways of the West and learned the arts of the trapper, the trader, and the wagonmaster. He seems to have taken naturally to the frontier life. On the trail along Timpas Creek in 1837, while on his way to Santa Fe with twelve pack mules, he was attacked by a roving band of Pawnees, with a loss of one man killed, three wounded, ten reams of paper, and a supply of printer's ink.[3] Since he had come through this rough affair with small loss, he was judged to be qualified for a more responsible assignment and was sent to the

---

[1] Paul A. St. Vrain, *Genealogy of the Family of De Lassus and Saint Vrain* (Kirksville, Missouri, 1943). The De Lassus family was a French family of some distinction, dispossessed by the French revolution. Marcellin's father, Jacques, added the St. Vrain designation to his name to distinguish himself from his brother Charles, who was Lieutenant-governor of Louisiana at the time of its acquisition by the United States. Despite his aristocratic origin, Jacques St. Vrain owned and operated a brewery near St. Louis.

[2] The Francis Whittemore Cragin Papers, The Pioneers' Museum, Colorado Springs, Colorado, Notebook IX, p. 27. Cragin's informant was Charles St. Vrain, second son of Marcellin. W. R. Sopris, Marcellin's grandson, gave the date of his grandfather's coming west as 1833, but this is almost certainly too early.

[3] David Lavender, *Bent's Fort* (New York, 1954), 177.

South Platte to take charge of a trading post which the company maintained there against several competitors.

Fort St. Vrain, as this post came to be called, was probably not fully completed when he arrived to take charge. It was located on the east side of the South Platte River, on high ground about a half mile from the stream. The three competing forts were south of Fort St. Vrain: first Fort Vasquez, then Fort Jackson, and farthest south, Fort Lupton. Fort St. Vrain was only about twelve miles to the north of Ft. Lupton. This was the homeland of the Arapaho Indians and the competition was for furs but more especially for buffalo hides.[4]

Young Marcellin St. Vrain sold all his buffalo robes to Sarpy and Fraeb at Fort Jackson in February, 1838. His policy was reversed by his employers when they heard about it. Bent Brothers and St. Vrain bought Fort Jackson and closed it down. Fort Vasquez was abandoned in 1841. Lancaster Lupton held on until 1845, when he finally gave up. Immediately after Lupton went out of business, Marcellin was ordered to close Fort St. Vrain as well. This he did and returned to Bent's Old Fort.[5]

With the resources of the big company back of him, he had managed to get the most of the Indian trade away from other firms. Also he had acquired a wife, Royal or Rel, a Sioux girl of thirteen when he married her in 1840.[6] During

---

[4] LeRoy R. Hafen, "Fort St. Vrain" in *Colorado Magazine* (October, 1952), XXIX, pp. 241-43. Fort St. Vrain was first called Fort Lookout and was also sometimes called Fort George. It was 109' by 128', with two corner bastions 19' in diameter. The walls were 2' thick.   [5] *Ibid.*

[6] F. W. Cragin Papers, notebook IV, p. 32. Throughout the Cragin Papers she is called Rel by those who knew her and whom Cragin interviewed, including her son Charles. Her grandson, W. R. Sopris, in an interesting article entitled "My Grandmother, Mrs. Marcellin St. Vrain" in *Colorado Magazine* (March, 1945), XXII, pp. 63-68, calls her Red. A possible explanation is that Red was the name used in the family by her second husband, William Bransford. The belief in the family is that she was a sister of Red Cloud, the Sioux Chief. For this there is no documentation. Dick Wootton always insisted she was a Blackfoot, but the common belief is that she was a Sioux. One story was that Rel had a twin sister, whom Marcellin also

his years at Fort St. Vrain, three children were born of this marriage.[7] At Bent's Fort, during the years 1845-1848, if not before, Marcellin had a second Indian wife known as Big Pawnee Woman, by whom he had two children.[8]

Marcellin St. Vrain was about 5'6" and weighed about 115 pounds. Not only was he reputed to have been a devil with the women, but he was an active sportsman, fond of hunting, riding, horse racing, and convivial drinking. It was said that to attract antelopes, who were noted for their curiosity, he would stand on his head and wave his legs in the air, to bring the game near enough to get a shot at them.[9]

The closing of Fort St. Vrain in 1845 did not mean that it ceased to be used altogether. The company continued to send out traders to the Arapahoes and these expeditions made temporary and seasonal use of the fort. On April 26, 1845, Alexander Barclay "stopt to breakfast above Gants' Fort and saw Marcellin St. Vrains Dearborn coming over the hills from the Platte." Again, on October 15, 1847, he records the fact that he saw St. Vrain's wagons setting out for the Platte, and again, on February 4, 1848, Marcellin St. Vrain's arrival from the Platte is noted at Barclay's houses near Pueblo. Thus, the adobe fort continued to be used for several years after the company had ceased to maintain it as a regular trading post all the year around.[10]

But not all of Marcellin's trips were to the north. Lieutenant James W. Abert, encamped at Bent's Old Fort with his army unit, noted on September 3, 1846, "In the evening

purchased and married but who hanged herself because of the jealous belief that Rel was the more loved by him of the two. Judge E. J. Hubbard to F. W. Cragin, June 8, 1908, Trinidad, Colorado, Notebook IX, p. 40. Wootton's opinion was given by his eldest daughter, Mrs. Eliza Walker, to Cragin, Notebook IX, p. 30.

[7] The children were Felix, b. June 17, 1842; Charles, b. October 17, 1844; Mary, b. March 9, 1846. All were born at Fort St. Vrain. See F. W. Cragin Papers, Notebook IX, pp. 19-21.

[8] Lavender, *op. cit.*, 310, 413.   [9] *Ibid.*, 182.

[10] Alexander Barclay Papers, The Bancroft Library, Berkeley, California. Diary entries for the dates specified.

Mr. Marcellin St. Vrain arrived from Captain Walker's camp above us." He reported that antelope were plentiful and that some deer were available, but that the sand flies were very bad. At this time, Bent's Fort was also the stopping point for James and Samuel Magoffin and their twenty-five wagons; Samuel's wife, Susan, had a miscarriage at the fort. On September 8, when Abert prepared to march on to Santa Fe, Marcellin announced that he would accompany them. He lived up to his reputation as a hunter and supplied them with fat antelope along the way.[11]

However, Marcellin's career as a Mountain Man was drawing to a close. In 1848, he returned to St. Louis. Two explanations are given for this. One story is that he had a wrestling match with an Indian at Bent's Fort in which the Indian was accidentally killed and that William Bent and Ceran St. Vrain thought it advisable for him to leave until the Indians, who did not regard the incident as accidental, had quieted down.[12] Another story is that his health failed and he thought he was losing his mind and so went to St. Louis, where Ceran paid his expenses in a sanitarium.[13] Some weight is given to the latter explanation by the fact that Alexander Barclay recorded on March 1, 1848, that he started from Bent's Fort in company with William Bent and that Marcellin St. Vrain was sick in his Dearborn.[14]

Whatever his ailment may have been, he quickly recovered in St. Louis and soon married an Irish woman, Elizabeth Jane Murphey.[15] Big Pawnee Woman went to

11 *House exec. doc. 41*, 30 Cong., 1 sess., 1847-1848, "Abert's Report, 1846-7," pp. 426, 432, 437. 12 W. R. Sopris, *op. cit.*, 63; Lavender, *op. cit.*, 310.
13 F. W. Cragin Papers, Notebook IX, p. 23.
14 Barclay Diary, entry of March 1, 1848.
15 By this marriage Marcellin St. Vrain had ten children: Isadora, b. November 21, 1851; Theresa Emma, b. July 4, 1854; William Eugene, b. March 7, 1856; María Felicité, b. May 10, 1858; Sarah Helen, b. April, 1860, d. July, 1862; Celeste, b. April 15, 1863; Leona, b. August 31, 1865; Paul Augustus, b. March 16, 1868; and posthumous twins, James Marcellin and Elizabeth Zelena, b. June 6, 1871. See F. W. Cragin Papers, Notebook IX, p. 26; also St. Vrain, *op. cit.*, which is less complete.

Pueblo with her two children, and no more is known of her or the children. Rel went to Santa Fe and then to Mora, where Ceran helped with her expenses until she married William Bransford. Marcellin came to Mora, in 1853, and took the two boys back to St. Louis with him for an extended visit. At that time, he had a farm in St. Louis County, Missouri.[16]

Later he established a mill in Ralls County and also had a farm there. Rel's daughter, Mary, visited her father there in 1866. Marcellin died, March 4, 1871, reportedly a suicide.[17]

Marcellin St. Vrain told his son, Charles, that he was nine years a trapper in the mountains. This coincides with the years he spent at Fort St. Vrain and excludes those he spent at Bent's Fort. At Fort St. Vrain, he had about fifteen men under him, but he was never a partner in the company.

Marcellin seems to have adapted very readily to the wild habits of the frontier, but he also retained the habits of his gentlemanly upbringing and put them to use on occasion. Travelers stopping at Fort St. Vrain speak of his courtesy, kindness, and hospitality.[18] He was sociably inclined, a ready talker, and knew several languages. He had a lively and expressive face and engaging manners but was of a rather mercurial disposition.[19] His desertion of his Indian wives seems inexcusable from the white viewpoint, but was acceptable according to Indian custom. For Rel, and for his children by her, he seems to have felt genuine affection and also to have felt some responsibility for their well-being.

16 F. W. Cragin Papers, Notebook IX, p. 25. Cragin's information came from Charles St. Vrain.

17 *Ibid.,* Notebook VI, p. 14.

18 See John C. Frémont, *Report of the Exploring Expedition to the Rocky Mountains* (Washington, 1845), 31; Charles H. Carey (ed.), *The Journal of Theodore Talbot* (Portland, 1931), 23, 27; also Hafen, *op. cit.,* 245, for William Gilpin's account of an Independence Day celebration at Fort St. Vrain, July 4, 1843.

19 A portrait of Marcellin St. Vrain appears herein at page 17.

Thomas L. Sarpy*

by GEORGE M. PLATT
University of Iowa

Thomas Lestang Sarpy (also called Thomas Laston and Thomas L. Sarpy) was born, according to his baptismal certificate, on March 7, 1810, in St. Louis, Missouri. He was the son of Gregoire Berald Sarpy, a member of a prominent St. Louis family well-known and honored in the Missouri fur trade, and Pelagie L'Abadie Sarpy. His father is credited with being the first person to navigate the Missouri with keelboats, and his brothers John B. and Peter A. followed successful careers in the trade and planted the family name on Sarpy County, Nebraska, and Forts John on the Laramie and Sarpy on the Yellowstone.[1]

Thomas L. began with perhaps two strikes against him, appeared to be on his way to success, and then by a literally explosive event was denied the chance to perpetuate his name on the map of the West. The available record of his life in St. Louis is brief and not too complimentary. It is reported that Gregoire Sarpy had a "n'er-do-well" son named Thomas Laston. He made an undesirable marriage while drunk, and his family sent him to the Far West to work for the American Fur Company.[2] The company assigned him as a $400-a-year clerk at the Oglala post, located on the Cheyenne at the mouth of Rapid Creek in what is

---

*This biography is based on a more extensive article concerning Thomas L. Sarpy and the location of the Oglala Post – Isaac H. Chase and George M. Platt, "The Missouri River Fur Trade: Thomas L. Sarpy and the Oglala Post," *The South Dakota Review,* II (Spring, 1965), 25-39.

[1] H. M. Chittenden, *American Fur Trade of the Far West* (New York, 1902), 390-91.

[2] Interview with Miss Eugenie Berthold by Charles van Ravenswaay, Director, Missouri Historical Society, January, 1949.

now western South Dakota, and his name is included in the company accounts for 1827. The *Journals* kept at Fort Pierre (Fort Tecumseh until 1832) make several references to him in 1830.[3]

APRIL 22. Three men left here in search of Mr. Thomas L. Sarpy who we presume is descending the Cheyenne in skin canoes and in want of assistance, as it is now a long time since we supposed he must have left his wintering grounds.

MAY 6. The men whom we sent in quest of Mr. Sarpy on the 22 of last month, returned without any intelligence of him. They followed the river Cheyenne as far as Mr. Chardon wintering ground, when they found themselves destitute of provisions and nearly barefooted, and consequently returned. We now think that both himself and those with him have been killed by some war party.

MAY 8. Louis Piton arrived from the Cheyenne River where he left Mr. T. L. Sarpy with his peltries. He has unfortunately lost a skin canoe loaded with robes. It is now about two months since he left his wintering ground, during which time the weather has been so unfavorable that he has not made more than 60 miles in two months. His canoes are rotten and he has sent in Piton for a supply of horses to bring his returns.

MAY 9. At noon Piton, Dickson, Degrey and LaChapelle with one man left here with 52 horses, mules and jackasses to bring in Sarpy's packs.

MAY 21. At 10 a.m. Mr. T. L. Sarpy and party arrived with 50 odd horses loaded with 108 packs of buffalo robes, a little beaver, merchandise, tallow, etc.

JUNE 24. Messrs. Sarpy, Juett, Pineau and Dumond left here with all our horses for Medicine River, where we intend keeping them a month or two because better grass and so many have been stolen here.

JULY 4. Dumond arrived from Medicine river where the horses are. They intend leaving Medicine river with the horses and to encamp somewheres in the Grand Detour for fear the Poncas will find their present situation.

---

[3] The remaining volumes of the *Fort Pierre Journals* are in the collection of the Missouri Historical Society, St. Louis. They have been published in slightly edited form in Doane Robinson (ed.), "Fort Tecumseh and Fort Pierre Journal and Letter Books," *South Dakota Historical Collections,* IX (Pierre, 1918), 69-239.

JULY 6.   T. L. Sarpy and Henri Ange came in from the Big Bend with 4 horses loaded with meat.

JULY 13.   T. L. Sarpy and L. Lagrave left here for the Brule's camp with a small equipment to trade what he may find.

OCT. 9.   Sent off goods for the Ogallallas, Sawons, and Cheyennes outfits.

The *Fort Pierre Journals* are missing from April 6, 1831, through January 26, 1832, but the next entry opens with the arrival of a party from the Oglala post bearing the news of Sarpy's death. Perhaps the best account of the tragedy is found in the following excerpt from a letter written January 31, 1832, by Jacob Halsey, then chief clerk at Fort Pierre, to Pierre Chouteau at American Fur Company headquarters in St. Louis:

It is with deep regret that I have to inform you of the death of Mr. Thomas L. Sarpy who was trading on a branch of the Cheyenne river, with a band of Sioux called the Ogallallahs. It appears that on the 19th inst. after he had been busily engaged trading throughout the day, he entered his store in the evening accompanied by two of his men with a lighted candle, for the purpose of putting it in order. The candle was placed on the counter, under which was a kettle containing about forty or fifty pounds of powder; either the candle or a spark from it, was accidently thrown in it, while they were in the act of passing some robes over the counter, which blew up the building, and the three persons engaged in it. Mr. Sarpy was found lying on his back some distance from where the building stood, he lived about an hour after the explosion took place, and his spirit fled into eternity. The other two were much injured, but they are now considered out of danger. Their names are Pierre Hebert and Francois M. Briot. From what we have been able to learn, the loss of property by the explosion was not so great as might have been expected. In consequence of this disturbing occurrence, Mr. Laidlaw left here yesterday morning for the purpose of arranging things in that quarter; he will visit the other Sioux stations before his return here, which may be expected about the 20th February.

I am happy to say the prospect in this part of the country is flattering. Buffalos have never been more pleanty in the Sioux country, than

they are now, and have been for the last month, consequently, we have
every reason to expect the robe return will fully equal, if not surpass
all made by the Sioux last year, say 2,000 packs. I am sorry the same
cannot be said of the Assiniboine and Mandan Posts, at which stations
Buffalo are said to be scarce.[4]

Thomas L. Sarpy, like many men who contributed to the
development of the West, lived but a short life. His blood
line however has not disappeared. Married to two Sioux
wives, because of the death of the first, he was survived by
two daughters who were later married to prominent employees of the company – Basil Claymore (Clement) and
Paul Narcelle.[5] Many descendants still reside in South
Dakota. Apparently Sarpy's bones were returned to St.
Louis, but there is no record of burial in the family lot.

If it were not for his untimely death, Thomas L. quite
possibly might have advanced in the fur trade, as did his
brothers, in spite of his questionable start. That his name
was not fastened to the area is perhaps explained by abandonment of the Oglala post within a few years and later
confusion over its location. The fur trade had already passed
its peak, and when in 1834 William Sublette and Robert
Campbell persuaded the Oglalas under Bull Bear to leave
Western Dakota and trade at Fort Laramie, need for the
Oglala Post was eliminated. In addition, the mistaken as-
sumption prevailed for years that the post was located at the
junction of Wounded Knee Creek and White River.[6] Even
though the *Fort Pierre Journals* do not give the exact position of Sarpy's post, it is difficult to understand how the
impression developed. Available records of the company
place the post on a branch of the Cheyenne, about sixty miles

[4] Missouri Historical Society, St. Louis.

[5] Basil Clement's name was corrupted to Claymore. A biography and picture are
available in Charles Edmund DeLand, "Basil Clement (Claymore): The Mountain
Trappers," *South Dakota Historical Collections*, XI (Pierre, 1922), 243-389.

[6] Robinson, *op. cit.*, 113.

from where the Cheyenne forks, or joins the Belle Fourche. This suggests a site at the mouth of either Rapid Creek or Spring Creek.

Two additional pieces of information tie the post to Rapid Creek. The diary of Lieutenant G. K. Warren, who escorted Dr. Hayden's expedition to the Black Hills in 1857, provides an identifiable description of the streams flowing east from the Black Hills. Warren records that while passing the mouth of what can only be Rapid Creek, his Indian guide, Morne, pointed out the remains of an old trading house built by LaChapelle about 1832.[7] This location was substantiated by Sarpy's eldest daughter, Mrs. Paul Narcelle, who stated when interviewed in 1899 that her father was at the mouth of Rapid Creek when "he blew up." Mrs. Narcelle further reported that her mother died five days after she was born at "Old Fort Pierre," and that her father "took" his second wife from Jacob Halsey.[8]

Thus a keg of powder, the competition of the trade, and a mistaken location, provide the interest and the drama for the story of Thomas L. Sarpy and the Oglala Post of the American Fur Company.

[7] The portions of Lieutenant G. K. Warren's diary concerning his 1857 trip to the Black Hills are published in Thomas E. Odell, *Mato Paha: The Story of Bear Butte* (Spearfish, South Dakota, 1942), 68-70.

[8] DeLand, *op. cit.*, 282-84.

George Semmes Simpson*

by HARVEY L. CARTER
and JANET S. LECOMPTE
Colorado Springs, Colorado

Although by no means a typical Mountain Man, George S. Simpson was a colorful character and a most interesting variation of the breed. He was born in St. Louis, Missouri, on May 7, 1818, the eldest surviving child of Dr. Robert Simpson and his wife, Bricia (Smith) Simpson. His father was a pioneer physician and druggist in St. Louis, who also held public office on several occasions, engaged in the mercantile business and in banking, and who, by all accounts, was a most substantial and respected citizen during the whole of his long residence in St. Louis.[1] George Simpson had a good education, as is evident from his writings. He

---

* The writing of this sketch was done by Professor Carter from his own notes and from the more extensive materials on Simpson assembled by Mrs. Lecompte, who read the manuscript and made suggestions which were incorporated in the final draft.

[1] Dr. Robert Simpson (1785-1873) was a native of Port Tobacco, Charles County, Maryland. He came of a family long established in America and studied medicine in Philadelphia at an early age. He entered the U.S. Army in 1809 and spent a year at Fort Madison on the upper Mississippi as an Assistant Surgeon, after which he settled in St. Louis and married, June 11, 1811, Bricia Smith (1784-1861), of Rome, New York. His wife was the sister of the wife of Rufus Easton, first postmaster of St. Louis. Dr. Simpson succeeded his brother-in-law as postmaster in 1814. During this time, he and Dr. Quarles operated the first drugstore in St. Louis. He practiced medicine for a number of years, beginning in 1821. He was elected a member of the Missouri Legislature (1822), appointed Collector of St. Louis County (1823), elected Sheriff of St. Louis County (1826). He also engaged in banking, ran a store on Main St. between Market and Chestnut for many years .He did not practice medicine in his later years. See: Reminiscences of Early St. Louis, Missouri Historical Society, St. Louis; Frederick L. Billon, *Annals of St. Louis in its Territorial Days* (St. Louis, 1888), 53ff, 77, 81, 85, 86, 87, 125, 132, 133, 139, 148, 164, 243ff; J. Thomas Scharf, *History of St. Louis City and County* (Philadelphia 1883), II, pp. 1463, 1520. Also *Missouri Gazette,* June 11, 1811 and October 3, 1812. His obituary is in *Missouri Republican,* May 3, 1873.

may have had some college training and there is reason to believe that he began the study of law.[2]

The family was well connected, for his cousin, Mary Easton, became the wife of Major George Champlin Sibley, who surveyed the road from Missouri to Santa Fe in 1825. His sister, Anna M. Simpson, married General Andrew Jackson Smith, who had a distinguished military career both before and during the Civil War. A cousin of Simpson's, Raphael Semmes, was captain of the famous confederate raider, the "Alabama," during the Civil War.[3] Despite these important family connections and his father's position in St. Louis, George Simpson pursued a path that diverged from the accepted pattern. He was what is known as "the black sheep" of the family. There are several slightly different versions of how and why he came to go west, but all agree in ascribing it to disagreement with his family over his behavior. One account says that his father sent him west to cure him of liquor and bad companions.[4] Another says that he had got in with a wild group of young people and his father thought it best to send him west.[5] Still another says that he had been disappointed in a love affair and had tried to kill himself with laudanum or opiates, and that his parents thereupon outfitted him to go west.[6]

Whatever may have been the precise nature of his juvenile delinquency, George Simpson turned up in the Rocky Mountains in 1838.[7] It seems more likely that he left home,

---

[2] Appleton's *Cyclopedia of American Biography* (New York, 1888), v, p. 538, makes the positive statement that "he received a college education and studied law." However, it may be doubted whether either was pursued to completion.

[3] Information given by Ralph Gordon, a grandson of George Simpson, to Mrs. Janet Lecompte, Colorado Springs, 1954.

[4] S. W. De Busk, De Busk Memorial, 295-96.

[5] E. B. Sopris, "Colorado before and during the Civil War," MSS. in Colorado Historical Society Library.

[6] F. W. Cragin Papers, Pioneers' Museum, Colorado Springs, Notebook VIII, p. 51. Interview of Cragin with Jesse Nelson, July 9, 1908. Probably all these accounts are an approximation of the truth.

on this first occasion, without the approval of his parents or much in the way of assistance from them.

Simpson describes his earliest western experience, without giving a date, in this fashion:

> There were five of us. Four were veteran beaver trappers, whom I met for the first time at Fort Hall, Wyeth's trading post on Snake River or Lewis' Fork of the Columbia. They were all middle-aged or past, while I was but a boy in years, and a greenhorn, but my recent arrival from "the settlements" made me welcome among these rough but kindly men, who were as young as I was when last they looked upon home and kindred. They were always going to the "states" "next spring" and never went. . . An instinct of vagabondism must have been in my nature, for besides falling into the rude ways of my comrades, I found a charm in an existence whose not the least attraction was freedom from conventionalities and a disregard of those social amenities to which I was accustomed.[8]

The four veteran trappers were Old Bill Williams; Charley Kinney (or Kenney), with his Piute squaw, Nancy; Calvin Briggs, a former Wyeth employee from Boston; and Lew Anderson, a former American Fur Company man. All

---

[7] Leonard K. Smith, "On the Old Frontier," MSS. in Colorado Historical Society Library. Smith's article is based on George Simpson's Scrapbook, which he had seen in the 1890s, when he was a newspaper editor in Trinidad, Colorado. Smith was later an Episcopalian clergyman. Smith gives the same date of 1838 in his article "George Simpson, Pioneer and Poet" in the *Denver Times* (Saturday Evening Times), November 21, 1903. Smith was the last of the tobacco chewing parsons of our acquaintance, and of such is the Kingdom of Heaven. It is true that Simpson himself testified in the Maxwell case that "he first came to this western mountain region" in 1841, "wintered at Bent's Fort and St. Vrain's." However, this was in response to a question designed to qualify him as one competent to testify because of long residence in the vicinity of the Maxwell Land Grant, and he would be correct in responding that 1841 was the beginning of such residence. If we take this to mean that 1841 was his first trip to any point in the West, then we must believe that he fabricated his early trapping experiences. See: *U.S. vs. Maxwell Land Grant Company et. al.,* U.S. Supreme Court, October term, 1886, No. 794, p. 142. Transcript supplied by Western History Department, Denver Public Library.

[8] Senex [George Simpson] "Pah-u-tah," III, in *Trinidad Daily News,* May 14, 1882. From the Colorado University Library, Boulder, Colorado. Simpson was 20 in 1838. He would probably not have referred to himself as a "boy in years" had he been over 21. Fort Hall was sold by Wyeth to the British in 1837, but Simpson's statement probably only means that it was built by Wyeth.

were now free trappers. When Simpson asked to join them, Old Bill Williams said, "Come along, sonny; you are as green as a gosling and as soft as a boiled turnip, but I'll make a beaver trapper of you in a few seasons."[9]

They trapped successfully on the Humboldt and other streams through the winter and accumulated five hundred pounds of prime beaver. But in the spring their horses were stolen by a band of Piutes and they were forced to cache their furs.[10] Williams located the Indian camp, and the four trappers, leaving Nancy and Simpson behind, recovered their horses. Williams told Simpson that he had first come west with Major Sibley and, knowing of their relationship, he had left him behind because he did not want him to get killed by the Piutes while he was under his guardianship, so to speak.[11]

After various incidents, they returned to the vicinity of their cache, where they met another party of trappers, which consisted of Jim Beckwourth, Tim Goodale, Maurice Le Duc, and a young man they had rescued from the Bannocks. With Le Duc was his Blackfoot or Shoshone squaw and two of her children.[12]

Early in June, 1839, they continued on, bound for the rendezvous on Horse Creek near Green River. In the Portneuf valley they encountered Henry Fraeb and John Burroughs, a particular friend of Briggs', who were also going to the rendezvous.[13]

---

[9] Ibid.

[10] Ibid., IV, in Trinidad Daily News, May 21, 1882. They considered going to California but decided against it.

[11] Ibid., V, in Trinidad Daily News, May 30, 1882.

[12] Ibid., VI, in Trinidad Daily News, June 18, 1882. Simpson digresses here to say that he had known Jim Beckwourth in St. Louis and that his mother had been a servant in the household of his uncle (probably Rufus Easton).

[13] Ibid., IX, in Trinidad Daily News, probably October or November, 1882. Found in Dawson Scrapbook, I, p. 409, in the Colorado Historical Society Library. Simpson says Fraeb was killed in 1843. This is an error of memory. It was in 1841 that his death occurred. This provides an additional reason for dating Simpson's arrival in the Rockies as early as 1838.

Simpson says little of the rendezvous but it may have been there that he and Williams formed another party, or they may have picked up an additional five trappers farther south.[14] At any rate, they attached to themselves Mark Head, Jimmy Daugherty, "Cut Rock" Brown, Robert Fisher, and Louis Ambroise and spent the next season in trapping on Grand River in western Colorado, and in Utah and Nevada, rambling over a vast territory and traveling more than two thousand miles.[15]

It must be assumed that, after this hunt, George Simpson returned to St. Louis in the latter part of 1840, for it is certain that he was a member of the well-known Bidwell-Bartleson party headed for California in 1841 and that he was considered to be one of those who was going all the way.[16] When this wagon train reached Ft. Laramie on June 22, 1841, George Simpson detached himself from it, and did not continue.[17] Apparently he struck up a conversation with "Colorado" Mitchell and Charley Raymond, a couple of trappers whom he may have known slightly, and they persuaded him to go with them to Bent's Fort. On arrival there, he sent word to his parents of his change of plan and asked

---

14 *Ibid.*, xi, in *Trinidad Daily News*, late April or early May, 1882. Simpson's story of Kit Carson, John Burroughs, and one other man holding off 300 Blackfeet occurs in Part x, which has not been found. Simpson also places the rendezvous on Snake River, probably in mistake for Green River.

15 Leonard K. Smith, "On the Old Frontier," 5-8. "Cut Rock" Brown has not been identified, unless it was John Brown, "the Medium of the Rockies." It should be said here that there is no very good reason why this may not have been Simpson's first trapping adventure, occurring in 1838-1839, and the one that has been related in detail would, in that case, be his second hunt, in 1839-1840. This would mean that he attended the 1840 rendezvous, which was also along the Green River near Horse Creek, instead of that of 1839. It all depends on whether he approached the mountains, in the first instance, by way of the Platte, as we have assumed, or by way of the Arkansas. The second group of free trappers was more closely associated with the Arkansas River region. Any means of determining this question of priority has been sought in vain from the available information.

16 John Bidwell, *A Journey to California* (San Francisco, 1937), 1. Jim Baker and William Mast are listed as trappers headed for the mountains.

17 *Ibid.*, 8. Mast also dropped off at Ft. Laramie.

them to send out a stock of goods. This they did, and Simpson rented a room at Bent's Fort and set himself up to be a trader with the Indians.[18]

While at Bent's Fort, Simpson became acquainted with two employees there, Alexander Barclay and Joseph B. Doyle, with whom, in one way or another, he was to be associated for many years. In the spring of 1842, Simpson moved up the Arkansas River to the mouth of the Fontaine Qui Bouille and there began the construction of a trading post which was called El Pueblo or, after a while, the Old Pueblo.[19] In August, he was joined in this enterprise by Doyle and Barclay, who appear to have replaced some earlier partners and who probably contributed some needed capital.[20] The new establishment was a *plaza;* that is, it consisted of adobe rooms on three sides of a courtyard with an adobe wall and gateway on the fourth side. The rooms all opened on the courtyard but were not inter-connected. There was a kitchen and common eating room, a blacksmith shop, a trading room, storage rooms and, of course, sleeping rooms.

A small amount of agriculture was carried on, but the Pueblo was mainly used as a base for trading operations with various Indian tribes. It soon became the gathering place for many free trappers of the area. On one occasion when Simpson's eccentric friend, Old Bill Williams, showed up, the two of them got into an argument in the blacksmith

[18] F. W. Cragin Papers, Notebook I, pp. 5, 6. Cragin's informant was Jake Beard, George Simpson's son-in-law.

[19] This spot was well chosen. Zebulon Montgomery Pike had built a log stockade there in 1806 and Jacob Fowler had built a log house and a horse corral there in 1822. It was where the main trail from the north leading to Santa Fe and Taos crossed the Arkansas River. The construction now begun was the beginning of what was to develop into the later city of Pueblo, Colorado.

[20] The original partners of George Simpson, as remembered by Mrs. Simpson in F. W. Cragin Papers, Notebook I, p. 11, were Robert Fisher, Matthew Kinkead, Francis Conn, and Joseph Mantz. Doyle was employed at Bent's Fort until August 1, 1842. Chouteau Papers, Missouri Historical Society, St. Louis, Entries in various ledgers.

shop and Simpson lost his temper and grabbed his gun. Old
Bill, who had a hatchet in his hand, jumped behind the door
and, taking the hatchet by the head, stuck the handle out to
resemble a pistol. He said, "Look out, George, this fellow
never snaps." Everyone laughed, including Simpson, and
there was no fight.[21]

Among those at the Pueblo was Teresita Suaso, the good-
looking widow of Manuel Suaso, and her four children.
Teresita had left Matt Kinkead for Alexander Barclay, and
Kinkead had left the Pueblo. George Simpson fell in love
with Juana Suaso, the eldest daughter and, on November
30, 1842, a marriage was carried out between the two without benefit of clergy or civil authority, since neither was
available. A man, who claimed to have been a notary in
Missouri, wrote out a certificate to which he attached a blue
ribbon with a gold seal to make it look more official.[22]

Early in 1844, Simpson, Barclay, and Doyle built another
plaza, this time on Mexican soil, about thirty-five miles
west of the Pueblo. It was located on the west bank of
Hardscrabble Creek, which the Mexicans called Penasco
Amarillo, about six miles above where it flows into the
Arkansas River.[23] The partners kept their rights to the Old
Pueblo, selling out in 1847. Simpson moved to Hardscrab-
ble, as the new establishment was called, at the close of
March, 1844.[24]

---

21 F. W. Cragin Papers, Notebook I, p. 24. Interview of Cragin with Jake Beard,
Trinidad, Colorado, October 31, 1904. Beard had the story from Ben Ryder, not
from Simpson.

22 S. W. De Busk, "Address at the Unveiling of the Kit Carson Statue, Los
Animas County" (Colorado). Pamphlet 359/24, 243 in Colorado Historical Society
Library, Denver. Also "Frontier Sketches" in *Field and Farm*, April 21, 1917.
Found in Dawson Scrapbook in Colorado Historical Society Library.

23 For a full account and description see Janet S. Lecompte, "The Hardscrabble
Settlement, 1844-1848," in *Colorado Magazine* (April, 1954) XXXI, pp. 81-98. The
reason for the removal to Mexican Territory was no doubt to circumvent certain
restrictions on trade enacted by the Mexican government.

24 Letter of George S. Simpson to George C. Sibley, dated February 7, 1844,
March 31, 1844, and April 10, 1844. Photostatic copy furnished by Missouri His-

On June 2, 1844, Juana Simpson gave birth to her first child, a daughter named Isabella. The event was notable because no child of white parents had been born on the fur trading frontier in this area prior to this time. Large numbers of Indians are said to have come to see the baby and to have performed dances in her honor.[25] In the fall, George and Juana Simpson and Joe and Cruz Doyle made a trip to Taos, where they were formally married by Padre Antonio Jose Martinez on October 14, 1844.[26]

In his interesting letter to George C. Sibley, Simpson had confessed his weakness for idleness and drink and had expressed the intention of not returning again to St. Louis "till I make *something*."[27] However, indolence came natural to him and roistering companions were to be found on the frontier as well as in St. Louis. He seems to have done no hunting and, though occasional business took him to Pueblo or to the Greenhorn settlement, these trips were likely to end up in a spree. Barclay's diary refers to him as hunting stray cattle and "cutting ice on the river all day," but also to his "playing cards and doing the loafer" and returning from Pueblo "having been there all night drink-

torical Society, St. Louis. The first portion of this letter was written at El Pueblo; the second and third portions were written at Hardscrabble. Thus, the time of the founding of Hardscrabble is definitely established. Simpson appears to have made a trip to St. Louis in June, 1843, where he posted bond for a license to trade with the Indians but recovered it and did not take out the license. Letter of D. D. Mitchell, Superintendent of Indian Affairs, St. Louis, to Major R. W. Cummins, Indian Agent, Council Bluffs, dated July 1, 1843. Simpson had a license already, granted by Mitchell, running from October, 1842, through September, 1843. A new license was also granted, dated July 5, 1843, to trade "at Ft. Juana – a point on the Arkansas River about a mile above Fontaine Qui Bouille. . ." Indian Department, National Archives, Washington, D.C., St. Louis File, 1843. It is interesting that Simpson, in this document, named the old Pueblo for his wife.

[25] For a highly colored account of this event, see "A Mountain is his Tomb," in *New York Sunday World,* June 17, 1888. Photostatic copy from New York Public Library.

[26] Matrimonial Records, Taos, 1833-1845, 270. Isabella Simpson had been baptized on the previous day.

[27] Letter cited in note 23, *supra.*

ing." [28] Trappers and traders came in to the two settlements from all around, and for a convivial man like Simpson the temptation was too great.[29]

Barclay, Doyle, and Simpson and their families apparently left Hardscrabble October 19, 1846, and built some houses on the Arkansas two miles above the Old Pueblo. But on March 27, 1847, Simpson moved back to Hardscrabble. Just how long he stayed there is not known. He put in a corn crop there and probably only stayed till it was harvested.[30]

Changes wrought by the Mexican War caused Barclay and Doyle to contemplate building a trading post farther south. Although Simpson went to Taos when Barclay went there and to Santa Fe to make arrangements for the new location, he does not seem to have had any share in the new enterprise of Fort Barclay, near the junction of the Mora and Sapello Rivers. But he and his growing family moved there with them in May, 1848, and resided in the fort when it was completed. He seems to have gone on errands to Taos and Santa Fe for them and, on one occasion, extended his time considerably and spent the money they had entrusted to him for purposes of his own.[31]

It seems probable that in the summer of 1849 Simpson returned to St. Louis for a visit. He seems to have ridden northeast to some point on the upper Missouri River and to

28 Barclay Papers, Bancroft Library. Memoranda of February 27, 1847; March 1, 1847; November 10, 1847; November 21, 1847; December 23, 1847.

29 Thomas Fitzpatrick estimated the population of the two places at 150 in 1847, probably about equally divided. About 60 were men, mostly with Indian or Mexican wives. He mentioned squaws of no less than ten Indian tribes as consorts of the trappers. He said further, "Those villages [Hardscrabble and Pueblo] are becoming the resorts of idlers and loafers. They are also becoming depots for the smugglers of liquor from New Mexico. . ." Report of Thos. Fitzpatrick, Indian Agent, September 18, 1847 in 30 Cong., 1 sess., *Sen. ex. doc. I*, p. 245 (series 503).

30 Barclay Papers. Memoranda of October 19, 1846; March 27, 1847; October 18, 1847.

31 *Ibid.* Memoranda of March 1, 1848; June 8, 1848; August 23, 1848; October 1, 1848.

have taken passage on a steamboat. Simpson noticed that every day the boat stopped at some sand bar and that men from the boat would hastily bury something in the sand. He inquired about this and found that they were burying victims of the cholera epidemic, about which he had been entirely ignorant. Not wishing to be buried on a sand bar and eaten by catfish, Simpson made the captain of the boat promise to deliver his body to Dr. Robert Simpson in St. Louis and, as the captain knew his father, he agreed. Simpson got the cholera and was thought to be dead. He was put in a box and covered with ice. Some time after, crew members saw the ice begin to move and Simpson crawled out. He had only fainted and now made a good recovery.[32]

On his return from St. Louis over the Santa Fe Trail, in company with Barclay, Spencer, and Isaac Adamson, Simpson noted the dead bodies remaining from the Indian massacre of Mr. White's party a few days before. This was at the Point of Rocks, three days' journey from Fort Barclay.[33]

A most interesting letter by George Simpson's mother, Bricia Simpson, to Alexander Barclay before they left St. Louis shows how he was regarded at home. She wrote, in part:

> Not seeing you again before you left induced me to address you a few lines. My object was to beg of you, if possible, to prevail on George to go home with you, and to express my thanks and gratitude to you for the interest you have always taken in my poor child. . . I am not ignorant of the trust you have many times placed in him, and he has deceived you . . . but he is my child still. . . You say

[32] This story occurs in the article cited in note 24, *supra*. No date is given in the article but we have placed it in the summer of 1849, because that was the year of the great cholera epidemic along the eastern part of the Oregon Trail and because Simpson is known to have returned from St. Louis, in company with Barclay, in the fall of 1849.

[33] Barclay Papers. Memoranda of October 25 to 28, 1849. Simpson later wrote of this experience in detail in an article entitled "Colorado – 1840" in *Trinidad Daily News*, May 20, 1881. This article appeared under his usual *nom de plume*, Senex.

his family will never suffer I know they will not. I hope and pray it will be through his exertions and industry more than it has been heretofore – I anticipate that what is intended for him will eventually produce something for his family. . . I have been reflecting on George's situation and I have concluded when you come in we will make some arrangements for his family. Say put in your hands whatever means we have to make use of it, the way you think proper. . .[34]

Simpson wrote, years later than the event, "In the year 1850 Kit Carson, Tim Goodale and the writer, were in camp near the upper crossing of the North Platte. The two first were engaged in trading with some emigrants, while the last was studying with interest the lights and shades of human life, the varied idiosyncrasies that the gold fever had developed among the ten thousand pilgrims that streamed along the road they fondly hoped would lead to fortune." Simpson was also reading aloud from a yellow-backed novel entitled *Kit Carson or the Prince of the Gold Hunters,* much to the amusement of Goodale and the disgust of Carson, who threatened to burn the "damn thing." They were approached by a stalwart "forty niner" from Tennessee, who had heard that Carson was there and who wanted to see him. They were unable to convince him that Kit was the man he was seeking, and he pulled a copy of the same book from his pocket to prove that they were lying. Simpson concluded: "Two months later I was wielding a pick in Deadman's Gulch near Hangtown, California."[35]

Simpson did go to California in 1850 but no details of his experiences there have been found, nor is it known precisely

[34] Barclay Papers. Letter of Bricia Simpson to Alexander Barclay, dated October 3, 1849. This letter makes clear the fact that Simpson's parents helped him over a period of many years. There is other independent testimony to the effect that he received goods or money from them fairly regularly. He was, in fact, what is known as "a remittance man." See citations under notes 4 and 5, *supra.*

[35] Senex [George Simpson] in "Pah-u-tah," VII in *Trinidad Daily News,* July 15, 1882. Colorado University Library, Boulder, Colorado. The incident is reported in DeWitt Peters, *Kit Carson* (Hartford, 1874), 355, without mention of Simpson. Simpson's account is a circumstantial one but he could have taken it from Peters.

when he returned. He is said to have returned by way of the Isthmus in 1852, and, if so, he must again have visited his parents in St. Louis before going back to Fort Barclay.[36] In the summer of 1854, Simpson's brother-in-law, Joe Doyle, took his family back to the Arkansas River but returned early in 1855 to Fort Barclay because of the Ute massacre of the inhabitants of the Old Pueblo on December 25, 1854. It is not clear whether Simpson and his family accompanied the Doyles or remained at Fort Barclay.

Somewhere on the Fontaine Qui Bouille, in 1858, he joined Col. Randolph B. Marcy's command, as a teamster, as it was returning to Fort Bridger after having made its famous winter march from there to Fort Garland. He was, consequently, with them during the famous sixty-hour blizzard, April 30 to May 2, while they camped on the divide between the Arkansas and the Platte. From May 5 to May 9, they were camped at the present site of Denver and, on May 7, Simpson took a mess pan and camp shovel and began washing for gold in Cherry Creek. He found a small amount of dust, gave it away, and forgot about it. When the Pikes Peak Gold Rush began, he concluded (as did Marcy) that he had been responsible for starting it, and so claimed for the rest of his life. He went back to Missouri, after leaving army employment; when he reached Westport, he was offered the job of guiding a party to Pikes Peak, but declined.[37] He was quoted, however, in some of the guidebooks of the time.[38]

In 1860, when Doyle brought his family to his newly-

---

[36] Article cited in note 24, *supra*.

[37] Letter to the Editor from George Simpson, *Daily Denver Times,* July 5, 1883. Copy provided by the Western History Department of the Denver Public Library. That Simpson's discovery did not produce the Pikes Peak Gold Rush is shown by LeRoy R. Hafen, *Pikes Peak Gold Rush Guide Books of 1859* (Glendale, Calif., 1941), 47ff.

[38] See *Pratt and Hunt's Guidebook* (Chicago, 1859), 49; Parker and Huyett's *1859 Pikes Peak Guide,* 59.

established ranch, on the Huerfano River south of Pueblo, the Simpsons accompanied them and they lived there till 1866, by which time both Joe Doyle and Cruz, his wife, had died.[39] In that year he moved to Trinidad, where he had a farm for several years about three miles below town on the Purgatoire River. His wife, who had taught a school in New Mexico, organized one in Trinidad in 1867.[40]

Simpson read a great deal, as he always had, and wrote occasional pieces for the local paper and for the Missouri papers, as he had done from time to time. He held office for a time as county clerk, as clerk of the probate court, and as secretary of the school district.[41] He was a familiar figure about town in his Prince Albert coat. He was thrilled when he saw the first Baltimore oriole he had ever seen in the Far West.[42] He was addicted to poetry, as well as to liquor, and some of his verse was published in various papers. He is said to have quit drinking before he died, but we do not know how long before.[43] Simpson was a small man, not over 5'7" in height and weighed about 130 pounds during most of his life.[44] He wore a full beard in his later years.[45]

Simpson was a dreamer, a romantic, and had a scholarly and philosophical turn of mind. But he was indolent, weak-willed, and completely undisciplined. He was utterly unable to write anything without indulging in a circumlocutory display of his vocabulary or without making devious divi-

39 John Dowd Kind, "George Simpson, Pioneer, Scholar, and Poet," in *El Porvenir* (August, 1904), III, p. 13.

40 Luis Baca, "The Guadalupita Colony of Trinidad," in *Colorado Magazine* (January, 1944), XXI, pp. 26-27.

41 De Busk Memorial, 235; Dr. M. Beshoar, *All About Trinidad and Las Animas County, Colorado* (Denver, 1882), 86-87; 98.

42 De Busk Memorial, 210.

43 F. W. Cragin, Notebook VIII, p. 51. Jesse Nelson (1825-1923) to Cragin, July 9, 1908.

44 Interview with Nicholas Vigil, Trinidad, December 7, 1934. Las Animas County, Pamphlet 359/12 in Colorado Historical Society Library, Denver.

45 A portrait of Simpson appears herein at page 18.

gations from the subject.[46] Yet he was witty and apt on
occasion. For example, he said of the Piute Indian, "Had
he been a little more human or a little less brute, Darwin,
if he had discovered him, would have rejoiced and proclaimed him the missing link." [47] And when someone started
a quarry on the site he had selected for his burial place, he
said, "When the average American sees a dollar in sight he
would be willing to work a graveyard for the marble." [48]

The site he selected for his final resting place was a
mountain overlooking Trinidad, which soon came to be
called Simpson's Rest. He wrote a poem of several stanzas,
the first of which runs thus.

> Lay me to rest on yon towering height
>   Where the silent cloud shadows glide,
> Where solitude holds its slumberous reign,
>   Far away from the human tide.[49]

He died on September 7, 1885, and was buried in a tomb
hewn out of the rock, where he desired to be. His children,
of whom eight survived him, erected a monument over it,
on top of Simpson's Rest.[50]

---

[46] We believe this sentence to be a fair imitation of the Simpsonian style. We
have noted quotations from Shakespeare and Keats and allusions from Fielding
and from the Bible in Simpson's writing. He was also fond of throwing in phrases
from Latin and French.

[47] Senex [George Simpson], "Pah-u-tah" in *Trinidad Daily News,* I, April 26,
1882. From Colorado University Library, Boulder.

[48] *Trinidad Daily News,* May 17, 1882. The remark is probably not original with
Simpson but it was aptly applied.

[49] See "A Mountain is his Tomb" in *New York Sunday World,* June 17, 1888. We
are unable to say whether Simpson ever took refuge from an Indian attack near
the site of his tomb, as was reported many times and as the third stanza of his
poem seems to indicate. We are inclined to believe that no such incident occurred
there. An incident, which may have given him some poetic license, is reported by
him in *Trinidad Daily News,* August 30, 1881.

[50] Juana Simpson, his much loved but long suffering wife, survived her husband
by many years and died, in her eighties, at Monrovia, California. Their children
were: Isabella (Mrs. Jacob Beard), b. June 2, 1844 at Hardscrabble; Robert, b.
March 19, 1846 at Hardscrabble; Pedro (Pete), b. August 1, 1848 at Barclay's Fort;
Merced, b. September 24, 1850 at Barclay's Fort; Alexander Barclay, b. October

Although George Simpson achieved some temporary recognition through his own efforts, the path to fame by way of newspaper columns is an ephemeral one. He appears to have been the only fur trader and Mountain Man, with the exception of Kit Carson, who was accorded space in Appleton's *Cyclopedia of American Biography,* which was first published soon after his death. Since that time his fame has declined, while that of others in the fur trade has risen. Had his industry been equal to his intellect, he might well have been the historian of the trappers and traders of the early Far West, for his knowledge of them was considerable, both from his reading and from his experience.[51] But though his inclination lay in this direction, his efforts to put it to purposeful execution were sporadic and disappointing. He was, as he said of himself, "a desultory man."[52]

29, 1853 at Mora; Jennie M. (Mrs. Ernest M. Camp), b. October 28, 1858 at Barclay's Fort; Ann Marina, b. July 18, 1860 at Mora; Virginia (Mrs. R. N. Cavalier), b. April 4, 1863 at Doyle's Ranch; Lucy (Mrs. Samuel L. Pawley), b. April 4, 1863 at Doyle's Ranch; Rafaela Semmes (Mrs. B. L. Gordon), b. March 25, 1867 at Doyle's Ranch. Colorado Historical Society Library, Denver.

[51] "Letter from Senex" [George Simpson] in *Trinidad Daily News,* January 2, 1882. Simpson said that in his youth he had read the narratives of Lewis and Clark, Pike, Long, and Ashley.

[52] The phrase occurs in his letter to George C. Sibley cited in note 24, *supra.*

William Tharp

by JANET LECOMPTE
Colorado Springs, Colorado

William Tharp, an offshoot of a wealthy St. Louis family, came west as a Cheyenne trader for Bent, St. Vrain & Co., became a highly successful independent trader at Pueblo, and was killed by Indians on the Santa Fe Trail in May, 1847. His death was neither the beginning nor the end of the disasters that plagued his family.

He was born in the city of St. Louis on July 20, 1817, and was baptized in the St. Louis cathedral on April 13, 1823, with his brother Louis, born in 1808, and a sister born in 1810. Another brother, Edward, was born April 5, 1824.[1] They were the children of William Tharp and Eleonora Dubreuil Tharp.[2] Their mother's father was Louis Dubreuil, the rich and respected St. Louis merchant whose estate they all shared after the death of their grandmother, Susan Dubreuil.[3]

William Tharp was scarcely two months old when his life was touched by the violence that dogged his family. On September 29, 1817, on a St. Louis street corner, his father got into an argument with a merchant named William Smith concerning the duel between Charles Lucas and Col. Thomas H. Benton the day before. Smith struck Tharp, whereupon Tharp drew his pistol and shot Smith dead.[4] A year later Tharp was tried for and acquitted of murder.[5]

Susan Santous Dubreuil, grandmother of William Tharp,

[1] St. Louis Cathedral records, microfilm copy, Missouri Historical Society, St. Louis.

[2] F. L. Billon, *Annals of St. Louis in its Early Days* (St. Louis, 1886), 434-35.

[3] *Missouri Republican,* Jan. 26, 1826, p. 3, c. 3.

[4] F. L. Billon, *Annals of St. Louis in Its Territorial Days* (St. Louis, 1888), 247.

[5] *Missouri Gazette,* Sept. 11, 1818, p. 3, c. 3.

was a *grande dame* of St. Louis society. She was also the grandmother of Ceran St. Vrain, which was probably one of the reasons Tharp came west and began trading with the Cheyennes for Bent, St. Vrain & Co. Tharp was at Bent's Fort at least as early as the winter of 1841-42. In the spring of 1842 he went east with his cousin Ceran and the wagons bringing the season's peltries, arriving at St. Louis on May 18. He was still at St. Louis in July and probably accompanied the wagons, again under Ceran St. Vrain's direction, back to Bent's Fort at the end of July. He was again in St. Louis in July of 1843, when he was paid his salary of $340.00 by Bent, St. Vrain & Co.[6]

By the winter of 1844-45, Tharp was no longer working for Bent, St. Vrain & Co. At that time, says Will Boggs, there was no post nearer to Bent's Fort than Fort Laramie, other than "a small log hut occupied by a man by the name of Tharp, who traded the Indians whiskey and sometimes he got a robe or two from some straggling Indian from the Cheyenne village, but his trade did not amount to much." [7] Tharp's "log hut" may have been a house erected within the walls of the Pueblo, an adobe trading post established in 1842 on the Arkansas at the mouth of the Fountain River. Two witnesses who knew Tharp at the Pueblo declared that he was a builder or founder of the post,[8] but since the fort was erected in the spring and summer of 1842, at the very time Tharp was on his way to St. Louis with Ceran St. Vrain's wagons, he could hardly have had much to do with its establishment. He did, however, use Pueblo as headquarters for the rest of his short life.

---

[6] Ledgers CC and GG, Chouteau papers, Missouri Historical Society.

[7] "The W. M. Boggs Manuscript About Bent's Fort, Kit Carson, the Far West, and Life Among the Indians," ed. LeRoy R. Hafen, *Colorado Magazine,* VII (March, 1930), 51.

[8] F. W. Cragin's notes of interview with Mrs. George Simpson, El Paso, Tex., Oct. 31, 1904, and with Pedro Sandoval, Mora, N.M., June 12, 1908, Cragin Collection, Pioneers' Museum, Colorado Springs, Colo.

In the spring, 1845, William Tharp left Pueblo with six wagons carrying 187 packs of skins and robes, arriving in St. Louis on the steamboat "Nimrod" on May 25.[9] In St. Louis he met Alexander Barclay of the Hardscrabble settlement, thirty miles up the Arkansas from Pueblo, and together they returned to the Arkansas in July.[10] By this time Tharp had formed a partnership for the Indian trade with Joseph B. Doyle, also from St. Louis and living at Hardscrabble. Sometime during 1845 the firm of Doyle & Tharp bought a wagon and cover, a yoke and chains, a yoke of oxen, and a mule from John Brown who had just opened a store on Greenhorn River fourteen miles south of Pueblo.[11] By the beginning of February, 1846, Doyle & Tharp had traded so successfully on the South Platte River in opposition to Marcellin St. Vrain, that Charles Bent wrote, "Doile & Tharp have traded all thare goodes, so we have an oppen field for the ballence of the trade. . ."[12]

The firm of Doyle & Tharp had been dissolved by the time Tharp went east in the spring of 1846 to take his furs to market. His old partner Doyle had formed a new partnership with J. B. Guerin, and on July 2, 1846, they were issued a trading license by the Superintendent of Indian Affairs at St. Louis on July 18, 1846. Tharp also applied for and was granted a one-year license to trade "at the Big Timbers on the Arkansas river; on the Platte river about five miles from Cache la poudre; on Horse creek north fork of the Platte river; and at Bayou Salade [South Park] near the headwaters of Arkansas river, with the Cheyennes, Sioux, Arrap-

---

[9] *Niles National Register,* June 7, 1845, p. 224, c. 2-3, quoting the St. Louis *New Era* of May 26.

[10] Letter of Robert H. Betts, St. Louis, July 9, 1845, Barclay papers, microfilm copy in Colorado State Historical Society, Denver, Colo.

[11] John Brown's account book, George Beattie papers, copy in Huntington Library, San Marino, Calif.

[12] Bent to Manuel Alvarez, Taos, no date [Feb., 1946], Alvarez papers, Benjamin Read Collection, Museum of New Mexico, Santa Fe.

ahoes, Eutaws and such other Indians as may frequent said places." The capital employed was $2,175.72; bond was set at $5000; securities were William Tharp, A. G. Boone and Richard Pearson; and the men employed numbered eight.[13] Tharp's license did not allow him to trade at the mouth of the Fountain, where Pueblo was situated, as Doyle & Guerin's license did; but Doyle's license did not specify "Bayou Salade" as a trading location; otherwise the licenses are the same and the ex-partners undoubtedly found themselves in sharp opposition at Big Timbers, Cache la Poudre, and Horse Creek.

By July, 1846, Tharp's brother Edward, now twenty-two, had come to Pueblo [14] and joined Bill Tharp's family, which now consisted of a wife and two children. His wife was Antonia Luna of Taos, commonly known as "Antonia Fool" because she was half-witted.[15] Nor did Tharp receive her in mint condition; she had previously lived in Taos, first with Jim Beckwourth and then with Kit Carson, who had promptly abandoned her when she told him she preferred Beckwourth as a lover.[16] In spite of her shortcomings, Tharp appears to have been devoted to her, taking her along on his trading trips, with their two little children, Mary and James.[17]

In January, 1847, Tharp was trading at the Upper Cheyenne village at Big Timbers, thirty-odd miles below Bent's Fort. He lived in an Indian lodge with his wife and their

---

[13] "Letters Received by the Office of Indian Affairs, St. Louis Superintendency, 1846-1847," Microfilm publication of the National Archives, Washington, D.C.

[14] F. W. Cragin's notes of an interview with Vicente Trujillo, Avondale, Colo., Nov. 9, 1907, Cragin Collection. An Edward Tharp was listed in the 1842 St. Louis city directory as a journeyman printer with offices at 2 North First street.

[15] F. W. Cragin's notes of an interview with Mrs. Felipe Ledoux, Las Vegas, June 19, 1908, and with Jesse Nelson, Smith Cañon Ranch, Colo., July 9, 1908, Cragin Collection.

[16] Cragin's interview with Jesse Nelson, *loc. cit.*, and with Albert Tison, Wagon Mound, N.M., March 14, 1908, Cragin Collection.

[17] Cragin's notes of an interview with Mrs. Felipe Ledoux, *loc. cit.*

children, a domestic scene that fascinated the young traveler Lewis Garrard, who had come to Tharp's lodges for a buckskin to make a pair of pants: "In the largest [lodge], was the owner, reclining on robes and smoking, and judge of my surprise, when before me sat a fair-skinned woman, and two children. She was the proprietor's Mexican wife. When Mr. Tharpe was getting the buckskins, I could do no less than stare at his wife, and the other appendages of civilization, hanging around, in the shape of dresses, etc. . ." But, Garrard concluded, Tharp's wife "did not compare, in point of symmetry of features" with a Cheyenne girl who had taken his fancy.[18]

When Tharp returned to Pueblo early in April [19] he brought with him a Mexican and an American Negro whom he had ransomed from the Kiowas.[20] On April 9, he left for Taos [21] and returned to Pueblo shortly thereafter to make preparations for taking his peltry east to market. He was to travel with a large number of Mountain Men and the young English writer, George F. Ruxton. Ruxton waited at the mouth of the St. Charles for Tharp's wagons to arrive from Pueblo. On May 2 Ruxton received word that Tharp could not leave until a trading party from the north fork of the Platte arrived at Pueblo, so he started on without him.[22]

Tharp and his wagons left the Pueblo on May 5, 1847. On the road he caught up with the Bent, St. Vrain & Co. wagons in charge of Ceran St. Vrain and George Bent, and on May 24 they all arrived together at Fort Mann at the trail crossing of the Arkansas, just west of present Dodge City, Kansas.[23] Tharp had decided to travel with the larger

---

[18] Lewis H. Garrard, *Wah-To-Yah and the Taos Trail,* ed. Ralph F. Bieber, Southwest Historical Series, VI (Glendale, Calif., 1938), 173.

[19] Alexander Barclay Diary, Barclay papers, *loc. cit.*

[20] George F. Ruxton, *Adventures in Mexico and the Rocky Mountains* (N.Y., 1848), 272.

[21] Barclay Diary, *loc. cit.*

[22] Ruxton, *op. cit.,* 272.   [23] Garrard, *op. cit.,* 338.

train because the Indians were now close by and danger-
ously hostile. On the evening of May 27, the train camped
at Walnut Creek with its wagons drawn in a circle as protection against possible attack. In the morning, however,
the number of buffalo in the vicinity seemed to indicate that
there were no Indians around, so William Tharp and Frank
DeLisle went out early to hunt. When they were not yet
three hundred yards from the wagons, mounted Indians appeared from every side, shooting at the men, the cattle and
the wagons. Tharp was wounded but managed to shoot back
for a time; DeLisle kept the Indians at bay until companions came to his rescue. By this time it was too late
for Tharp, who was killed, scalped and mangled before the
Indians rode off. He and another victim named McGuire
were buried on the north bank of the Arkansas.[24]

Tharp was thought to have cleared a profit of $5,000 on
his winter's trade, but the Indians who killed him (probably
Comanches) rode off with sixty of his mules, worth about
half of his earnings.[25] His gun later showed up at Westport
in possession of a renegade Delaware Indian named Big
Nigger,[26] but the rest of his property was lost.

William Tharp's elder brother Louis came out to Pueblo
the November after William's death with a wagon-load of
goods and opened a store, hoping, perhaps, to pick up the
pieces of William's successful trade and at the same time
keep an eye on young Ed Tharp, whose tragic end may
have been foreseen by those who knew his temperament. On

---

[24] *Ibid.,* 373-74; Ruxton, *op. cit.,* 272f; *Daily Missouri Republican,* June 14, 1847,
p. 2, c. 3. Other less reliable sources for Tharp's murder include Henry Inman, *The
Old Santa Fe Trail* (N.Y., 1897) 283f, who gives us an interesting assortment of
demi-truths about "Thorpe," purporting to be out of the mouth of John Smith; and
H. L. Conard, *"Uncle Dick" Wootton* (Chicago, 1890), 107-8. Wootton claims that
the entire wagon train was destroyed and with it his own peltry. He is, as he often
proves to be, mistaken.

[25] *Daily Missouri Republican,* June 14, p. 2, c. 3; Garrard, *op. cit.,* 374.

[26] Report of Thomas Fitzpatrick, Bent's Fort, Sept. 18, 1847, *Sen. exec. doc. 1,*
30 Cong., 1 sess., 246.

February 2, 1848, Ed Tharp got into a quarrel with Jim Waters at Louis Tharp's store, over Waters' wife Candelaría, a dark, half-Indian woman, and Ed was killed.[27] He was buried the next day on Tenderfoot Hill in present east Pueblo, and the grave had a paling around it that was still standing as late as 1863.[28] William Tharp's unfortunate wife continued to live at the Pueblo; on November 6, 1847, she spent the night with Barclay's family and "amused us with fitts all night." [29] Even Tharp's widow was to partake of the Tharp family misfortunes. Her two children by William Tharp were captured by Jicarilla Apaches on June 20, 1848, in the Manco de Burro pass of the Raton Mountains, while they were being taken from Pueblo to live with Antonia's family at Taos. Three months later they were redeemed at Abiquiu, either by relatives [30] or by merchants of Taos, for the ransom of $160,[31] but the little girl died shortly after. The boy, James, went to work for his cousin Vicente St. Vrain at Mora [32] and died at Cimarron in about 1898.[33] During the winter Louis Tharp had been robbed and three of his men killed by Indians. Discouraged, he left Pueblo for St. Louis on February 25, 1848, with eight men and a pack train, and never returned.[34]

---

[27] Barclay Diary, *loc. cit.;* Cragin's notes of interview with Tom Autobees, Avondale, Colo., Nov. 8 and Nov. 10, 1907; Mrs. Felipe Ledoux, Las Vegas, N.M., Feb. 13, 1908.

[28] Tom Autobees, who only heard the story second hand and years later, says the duel (if such it was) was over Nicolasa, but Mrs. Ledoux who was at Pueblo at the time and is a better witness anyway, insists that the lady was Candelaría and that Nicolasa then lived with Rube Herring.

[29] Barclay Diary, *loc. cit.*

[30] Cragin's interview with Mrs. Ledoux, *loc. cit.*

[31] "Maxwell's Fight with the Apaches, June 20, 1848," notes of John Greiner, Ritch Papers, Huntington Library, San Marino, Calif.

[32] Cragin's notes of an interview with Pedro Sandoval, *loc. cit.* James Tharp and Vicente St. Vrain were cousins twice over, for Vicente's mother Paula Luna was James's mother's sister.

[33] Cragin's notes of an interview with Mrs. Felipe Ledoux, *loc. cit.*

[34] Louis Barry, "Kansas before 1854: A Revised Annals," in *Kansas Historical Quarterly,* XXXI, no. 2 (Summer 1965), 147-48.

In 1853 he drove a flock of sheep to California[35] and there, let us hope, he shook off the bad luck of the Tharp family and lived happily ever after.

[35] Garrard, *op. cit.*, 173n.

David Thompson

by ALVIN M. JOSEPHY, JR.
American Heritage

David Thompson was essentially a fur trader and surveyor. But by many of those familiar with his career he has
been called – perhaps not extravagantly – one of the greatest
practical land geographers the world has ever known.[1] During a twenty-year period, between 1792 and 1812, he crossed
and recrossed much of the unknown wilderness of the present-day northwestern United States and western Canada,
usually accompanied only by Indians or half bloods – partly
intent on trading, but also exploring and mapping the principal features within an area of more than a million and a
half square miles, from Hudson Bay to the Pacific Ocean
and from the Great Lakes to the Athabaska country of
northern Canada. On the maps, when he began his explorations, much of that vast region was a blank.

He was the first known white man to locate the source of
the Columbia River, explore its entire length, and build a
post on its upper waters. He was the first known to erect
white establishments in the present states of Idaho and
Washington, and in Montana west of the continental divide.[2]

---

[1] M. Catherine White (ed.), *David Thompson's Journals Relating to Montana
and Adjacent Regions, 1808-1812* (Missoula, 1950), cxxix; W. M. Stewart, "David
Thompson's Surveys in the North-West," *Canadian Historical Review*, XVII (1936),
289-303, etc.

[2] Members of the mysterious "Jeremy Pinch" expedition, possibly led by ex-
artillery captain John McClallen and dispatched secretly from St. Louis in 1806 by
General James A. Wilkinson, may have built ahead of him in western Montana. But
no proof of this yet exists. See Alvin M. Josephy, Jr., *The Nez Perce Indians and
the Opening of the Northwest* (New Haven, Conn., 1965), 656-60, and pp. 325-26
of this text. The first post known definitely to have been built anywhere in Montana
was erected at the mouth of the Bighorn River, east of the Rockies, by Manuel
Lisa's men in the fall of 1807.

He was the first to make a survey of almost the full shoreline of Lake Superior, and the first to map reliably the relationship between the Missouri River and the principal streams of the central Canadian plains. In addition, he was the first, and in some cases the only man to gather and record certain information that is today considered indispensable for an accurate history of the early Northwest. He met Blackfeet and other Indians of the northern plains and Rocky Mountains who told him what it was like when they first got guns and when they saw their first horse. He heard anecdotes and learned the history of Indian warfare and tribal movements before other white men were aware of the existence of those tribes. And along the upper tributaries of the Columbia, he was the first to open trade with tribes only recently met by Lewis and Clark, the first to give them firearms, and the first to learn and map their principal routes of transportation, which were later utilized by succeeding generations of fur traders and other whites in the Oregon country. With this important pioneering work, he laid the foundation for much of the great fur trade in the Columbia Basin.

And yet it must be noted that Thompson has had modern-day detractors, few in number but eminent in reputation. During his lifetime Thompson was relatively obscure, and for half a century after his death his accomplishments were scarcely known. When recognition finally came, the appreciation of his "discoverers" was so great that criticism, when it arose, may be said to have stemmed partly as a reaction to the enthusiasm of his Boswell, Dr. Joseph B. Tyrrell, and others who edited, published, and evaluated his long-overlooked journals. Some of the criticism, having to do with alleged defects in his personality (his "over-virtuousness," for example), is niggling. Some, which will wither away inevitably as time adds perspective, is little more than continued Hudson's Bay Company versus North West Company partisanship and has the petulant sound of spankings administered to an HBC servant who dared turn Nor'Wester. But some is quite serious and has given birth to controversies which, as will be noted later, have not yet been settled: Are Thompson's journals and writings so self-righteous that they obscure opposing points of view and thus distort true situations? Did Thompson lack boldness and determination at certain critical times and thus muff assignments of great importance? Was he responsible for the fact that the Astorians beat him to the mouth of the Columbia River in 1811, thereby laying him open to the charge that "if any one person was to blame for the British failure to state an effective claim [to the Columbia River] it was David Thompson. . .."?[3]

Such questions are grist for further study. But in the main, while adding interest to the man who is still so little known, they do not in the least deny the achievements of Thompson's remarkable career.

Thompson was active during some of the most aggressive days of the Canadian fur trade, when rival companies were leapfrogging each other westward across the unexplored forests and plains of Canada, competing with guns and alcohol for the beaver trade of newly discovered tribes. He was described as a short, stocky man with a snub nose and hair worn long and "cut square" across his forehead in a way that made him resemble John Bunyan.[4] Little more is known of his looks, for there is no known contemporary likeness of him. He was unassuming, reserved, and apparently introspective; a resourceful, intelligent man of keen intellect; a good observer who loved nature, respected most men, including Indians, and accomodated himself expertly to wilderness life. In addition, he was deeply pious, did not swear, smoke, or drink, and behaved so virtuously in the

[3] E. E. Rich, *Hudson's Bay Company 1670-1870*, (London, 1959), II, p. 241. See also pp. 152-55 in the same volume.

[4] John J. Bigsby, *The Shoe and Canoe* (London, 1850), I, pp. 111-14.

context of a rough and rugged life and profession that, as already stated, he has aroused scorn among a few modern critics – although strangely there is no evidence that he did so among his contemporaries in the fur trade.

The conditions of his youth probably had much to do with the qualities of his character. He was born on April 30, 1770, in Westminster, England, of Welsh parents whose name was originally Ap-Thomas. He had one brother, John, born after him, who seems to have become a sea captain in later life.[5] The Thompsons were poor and obscure, and when the father, also named David, died on February 28, 1772, he was buried evidently at public expense. Rearing the sons must have been difficult for the widow, and on April 29, 1777, when David was seven years old, he was entered in a charitable institution, the Grey Coat School, in London to

---

[5] David Thompson, *Narrative of His Explorations in Western America, 1784-1812,* ed. J. B. Tyrrell (Toronto, 1916), xxiii. Acknowledgement is made to the work of the late Dr. Tyrrell for much of the biographical material I have used on Thompson. The *Narrative,* with Tyrrell's excellent biography of Thompson's life, is still the basic volume on Thompson. In addition, portions of Thompson's journals, some with valuable biographical material and notes by the persons who edited them, were published at various times. Two of the most important works that contain sections of the explorer's journals, are Elliott Coues (ed.), *New Light on the Early History of the Greater Northwest* (New York, 1897), 3 vols., and White, *op. cit.*

Other parts of Thompson's journals and writings have been published as follows: F. W. Howay (ed.), "Account of an Attempt to Cross the Rocky Mountains, by Mr. James Hughes, Nine Men & Myself, by David Thompson," *Queen's Quarterly,* XL (1933), 333-56; T. C. Elliott (ed.), "Narrative of the Expedition to the Kootanae & Flat Bow Indian Countries, on the Sources of the Columbia River, Pacific Ocean, by D. Thompson on Behalf of the N.w. Company 1807" in "The Discovery of the Source of the Columbia River," *Oregon Historical Quarterly,* XXVI (1925), 23-49; Elliott (ed.), "David Thompson's Journeys in Idaho," *Washington Historical Quarterly,* XI (1920), 97-103, 163-73; Elliott (ed.), "David Thompson's Journeys in the Pend Oreille Country," *Washington Historical Quarterly,* XXIII (1932), 18-24, 88-93, 173-76; Elliott (ed.), "David Thompson's Journeys in the Spokane Country," *Washington Historical Quarterly,* VIII (1917), 183-87, 261-64; IX (1918), 11-16, 103-06, 169-73, 284-87; X (1919), 17-20; Elliott (ed.), "Journal of David Thompson," *Oregon Historical Quarterly,* XV (1914), 39-63, 104-25; Hugh A. Dempsey (ed.), "Thompson's Journey to the Red Deer River," *Alberta Historical Review,* XIII, no. 1 (1965), 1-8; Dempsey (ed.), "Thompson's Journey to the Bow River," *ibid.,* XIII, no. 2 (1965), 7-15.

receive his education. Like Oliver Twist, he would have been subjected to a strict and exacting rule, but he would also have learned piety and simple virtues. An industrious youth with ability in mathematics and writing, he remained at the school for seven years, and then on May 20, 1784, at the age of fourteen, was bound to the Hudson's Bay Company as a seven-year apprentice.

The school seems to have given him a good recommendation. He was shipped on the "Prince Rupert" to the bleak and lonely Churchill Factory post on Hudson Bay, but was accompanied by instructions that his mathematical ability be put to use, and that he be kept from the common men and his morals and behavior protected. After a year at the post, during which he served under Samuel Hearne but had little to do, he was sent on foot with two Indian guides to York Factory, 150 miles away. He had a gun, but was given no provisions for the trip, and the difficult journey along the lonely, windswept shore of the bay taught the fifteen-year-old boy how to live off the land.

His wilderness education continued at York Factory, where he served as a clerk and hunter under Humphrey Marten. A year later, in the summer of 1786, he was sent with an expedition led by Robert Longmoor deep into central Canada to help establish a new Hudson's Bay Company trading post, the South Branch House, on the south fork of the Saskatchewan River. He wintered there, 1786-87, under Mitchell Oman, competing with nearby posts of Montreal traders for the furs of Cree and Assiniboine Indians.[6] In the fall of 1787 he was transferred to the newly-built Manchester House on the North Saskatchewan, almost as far west as traders had yet penetrated, and a few days later was detailed to accompany a party of six men under James

[6] V. G. Hopwood, "New Light on David Thompson," *The Beaver,* Summer, 1957, pp. 26-31, and "More Light on David Thompson," *The Beaver,* Autumn, 1957, p. 58.

Gaddy. The group's mission was to travel southwestward across the little-known plains, find the Blackfeet Indians, teach them to trap beaver, and urge them to become providers of furs to the Hudson's Bay Company – something that Anthony Henday had been unable to accomplish thirty-three years before during a pioneer excursion to the edge of the Blackfeet country.

Although only seventeen, and a quiet, unobtrusive youth, Thompson was already considered an able wilderness man, reliant and quick to learn, a trustworthy servant with a sense of responsibility to his companions and a devotion to work and duty. The party left Manchester House in October, and southwest of Bow River, probably close to present-day Calgary, met a band of Piegans. Thompson spent the winter, 1787-88, in the lodge of a friendly and aged chief who instructed him in the life and traditions of the Indians inhabiting the country along the eastern side of the Rockies. Much of what the youth learned that winter, and recorded later in his narrative, is the only known account of Indian history in that part of the continent before the arrival of white men.

The Blackfeet agreed to open trade with the newcomers, and Thompson and his companions returned to Manchester House on the North Saskatchewan River in the spring of 1788 with about thirty Piegans and their furs. He spent the summer at Hudson House, a post also on the Saskatchewan, and then returned to Manchester House where on December 23, 1788, he broke his leg in an accident.[7] In the spring of 1789 he was sent downriver to Cumberland House to recover. Adversity led to good fortune, for Philip Turnor, official surveyor of the Hudson's Bay Company, also arrived there, and during the winter of 1789-90, while Thompson continued to recuperate, Turnor instructed him in the theory

[7] Hopwood, "More Light . . . ," 58.

and practice of astronomy. It was an important turning
point in Thompson's life. His interest in meteorology and
surveying increased, and under Turnor's tutelage he commenced keeping daily records of weather, temperature, and
wind, and began to take astronomical readings and learn to
solve problems of time, latitude, longitude, and variations
of the compass. Later, he acquired a ten-inch brass sextant
and thereafter, wherever he traveled, made careful observations with compass, watch, and a crude artificial mercury
horizon. His thoroughness and skill, in time helped him
attain a high degree of precision in his calculations. Many
geographers and surveyors, who in later years with better
instruments retraced ground first mapped by Thompson,
were surprised by the accuracy of his work.

Thompson remained at Cumberland House throughout
1790 and during the winter of 1790-91, trading and improving his skill at surveying. In May, 1791, his term of
apprenticeship ended. He journeyed to York Factory, making a survey of 750 miles of the Saskatchewan and Hayes
rivers en route, and at the post on the bay signed a contract
as a servant of the company at a salary of fifteen pounds per
year. He was also entitled to a set of clothes but, instead of
accepting them, asked for and received the brass sextant and
surveying instruments mentioned above. He remained at
York over the winter of 1791-92, and in 1792 was sent by
Joseph Colen to explore a Nelson River route toward Athabaska Lake via Reindeer Lake.

Thompson, now infatuated with surveying and exploring,
felt a lack of support from Colen. He started on his way,
wintered, 1792-93, at Sipiwesk Lake, then, short of supplies
and unable to find Indians to accompany him on his survey,
returned to York.[8]

---

[8] Even Thompson's severest critics find no fault with him for not having pressed
on to Athabaska at this time. What criticism arose was directed at Colen, Thompson's superior.

In 1793 Thompson went up the Saskatchewan again to Cumberland House, then wintered, 1793-94, far up the North Saskatchewan at Buckingham House, trading, traveling through the countryside, surveying, and mapping. He returned to York in the summer of 1794 and went back to the "muskrat country" to survey and winter, 1794-95, at Reed Lake. In the summer of 1795 he was once more at York.

Now, for the second time, he was assigned to seek the short route to Lake Athabaska from the bay. He set off in July, 1795, wintered at Duck Portage near the junction of the Churchill and Reindeer rivers, and departed on June 10, 1796. He reached Lake Athabaska on July 2, traveling via Reindeer and Wollaston lakes, and made a rapid return, arriving at Fairford House on July 21.

At the latter post he induced Malchom Ross to agree to go back with him to Athabaska where they would trade, and where Thompson could continue his surveys. Colen sent a letter directing Thompson to halt further surveys and open a trading post on Reindeer Lake. They spent a difficult but busy winter there, 1796-97, at a rough post they built on the west shore and called Bedford House.

By spring Ross was disenchanted with the trade potential of the country, thought he had been foolish to let Thompson induce him to leave Fairford House for the north, and did not share Thompson's enthusiasm for the route the latter had found to Athabaska.[9] At York, Colen apparently felt the same way about the route, and, in fact, it was neither an easy nor a very practicable one. Thompson, however, was proud of his discovery (and failed in his writings to reflect the opposing views of Ross and Colen regarding the route's feasibility), and had had enough of an employer who did not seem to appreciate his principal interest. Anxious to

---

[9] Rich, *op. cit.*, II, pp. 152-53.

continue surveying, he looked toward the more aggressive North West Company, whose partners would welcome his special skills.

On May 23, 1797, when his term with the Hudson's Bay Company ended (he was now being paid sixty pounds a year plus a bonus for inland service), he left Ross at Bedford House, journeyed to the nearest North West Company post, and joined that firm.[10]

At twenty-seven, Thompson was now a seasoned surveyor. For five years he had carried out assignments in the great wilderness west and southwest of Hudson Bay. He had traveled through thick forests sown with lakes, streams, and mosquito-filled bogs, and across treeless barrens stretching in cold and lonely silence toward the Arctic horizon. No white man had been in much of the country before him, and wherever he had gone, he had surveyed and mapped. He had built log huts in the forested areas for the trade of small, isolated groups of Indians, had explored canoe routes through muddy, marsh-choked ends of lakes, and had charted difficult portages around rushing falls and boulder-strewn whitewater.

Often his only companions had been Indians or half bloods who had helped him find passages for his canoe and had supplied him with fish and deer and caribou meat. In the face of unending hardships and close calls with death, he had learned to live and travel like the natives, moving with speed and exactness across huge reaches of land, pausing only to seek protection from gales and blizzards or to gum the leaking seams of his canoe with pine pitch.

---

[10] Thompson's narrative of this portion of his life, Rich charges, illustrates the "defect" in the man and his writings. Colen was right about the route, and Thompson was wrong, says Rich; but Thompson, "the man of all the virtues and none of the vices . . . who was always right," would not accept the verdict and not only quit the company but obscured the truth in his writings by omitting relevant information and failing to present objectively the points of view of Colen and Ross. — Rich, *op. cit.*, II, pp. 152-55.

Having joined the North West Company, he now in the summer of 1797 went down to the partners' annual meeting at Grand Portage. The terms of his employment are not known, but he was at once given an important assignment by Alexander Mackenzie and William McGillivray. It sent him off on a large-sized mapping tour for his new employers, locating the geographical positions of North West Company posts in relation to the border between the United States and Canada immediately west of Lake Superior.

Leaving Grand Portage on August 7, 1797, he traveled to Lake Winnipeg and the lower Assiniboine River, and then struck south on foot across the plains to the Mandan Indian villages on the Missouri River, near where Lewis and Clark would winter in 1804-05. Returning to the Assiniboine and then the Red River, he went south along the Red and then east, charting the watery wild rice district of northern Minnesota and coming within a few miles of correctly identifying the source of the Mississippi River (it was not found until 1832). Going on, he surveyed the south shore of Lake Superior, reaching Sault Ste. Marie in May, 1798. He continued around the lake, mapping the east shore and most of the north, and arriving finally at Grand Portage, where Alexander Mackenzie told him he had accomplished more in ten months than the company could have expected in two years. It had indeed been a remarkable exploit; in those months, which included the worst traveling seasons of the year, Thompson had mapped approximately four thousand miles. During the next two years, 1798-99, he surveyed northward for the North West Company in the Churchill district and from the Saskatchewan toward the Athabaska country and Lesser Slave Lake, once again probing cold and remote regions.

On June 10, 1799, at Ile-à-la-Crosse Lake he married Charlotte Small, the daughter of Patrick Small, a Scotch trader, and a Cree or Chippewa woman. In time, they had five children born in the West, and eight more born later in the East.[11] Thompson took his family with him on most of his travels and, unlike many traders, remained loyal and devoted to his half blood wife until his death.

In the fall of 1800, after a visit to Grand Portage for the annual meeting, Thompson went up the North Saskatchewan toward the eastern slopes of the Rocky Mountains, directed to help lead a North West Company party across the mountains and open trade with Indians in the upper Columbia Basin, where whites had not yet been.

Interest in a trans-mountain push had been growing among British fur men for almost ten years. In January, 1793, Peter Fidler and John Ward of the Hudson's Bay Company, guided by Piegans, had met some Kutenai Indians "who had never seen an European before" on the Oldman River in present-day southwestern Alberta.[12] Those Indians, who had crossed from west of the Rockies, had told the traders about tribes and geography in the upper Columbia Basin and had excited their interest in that region. At the same time, also in 1793, Nor'Wester Alexander Mackenzie had made the first crossing of the Canadian Rockies to the Pacific Ocean. Mackenzie's route had been too far north and too rugged and difficult to serve the fur trade, but the explorer had been confident that an easier passage would be found to the Columbia farther south.

On his return, Mackenzie had proposed a grand scheme for the reorganization of the British fur trade and its expansion to the Pacific and China. Under its charter the Hudson's Bay Company held monopoly rights to trade at the bay and in all territories drained by waters that flowed into it. The North West Company, which was barred from

---

[11] For the names and dates of birth and death of Thompson's children, see White, *op. cit.,* 244-45.

[12] Hudson's Bay Company Archives E.3/2, fol. 16-16d. Published by permission of the Governor and Committee of the Hudson's Bay Company.

the bay, had shown a dynamic ability to expand and could move westward across the mountains and open trade in the Columbia country. But both companies were prohibited from trading in the Pacific or selling their furs in the rich Chinese market, since the South Sea and East India companies held monopolies in those areas. Mackenzie's plan proposed the amalgamation of the Hudson's Bay and the North West companies, or at least an agreement between them that would allow the Nor'Westers to be supplied at Hudson Bay. Then the new combine, he suggested, should be granted licenses or privileges to trade in the Pacific and at China ports from depots on the Northwest American coast. Several posts, including one at the mouth of the Columbia, would serve as collection points for furs taken from the interior of the continent, and would also secure for the British the fisheries and sea otter trade of the coast.

The Hudson's Bay Company had shown little interest in the idea, and Mackenzie had received scant support from his own partners in the North West Company. Soon afterward, internal dissension had split the latter firm and led to the formation of a rival Montreal group, the X Y or New North West Company; and Mackenzie, quarreling with Simon McTavish, the domineering senior partner of the old North West Company, had eventually retired from that organization.

By the end of the eighteenth century, Thompson's surveys in northern Minnesota had shown McTavish that the North West Company had been operating in considerable territory from which it might one day have to withdraw, since it was owned by the United States. To compensate for the abandoned regions, McTavish decided to expand the trade toward the north and the Pacific, and in 1800 directed at last that an attempt be made to try to find a suitable fur route across the Rockies to the tribes in the Columbia Basin.[13] His nephew, Duncan McGillivray, who had had

[13] Rich, *op. cit.*, II, p. 226.

trading experience on the Saskatchewan River, was placed in command of the exploring expedition, and Thompson was assigned to accompany him.

In October of 1800, Thompson, seeking some Kutenais, moved toward the mountains from the Rocky Mountain House, the company's most westerly post on the North Saskatchewan. Traveling in a southwestwardly direction and accompanied by five half bloods, a Cree Indian, and a Piegan guide, he moved up the Red Deer River with trade goods worth three hundred beaver skins, and in the foothills of the Rockies met a band of Piegans. From them he heard of a Kutenai party a little to the west, and on October 14 he slipped past the Piegans and rode twenty-two miles into the mountains, where he met a Kutenai chief and his party. He spent two days trading and counciling with them, and persuaded them to return with him to the Rocky Mountain House.

When the Kutenais were ready to go back to their own people, Thompson sent two French-Canadian engagés, known to us only as La Gasse and Le Blanc, to help them evade the Piegans and to winter with them in their homeland. These were the first two men of white blood known to have crossed the Rockies south of Mackenzie's route. Although neither they nor Thompson left a record of the knowledge they acquired during that first winter in the upper Columbia Basin, Peter Fidler at the nearby Hudson's Bay Company's Acton House recorded bits of information that he learned about their historic trip after their return.

The men, Fidler noted, traveled seventeen nights by way of "the Source of the Saskatchewan in an oblique direction" before reaching the Kutenai camp. They apparently crossed the divide via present-day Howse Pass and when west of the mountains and "opposite to the Head of the Saskatchewan," traveled "along an old Track formerly cut by the Cottonahouse [Kutenais] – being the Northern most track they have." During the greater part of the winter the two men "tented opposite to the King or Nin nare tock que in the fine open country," which would have put them near the very head of the Columbia River or even farther south on the Kootenay River, since "the King," according to Fidler's maps, was a distinguishing peak in the Rockies opposite the headwaters of the Oldman River. The two Canadians, Fidler finally noted, returned to Rocky Mountain House on May 23, 1801, having taken twenty-eight nights to reach "this [east] side [of] the Mountain betwixt the Sources of the Red Deers river & Saskatchewan." [14]

Thompson's own attempt to follow across the mountains with McGillivray met with failure. In February, 1801, McGillivray, according to Thompson, came down with rheumatism and ordered James Hughes to take his place and "cross the Mountains and discover the Columbia River" with Thompson.[15] On June 6, Hughes and Thompson finally set off with seven men and trade goods for the Columbia River tribes, but their guide got lost and led them into gorges that ended abruptly in steep rock walls, and they had to return on June 30 without finding a pass. The next spring Thompson was ordered elsewhere, and McTavish postponed further attempts to establish North West Company posts across the Rockies.[16]

14 Hudson's Bay Company Archives E.3/2, fols. 19d, 20, 20d. Extended discussions of the significance of this material may be found in Josephy, *The Nez Perce Indians*. . . 654-55, and Josephy, "New Light on the Early Northwest," *New York Westerners Brand Book*, XII, p. 3.

15 J. B. Tyrrell, "David Thompson and the Rocky Mountains," *Canadian Historical Review*, XV, p. 43.

16 In "The North West Company's Columbian Enterprise and David Thompson," *Canadian Historical Review*, XVII, no. 3, pp. 266-88, the late Arthur S. Morton contended that during the summer of 1801 Duncan McGillivray and David Thompson had made another trip together, at which time they had actually gotten across the Rockies via White Man's Pass. They had then, according to Morton, descended Cross River to the Kootenay, continued down that river to Kootenay Lake, retraced their way to the portage to Columbia Lake, crossed it to the Columbia, and (McGillivray at least) descended the Columbia to the Wood River, returning to the east

Thompson remained at Rocky Mountain House until the spring of 1802, meantime making short trips on the east side of the mountains. In 1802 he traveled to Fort William, the North West Company's new base post on Lake Superior, and then headed to Lesser Slave Lake to continue his northern surveys. In 1803 he was in the Peace River country, and in 1804 he returned to Fort William where on July 10 he was made a partner of the company. From Fort William he traveled to the "muskrat country" between the Nelson and Churchill rivers and remained there, 1804-06, surveying and trading in a region in which he had formerly been employed by the Hudson's Bay Company.

by way of Athabaska Pass. Arguments against this reasoning were quick to come from J. B. Tyrrell in "David Thompson and the Columbia River," *Canadian Historical Review,* XVIII, no. 1, pp. 12-27. Morton made rebuttal in the same publication, XVIII, no. 2, pp. 156-62, and there the matter still stands, at least with regard to McGillivray. Although Rich, *op. cit.,* II, p. 227, states bluntly, without explanation but apparently in an unquestioning acceptance of Morton's thesis, that McGillivray crossed the Rockies in 1801 (via White Man's Pass, with a return trip over Athabaska Pass), and then, p. 239, says "though Thompson [in 1811] was with the possible exception of Duncan McGillivray the first white man" to get across the Athabaska Pass, the best conclusion, for the present at least, seems to be that of M. Catherine White, *op. cit.,* pp. lxxxvii-xci: ". . . the evidence in the records available at the present time is not sufficient that Thompson and McGillivray crossed the mountains to the main stream of the Kootenay River or to the Columbia in 1801, as all the arguments in favor of the contention are either refutable or at least open to dispute."

Unfortunately, Thompson's journals are incomplete for 1801 and cannot throw light on the matter. But the record concerning Thompson can be clarified by newly-found material. In 1844, Sir George Simpson wrote to the British Minister in Washington: ". . . in a conversation two years ago he [Thompson] informed me he did not cross the mountains until the year *1806.* . ." (See Josephy, *The Nez Perce Indians* . . . , 655). Thompson's memory in 1842 had his first crossing wrong by a year. But the statement seems to be a clear indication that he did not cross in 1801, and it would appear to imply that no one else did either. The absence of references to a McGillivray crossing in the journals and records of any of the fur companies or of the various traders, together with Simpson's silence concerning such a trip, outweigh, I think, Morton's claim.

If there is any questioning to be done, incidentally, it may be why Thompson could not have been led back successfully over the mountains in 1801 by La Gasse and Le Blanc. According to Fidler, they had returned to the Rocky Mountain House on May 23, two weeks before Thompson and Hughes set off on their ill-fated attempt.

At the 1806 annual meeting at Fort William, he was assigned to the Fort des Prairies, or Saskatchewan, department under John McDonald of Garth. Simon McTavish had died in 1804, and McDonald and other Nor'Westers, stirred to action by the Lewis and Clark Expedition's threat to flank their traders in the West and establish American control on the Columbia, now directed Thompson to try again to cross the continental divide.

By then, a number of French-Canadian, mixed blood, and eastern Indian hunters and trappers who worked part time as employees of the companies, but more often struck off on their own, had undoubtedly got west of the mountains. Between 1801 and 1806, following perhaps the route of La Gasse and Le Blanc but also finding other passages, including the Athabaska Pass, they had made their way to the Columbia and Kootenay rivers, where La Gasse and Le Blanc seem to have wintered with the Kutenais. They were illiterate and left no records, but Thompson's actions and movements in 1807 indicate reliance on knowledge first acquired by La Gasse and Le Blanc and increased by others who followed after 1801.

During the summer of 1806, John McDonald of Garth sent an advance party headed by Jacques Raphael Finlay, a half blood trader known as Jaco, over the mountains to clear a trail and build canoes on the Columbia for Thompson. Finlay's route, apparently already a familiar one, climbed through present-day Howse Pass and followed the rushing Blaeberry River down to the Columbia; but Finlay did a poor job of clearing the trail, and Thompson the next year was irritated by his inefficiency.

Thompson himself, with his wife, three small children, three engagés, and a load of trade goods, set out from the Rocky Mountain House on May 10, 1807. In one respect fortune favored him, for many of the Piegans, who normally would have tried to prevent him from bringing guns and trade goods to their western enemies, the Kutenais and various Salish-speaking peoples of the Columbia Basin, had ridden south that year to try to intercept Americans whom Meriwether Lewis the previous year had informed them he would send to trade with the western Indians. Near the foot of the Rockies, Thompson joined another advance party of six men, including his clerk, huge, red-bearded Finan McDonald, and then climbed toward Howse Pass. After being delayed by snow for two weeks, the men crossed the summit on June 25 and five days later, following down the Blaeberry, reached the upper Columbia. Since its current ran north, Thompson apparently did not recognize it as the Columbia, and he named it the Kootanae. Moving up it, using geographic knowledge acquired presumably by predecessors, he finally halted near present-day Invermere on Windermere Lake and built the Kootanae House, a crude storage post for his trade goods and furs. He wintered there, 1807-08, with Finan McDonald among Kutenais Indians whom he encouraged to bring in furs.

Thompson's post was the first one known on any of the upper waters of the Columbia, and news of its establishment traveled to various tribes in the region. On August 13 some Kutenais arrived with word that a party of Flatheads had started toward the post, but had been turned back by Blackfeet. The Flatheads had then ridden off "to a military Post of the Americans," who had reached the Northwest about three weeks before "to settle a military Post, at the confluence of the two most southern & considerable Branches of the Columbia." Who those Americans were is not definitely known, but it may be guessed from the evidence presently available that they were members of an exploring and trading expedition possibly led by an ex-artillery captain named John McClallen, and dispatched privately up the Missouri River in 1806 by General James Wilkinson, governor of upper Louisiana Territory. Thompson received communications from them on two occasions, warning him to leave the region. But he never met them, and in various of his writings he indicated that most, if not all, of them were eventually wiped out by Blackfeet Indians near the Clark Fork River in northwestern Montana.[17]

During the fall and winter, Piegans, Flatheads, Nez Perces, and other Indians all visited Thompson's post. The western natives added to his store of geographic knowledge about their homelands, and on April 20, 1808, he started for their countries, intending to open trade with as many of their bands as possible. With four engagés, he portaged from the head of the Columbia to the southward-flowing Kootenay River, descending that stream across the present-day international border and on May 8 reaching the vicinity of today's Bonners Ferry in northern Idaho. He dispatched a Kutenai messenger south on "the Great Road of the Flatheads" to Lake Pend Oreille, hoping to draw Flatheads to him, then explored farther along the Kootenai River (so-spelled today south of the border). Returning to the Bonners Ferry site, he was unable to wait for the return of his messenger, but, obliged to get his furs back east before the end of the season, returned by packhorse and canoe to the Kootanae House. He crossed the divide with his furs, traveled eastward for two months (at so rapid a pace that on one day he made 132 miles down the Saskatchewan), and delivered the pelts at Rainy Lake House, almost at Lake Superior. Shortly afterward, on August 4, 1808, he started west again, retracing the full route to the Columbia River.[18]

He spent the turn of the year once more at the Kootanae House, but that winter sent Finan McDonald with several companions down the Kootenai River to build a post at the

---

[17] Josephy, *The Nez Perce Indians* . . . , 41-43, 656-60.

[18] On the return trip he was directed, against his will, to take two kegs of liquor to trade with the Columbia Basin Indians. He recorded his pleasure when the kegs were so damaged during the journey that their contents leaked away.

falls of that stream in Montana. McDonald pitched two skin tents and built a log storehouse almost opposite present-day Libby, and opened trade with Salish-speaking Indians in the vicinity. During that winter of 1808-09, two of McDonald's men visited Idaho's Lake Pend Oreille, and others, including Jaco Finlay, explored south and east through Montana along the Clark Fork River and toward Flathead Lake.

In the spring of 1809 Thompson once more went east with his furs, but was back on the Columbia in July. He descended the Kootenai River again to the Bonners Ferry site, and in September moved south along the "Great Road of the Flatheads" to Lake Pend Oreille. There he set to work near present-day Hope, at the eastern end of the lake, building Idaho's first white establishment, Kullyspell House, for the trade of Flatheads, Coeur d'Alenes, Kalispels, Spokans, and other natives who frequented the area.

Toward the close of September, Thompson with one man and an Indian boy explored down the Pend Oreille River from the western end of the lake to a point near present-day Cusick, Washington. Retracing his route, he then rode up the Clark Fork River from the eastern end of Lake Pend Oreille, recognizing the valley of that stream as one of the Indians' principal transportation routes through the Bitterroot Mountains. After meeting his clerk, James McMillan, on the Kootenai River and escorting McMillan's store of trade goods to the Kullyspell House, Thompson led a party up the Clark Fork and in early November near present-day Thompson Falls, Montana, built another post, which he called the Saleesh House, for the Flathead trade.

Wintering there, 1809-10, Thompson conducted a brisk trade with Flatheads and their allies, including members of buffalo-hunting bands of Sahaptin-speakers, some of whom wore small dentalium shells in their noses. Thompson's

French Canadians gave them their historic name, Nez Perces, and Thompson first referred to them as such in his journal on March 11, 1810. In February, Thompson also noted the slaying by Blackfeet at the nearby site of present-day Dixon, Montana, of an American hunter named "Courter," who was probably Charles Courtin, a French-Canadian trader who had taken American citizenship and is believed to have preceded Manuel Lisa up the Missouri in 1807. Courtin had apparently reached the Three Forks, built a post there, and then moved across the continental divide to erect another post near present-day Missoula, Montana.[19]

On April 19, 1810, Thompson set off from the Saleesh House with twenty-eight packs of furs. He stopped briefly at the Kullyspell House, sent Finan McDonald and five men back to spend the summer with the Flatheads at the Saleesh House, and then went down the Pend Oreille River almost to its mouth, trying to find a shorter route to the Columbia. Rapids stopped him short of the juncture of the two rivers, and he returned to the Kullyspell post on May 1 and took the familiar route back to the Kootanae House. From there he crossed to the eastern side of the Rockies, and on July 22 delivered the year's Columbia Basin fur harvest to the North West Company post at Rainy Lake.

Meanwhile, his trade had put firearms for the first time in the hands of various of the western tribes,[20] and in July, 1810, a hunting group of some 150 Flatheads and their allies, accompanied by several of Thompson's men, traveled to the Montana plains where they effectively defended themselves with their guns against a Piegan war party. The Piegans, with seven killed and thirteen wounded, rode off, furious at the whites who had given firearms to their enemies, and

---

[19] Josephy, *The Nez Perce Indians* . . . , 45, 660-63.

[20] By April, 1810, he had distributed more than 20 guns and 100 iron arrowheads to the natives around the Saleesh House.

determined to halt Thompson's trade with the western Indians. That September, when Thompson tried to return to
the Columbia after his trip to Rainy Lake, he found angry
Piegans blocking the route to Howse Pass, having already
turned back his advance canoes on the headwaters of the
Saskatchewan.

It has been argued by Thompson's most serious critics
that his mission that winter of 1810-11 was one of great importance and urgency, that the North West Company partners had ordered him to cross the mountains as quickly as
possible, hurry directly to the mouth of the Columbia, and
establish a North West post there before an American
group, being dispatched from New York by John Jacob
Astor, occupied the region. Since he did not accomplish
that end, but arrived at the mouth of the Columbia after
the Astorians, great blame has been heaped on him. Some
of his critics spare no opportunity to question why, from
1807 onward, he dawdled on the upper Columbia and did
not in any one of those years go all the way to the Pacific,
and one of them even states baldly that Thompson "took
ten years to complete the project on which he had embarked
in 1801," as if that had been his steady purpose and goal
from 1801 to 1811.[21]

The truth is that, as yet, no evidence has been revealed,
either in company records or in the journals of Thompson or
anyone else, that he had been given the mission of reaching
the Pacific prior to 1810 or that, even in that year, he had
been directed to reach the mouth of the Columbia before
the Astorians. He had been a trader as well as an explorer;
he had had to build posts, conduct trade, and get his furs
back east each year. When one compares his parties of scant
personnel with the large complement that accompanied
Lewis and Clark and remembers that they both moved

[21] Rich, *op. cit.*, II, p. 241.

through the same sort of unknown and potentially hostile environment, one is more ready, perhaps, to accept Thompson's record without complaint.[22]

At any rate, after an unsuccessful attempt to steal past the Piegans in the late fall of 1810, Thompson was forced to make a hazardous detour north, crossing back into the Columbia Basin via Athabaska Pass, which Nipissing and Iroquois trappers had already discovered.[23] It was one of Thompson's most difficult trips, for the journey took him in below-zero temperatures, into a high, unmapped wilderness and across frigid, gale-blown glacier fields and ranges of granite-walled mountains through part of what is now Jasper National Park. His route led up the snowbanks along the Athabaska and Whirlpool rivers to the pass, then down the Wood River to the Canoe River, and so to the great northern bend of the Columbia. Guided by an Iroquois who had traveled the route before, Thompson and his engagés topped the pass on January 10, 1811, and eight days

[22] The criticism of Thompson, first raised in A. S. Morton, "The North West Company's Columbian Enterprise and David Thompson," *op. cit.*, 266-88, and furthered by Rich with additional barbed shafts that question Thompson's personal courage (pp. 236, 238, 250), seems to this writer effectively answered in Thompson's favor by White, *op. cit.*, 247-55. For the lengthy arguments, pro and con, including pertinent parts of Morton's writings, the reader is referred to White. In addition, it should be noted that David Lavender, *The American Heritage History of the Great West* (New York, 1965), 94, provides a new, third dimension to the question. According to Lavender, Thompson started for the Rockies in 1810 with the information that the North West Company held a one-third interest in Astor's venture, and that the North West Company backed out of the deal after it was too late to inform Thompson. Thus, the latter would have thought that he had no need to beat the Astorians to the Pacific, and, says Lavender, when he did reach the mouth of the Columbia, he still carried letters saying that the North West Company owned a third of the enterprise. Thompson himself gives no hint of any of this, but his various writings, as Rich justly observes, are guilty in several places of omitting information which historians require for proper perspective and a true understanding of the context surrounding Thompson's activities.

[23] And which Morton, *op. cit.*, 271-76, and in "Did Duncan M'Gillivray and David Thompson Cross the Rockies in 1801?" *Canadian Historical Review*, XVIII (1937), 156-62, as well as Rich, *op. cit.*, II, 227, say Duncan McGillivray used in 1801, though, to repeat, evidence seems against the contention.

later, worn from their toil, arrived on the Columbia. The
engagés had had enough. Thompson tried to get them to
go on with him and ascend the Columbia to the Kootanae
House, but three of the men deserted and the others refused
to go farther until spring.

After wintering at the confluence of the Canoe and Columbia rivers, the group finally set off up the Columbia on
April 17. Thompson made it plain that he would have
preferred trying to descend the river, exploring its course
all the way to its mouth, but he deemed that his party, now
reduced to three men beside himself, was too small to risk
encounters with unknown tribes along the route. Instead, he
decided to return to familiar country around his trading
posts, where he could recruit more men to accompany him
down the Columbia.

Traveling south to the Clark Fork River, he discovered
that in his absence his men had abandoned both the Saleesh
and Kullyspell posts because of danger from raiding Piegans. Crossing west of Lake Pend Oreille, he at last found
Finan McDonald and Jaco Finlay living at a new post, the
Spokane House, which they had built during the winter
among the Spokan Indians near the confluence of the
Spokane and Little Spokane rivers, about ten miles northwest of the present city of that name.

Thompson now turned to the business of exploring the
Columbia River and reaching its mouth. On June 17, he
left the Spokane House, traveling by horse across present-
day northeastern Washington to a fishing settlement of
Sanpoil Indians at Kettle Falls on the Columbia. There he
built a stout cedar canoe, and on July 3, 1811, with two
Sanpoil interpreter-guides, two Iroquois hunters, and five
French Canadians, he embarked on the downriver voyage.
Although the travelers met many riverine, fishing bands
that had never before seen a white man, the trip was without serious incident. On July 9 Thompson halted briefly at

the mouth of the Snake River, where Lewis and Clark had entered the Columbia six years before, and erected a pole and a note that laid claim to the region for Great Britain and signified the trader's intent to build a post at the site for the North West Company. Continuing on, Thompson reached the Columbia's mouth on July 15, 1811, finding that the Astorians had already landed there in March and had begun construction of their own post in April.[24]

The Astorians had planned to move inland to compete with the Nor'Westers, and on July 23 David Stuart started an American party upriver to build a post on the Okanogan. Thompson and his men accompanied the Astorians as far as the Dalles, then hurried on ahead to the mouth of the Snake. There, a large group of Sahaptin-speaking Indians, probably Palouses and Nez Perces, told him of a shorter route to the Spokane House, and he turned up the Snake. At the mouth of the Palouse River he secured horses from Indians, left his canoes, and rode quickly overland to the post, thus finding still another important avenue of transportation which succeeding generations of traders and other whites would utilize.

Collecting the season's furs, Thompson almost immediately went on to Kettle Falls, where he built a new canoe in which to ascend the Columbia toward Athabaska Pass, which he would have to take again in order to avoid the Piegans. On September 2, he set off up the Columbia, exploring the only part of the river he had not yet traveled. Passing through the Arrow Lakes and navigating a series of dangerous rapids, he left his craft at the Canoe River, crossed Athabaska Pass, exchanged his furs for trade goods

---

[24] The feelings of Thompson and the Astorians, on seeing each other, have been variously described – from warmth to hostility – by different writers. Present evidence would indicate to this writer that Thompson was disappointed, but not surprised, to find the Astorians ahead of him, and that the Astorians were friendly but dismayed by the proof he furnished of how well entrenched he was in the interior – hints of which they had already received.

at the North West Company's Henry House, and hastened directly back to the Columbia. Recrossing Athabaska Pass and hurrying down the Columbia, he was back at his starting place, Kettle Falls, on October 31. The area was deserted, all the Indians having gone off hunting, and Thompson was forced to backpack his goods on foot to Spokane House, and then over an old Indian trail to the Pend Oreille River. He hurried on, all the way to the sagging, weed-grown ruins of his old Saleesh House on the Clark Fork River, where prior to his trip east he had promised on his return to meet the Flatheads and their allies.

His men at once began to rebuild the post, and the next week, on November 25, 1811, the first large reinforcement of North West Company traders, following one of the routes that Thompson had pioneered from east of the Rockies, came paddling down the Clark Fork River. These were fifteen men under John George McTavish and James McMillan, ordered hurriedly into the Columbia country as a result of Thompson's report at Henry House that Astor's traders were already in the region. After two days with Thompson, McTavish and his men left for the Spokane House and the mouth of the Columbia. A struggle for the fur empire of the Columbia was in the offing, but Thompson was not destined to be a participant.

Up to then, Thompson and his companions had been the only Nor'Westers in the upper Columbia Basin. They had explored a vast land, mastered much of its tangled geography, mapped many of its routes, brought the fur trade to many tribes (most of which had never before seen a white man), and prepared the way for traders who would have neither the time nor the ability to start from scratch. Thompson's role was almost finished. He spent the winter of 1811-12 at the rehabilitated Saleesh House, sending his men out to trap beaver, and making several exploratory trips of his own through the country east of the post. On one of those excursions, during February and March, 1812, he rode up the Flathead and Jocko rivers (the latter named for Jaco Finlay), then turned south, and reached the site of present-day Missoula, Montana, where he climbed a "high Knowl" and made out the area of the start of the Lolo Trail by which Lewis and Clark had so laboriously crossed the Bitterroots.

After traveling farther north to view Flathead Lake and the Mission Mountains (March 1), the trader returned to the Saleesh House, packed his winter furs in two canoes, and on March 13 started down the Clark Fork River. He crossed Lake Pend Oreille and, pausing at the Spokane House to pick up John George McTavish, went on to Kettle Falls. On April 22, he and McTavish departed from that point up the Columbia with a brigade of six canoes, each manned by five men, and a total of 122 packs of furs. On May 5 they reached the Canoe River, and Thompson and his men set off on foot over the Athabaska Pass. On May 11 they were at Henry House, and two months later, on July 12, Thompson arrived at Fort William, in time for the annual partners' meeting.

Thompson never again returned west. From Fort William he left for Montreal to work on a great map of all the western lands that he had explored and surveyed. He finished it in 1814, and for a while it hung in the dining hall of the company's post at Fort William, where it was seen only by company partners and employees.[25] The firm had no interest in having the map circulated while its members were engaged in intense competition with the Hudson's Bay Company, whose traders would have valued the detailed information it contained.

After Thompson retired from the fur trade, he tried on a number of occasions to have his map published, but never

---

[25] The map was huge, measuring 10' 3½" x 6' 6".

succeeded. He settled, 1813-14, at Terrebonne in Quebec Province with his wife and children. In 1815 he moved to Williamstown, Ontario, where he maintained his home until 1829. In that year he moved again, this time to Longueuil opposite Montreal. From 1817 to 1827 he was employed by the British Boundary Commission to survey the international border between Canada and the United States from St. Regis on the St. Lawrence River to the Lake of the Woods, north of Minnesota. Later, from 1834-40, he surveyed extensively in eastern Canada.

As the years passed, he was overcome by a series of misfortunes. Most of his savings disappeared in unprofitable business ventures of his sons. His eyesight failed. Further difficulties forced him to sell his scientific instruments – and at one time even pawn his coat – in order to eat. When the North West and Hudson's Bay companies merged, a new generation of fur men forgot the name and achievements of David Thompson, the Nor'Wester. Even the pass by which he had first crossed the Rockies in 1807 was named for a johnny-come-lately, Joseph Howse, a Hudson's Bay Company clerk who had crossed the pass on a brief visit to the upper Columbia country in 1810-11.

Thompson's own modest character contributed to his obscurity. Quiet and unobtrusive, he failed to push himself forward or seek recognition. In extreme poverty, on the edge of complete blindness, he managed when more than seventy years old to write a gripping and detailed narrative of his explorations, hoping to make a little money from its sale. In some way Washington Irving heard of it and tried to buy it but, according to Thompson's daughter, failed to offer enough money or to satisfy Thompson with regard to acknowledgement of its authorship. There were no other bidders. The narrative, like the great map, remained unpublished. Finally, at the age of eighty-seven – poor, blind, and unknown – Thompson died on February 10, 1857, at Longueuil and was buried in an unmarked grave in Montreal's Mount Royal Cemetery.[26]

Thompson's discoveries and surveys had enriched the world with knowledge of the northwestern part of the continent. But during his lifetime the professional cartographers and engravers who used the information he had gathered for his employers failed to acknowledge him as their source, and the people who in later years followed the routes he had pioneered were unaware that he was the original author of the maps they used. It is not inconceivable that the scope of his work might still be little known had it not been for the curiosity of a Canadian geologist, Dr. Joseph B. Tyrrell, who was working in the West during the 1880s as a member of the Geological Survey of Canada. Tyrrell was struck by the completeness and accuracy of the old government maps he was using, and he became interested in trying to discover their source. His search led him ultimately to the files of the Crown Lands Department of the Province of Ontario at Toronto, where he uncovered a group of weathered journals and notebooks of David Thompson, as well as Thompson's huge manuscript map of the western half of North America between the latitudes of forty-five and eighty degrees, which the explorer had finished in 1814. The journals and map had been deposited in the provincial files sometime after Thompson's death, and the map had been used from time to time to help in the preparation of charts of western Canada.

Dr. Tyrrell's study of the diaries and notebooks revealed for the first time the hitherto unsuspected extent of Thompson's many journeys, and the map quickly confirmed him as the original source for the charts Tyrrell had been using. In the years that followed, Dr. Tyrrell continued his quest

[26] Three months later his wife died and was buried beside him.

for further information, and eventually learned that while Thompson had been in the service of the fur companies, his field maps and reports had been sent by his superiors to the English cartographer, Aaron Arrowsmith, who had used them to help prepare his maps of North America but had never acknowledged Thompson as a source of information.

Tyrrell gradually embarked on a life's mission of making Thompson's achievements known. The high point of his labors was reached in 1916 when he finally published Thompson's rich and revealing narrative. The piecemeal publication of the explorer's field journals in the years that followed ultimately won the recognition that is at last accorded David Thompson.

Philip F. Thompson

by LeRoy R. Hafen
Brigham Young University

Philip F. Thompson is best known in the western fur trade as a partner in the ownership and operation of Fort Davy Crockett. This post was in Brown's Hole, on Green River, northwestern Colorado. Thompson's partners in 1839 were William Craig and Prewitt Sinclair (see their biographical sketches in volumes II and IV of this *Series*).

Of Thompson's early life little is known. He was born in Tennessee in 1810 or 1811,[1] "of Scotch-Irish ancestry."[2] According to his obituary, he "went in early life to the Rocky Mountains."[3] How early and just where he went have not been determined. The first contemporary record we have found places him at Fort Vasquez on the South Platte River with Robert Newell in May, 1837.[4] Newell says they went from there northwestward to the Green River and up that stream to the summer rendezvous at the mouth of Horse Creek.

> In twenty days the rendezvous broke up, [says Kit Carson] and I and seven men went to Brown's Hole, a trading post, where I joined Thompson and Sinclair's party on a trading expedition to the Navajo

---

[1] In his sworn statement in Washington County, Oregon Territory, on October 22, 1853 ("Affidavit of Settlers on unsurveyed Lands" in "Records of the General Land Office, Oregon City Donation Certificate 3874," National Archives), he says he was born in Williamson County, Tennessee, in 1811. His obituary in the *Oregonian* (weekly, Portland), Feb. 25, 1854, says he was born in Tennessee, April 22, 1810.

[2] According to the biographical file in the Oregon Historical Society, as reported to me in a letter of October 10, 1949.

[3] Obituary in the *Oregonian, op. cit.* This and other data were supplied to the writer in 1949 by Priscilla Knuth of the Oregon Historical Society, Portland.

[4] *Robert Newell's Memoranda,* etc., edited by Dorothy O. Johansen (Portland, Ore., 1959), 34 (hereafter cited as Newell). This is one of our most reliable chronologies of the period.

Indians. We procured thirty mules from them and returned to Brown's Hole. After our arrival Thompson took the mules to the South Fork of the Platte, where he disposed of them to Sublette and Vasquez and returned with goods suitable for trading with the Indians. I was now employed as hunter for the fort and I continued in this service during the winter, having to keep twenty men supplied with meat. In the spring of 1838 I joined Bridger.[5]

For the period 1839-40 there is abundant contemporary information about Thompson and events at Fort Davy Crockett. By this time the trading post in Brown's Hole was in regular operation, in the hands of Thompson, Craig, and Sinclair. The date of founding has not been definitely determined. But Brown's Hole, the mountain-walled valley that was the site of the post, had long been a favorite winter resort for Indians and for whites. In this grassy retreat the bands sought shelter from the storms that swept the surrounding mountains.

White man records regarding the site go back to May, 1825, when William H. Ashley boated down Green River in search of beaver. He noted the remains of an Indian camp "where several thousand Indians had wintered the past season." [6] Conical lodges made of poles and cedar bark were still standing. Farther down the Green River, in the Uinta country around present Vernal, Utah, Ashley met Etienne Provost and other fur gatherers from New Mexico.[7]

Prewitt Sinclair and other members of the Bean-Sinclair trapping party from Arkansas wintered in Brown's Hole in 1831-32.[8] They may have erected cabins or some form of shelter for winter quarters. This good location continued as a favorite resort for trapper bands. References to it appear

[5] *Kit Carson's Autobiography,* edited by M. M. Quaife (Chicago, 1935), 54-55. Carson's dating of events 1837 to 1840 is very undependable, but this statement appears to fit in correctly.

[6] H. C. Dale, *The Ashley-Smith Explorations,* etc. (edition of 1841), 142.

[7] D. L. Morgan, *The West of William H. Ashley,* etc. (Denver, 1964), 113, 116.

[8] *Life and Adventures of George Nidever,* edited by W. H. Ellison (Berkeley, California, 1937), 23.

in the licenses given by William Clark, Superintendent of Indian Affairs, during the 1830s. These licenses, issued to various traders, 1833-38, give permission to trade "at a post near the mouth of Bear river on the waters of Grand river or the Colorado of the West." [9]

No contemporary accounts of Brown's Hole, except the record of licenses, have been found for the years 1832-36. And these give no name for the post. When the name, Fort Davy Crockett, was applied is not known, but it is likely that it was given in 1836, the year of the dramatic death of Crockett at the Alamo.

The fort as it appeared in 1839 has been described by contemporary visitors, T. J. Farnham, Obadiah Oakley, F. A. Wislizenus, E. Willard Smith, and Sidney Smith. There are also reminiscent accounts by Robert Shortess and Kit Carson.[10]

In the spring of 1839 Thompson went down the Arkansas River and to the Missouri frontier for supplies. He returned with his goods in the supply caravan of Sublette and Vasquez, leaving Independence, Missouri, on August 6, 1839, and reaching Fort Vasquez on the South Platte September 13.[11]

In the meantime William Craig had headed eastward across the mountains in July to meet Thompson, leaving Sinclair in charge of the fort. During August, Sinclair, already short of supplies, was visited by two parties of travelers. Thomas J. Farnham, westward bound to "conquer Oregon," arrived on August 12, and five days later Dr. F. A.

9 See a detailed discussion in LeRoy R. Hafen, "Fort Davy Crockett, its Fur Men and Visitors," in the *Colorado Magazine*, XXIX (1952), 17-33.

10 *Ibid.*, and L. R. and A. W. Hafen, *The Far West and the Rockies* (Glendale, Calif., 1955), III, pp. 77, 106, 173-74.

11 E. Willard Smith, an excellent diarist, accompanied the Vasquez and Sublette caravan westward to the South Platte and then journeyed on to Brown's Hole with Thompson and Craig. His "journal" is printed in Hafen and Hafen, *The Far West and the Rockies,* III, pp. 151-95.

Wislizenus and party traveling in the opposite direction came in. No wonder they had to thin the dog soup and that the visitors labeled the post "Fort Misery." [12] Other traders soon came to the area. Doc Newell reported that Kit Carson and Dick Owens arrived on September 1; [Abel] Baker to trade for Bent and St. Vrain, on the 23rd, and [Thomas] Biggs for Vasquez on the 25th.[13]

Thompson and Craig, with their fresh supplies, set out from the South Platte on September 16, 1839. The young adventurer into the West, E. Willard Smith, accompanied them, and gives a detailed account of experiences. His entry of September 16, 1839, reads:

> Today we left our encampment, and started to cross the mountains. Our party consisted of eight men, two squaws, and three children. One of the squaws belonged to Mr. Thompson, the other to Mr. Craig. They were partners & have a trading Fort at Brown's Hole, a valley on the west side of the mountains.[14]

They arrived at Brown's Hole on October 1st. There Kit Carson told Smith of a fight that hunters from Fort Davy Crockett had had on Little Snake River some days before with a band of Indians. The head chief, while a peacemaker near the white men's camp, was treacherously killed.[15] This doubtless was the cause of a subsequent raid on the whites at Brown's Hole.

A second, big expedition for "making meat" went out from the fort on October 10. The party of thirty, about half of whom were squaws of the white trappers, found ample game on Snake River near the mouth of the Muddy. They killed and dried the meat of one hundred buffalo, and bagged six grizzlies.[16]

---

[12] F. A. Wislizenus, *A Journey to the Rocky Mountains in the Year 1839* (St. Louis, 1912; translated from the original German edition, published in St. Louis in 1840), 129. See also T. J. Farnham, *Travels in the Great Western Prairies*, etc., in R. G. Thwaites, *Early Western Travels*, XXVIII, pp. 252-53.

[13] Newell, 38.   [15] *Ibid.*, 174-75.   [16] *Ibid.*, 175-76.

[14] Smith's Journal in *The Far West and the Rockies*, III, p. 168.

On the very heels of the returning band of meat-laden hunters came a small band of Sioux. On November 1 they crept into the supposedly safe retreat of Brown's Hole, where the trappers "had been in habit of letting their horses run loose in the valley, unattended by a guard, as this place was unknown to any of the hostile Indians." The Sioux succeeded in running off about 150 horses. "This event caused considerable commotion at the Fort," wrote E. W. Smith, "and they [the whites] were determined to fit out a war party to go in search of the stolen horses, but the next morning this project was abandoned."[17] The traders doubtless realized that once the horses had been driven through the narrow passageway leading from Brown's Hole the Indians could block the trail and prevent successful pursuit by the whites.

So, instead of attempting to recover their stolen horses, some of the traders decided to recoup their losses by stealing from someone else. Accordingly, they went to friendly Fort Hall, Hudson's Bay Company post, and stole fourteen horses. On the way back, after enjoying the hospitality of some peaceful Snake Indians, they stole some thirty head from the unsuspecting friendlies. Doc Newell gives the number of animals stolen and names Thompson and Michel as leaders of the renegades.[18]

The majority of the whites at Fort Davy Crockett roundly condemned this breach of mountain etiquette. Their attitude was prompted not only by the ethical breach, but by the fear of just retaliation. And in such an eventuality, avenging Indians would not distinguish between the guilty and innocent at Fort Davy Crockett.

The horse thieves took their booty to an old trapper fort on Green River at the mouth of the Uinta. When the robbed Snakes came to Fort Davy Crockett and complained of their

[17] *Ibid.*, 176.   [18] Newell, 39.

loss, the whites at the fort decided to attempt a recovery of the stolen stock. "This party consisted of Meek, Craig, Newell, Carson, and some twenty-five others under the command of Jo Walker," Meek told Mrs. Frances F. Victor:

> The horses were found on an island in Green River, the robbers having domiciled themselves in an old fort at the mouth of the Uintee. In order to avoid having a fight with the renegades, whose white blood the trappers were not anxious to spill, Walker made an effort to get the horses off the island undiscovered. But while horses and men were crossing the river on the ice, the ice sinking with them until the water was knee-deep, the robbers discovered the escape of their booty, and charging on the trappers tried to recover the horses. In this effort they were not successful; while Walker made a masterly flank movement and getting in Thompson's rear, ran the horses into the fort, where he stationed his men, and succeeded in keeping the robbers on the outside. Thompson then commenced giving the horses away to a village of Utes in the neighborhood of the fort, on condition that they would assist in retaking them. On his side, Walker threatened the Utes with dire vengeance if they dared interfere. The Utes who had a wholesome fear not only of the trappers, but of their foes the Snakes, declined to enter into the quarrel. After a day of strategy, and of threats alternating with arguments, strengthened by a warlike display, the trappers marched out of the fort before the faces of the discomfitted thieves, taking their booty with them, which was duly restored to the Snakes on their return to Fort Crockett, and peace secured once more with that people.[19]

The horse-stealing raids by Thompson and his cohorts and the consequent division among the white traders appear to have ended the partnership of Thompson, Craig, and Sinclair. Craig went to Oregon in 1840 and Sinclair subsequently moved to California.

But Thompson and others decided to go to California, where horses were plentiful, and obtain a supply. Their raid in the spring of 1840 was the most extensive and notorious of many such ventures. The Californians, smart-

---

[19] F. F. Victor, *The River of the West*, etc. (Hartford, Conn., 1870), 259-60.

ing from previous losses, made their boldest and greatest effort to punish the marauders and recover their horses.[20]

Leadership of the 1840 raid has been charged, or credited, to three Mountain Men – Philip Thompson, Old Bill Williams, and Pegleg Smith. All three were doubtless in the band, but it is probable that no one was an elected leader.

A good, though brief, account of the venture is given by Rufus B. Sage, who met Philip Thompson and his party driving horses to the Missouri River in 1841:

> Their horses had been mostly obtained from Upper California, the year previous, by a band of mountaineers, under the lead of one Thompson. This band, numbering twenty-two in all, had made a descent upon the Mexican ranchos and captured between two and three thousand head of horses and mules. A corps of some sixty Mexican cavalry pursued and attacked them, but were defeated and pursued in turn, with the loss of several mules and their entire camp-equipage: after which the adventurers were permitted to regain their mountain homes, without further molestation; but, in passing the cheerless desert, between the Sierra Nevada and Colorado, the heat, dust, and thirst were so intolerably oppressive, that full one half of their animals died. The remainder, however, were brought to rendezvous, and variously disposed of, to suit the wants and wishes of their captors.[21]

Thompson returned to the mountains and then moved to Oregon in 1842. With him went his Indian wife and family. In an affidavit for proving title to a land claim Thompson stated that he arrived in Oregon on October 15, 1842,

---

20 For accounts of the raid and pursuit see Department State Papers, Los Angeles, IV, pp. 88-106 (May 14 to June 9, 1840). A full story of the raids into California for horses is given in L. R. and A. W. Hafen, *The Old Spanish Trail* (Glendale, Calif., 1954), 227-57.

21 As reprinted in Hafen and Hafen, *Far West and Rockies*, IV, p. 148. Other accounts of the raid are found in G. D. Brewerton, *Overland with Kit Carson* (New York, 1930), 70-72, crediting leadership to Old Bill Williams; and in Horace Bell, *Reminiscences of a Ranger* (Santa Barbara, 1927), 289-91, naming Pegleg Smith as leader. It was probably this raid of 1840 that was the principal basis for the interesting fictionalized account of a horse-stealing foray that George F. Ruxton gives in his *Life in the Far West,* edited by L. R. Hafen (Norman, Okla., 1951).

and that he legally married Martha Thompson in November following.[22]

Of their trek to Oregon and subsequent life there we have this revealing human-interest story from H. S. Lyman, Oregon historian:

> The story of Phil Thompson and his family would afford material for a romance. After trapping many years in the Rocky Mountains and marrying a native woman of the Snake Indians, he saw his oldest daughter beginning to grow up to womanhood, and concluded that he must follow the missionaries who had come into the Willamette Valley that the girl might be educated. He talked the matter over with his Indian wife, who perceived the advantage of the child becoming a white woman; but could not bring herself to leave her country. She bade him and the girl a sad farewell, and Thompson set out, and after one day's journey made camp. In the morning the mother appeared to say good-bye again. Another day's march was made; but once more, as morning came, the Snake Indian mother was there to say good-bye. This continuing several days she finally gave up her tribe to follow her child; and in the Willamette Valley became known as one of the most careful of housewives. She tried to learn the white woman's ways, and visited her white neighbors, noticing all the home arrangements and ways of cooking, washing, and keeping house, and introduced these at home, to please her husband, and that her children might grow up like white people. Mrs. Doty (Doughty), who was of the same Indian tribe, became a Baptist; but Mrs. Thompson died before the Baptist missionary reached the neighborhood.[23]

When the Cayuse Indian War broke out, following the Whitman massacre, Philip F. Thompson was appointed captain of the Fifth Company. He took a prominent part in the campaign and especially distinguished himself in the Battle of Touchet in March, 1848.[24]

[22] Records of the General Land Office, National Archives, *op. cit.*

[23] H. S. Lyman, *History of Oregon* (Portland, 1903), III, pp. 266-68.

[24] *Oregon Spectator* (Oregon City), Jan. 20, April 6, 20, July 13, 27, 1848. See also F. F. Victor, *Early Indian Wars of Oregon*, 144, 168, 188, 214, 216. This and other data, including a photograph of the Touchet battlefield, were supplied by John R. White of Waitsburg, Washington.

Thompson was appointed sub-Indian Agent in 1853,[25] but did not long hold the position. He died of tuberculosis at Wapato Lake on January 22, 1854.[26] His wife had passed away in February of the preceding year.[27] When their daughter Mary died on February 27, 1856, at the age of eleven, the report stated that "all her family died of tuberculosis." [28]

[25] *Oregon Statesman* (Salem), June 21, 1853.

[26] *Oregonian* (weekly, Portland), Feb. 25, 1854. Also information from Harvey E. Tobie, Portland. Philip F. Thompson's uncle, Philip W. Thompson, of Arrowrock, Missouri, was a trader over the Santa Fe Trail to New Mexico in 1828-29 (Ritch Collection of MSS in the Henry E. Huntington Library, San Marino). The Oregon Historical Society has three MS letters concerning Thompson and his uncle and which refer to a loan of $500 from the uncle.

[27] Thompson's affidavit in Land Claim papers, *op. cit.*

[28] *Oregon Weekly Times,* March 15, 1856 (Oregon Historical Society reference card files).

Courtney Meade Walker*

by Jo Tuthill
Tillamook, Oregon

Courtney Walker was born in Nicholasville, Kentucky, on April 14, 1812. This was the same year that General Andrew Jackson, Courtney Walker's grand-uncle-in-law, was to write to his wife Rachel, "Have a house built for your sister Mary" (who had lately become widowed by an arrow of the Indians that her husband, John Caffery, was fighting in the Louisiana country). Mary Caffery was Rachel Jackson's eldest sister and the maternal grandmother of Courtney Walker.

Courtney's father, George Walker, was a lawyer, a state senator in Kentucky, for a short time a United States senator, and a veteran of the Revolutionary War and the War of 1812. Courtney's mother, Rachel, died when he was very young, and his father married her sister Katherine.[1]

Courtney Walker attended the schools in Nicholasville, and probably the college at Lexington, where he and his brother, Joseph, lived after their father's death in 1819. Courtney knew the Austin boys, James and Stephen; and his relatives thought that Courtney may have gone into Texas territory during the years 1829-1834. His brother, John Walker, noted in the family records that Courtney left his home in Nicholasville to go to Oregon in 1829. That year his grand-uncle, Andrew Jackson, was inaugurated as president of the United States, and soon filled his cabinet and his household at the nation's capital with numerous

---

* A portrait of Walker appears herein at page 18.
1 Photostatic copies of records of the George Walker family, from a grand-niece in New Orleans, La., 1964.

"cousins" of Courtney Walker. His Aunt Jane Caffery was the wife of the artist, R. E. W. Earl, much in the home of Andrew Jackson as a personal friend.[2]

When the missionaries, Jason Lee, Daniel Lee, and Cyrus Shepard, stopped off at St. Louis, Missouri, to get supplies and to see General William Clark (of the Lewis and Clark expedition), they may have mentioned their difficulty in finding anyone willing to accompany them to Oregon as their assistants. General Clark, who knew Courtney's family and also knew that Courtney was then at his brother Andrew's home near St. Louis, probably suggested Courtney Walker as an assistant. At any rate, Courtney was hired on a one-year contract, and Daniel Lee found another assistant in Philip Edwards.[3]

The party assembled at Independence, Missouri, in April, 1834, and joined Nathaniel Wyeth on his second expedition to the West Coast. Milton Sublette, with his spring fur brigade, and the two scientists, Nuttall and Townsend, were in the caravan. At the Snake River in Idaho, Wyeth raised the cottonwood cabins that he dubbed "Fort Hall." The group then proceeded northwestward.

In Oregon, Courtney Walker and the missionaries constructed buildings, broke a bit of land for gardening, and by the spring of 1835 the mission was fairly well established on the bank of the Willamette River, eight miles northwest of present-day Salem, Oregon.

Courtney Walker entered the fur trade of the Far West as the business agent (clerk) for Nathaniel Wyeth and his Columbia River Fishing and Trading Company, situated at Fort William on Wappatoo Island, when his year's contract with the Methodist Mission expired. This was prob-

[2] Marquis James, *Andrew Jackson, Portrait of a President* (Indianapolis, 1937), 21, 23, 249, 268, 270, 292, 327, 444, 461-62; and family records.

[3] C. J. Brosnan, *Jason Lee, Prophet of New Oregon* (New York, 1932), 46.

ably in April of 1835, as the site of Fort William was moved to a new location opposite the Old Logie Trail by the first of May, 1835.

There Wyeth and his men constructed sturdier buildings. Most of the first buildings had been "wikiups," or three-sided huts with slant roofs and set on poles. These huts never ceased to amaze the "Easterners" from the states during the first half century of the taming of the Pacific Coast. Used by the natives along the coast, the huts were sturdy and easily assembled, and are still used as temporary shelters in the coastal back country.

In the summer of 1835, Wyeth and Walker tried valiantly to obtain enough furs, and to pack enough salmon, to make a decent showing of cargo, but with very little success. This was due to lack of experience in the use of their fishing equipment, and also to the opposition of the British at Fort Vancouver, who took most of the Indian trade away from the inexperienced Americans at Fort William. In the fall of 1835, Wyeth went to his other establishment, Fort Hall, to take charge of his fur trade in the Snake River region, leaving Courtney Walker in charge of Fort William.

Nothing seemed to turn out right for Courtney that year. The Indians either refused to trade with him or sold him inferior goods. The nets were not correctly made to catch salmon, and most of the men at the island were ill a great deal of the winter. In fact, the supply of workers was fast becoming depleted. Some drowned in the river and sloughs, some were killed in drunken brawls with the natives of the island. The tailor of the fort, Mr. Thornburg, was shot by the gunsmith, Hubbard, when Thornburg attempted to put a bullet through the head of Hubbard while he was asleep on July 4, 1835.

Nathaniel Wyeth had no better luck in the Snake River country. When the "May Dacre" returned to Fort William, only half a cargo of salmon and furs had been collected. Wyeth decided he must return to the East Coast and obtain both men and money if his company was to succeed.[4]

Wyeth made several trips to Fort Vancouver and talked with its chief factor, John McLoughlin, and the other gentlemen of the Hudson's Bay Company, trying to find some workable compromise in the fur trading competition. The British offered little help to Wyeth's depressed condition, and he soon learned through the grapevine that the H.B.C. office in London was determined to drive him and his American concern out of the Oregon country. But before Wyeth left for the States in May, 1836, he and Courtney Walker did some conniving on their own. Although historians have hitherto given Dr. McLoughlin credit for out-maneuvering Wyeth, this writer is not quite sure that was the case.

Nathaniel Wyeth was hardly out of earshot when Walker set their plan in motion. He hied himself over to Fort Vancouver and asked for a job with the Hudson's Bay Company, stipulating that he wanted to become a trapper. If there was one thing John McLoughlin did not need or want, it was one more American fur trapper – especially not in the regions to the north or south indicated by Walker, for there lay the untapped fur resources.

The following letter, written by the Hudson's Bay factor to the Governor and Committee, clearly states McLoughlin's suspicions of the young would-be trapper:

When Mr. Wyeth was here in 1834, he Engaged a young Man as a clerk of the Name of Walker (who came here with the American Methodist Missionaries). But this spring his time being Out he refused to Engage to Wyeth to go to the Snake Country and remained here giving out that he Intended to become a Trapper (Wyeth Equipped him with traps). But as it might be that Wyeth had

---

[4] "Correspondence and Journals of Captain Nathaniel J. Wyeth," 255, in *Sources of the History of Oregon* (Eugene, Ore., 1899).

Equipped him thus to go about and acquire a knowledge of the Country Which would be of Great use to Wyeth if he comes back to oppose us again, I tried at first to Engage him for the Snake Country but he would not Engage for that place (where all the information he would acquire would do us no more harm than that which his Country-men Already have). At last however I Engaged him for any place we may Want him (Except the Snake Country) for three years at forty pounds p. Annum and to be Increased if found Deserving, and Imme-diately sent him to Nisqually and to be sent from there to Fort McLoughlin, Where he could Acquire no information Advantageous to Wyeth or Detrimental to us. But he has sent me Word he would now on Condition of an Increase of Wages go the Snake Country: he will therefore be sent to the Snake Country or Fort McLoughlin as May [be] considered most Expedient and as My engaging him as a clerk is contrary to Rule, I trust your Honors will take into considera-tion My object in assuming this Responsibility.[5]

On July 1, 1836, Courtney Walker left for Fort Nisqually and Fort McLoughlin, but was back at Fort Vancouver in September. On November 26 he was sent, with the steamer "Beaver" and its crew, to help them over the portages; he returned with Duncan Finlayson just in time to greet Andrew Jackson's secret agent, William Slacum. By Feb-ruary, 1837, he was at Fort Nisqually again, but was ordered to the Snake River country that spring with the Hudson's Bay fur traders serving under Thomas McKay.[6]

Meanwhile in the East, Nathaniel Wyeth was becoming concerned because he had received no word from Walker. Courtney's letters were being intercepted, as were those of the missionaries in the Rocky Mountains. In desperation, Wyeth wrote to John McLoughlin, and having had no success in his attempt to raise enough capital to tide him over in the Far West, he returned to the Columbia River region to find out what had happened to Walker and his

[5] E. E. Rich (ed.), *The Letters of John McLoughlin from Fort Vancouver to the Governor and Committee, First Series, 1825-38* (London, 1941), 171.

[6] Extracts of letters from archives of Hudson's Bay Company, London, received in August, 1964.

fur trade. When he reached the Snake River region, he found worse news than he had anticipated. The fur trade of the Rocky Mountains was in a sorry state, and when Walker told Wyeth about the situation, the trouble with the Indians, and the plan of the Hudson's Bay Company to establish more trading posts to oppose the American fur traders, Wyeth decided to sell Fort Hall to the H.B.C. However, Fort William, which he wanted as a future land enterprise, he left for Walker to dispose of by leasing it to a responsible party.[7]

Walker spent most of the next two years at Fort Hall or at Fort Boise. James Douglas and McLoughlin sent orders for Thomas McKay and Courtney Walker to proceed two hundred miles south of Fort Hall into Yuta country and establish a fort. When finished, it was to be left in charge of Courtney Walker with as many fur trappers as he could muster. This was in the spring of 1838, but the plan never materialized.[8]

Courtney Walker by this time was married to Margaret McTavish, daughter of John George McTavish and Nancy McTavish LeBlanc. (It was McTavish who persuaded the Astorians' Donald McKenzie and his associates to turn over Fort Astoria to the British during the War of 1812.) Margaret's mother, Nancy, was the niece of Donald McKenzie, and was the wife cast off by John G. McTavish after he and Sir George Simpson brought back from the British Isles their bigamous wives in 1830. Although historians have pictured her as a "squaw," she certainly had no more than a trace of Indian blood.[9]

During 1838 and 1839, Courtney Walker was to play a courteous host to many travelers who stopped at Fort Hall,

---

[7] Journals of Wyeth, op. cit., 255.
[8] Extracts from the Hudson's Bay Company records.
[9] Arthur S. Morton, Sir George Simpson (Portland, 1944), 41, 159, 165, 283.

and who spoke in glowing terms of the hospitality of Francis Ermatinger and Courtney Walker.

Walker retired from the service of the Hudson's Bay Company in the summer of 1840, when he and Joe Meek, Caleb Wilkins, and others, quit the mountains to go to the Columbia River region to settle down with their families.[10]

Walker returned to Sauve (Wappatoo) Island, salvaged what supplies he could find at the old fort, and then moved over near his friend Tom McKay, near Scappoose, Oregon. His friends had begun to build a ship, and Walker did all he could to help this project. When Lieutenant Wilkes, of the United States Naval Squadron, gave Joseph Gale the necessary sea papers, Walker bought Gale's farm and equipment on the East Tualatin Plains in 1841.

On November 1, Walker and George LeBreton leased the then-deceased Ewing Young's estate, and by 1844 Courtney showed 150 horses and 240 cattle on the tax book records.

From 1841 to 1849 Courtney Walker moved about a good bit, surveying land, buying land, and farming. He took part in shaping the provisional government, and was elected chief clerk of the territorial government in 1849. He served under Major Kearny, Governor Gaines, and Joseph Lane in suppressing the Rogue River Indian uprising against the settlers and gold miners in southern Oregon in 1851. He ran unsuccessfully for several offices, taught school for a short while at Dundee, but was ousted by the sanctimonious "click" then in power at Salem.[11]

Courtney and Margaret Walker had six children: Jacob, Helen, Dougall, John, Rachel, and Nancy. Except for their

---

[10] Extracts of letters, Hudson's Bay Company; and Bancroft's *History of Oregon,* vol. 2.

[11] From records at the Oregon Historical Society, Portland, Oregon. He was charged with drinking.

daughter Helen, who married John Cummins, a legislator and lawyer, and moved to Washington, D.C., nothing is known of their descendants. In the early part of the 1870s, Courtney Walker moved to Tillamook County alone and bought William Squires' place on the Trask River.

He later took up his homestead near Blaine, Oregon. There he spent the remaining years of his life, in the mountains with his mare "Nelly," who once almost drowned in the rapids of the Nestucca River, but floated downstream and was brought home the next day by a neighbor.

Walker wrote several sketches of the men of early Oregon, including Ewing Young and John McLoughlin, and he sent numerous letters to his niece in Texas, which correspondence this writer has discovered in her research.

Sometime in the year 1887, Courtney Walker became ill and walked to his neighbors, the Hugheys, who put him to bed. There he died. His friends buried him on the hillside behind their house. He lies there in an unmarked grave, close to the sunset of the Far West.

Seth E. Ward

by MERRILL J. MATTES
National Park Service, Omaha, Nebraska

The life of Seth Edmund Ward, 1820-1903, spans the era of historic upsurge of the trans-Mississippi frontier. When he was born, William Ashley was poised for his many-pronged invasion of the unknown West. When he died, the "geography gap" was closed, the Indians subdued, the West settled, the United States embarked on a career as a world power. During his eighty-three full years, Ward was successively a runaway apprentice, a Rocky Mountain trapper, an Indian trader, post sutler at Fort Laramie, merchandising magnate of Nebraska City, and a patriarch of Westport (Kansas City, Missouri). He was a citizen of sufficient prosperity and influence to be memorialized today in Kansas City by one of the most stately thoroughfares in one of the most resplendent residential areas – Ward Parkway.*

By monumental energy, personal integrity and a knack for capitalizing on the lucky chance, Seth Ward became a Horatio Alger of the fur trade, rising from penniless boy trapper to the status of a merchant prince. Along the way he trapped with Jim Bridger, Thomas Fitzpatrick, Joe Meek and Kit Carson; crossed pathways with William Bent, Captain Fremont and Father DeSmet; and served as both creditor and confidante to a whole generation of soldiers and Indians, emigrants and freighters. His rise was not as meteoric as Ashley's, and he did not quite achieve the stature of his best friend, Robert Campbell; but he is the classic example of the rare Mountain Man who achieved both wealth and beneficent old age.

---

* A portrait of Ward appears in this volume at page 19.

Despite his story-book career, Seth Ward has remained obscure and enigmatic. Unlike Bridger, Carson and Ashley, he had no biographer. He appeared on the scene just a trifle late to get in on the golden age of the mountain fur trade, and he did not manage to get himself involved in any lurid publicity. By the standards of his time he was a man of high moral principles, avoiding violence, quietly concentrating on becoming one of the frontier's first millionaires. He kept no journal, and few of his papers have been preserved. Even after he retired from the frontier to become the dignified country squire of Westport he managed to remain in the background, politically. His descendants in the Kansas City area have no illuminating family tradition or documents. Most of what we know of him survives in scattered references in other journals; Missouri's Jackson County archives; official records of the War Department and the Indian Bureau, plus one small batch of Ward-Bullock commercial correspondence; and his own limited reminiscences, repeated, with only minor variations, in Missouri contemporary newspapers and hack biographies.[1]

Seth E. Ward was born on March 4, 1820, in Campbell County, Virginia. The given name of his father, Seth, was borne by the oldest sons of five generations of the Ward family, the earliest Seth Ward appearing as a Bishop of the Church of England. His parents were married in 1818, the mother, Ann Hendrick, being a descendant of John Goode of Virginia Colony. Of their four children Seth E. was the only son. In 1832 his father died, leaving only meager resources, so at age twelve Seth was left pretty much on his own, equipped only with the paltry education the common rural schools of that day afforded. At fourteen he was placed by his grandfather with a Mr. Jacob Haas of La Porte, Indiana, "for the express purpose of having him

---

[1] The present article is the first known effort to make an exhaustive scholarly documented study of Seth E. Ward.

trained to labor," presumably in the pursuit of agriculture. This kind of a career held no charms for the future tycoon of Westport, and within two years he hiked back to his home in Greencastle, Virginia. Thereupon his mother endowed him with twenty-five dollars and her blessing, and for three years "he wandered through Kentucky, Missouri and Illinois without settling himself to any specific business." [2]

In 1836 he found himself in St. Louis, bustling gateway of the frontier West, and the hand of destiny was upon him. According to one account, he served here as a clerk in a tobacco factory.[3]

In the spring of 1838 he traveled by steamboat to Lexington, which was as far as his funds would carry him. Here the Seth Ward magic – doubtless compounded of a little bit of luck and a large measure of personal charm – first comes into focus. As he told his interviewers, "his money being expended, a stranger divided his purse of eighteen dollars with him." With these proceeds, Seth journeyed on to Independence, expending $4.50 for stage fare and a like amount for his first week's bed and board in this historic jumping-off point for Santa Fe. This left him "again without money." At this point another kindly stranger appeared providentially, this time identified as a Mr. Wilson Roberts, who became surety for his keep until he could find employment. Shortly thereafter he ran into Captain Lancaster P. Lupton, army officer turned fur trader, bound for the Rocky Mountain West.

On July 12, 1838 the Lupton train left Independence. Ward, the youngest and greenest member of the crew, was equipped only with "butcher knife, belt and scabbard, a checked shirt and a hat," and it was his lot to tramp along to

2 *U.S. Biographical Dictionary – Missouri* (1879), 466; *Memorial and Biographical Record of Kansas City and Jackson County, Missouri* (Chicago, 1896), 567-70; *Encyclopedia of the History of Missouri,* (New York, 1901), VI, pp. 372-73.

3 *Memorial and Biographical Record.*

the rear, herding loose stock. In his halcyon days Ward was fond of recalling that his first night out of Independence he slept without any covering, in the tall prairie grass. The next day he purchased a pair of blankets from Captain Lupton for thirty dollars credit, and that night he slept royally, near the site of his future luxurious home, where the Santa Fe Trail out of Missouri intersects the Kansas border. By performing extra night guard duty for pay the young capitalist was well launched.[4]

The Lupton train went to "Fort Lancaster" (Lupton) on the South Fork of the Platte, north of present Denver.[5] Ward soon left Captain Lupton to take service with the fur company of Thompson and Craig, with headquarters at Fort Davy Crockett in Brown's Hole.[6] This was on the left bank of Green River, above the mouth of Vermillion Creek, in the extreme northwestern corner of Colorado.[7] In 1839 this was described by Oregon-bound Thomas Farnham of Peoria, Illinois, as "a hollow square of one story log cabins, with roofs and floors of mud." [8] Another traveler of that year, Dr. F. A. Wizlizenus of St. Louis, described it as a "low one-story building, constructed of wood and clay, with three connecting wings, and no enclosure." He labeled it "the worst thing of the kind that we have seen on our journey." [9]

In any event this was Seth Ward's base of operations for at least three years, 1838-1840. According to one account,

[4] *U.S. Biographical Dictionary, op. cit.*

[5] "A Trapper's Tale," special correspondence of the St. Louis *Globe-Democrat,* Nov. 4, 1888.

[6] See LeRoy R. Hafen, "Fort Davy Crockett: Its Fur Men and Visitors," in *Colorado Magazine,* XXIX (Jan. 1952), 17-33. Hafen identifies Sinclair as a third member of the outfit.

[7] John C. Fremont, *Report of the Exploring Expedition to the Rocky Mountains* (Washington, 1845), 279-80. This site has never been identified archaeologically. See this *Series,* II, p. 101.

[8] T. J. Farnham, *Travels,* in R. G. Thwaites (ed.), *Early Western Travels,* XXVIII, pp. 252-53.

[9] F. A. Wislizenus, *A Journey to the Rocky Mountains* (St. Louis, 1912), 129.

Ward was "made a clerk in the trading house of Thompson and Company at Brown's Hole, at a salary of $25 per month." [10] The only concrete glimpse we have of a "Ward" in the Colorado mountains during this period appears in the journals of Obadiah Oakley and Sidney Smith, of the 1839 Farnham party. It was on August 2, 1839, in the Upper Bear or Yampa valley, near Steamboat Springs, that the Peorians encountered a band of trappers under Captain Craig, enroute to the South Fork of the Platte to meet Thompson with trade goods. Both of these journals identify two men – Burroughs and Ward – accompanied by a squaw who was skilled at making "Mogasons." [11]

In the spring of 1839, according to himself, Seth Ward

went on a trapping expedition into the Navajo and Digger Indian country as camp keeper, but the enterprise was not successful. Many of their horses were shot by Indians and one of the trappers, Dick Owens, was badly wounded in the knee. On foot, in an almost starved condition, and carrying their comrade on a rude litter, they started for the settlements. Overtaking a poor donkey that had been left by a Spaniard, the animal was killed and his flesh eaten with relish; finally after many privations, they reached Taos. . .[12]

Kit Carson was among his early associates, beginning on this trip to the Navajoes. According to tradition,

The acquaintance between Carson and Ward soon ripened into a strong friendship, each recognizing the traits of manhood in the other. Mr. Ward's first horse was a present to him from Carson, who had won it upon a wager with Philip Thompson, an old mountaineer, who maintained that no greenhorn . . . could bring down a buffalo at first dash. Ward accomplished the feat, but his horse coming in collision with the wounded buffalo he was thrown heavily to the ground and carried to camp in an unconscious condition.[13]

---

10 *U.S. Biographical Dictionary, op. cit.*

11 LeRoy R. Hafen and Ann W. Hafen, eds., *To the Rockies and Oregon in 1839-1842 (Far West and Rockies Series,* III; Glendale, 1955), 57, 76. Although there was a Barney Ward in the mountains also at this time, it was Seth Ward who joined Craig and Thompson.

12 *U.S. Biographical Dictionary, op. cit.*   13 *Ibid.*

Seth Ward's first seven years on the frontier were passed largely in intercourse with Indian tribes, extending from the Red River on the south to the upper waters of the Columbia and Yellowstone on the north.[14] In his 1888 interview, Ward reminisced freely about Indians, their upright character before corruption by whites, their firearms, method of hunting buffalo, sign language, marriage customs, and treatment of prisoners. He also descanted authoritatively on the thriftlessness of the mountaineers, their methods of entrapping beaver, and the pet beaver at Bent's Fort which fell into a vat of molasses.[15]

We know little of Seth Ward's actual movements during this period. In 1843 Theodore Talbot, with Fitzpatrick on the Fremont expedition, identified a "Mr. Ward" as chief trader at Fort St. Vrain, an adobe post of the usual quadrangular design on the South Platte.[16] That this was indeed Seth Ward (instead of some other Ward) seems supported by the fact that Seth was definitely associated with Colonel St. Vrain in 1845 and subsequently in the Arkansas trade. In 1844 Solomon Sublette reported from Fort Lupton that he hunted bighorn sheep with "M. St. Vrain, Ward and Shavano." [17]

John Hunton, a trusted employee of Seth Ward in later years at Fort Laramie, says that Ward frequented "the Narrows," twenty miles east of Fort Laramie, as early as 1836, an obvious error as to date. However, he continues,

[14] Alexander Majors, *Seventy Years on the Frontier* (Chicago, 1893), 119-20. Majors and Ward were contemporary residents of Nebraska City.

[15] "A Trapper's Tale," *loc. cit.*

[16] Charles H. Carey, ed., *Journals of Theodore Talbot, 1843* (Portland, 1931), 23; LeRoy R. Hafen, "Fort St. Vrain," in *Colorado Magazine,* XXIX (Oct. 1952), 241-255. This fort was on the right bank of the South Platte, six miles northwest of present Platteville, Colorado.

[17] Letter of June 6, 1844, S. P. Sublette to brother Andrew, in Sublette Papers, Missouri Historical Society. "Shavano" is believed to be Charbonneau, of the Lewis and Clark Expedition.

"in 1844 while Mr. Ward was still at the Narrows with his employer, they accumulated a great many more furs than they expected at that place and did not have enough ponies to move them over to the Platte, so Ward and two Indians were sent to Fort Lupton to get others," camping with Crow Indians on the site of future Cheyenne, and being trapped in a fierce blizzard that left the plains littered with dead buffalo.[18]

In 1845 Ward turned up in St. Louis

in company with Colonel St. Vrain, a former employer . . . who there paid him his first $1,000. Colonel St. Vrain had come to St. Louis for the purpose of purchasing goods to load a train which he was about to start from Westport Landing for the southwest. Mr. Ward was employed by the Colonel to accompany the train with the privilege of shipping as many goods as his capital would purchase. With one wagon loaded with goods, drawn by two yoke of cattle, he took his first place in the train, and committed his venture to the fortunes of the trade. His goods arrived in safety and were profitably exchanged for horses and mules, which he sold to the United States Government, then (1846) at war with Mexico. . . In 1847 he made a trip into the Indian country, purchasing his goods of Boone & Hamilton, Westport, which were loaded in one large wagon drawn by five yoke of cattle, and were all sold at the Arkansas River to good advantage. Returning to Westport in 1848 he formed a partnership with William Le Guerrier in the Indian trade, each of them having about $1,500 in cash. From purchases made of Boone & Hamilton on ten months credit, they loaded five large wagons and made a very successful expedition, securing six thousand buffalo robes, with which they returned to Westport, May, 1849. From this point the robes were shipped to New York, Mr. Ward going East to attend to their sale in person, disposing of them at a very good profit. . . He next purchased from Grant & Barton goods to the amount of $10,000, which he shipped to Westport; Boone & Bernard furnished the outfit, and the results were once more highly satisfactory. In 1850 he began purchasing goods of Robert Campbell, St. Louis . . . with whom he continued to trade until Mr. Campbell retired from business.[19]

[18] John Hunton, "Seth Edmund Ward," *2nd Biennial Report* of the State Historical Department of Wyoming, 1922, pp. 99-100.
[19] *U.S. Biographical Dictionary, op. cit.*

Aside from the above autobiographical data, references to Ward in the Arkansas trade are scarce. In his journal of September 13, 1846, while camped on the Purgatoire River, Lieutenant Abert of the U.S. Army noted that, "Mr. Ward who had gone to Santa Fe and who promised to be at the fort [Bent's] some time since, had not arrived." [20] Thomas Forsyth's journal of 1849 refers to Ward with Fitzpatrick on the Arkansas. [21]

Thus, during the climax years of the California Gold Rush, 1849-1850, the partners seemed to have remained in the Southwest. However, the heavy traffic up the Platte River could not be ignored. The first indication we have of Ward and Guerrier again operating in the Platte Valley is in a letter of May 5, 1851, from the Fort Laramie sutler: "Ward and Guerrier have bought and moved to Ash Point." [22] This was a trading post twenty miles east of Fort Laramie (apparently synonymous with "the Narrows," in the vicinity of Torrington, Wyoming) which in 1850 had been managed by John Richard of the American Fur Company. [23] Thus it may be safely assumed that Ward and Guerrier were among those present at the great assembly of northern Plains tribes at Horse Creek near Scott's Bluff, in September, 1851. Engineered by Tom Fitzpatrick and Father DeSmet, this was the first Fort Laramie Treaty Council. [24]

For reasons not specified, in 1852 these partners removed to Sand Point (the Register Cliff of Oregon Trail fame, near present Guernsey, Wyoming), nine miles west of Fort

---

[20] Lieutenant Abert's journal of 1846, p. 437, *Abert's New Mexico Report, 1846-47* (Albuquerque, 1962), 31.

[21] John R. Forsyth, "Overland Journal of 1849," MS., Peoria, Illinois, Public Library.

[22] John S. Tutt to John Dougherty, Dougherty Papers, Missouri Historical Society.

[23] Howard Stansbury, *Exploration and Survey of the Valley of the Great Salt Lake* (Philadelphia, 1852), 288.

[24] LeRoy R. Hafen and Francis M. Young, *Fort Laramie and the Pageant of the West* (Glendale, 1938), 177-96.

Laramie. This date seems valid, since there is no reference to such a post in the hundreds of overland journals prior to that date. And on September 27, 1852, the wife of Benjamin G. Ferris, U.S. official bound for Utah, says that her mule-drawn party recruited for a day at "Ward and Garay's Station" seven miles west of Fort Laramie. She describes it thus: "We are now encamped directly on the bank of the river, under two fine trees. The station, about a mile below, is in a handsome bend of the stream, and consists of two or three log buildings, with a large one of stone, about half erected." [25]

The enterprise of Ward and Guerrier (often spelled Guerrieu or Guarriou) is reflected in the Tutt-Dougherty correspondence of 1852. They contracted with Tutt to transport four hundred packs of furs to the settlements. They traded with the Kiowas and Comanches, obtaining valuable mules (probably stolen from Santa Fe traders). With Joseph Bissonette they went into the then flourishing "boat business," which means that they may have operated one of the several North Platte ferries. [26]

In 1851, by agreement with the army, John Richard and others had built the first bridge across the Laramie River, charging up to three dollars per wagon. It was poorly constructed, and vanished in the spring rise of 1853. In July of that year Richard Garnett, post commander, recommended that "two responsible men," Ward and Guerrier, be permitted "to build a substantial bridge . . . and charge the same rate of toll as the old company." [27] Accordingly,

---

25 Mrs. Benjamin G. Ferris, *The Mormons at Home* (New York, 1856), 62-63. Sand Point station is marked by a stone monument about one-fourth mile west of Register Cliff. The site is authentic, according to Paul Henderson, Field Historian, Wyoming State Parks Commission, but is jeopardized by new road construction. Its stated distance from Fort Laramie varies from seven to ten miles, depending on whether the traveler took the "river road" or the upland branch of the Oregon Trail.

26 Letter of April 14, 1852, John S. Tutt to Major John Dougherty, Dougherty Papers, Missouri Historical Society.

in the autumn of 1853, the two partners erected such a bridge, which apparently survived heavy use and spring floods for many years.[28]

Another sideline of Ward and Guerrier was the cattle business. Because of their operations in this field, a case can be made that their layout at Sand Point was the first cattle ranch in the state of Wyoming. This got started with the practice of trading oxen with the covered wagon emigrants, usually on the basis of one good oxen for two or more lame ones. Alexander Majors credits Seth Ward, "partner of Campbell," with wintering the first large work herd in the sheltered valley of the Chugwater in 1852. His example inspired others, and the Wyoming cattle industry was born.[29]

It is known that in 1853 the Ward and Guerrier post was also a station on the pioneer mail route to Salt Lake City. The operator of this line, J. M. Hockaday, speaks of keeping a relay of mules here. In December, 1853, he bought a span of mules of S. E. Ward, only to have them stolen by Indians at Ash Hollow; whereupon he petitioned Ward to recover them from his Indian relatives! [30]

We do not know the exact year that Seth E. Ward fell in

[27] Merrill J. Mattes and Thor Borresen, "Historic Approaches to Fort Laramie," National Park Service, MS.; Letter of July 24, 1853, Lt. R. B. Garnett to Col. S. Cooper, Records of Adjutant General's Office, National Archives.

[28] Mattes and Borresen, op. cit.; excerpt from the Missouri Republican, Nov. 21, 1853, in Publications of the Nebraska State Historical Society, XX, p. 253; Letter of Mar. 5, 1860, Henry F. Mayer, Wyoming Historical Society.

[29] Virginia C. Trenholm, Footprints of the Frontier (Douglas, 1954), 126. Trenholm credits W. G. Bullock and B. B. Mills, employees of Ward, with establishing "the first permanent range herd in Wyoming" in 1868, grazing them "about six miles from Fort Laramie, where they remained for about two years in spite of numerous Indian raids." John Bratt, Trails of Yesterday, 118, says that in 1867 "I drove steers [from Fort Mitchell] to Fort Laramie, and later turned them over to Ben Miles [sic], Seth Bullock's [sic] clerk." See fn. 54. In 1884 Bill Reid, famous stage driver and wagon master, established a cattle ranch at Ward's old station: "Reminiscences of Sarah Picknell Reid," in The Pony Express, Sept. 1949.

[30] Letter of October 29, 1855, Hockaday to Smoot; letter of June 12, 1856, Hockaday to Mannypenny, Commissioner of Indian Affairs; Records of Upper Platte Agency, National Archives.

with the frontier custom and married a native girl. We know that it was before September, 1853, since the account books of John S. Parker of Westport show medical attention to S. Ward and family beginning at that time.[31] It seems probable that this alliance with the Sioux took place some years before that date, perhaps during the first trading episode on the Platte in the mid-forties, since his half-breed son, Seth Ward, was himself married in 1866. According to James Bordeaux's daughter, Susan Bettelyoun, the Indian bride of Seth E. Ward was "a beautiful woman, Wasna of the Wajai band of Brules, given him by her brothers." She bore Ward four children, but died young of tuberculosis.[32]

The existence of an Indian family is confirmed by Edison G. Ward of Martin, South Dakota, great-grandson of Seth E., and grandson of half-breed son Seth. The latter, the only one of the four offspring identified, on October 15, 1866, married Elizabeth Gerry, daughter of a South Platte trader and granddaughter of the Elbridge Gerry who was a signer of the Declaration of Independence and a vice-president of the United States.[33]

The most significant event of the 1850s was the so-called

---

31 John S. Parker, MS., Kansas City Public Library.

32 Susan Bordeau Bettelyoun, MS., Nebraska State Historical Society; Letter of Dec. 27, 1952, Mari Sandoz to LeRoy R. Hafen, based on "the story as I heard it told by Old Provo to my father." One variant of the story is that Wasna had an Indian sweetheart and deserted Ward, who was "furious that she deserted her children, swore he would get her back," etc.

33 "To this union three children were born, Martha, my father Elbridge Gerry Ward, and Mamie. My father was born May 28, 1869 . . . passed away in March of 1950. I am the first born, the next, Vincent died as an infant, Irene, Genevieve, Eileen, Woodrow, and Gerald, all living. I was born May 23, 1907." (Letter of Aug. 31, 1965, Edison G. Ward to Merrill J. Mattes.) The Seth Ward who appears on an 1867 list of petitioners, "all heads or members of Indian families" who request the Congress and the Commission of Indian Affairs for a grant of 320 acres each in South Dakota, is thus established as the son of Seth E. (Affidavit, dated at Fort Laramie Nov. 16, 1867, Records of Upper Platte Agency.) According to an interview with Elizabeth Doten of Greeley, Colorado (LeRoy R. Hafen files), son Seth died at Evans, Colorado in 1871. After the death of grandson Elbridge G. Ward, great-grandson Edison presented to the Colorado Historical Society two ancestral documents and the gold band ring of 1866.

Grattan Massacre, wherein Lieutenant Grattan with twenty-eight enlisted men and a drunken interpreter from Fort Laramie foolishly attempted to arrest an Indian who had allegedly stolen a Mormon's cow; the lieutenant and his entire command were annihilated by Sioux bands waiting for Indian Agent Whitfield to arrive and distribute annuity goods. This was at a point eight miles east of the fort. Although the Sioux subsequently rampaged around the nearby posts of Bordeau and Gratiot, there is no evidence that they molested Ward's.[34] However, in 1855, after his victory over Little Thunder's band at Ash Hollow, General Harney of the Sioux Expedition ordered all Indian traders into the fort.[35] In consequence, we find on Lieutenant Kelton's map of Fort Laramie of 1856 a new "Ward and Guerrier's trading post" on the right bank of the Laramie River, directly opposite the ruins of Fort John (the adobe Fort Laramie of the American Fur Company).[36]

After the Grattan Massacre and the Harney reprisal, the system of distributing Indian annuities in the Upper Platte Agency was resumed, and the Ward establishment was a prime beneficiary. An inventory of March, 1856, receipted by Joseph Bisonette, shows a government order on Ward and Guerrier for copious provisions, including coffee, sugar, flour, white blankets, red flannel shirts, scarlet cloth, knives and "Japan kettles." [37] Through their recurrent trade li-

---

[34] Hafen and Young, *op. cit.,* 221-45; Lloyd E. McCann, "The Grattan Massacre," in *Nebraska History,* vol. 37 (Mar. 1956), 1-25; an affidavit of July 10, 1854, in the Hunton Collection, Wyoming Historical Society, attests to the fact that Lieutenant Grattan owed Seth Ward $500, secured by five fellow officers.

[35] Letter of May 9, 1857, Ward to James W. Denver, Commissioner of Indian Affairs.

[36] Lt. J. C. Kelton, "Plot of Fort Laramie," Map in Cartographic Section, National Archives. The date is not given but may be deduced from the structural record documented in Merrill J. Mattes, "Evolution of Buildings at Fort Laramie," National Park Service MS. Other trading posts in evidence in the immediate vicinity of the fort are those of "Beauvais" and "Bissonett."

[37] Affidavit of Mar. 28, 1856, by Joseph Bisonette, Records of the Upper Platte Agency.

censes the traders were then able to retrieve some of these articles. One such license to "William Guernier" authorized trade with Sioux, Cheyenne and Arapahoe at Raw Hide Creek, at White River, at Upper Platte Bridge and at the Cache la Poudre – a territory embracing much of Colorado, Wyoming and South Dakota.[38]

However, while Indian warfare subsided, a squabble broke out in 1856 between Indian agent Thomas Twiss and the squawman traders. Twiss considered Seth E. Ward one of the chief trouble-makers, allegedly violating the Intercourse Law and "exciting the Indians against themselves." He pronounced Ward an improper and unfit person and suspended his trading license. Thereupon Ward charged Twiss with malfeasance of office. Colonel Hoffman, the Fort Laramie commander, showed the normal military distrust of civilian Indian agents and, siding with Ward, ordered Twiss stripped of his powers, but this was rescinded upon appeal to the Commissioner of Indian Affairs.[39] The feud between Twiss and Ward was apparently settled by November 1857, for on that date he issued Seth E. Ward a license to trade "within the boundaries of Upper Platte Agency," citing there "especial trust and confidence in the patriotism, humanity and correct business habits of the said applicant."[40]

In 1857 Seth Ward became the dominant figure in the Platte Valley trade by gaining the coveted post sutlership at Fort Laramie, the principal white settlement between the Missouri River and Salt Lake City. That he enjoyed the confidence of the army officers is evidenced by the fact that

---

38 Affidavit by Twiss, Dec. 20, 1856, Records of Upper Platte Agency.

39 Letter of Jan. 12, 1856, Twiss to Cuming; Letter of May 19, Cuming to Manypenny; Letter of May 24, Twiss to Mannypenny; Letter of Feb. 19, 1857, Twiss to Colonel Hoffman; Letter of Feb. 1, 1857, Twiss to CIA; Records of Upper Platte Agency.

40 *Annals of Wyoming,* vol. 5, no. 1. The license was approved by Charles E. Mix, Acting Commissioner of Indian Affairs, Jan. 13, 1858.

in March the post council of administration "elected" or
rather nominated him to a three-year term as sutler vice
John S. Tutt.[41] His first three-year term was proclaimed on
April 30, 1857, by John B. Floyd, Secretary of War.[42] That
Seth Ward was able to retire at age fifty-two a millionaire
is due in large measure to the fact that, while enjoying the
monopoly of a sutlership at the busiest post on the frontier,
he continued also to operate as a licensed trader with the
biggest buffalo-hunting tribe on the plains.

Several 1857 documents are revealing. On March 19
Tutt and Lewis B. Dougherty sold their entirestock to
Ward for $3,000, with Robert Campbell as surety.[43] In
May there was talk of abandoning the fort, and Ward wrote
an impassioned letter to James W. Denver, Commissioner
of Indian Affairs, requesting permission to remain in the
Indian country to trade off his merchandise to "avoid injury." Because of the threatened abandonment also, the
garrison went unpaid for months, and Major Hoffman
commended Ward: "Were it not for the charity of the sutler
many soldiers would suffer."[44] However, the idea of abandonment was soon dropped when in the summer the Cheyennes went on a rampage, and the Mormons threatened
rebellion. Fort Laramie now became a focal point of major
campaigns and the mecca for the long freight trains of
Russell, Majors and Waddell.[45] The rising star of Ward's

[41] Letter of Mar. 4, 1857, Colonel Hoffman to Adjutant General, National
Archives.
[42] Appointment registered by Adjutant General S. Cooper. Reproduced in *Annals
of Wyoming,* vol. 13, no. 4 (Oct. 1941), 317. The early biographical sketches published in Missouri erroneously identify Jefferson Davis as the Secretary of War
who appointed Ward.
[43] *Annals of Wyoming,* v, no. 1 (1927).
[44] Ward to Denver, *ibid.;* Letter of Mar. 4, 1857, Major Hoffman to Adjutant
General, War Records, National Archives.
[45] On June 23, at Fort Laramie, Quartermaster Sergeant Percival G. Lowe notes:
"Everybody getting ready for the Cheyenne campaign. This is the last chance for
any sort of outfit until it is over. Mr. Seth E. Ward, the sutler here, has a good
stock of campaign goods." *Five Years a Dragoon* (Kansas City, 1906), 253.

prosperity was evidenced by Kansas City newspaper notices that August:

> The Fort Laramie trains arrived the present week, with 12,000 buffalo robes, besides furs, peltries, etc. The trains belonged to Messrs. Ward & Geary, extensive traders in the mountains, and filled the streets lead-into town. . . The wagons looked like immense elephants, being filled high above the beds and tightly covered with tarpoulins. This is the richest received at any one time the present season.[46]

While Ward played the genteel proprietor in the adobe sutler's store at Fort Laramie, William Guerrier conducted the profitable Indian trade, assisted by B. B. Mills, Antoine Janis and others.[47] The famous partnership came to an abrupt end on February 16, 1858. On that date Guerrier was blown up when sparks from his pipe ignited a powder keg at a trading camp on the Niobrara River near present Lusk, Wyoming.[48] Thereafter it appears that Mills and Janis managed the Indian trade, with headquarters at Ward's old location at Sand Point.[49] This post must have required extensive rehabilitation, for in 1857 Ward had complained to Commissioner Denver about Harney's order requiring the abandonment of this post, "on which he had expended between six and seven thousand dollars and which has since been reduced to ruin by the necessities of imigrants who used them for fuel." [50] In 1860 Richard Burton, riding with the mail wagon, reported a change of mules "at Ward's Station, alias the Central Star." [51] In 1861 this became the

---

[46] *Missouri Republican,* Aug. 5, 1857, reprinted in the *Kansas City Enterprise,* n.d.

[47] J. Aymond and Chas. Gurue are also listed as traders with Guerrier.

[48] *The Goshen News and Fort Laramie Scout,* Sept. 1, 1927. The story is based on recollections of John Hunton. Guerrier had a Cheyenne wife while on the Arkansas. His son, Ed Guerrier, married Julia Bent, daughter of William Bent and Yellow Woman, according to Dwight Stinson, Historian, Bent's Old Fort National Historic Site.

[49] The Ward-Guerrier trading post on Laramie River, opposite the fort, was short-lived. It is not in evidence in post ground-plans of the 1860s. The National Park Service has identified the site archaeologically.

[50] Ward to Denver, *ibid.*

[51] Richard Burton, *City of the Saints* (London, 1861), 113, 612. According to *Wyoming, A Guide (American Guide Series)* (New York, 1941), 295, "near the

first Pony Express station west of Fort Laramie.

Ward made semi-annual trips to Westport, primarily for supplies, but also to court a comely young widow, Mrs. Mary Frances McCarty, daughter of Colonel Harris, proprietor of Westport's leading hotel. On February 2, 1860, they were married in Westport, despite strong objections by the bride's mother who understood, correctly, that Ward already had an Indian family.[52] The marriage, destined to last a lifetime, was further jeopardized when Ward took his bride to Fort Laramie. The refined Westport belle was unhappy in this primitive and dangerous environment; accordingly, in 1863, Seth Ward moved his home to the steamboat town of Nebraska City, where he could coordinate overland freight shipments.[53]

In 1858 Ward had hired William G. Bullock of St. Louis as his general manager; and, while Ward made frequent and extended visits to Fort Laramie after 1863, from this time onward Bullock became the more visible factotum of the sutler's store.[54] Like Ward he was the lordly executive type, with flashing diamonds, looked upon with awe by the clientele of soldiers, Indians, emigrants, bull-whackers and assorted renegades. They were an impressive pair. In 1864 Captain Eugene Ware of the 7th Iowa Cavalry observed

[Register] Cliff, Jules E. Coffey [Ecoffey] operated a stage station in the 1850's. For many years a remnant of the stage station marked the site." It seems probable that Ecoffey was a Ward employee; there is no evidence of a rival post or station at this place.

[52] Edward R. Schauffler, "Old Seth Ward Home," in *Kansas City Star,* May 2, 1848, based on interview with Frank C. Wornall.

[53] *Memorial and Biographical Record.* Mrs. Ward probably returned to Westport in 1861 to have her first child. According to *ibid.,* the Wards lived in Westport, 1861-1862.

[54] William G. Bullock's story is briefly told by Agnes Wright Spring, "Old Letter Book," in *Annals of Wyoming,* vol. 13, no. 4 (Oct. 1941), 242. A man named Seth Bullock figured prominently in the Black Hills Gold Rush and is sometimes confused with the partners, Seth Ward and William Bullock. For an accurate portrayal of Seth Bullock see Harry Anderson, ed., "An Account of Deadwood in 1876," in *South Dakota Historical Collections,* XXXI, pp. 287-364.

(above) SUTLER'S STORE (RESTORED) AT
FORT LARAMIE NATIONAL HISTORIC SITE
Photo by Robert Murray, 1964.

(left) FORT LARAMIE TRADE TOKEN,
ISSUED BY SETH E. WARD
Stamped on one side only. Courtesy of Robert Murray,
Fort Laramie National Historic Site.

(below) SITE OF THE SETH WARD
TRADING POST AND STAGE STATION
Register Cliff or "Sand Point" in the background.
Photo by Merrill J. Mattes, 1965.

THE OLD SETH WARD HOME IN KANSAS CITY, MISSOURI
Photo by Ray H. Mattison, 1956.

that while Ward gave no personal attention to the store, "he was making a great deal of money out of it." He thought Bullock "the most courteous old-school gentleman I ever saw. He was dignified as a major-general," whose specialty was whisky toddies that "none might hope to equal." [55]

In 1866 young Julius Birge, bound for Montana gold fields, writes that he approached "the pompous Mr. Ward who we were told was the sutler. He wore fine clothes, and a soft easy hat. A huge diamond glittered in his shirt front. He moved quietly around as if he were master of the situation." [56] At the same time treaty negotiations were going forward at the fort, and the place swarmed with Indians. The colorful scene is vividly described by Margaret Carrington, wife of the ill-fated commander of the 18th U.S. Regiment of Infantry:

> The long counter of Messrs. Bullock and Ward was a scene of seeming confusion not surpassed in any popular, overcrowded store of Omaha itself. Indians, dressed and half dressed and undressed; squaws, dressed to the same degree of completeness as their noble lords; papooses, obsolutely nude, slightly not nude, or wrapped in calico, buckskin, or furs, mingled with soldiers of the garrison, teamsters, emigrants, speculators, half-breeds, and interpreters. HERE, cups of rice, sugar, coffee, or flour were being emptied into the looped-up skirts or blankets of a squaw; and THERE, some tall warrior was grimacing delightfully as he grasped and sucked his long sticks of peppermint candy. Bright shawls, red squaw cloth, brilliant calicoes, and flashing ribbons passed over the same counter with knives and tobacco, brass nails and glass beads, and that endless catalogue of articles which belong to the legitimate border traffic. The room was redolent of cheese and herring, and "heap of smoke;" while the debris of mounched crackers lying loose under foot furnished both nutriment and employment for little bits of Indians too big to ride on mamma's back, and too little to reach the good things on counter or shelves. [57]

A. B. Ostrander, an enlisted man of this regiment, gives

[55] Eugene F. Ware, *The Indian War of 1864* (Topeka, 1911), 274.
[56] Julius Birge, *The Awakening of the Desert* (Boston, 1912), 178-79.
[57] Margaret Carrington, *Ab-Sa-Ra-Ka* (Philadelphia, 1869), 76-77.

another sidelight on Ward's emporium as a latter-day fur trappers' rendezvous: "I spent hours in the store of the post trader, Col. Bullock, listening to the conversation and stories told by the mountain men. They all made Col. Bullock's store their headquarters. Old Nick Janis seemed to be the leading spirit." [58] Another old Mountain Man who haunted Seth Ward's store was the aging Jim Bridger. After helping to pilot the Carrington expedition up the Bozeman Trail to its fatal rendezvous with Red Cloud's warriors, Bridger retired to the fort to recuperate. John Hunton says that he "became acquainted with Jim Bridger in October, 1867," and that, "until April, 1868, Bridger occupied a bunk in the same room in the sutler's store with himself and other employees." [59]

In 1860 Indian Agent Twiss was replaced by J. A. Cody, who extolled Ward for loaning him storage space for annuity goods. [60] However, Cody and his successors continued to be thorns in Ward's side, since his dual function as sutler and Indian trader conflicted with the Indian Office policy of persuading the Sioux and Cheyennes to keep away from Fort Laramie. Among alleged evils confronting the tribesmen here were slothfulness, intoxication, and the availability of squaws to soldiers. There was a considerable quarrel in 1863-64, while Colonel Collins of the 11th Ohio Cavalry was in command, between Ward and Indian Agent John Loree. In addition to the above indictments, Loree complained that condemned military provisions found their way into the hands of the sutler and were then sold to the Indians at extortionate rates; and that, in any event, it was improper for a post sutler who was guaranteed all the busi-

---

[58] Alson B. Ostrander, *An Army Boy of the Sixties* (New York, 1924), 102, 227.

[59] J. Cecil Alter, *James Bridger* (Salt Lake City, 1925), 471.

[60] Letter of Dec. 18, 1861, J. A. Cody to Commissioner of Indian Affairs, Records of Upper Platte Agency.

ness around the post, to be licensed to trade also in the surrounding territory. The most serious charge was that Ward
was the receiver of money that the Indians had obtained by
murder and robbery of the U.S. mails.[61]

Ward countered all this with charges that Loree was un-
ethically lining his own pockets from the Indian trade, by
issuing licenses to "certain friends and former schoolmates."
It was Loree's prerogative to issue licenses, and his exclusion
of Ward and other "old traders" caused an uproar that was
heard, through the intercession of the influential Robert
Campbell, in Washington, D.C. Acting on his own, Colonel
Collins "arrested" those "lawfully licensed." The enraged
Loree saw this as a foul plot by Ward the sutler, who
liberally plied the officers with "hot whisky punch," and
the latter, angered because "they cannot enjoy the company
of squaws." [62] We must give the benefit of the doubt, if not
to Ward, at least to Colonel Collins. Aside from his known
high integrity, Collins received two petitions that strongly
supported the anti-Loree forces. One was from the Sioux
Chief Brave Bear, requesting that licenses be restored to
"the old traders." The other was signed by the post officers,
asking that Loree be replaced by ex-agent Twiss, now seen
in retrospect as "one in whom all repose entire confidence
both in his integrity and patriotism"! [63]

The friendless Loree got unexpected aid and comfort
from none other than Colonel J. M. Chivington of Denver,
commander of the military district, who promulgated an
order specifically excluding post sutlers from the Indian

[61] Letters of Nov. 5, 1863, and Feb. 10, 1864, Loree to Commissioner of Indian
Affairs and "Hon. Julian" respectively. Records of the Upper Platte Agency.

[62] Letters of Aug. 19, 1863, Beauvais to Ward; Sept. 10, Ward to Campbell;
Sept. 24, Campbell to Hon. Frank Blair; Sept. 25, Campbell to Dole (CIA); Feb. 29,
1864, Loree to "Hon. Julian."

[63] Letters and enclosures, Collins to Dole, Commissioner of Indian Affairs, Feb.
1 and 18, 1864. Collins himself did not sign the petition of the officers. Records,
Upper Platte Agency.

trade.[64] It was an empty victory for Loree, however, who in 1865 was replaced by Vital Jarrott of St. Louis.[65] During Jarrott's brief and luckless tenure Indian hostilities deepened. Chivington's volunteers butchered the Cheyennes at Sand Creek, Colorado, and, despite Bullock's pleas, the Fort Laramie commander, Colonel Moonlight, hanged two chiefs who had, with honorable intentions, brought in two captive white women. The Indian war was again at the boiling point. The hostiles attacked and burned Julesburg, skirmished with soldiers at Mud Springs, and raised havoc along the Platte, killing many soldiers, including Lieutenant Caspar Collins, at Platte Bridge.[66] In December the Indians ran off most of Ward's mule herd. Other traders who had losses gave S. E. Ward power of attorney to collect claims. In August 1866, E. B. Taylor recommended Ward as a U.S. Indian Peace Commissioner, for "he speaks the languages of Sioux, Cheyenne and Arapahoes perfectly, and is a gentleman of high character." [67]

The Bozeman Trail War and related treaty parleys of 1866-68 and the transitional years following were climactic in Fort Laramie history, and the Ward-Bullock place was headquarters for all visitors, from General W. T. Sherman and Chief Red Cloud on down. In addition to its function as a store and social center, "the sutler's store at the fort served as general supply house and was the chief banking institution for the outlying posts for hundreds of miles around." [68] S. E. Ward trade tokens used to facilitate the

[64] Special order of Sept. 22, 1863; Letters of Nov. 15, Ward to Collins, and Nov. 16, Collins to Dole, CIA. Records, Upper Platte Agency.

[65] Letter of July 15, 1865, at California Crossing, Nebraska, Jarrott to Dole, Commissioner of Indian Affairs.

[66] Hafen and Young, op. cit., 325-333.

[67] Letter of Dec. 26, 1865, Jarrott to Hon. D. Cooley; Letter of Mar. 2, 1866, A. H. Young to Hon. W. E. Chandler. Records, Upper Platte Agency. Ward did not receive an appointment as a Commissioner.

[68] Spring, op. cit., 238.

trade are treasured by coin collectors. Many have been recovered by the National Park Service in the course of
archaeological excavations.[69]

An old letter file of Bullock and Ward, preserved by
French ink copying process and providentially rescued from
the sutler's store ruins about 1920, illuminates the period.
Although most of the letters concern payment of debts and
inventories of merchandise, there is much in the way of
colorful fact and opinion, particularly about the Indian
crisis. Robert Campbell of St. Louis, a prime financial
backer, is the principal correspondent, but the list of names
involved is a rollcall of famous frontiermen, from Bridger,
Beckwourth and Bordeaux to Pourier, St. Vrain and Wig-
gins.

A letter of May 13, 1868, from Ward to Collins Dixon,
offering to sell out, constitutes a fascinating inventory of
Ward's assets – corn, mules, oxen, wagons, "a comfortable
dwelling house" and "a store with two warehouses and a
sitting room and sleeping room for the clerks." On these
items Ward placed a total valuation of approximately
$25,000. Apparently most of the livestock and rolling equip-
ment was sold at this time; but the stock of merchandise
remained intact, and Ward hung on as sutler until 1871.
The last pertinent document to be found is a letter of May
20, that year, Ward to Bullock, deploring the poor quality
of buffalo hides, and mentioning E. B. Taylor as incoming
sutler.[70]

[69] "According to the late John Hunton, then a clerk in the Sutler's Store at Fort
Laramie, but later to become Post Trader himself, 1888-90, these tokens or trade
pieces were first issued in October 1867, for the use of the soldiers in their dealing
at the sutler's store in order to cut down the use of the 5¢, 10¢, 25¢ and 50¢ paper
notes known as 'shinplasters' which were in use at that time and which caused considerable losses and bookeeping difficulties. The trade pieces were issued in 10¢, 25¢
and 50¢ denominations." Letter of Feb. 13, 1950, David L. Hieb, Superintendent,
Fort Laramie National Historic Site, to John R. Spillman. National Park Service
files.

In 1871 Ward made his last visit to Fort Laramie, and in the same year he also relinquished his holdings in Nebraska City and moved to Westport, which would be soon swallowed up by metropolitan Kansas City, Missouri. Here he crossed paths again with William Bent of Arkansas fame, at least in memory, for on November 11, 1871, he and Mary F. Ward purchased from the Bent estate a farm of some 450 acres, located on the edge of the prairie about two miles south of Westport and within shooting distance of the historic road from Westport to Santa Fe, Oregon and California.[71] This land is now in the old country club residential area of Kansas City; the Ward estate would be bounded today by State Line Road, Wornall Road, 51st Street and 55th Street.[72]

The Ward acres had a prestigious history, being owned successively beginning in 1833 by a Mormon bishop named Partridge who, with others of his faith, was banished from Missouri in 1838; Alexander W. Doniphan of Mormon Battalion fame; Dr. Johnston Lykins, Westport postmaster and mayor; a Mr. Edmund Price and, in 1858, William Bent, whose Cheyenne wife, Owl Woman, provided much Westport gossip with her dashing equestrian habits and preference for sleeping in a tepee. In 1864 this farm was on the periphery of the Battle of Westport, which marked the decline of the Confederacy in the West. From 1897 to 1926 part of the Ward land was used as a golf course of the Kansas City Country Club.[73]

[70] Spring, *op. cit.*, 243-315; Letter of May 20, 1871, Omaha, Neb., Ward to Bullock in Fort Laramie Letters donated by Agnes Wright Spring to the National Park Service. This item is among a few of the letters not published in Spring, "Old Letter Book," *loc. cit.*

[71] Letter of June 6, 1956, James Anderson, Historian, Native Sons of Kansas City, to Ray Mattison, National Park Service. In the several biographical sketches the Ward acreage varies between 400 and 500. The Santa Fe and Oregon-California Trails were one until they split off near present Gardner, Kansas.

[72] Notes by James Anderson in files of the Native Sons of Kansas City, Missouri.

When Seth Ward acquired the property there was a two story square brick house which had been the William Bent home, supposedly built in 1858. In 1872 he proceeded with the construction of a much larger brick house, of stately Southern colonial style, retaining the Bent place to the rear as kitchen and servants' quarters.[74]

In 1873 Seth Ward put his capital to work and became president of the Mastin Bank. He belonged to Odd Fellows and was a Mason, affiliated with the Golden Square Lodge of Westport.[75] As a pillar of the Westport Baptist Church, he became a trustee of the denominational William Jewell College of Liberty, Missouri.[76] The 1879 biographical sketch describes Ward, "a practical Christian," at that time as a man

of medium height, strongly formed, erect bearing, with but few traces of his early hardships; he has light blue eyes, and his once dark hair is now turned to gray; his complexion is fair, features large and of shapely outline; in his manners dignified, unobtrusive and always welcomed among those who appreciate an earnest, upright and self-reliant nature. . . His fireside is the place where all domestic affections and qualities find happy expressions. His grounds embrace about four hundred and fifty acres, and remind one of the rich blue grass region of Kentucky – the green sward dotted with trees and groves. He has one of the finest herds of short horns in western Mis-

[73] Schauffler, *op. cit.;* interview with Kate Bernard, by James Anderson, reported in Anderson letter of June 6, 1956.

[74] Schauffler, *op. cit.,* says that the construction dates are lost and hints at greater antiquity, that somebody else built the older house and Bent built the big house. But James Anderson, in his letter of June 6, 1956, suggests 1858 and 1872, on the basis of all evidence and reasoning. There is no evidence whatever of a house before 1858. In other words, Bent built a house when he bought; and Ward built a better house when he bought. According to Nelly McCoy Harris, "When Col. Bent completed the brick mansion he gave a housewarming," etc., but she fails to offer a date. (Westport Scrap Book, files of Native Sons of Kansas City.) When William Bent married his third wife, Adelina Harvey, in 1867 the family left Westport.

[75] *Memorial and Biographical Record; Missouri Lodge of Research* (Masonic), III, p. 85.

[76] *Encyclopedia of the History of Missouri, op. cit.*

souri, and deserves commendation for his efforts to introduce these valuable cattle into the country.[77]

In 1888 a correspondent of the *St. Louis Globe-Democrat* found him "now, at 68 years . . . about twice a millionaire and one of the most respected citizens of western Missouri, . . . as fine-looking a gentleman of the old school as the State can present." At this stage of his life there was little about the opulent Mr. Ward to suggest the bronzed young apprentice of Fort Davy Crockett, but the article proceeds glowingly about Ward's early adventures among trappers and Indians.[78]

Seth Ward died in Kansas City on December 9, 1903.[79] His wife Mary died in 1910.[80] They were survived by two sons, John Edmund and Hugh Campbell, born respectively in 1861 and 1863.[81]

The Bent and Ward homes survive to this day, two of the most historic places in Kansas City. The Ward mansion fronts on 1032 West Fifty-fifth Street, a mellow but still fashionable neighborhood. The place was purchased in 1942 by Mr. and Mrs. Leland W. Browne, who undertook ex-

---

[77] *U.S. Biographical Dictionary, op. cit.*

[78] "A Trapper's Tale," *op. cit.* All of the Missouri biographical sketches are silent about Ward's Indian family. This particular adventure is revealed especially in the Bettelyoun MSS., Mari Sandoz notes, and the 1867 petitions to Congress to "heads or members of Indian families" at Fort Laramie, *op. cit.*

[79] Hoyle Jones, MS., Wyoming Historical Society.

[80] Schauffler, *loc. cit.*

[81] *U.S. Biographical Dictionary, op. cit.;* according to *Annals of Wyoming,* v (1927), 11, John Edmund, deceased, left two sons, Seth E. and Robert Campbell. In a letter of June 10, 1965 to the writer, Robert Campbell Ward, 221 West 48th Street, Kansas City, Missouri, advised that he and Mrs. David T. Beals, also of that city, are the surviving children of John Edmund. Other grandchildren of Seth E. Ward, *viz.* Hugh Campbell, are Hugh C. Ward, Jr., and Mrs. George Olmstead of Boston, James C. Ward of Nashville, and John Harris Ward of Chicago. Seth R. Ward of Greeley, Colorado, a grandson of R. C., is a great-great-grandson of Seth E. According to the *Kansas City Times,* Jan. 18, 1966, informant R. C. Ward died on November 22, 1965, age 69, leaving a comfortable fortune.

tensive restoration work.[82] They are now owned and occupied by Dr. and Mrs. Frederick B. Campbell; they are not open to the public.[83] The Ward home was feelingly described in 1948 by a *Kansas City Star* reporter:

> It is a gracious place, mellowed by generations of comfortable living. Great elms arch over the house. There are evergreens in the back garden, reminiscent of old Missouri farmhouses; brick walks, with green moss growing on them; second-floor "galleries," such as Southern colonial houses had, for resting on hot days. There is a west gallery for morning comfort, and an east gallery for afternoon use. At the back of the wide, deep lot is a separate 2-story brick house, which was the house servants' quarters in slavery days, and which had covered access to the "big house." This building serves as a garage today. The "big house" is big, indeed – fifteen rooms. . . A 1-story front porch, the roof of which is supported by clustered columns, runs the length of the front section of the house. Peacocks once paraded there, to see their splendor reflected in the windows. A curving stairway welcomes the guest arriving in the central hallway. It is a beautiful stairway for a bride to descend.[84]

An even more significant and vivid reminder of Seth E. Ward is the sutler's store at Fort Laramie National Historic Site, which is an area of the National Park System, twenty miles west of present Torrington, Wyoming, via U.S. Highway 26. Like certain other of its venerable companions which date back to the California Gold Rush and the Sioux Wars, the sutler's store has been stabilized and restored structurally and provided with interior fixtures and furnishings. The ancient adobe and stone portions of this building are the same which sheltered Ward and Bullock, and

---

[82] Schauffler, *loc. cit.*

[83] In company with James Anderson, the writer was privileged to visit the "William Bent and Seth Ward homes" in 1956, courtesy of Mrs. Campbell. "The Campbell family's intentions are to turn over the homes to the Daughters of the Confederacy, when they give it up as their residence." Letter of June 10, 1965, R. C. Ward to M. J. Mattes.

[84] Schauffler, *loc. cit.*

the stocked shelves of merchandise and the refurnished offices are as accurate historically as research can make them.[85] The imaginative visitor can easily picture "the pompous Mr. Ward," diamonds a-glitter, keeping an eye on his busy young clerks; soldier, civilian and Indian customers; and weather-beaten bewhiskered old Mountain Men lounging around, reliving their days of glory.

[85] Merrill J. Mattes, "The Sutler's Store at Fort Laramie," in *Annals of Wyoming,* vol. 18, no. 2 (July 1946), 93-138; David L. Hieb, "Preliminary Report on Rehabilitation of the Sutler's Store during 1952-53," MS., National Park Service files; Sally Johnson, "Furnishing Plans for Sutler's Store, Fort Laramie National Historic Site," MS., National Park Service files.

Caleb Wilkins

by Harvey E. Tobie
Portland, Oregon

Having been born in Zanesville, Ohio, July 10, 1810, Caleb Wilkins was only a few months younger than his more famous brother-in-law, Joe Meek, and only a few weeks the junior of George Ebbert, his closest friend in the Oregon colony they had helped to found. Though never well remembered in history, his associates, because they respected his outstanding coolness, personal bravery, indefatigible independence and integrity, often looked to him for leadership in practical matters.[1]

When Nathaniel Wyeth added reenforcements at Fort Hall, December 9, 1835, Caleb Wilkins was one of those coming to the aid of the Yankee trader's brilliant but precarious enterprise. Within days after arrival of the new men, excitement was plentiful. On December 14, each man was issued four pounds of gunpowder and eight pounds of musket balls and ordered to prepare for a Bannack Indian attack. Fortunately, Wyeth's negotiations eliminated the alarming possibility of conflict. Also, Christmas was coming and a great celebration was scheduled. For employee enjoyment, the company contributed fifteen pints of alcohol, six pints of flour, a pint of sugar and three pints of rice.[2]

Previous to his arrival at Fort Hall, Caleb (usually called Cale) had been one of a small party whose furs and steeds were stolen on the headwaters of the John Day River in 1835. Since one of the men had abducted a woman from Fort Walla Walla, and since they had refused to trade their

---

[1] Caroline C. Dobbs, *Men of Champoeg* (Portland, 1932), 148-49.
[2] Richard G. Beidleman, "Nathaniel Wyeth's Fort Hall," in *Oregon Historical Quarterly*, LVIII (Sept. 1957), 237-39, 238n.

furs to the Hudson's Bay Co., the supposition was that trader Pierre Pambrun had ordered a retaliatory seizure. To an American Mountain Man, such action, proven or not, was a high-handed confiscation and wholly unjustified. "What we call stealing a woman," said Joe Meek, commenting on the incident in 1866, "is taking a wife when you can get her; that's what we call petit larceny in the mountains." [3]

For services prior to February 24, 1836, Cale was credited with $95.62½. However, a debit of $313.21 was carried over from the "old ledger," and in May and June of 1836 he required merchandise totaling $88.25. The fact that he was an expert hunter helped him to make progress toward balancing his account. From May 26 to June 21 he was credited with $182.45 for buffalo and other contributions to the commissary. In 1837 he was given $179 credit for entries in chief hunter Paul "Richardson's Book." On the other side of that ledger, Wilkins was charged with only $92.68. When he finally severed his Fort Hall connections, Cale was in arrears $50.18½. When the fort and other Wyeth assets were purchased by the Hudson's Bay Co. in 1837, the Wilkins account was not included, as was that of Ebbert, because of Cale's desertion to Jim Bridger. Ledger no. 1 suggests a date for the defection, for his account was first closed in February, 1836, apparently on expiration of a contract.[4] Sixteen of the Wyeth men joined Bridger at about that time. Osborne Russell, using nicknames, probably named "Major" Joe Meek and "Squire" Ebbert among Gabe's (Bridger's) associates who were then camped near the mouth of Blackfoot River.[5]

---

[3] "Evidence for the United States in the Matter of the Claims of the Hudson's Bay Co.," VIII, pp. 63-64, 71; Dobbs, op. cit., 149.

[4] "Account Books of Fort Hall," Ledger no. 1, pp. 375-76; Ledger no. 2, pp. 40-41, Oregon Historical Society.

[5] Harvey E. Tobie, No Man Like Joe (Portland, 1949), 55; Osborne Russell, Journal of a Trapper (Boise, Idaho, 1921), 34-35.

Free trapper independence did not entirely terminate Cale's social visits to the fort nor his barter transactions involving supplies and delivery of the game that reduced his indebtedness. Hunter Richardson's departure for the East in the summer of 1837 and the sale of Fort Hall were two factors that ended all recorded transactions at the supply depot.[6]

The rendezvous of 1837 at Green River was the last gay fair at which unworried relaxations ran riot. Thereafter, adding to the general difficulties of the declining fur trade, a smallpox scare became a barrier to fall and winter operations in the Crow country. Wilkins and his associates wisely headed for the Northwest to ply their trade among the Flatheads and Nez Perces. Joe Meek's account in *River of the West* of the fall expedition of some free trappers has all the suspense and stately eloquence of a native narrative spiced with sly, incongruous mountaineer humor. It was a thirsty trip for Joe, Cale, "Cotton" Mansfield, and their guide, an old Flathead woman whose wilderness prowess put the men to shame. Reaching Godin's Fork (Big Lost River), ". . . they crossed over to Salmon River, and presently struck the Nez Perce Trail" along which they proceeded to an Indian village on the Beaverhead Fork of the Missouri near the site of Virginia City, Montana. With the village they traveled the short distance to Madison Fork, which they followed to its source, "Missouri Lake," near which they joined in the fall hunt for buffalo.[7]

By 1837, Wilkins made his home with a Nez Perce wife to whom a son, George, was born in Indian country in 1838 or 1839. Even earlier, in 1833, Robert Newell had contracted a Nez Perce marriage, but Joe Meek's third recorded marital union came somewhat later than Cale's. By

---

[6] *Oregon Historical Quarterly,* LVIII, p. 248.

[7] Frances Fuller Victor, *The River of the West* (Hartford, 1870), 242-45, chap. XIX; Tobie, *op. cit.,* 74-75.

1840, when the three men moved together into the Willamette Valley, they were married to sisters, daughters of Nez Perce chief Kowesote.[8]

More than native marriage alliances bound the three men with close ties. Wilderness experiences cemented friendships permanently. David-Jonathan partnerships became till-death-do-us-part relationships. Wyeth-men Joseph Gale and Wilkins, and their pals "Squire" Ebbert, William Doughty, "Doc" Newell and Joe Meek made an agreement among themselves to move eventually to the plains west of the Willamette River and live together there in friendly intercourse.[9]

And more than mountain miseries and Oregon attractiveness impelled the fraternity westward. Emigrants from the States, who were now trickling toward sea level, needed help for which they could sometimes pay. The newcomers had an attraction of their own for civilization-starved wilderness hunters. White women were much more appealing than whiskey. Even preachers inspired nostalgic interest and, frequently, respect. The new society which the mountaineers envisioned, needed the influential forerunners who were passing. The missionary efforts at Waiilatpu, Chemekete and The Dalles were about to be supplemented by the endeavors of unsubsidized independent crusaders. Some of them would settle near the Mountain Men. The Peoria party, the Quincy group, the Joel Walker family, and others merged their westward movements with those of the footloose trappers.

About fifteen Mountain Men went down the Columbia in the fall of 1839 with Farnham, Shortess, Munger and

---

[8] *Ibid.*, 76; Victor, *op. cit.*, 242, 252-53; Oregon Census of 1850, 1860, Oregon Historical Society; *Dictionary of American Biography*, XIII, p. 458; Judith G. Goldman, "The Mountain Flowers . . . ," Genealogical Forum of Portland, Oregon, Jan. 1965, pp. 49, 58.

[9] Oregon Pioneer Assn., *Transactions* (nineteenth, 1891), 182.

Griffin. Newell, Meek, Wilkins and others wintered at Brown's Hole in 1839-40 with other Peoria migrants.[10] Lacking organized support, Congregationalists Rev. Harvey Clark, Alvin T. Smith and P. B. Littlejohn felt the pinch of poverty even before they were out of the mountains. Learning that remuneration asked by Moses "Black" Harris for guiding them beyond the rendezvous would have seriously depleted the resources of the independents, Cale and his friends came to the rescue of the would-be missionaries. When Newell, who was in a limited business for himself, undercut the stipulated pilot's fee, the enraged Harris took a shot at him. With the assistance of Newell, William Craig, Wilkins and others, the strangers made their way comfortably to Fort Hall. When Indians stole a couple of horses, Cale talked to the suspects in language they could understand and, when ". . . he received an impudent reply, he knocked the Indian down and ordered him to bring back the horses, which he did." [11]

In the trading which accompanied the change from four-wheeled to four-legged transportation, emigrants who reached Fort Hall with wagons abandoned them there. Thus Newell acquired two vehicles. Also in 1840, Joel Walker of the one-family immigration left behind two wagons, of which Wilkins acquired one. Hudson's Bay Co. trader, Francis Ermatinger, was certainly involved in some of these transactions. The important point is that Newell, Wilkins and associates now had in their possession equipment for a daring enterprise.

At first only Newell and Wilkins were ready to undertake the wagon experiment. Joe Meek, the third brother-in-law, was absent with a trapping party and did not arrive at

10 Tobie, *op. cit.,* 81, 84; R. C. Clark, *History of the Willamette Valley, Oregon* (Chicago, 1927), 254; "Memorandum of Robert Newell's Travels in the Territory of Missouri, 1829-1841," MS, University of Oregon; Oregon *Herald,* Mar. 3, 1867.
11 Dobbs, *op. cit.,* 149, quoting Alvin T. Smith; Newell, "Memorandum."

Fort Hall until September 22. Another recruit was "Nicholas," who has not been definitely identified. If Nicolaus Altgeier drove a wagon to Fort Walla Walla, it must have been earlier in the season, for he arrived in California in mid-August, 1840. Though his name does not sound German, Meek's bear-escapade partner, Fort Hall visitor and later Tualatin Plains resident, Nicholas U. Sansbury, might qualify for the honor. Wilkins, Meek and Nicholas drove the first three wagons whose running gears rolled as far as Fort Walla Walla. Newell, William Craig, John Larison and other Mountain Men rode along and did their part in the accomplishment of a very difficult feat.[12]

November was "far advanced" by the time the party arrived at Willamette Falls. "Rain, mud and an empty stomach" were the afflictions of each new colonist. The Hudson's Bay Co., Methodist missionaries, and ex-mountaineer friends came to the assistance of the newcomers. William Doughty, who had preceded the Newell party into the Willamette Valley, was the first to rejoin his old friends, and George Ebbert, another earlier arrival, was also one of the six who established a camp for the winter, overlooking the falls from the west. Doughty already had a small cabin in the Chehalem Creek vicinity that was dominated by fur trader Ewing Young.[13] Gradually, the friends, having survived a winter too wet for Rocky Mountain residents, established locations of their own, built cabins, and began farming. Wilkins, in partnership later with close friend George Ebbert, occupied about 1280 acres of excellent land near the present village of Orenco.

Cale did not limit his activities to farming, but continued to hunt and trap and carry on other transactions necessary

---

[12] Tobie, *op. cit.*, 84-87; Census of 1850; Victor, *op. cit.*, 279-83; James Peter Zollinger, *Sutter: the Man and His Empire* (New York, 1939), 77; Harvey W. Scott, *History of the Oregon Country* (Cambridge, 1924), I, p. 326; II, pp. 226-27.

[13] Victor, *op. cit.*, 284-87; Tobie, *op. cit.*, 93ff, 292.

for survival and self-betterment. Records kept for Ewing
Young and his estate reveal Cale's continued traffic in
beaver. But farming was not neglected. Unlike Joe Meek,
he was able to secure seed wheat from the Hudson's Bay
Co., as did Newell, Doughty and Courtney Walker. These
men, including Meek, helped each other, and all pitched in
to assist Alvin T. Smith and anyone else who needed extra
hands, frontier know-how or employment.[14]

Though omitted from one list of those voting for the
establishment of provisional government on May 2, 1843,
Wilkins doubtless deserved to have his name included on
the Champoeg monument. The Daughters of the American
Revolution have placed a plaque on Cale's tombstone in the
West Union Baptist cemetery, honoring his participation in
the historic event. For the most part, he was occupied with
the exacting and formidable processes of farming, and with
road building and repair, cooperative neighborhood enterprises, and raising a large family. With Hugh Burns he was,
in 1844, named by the legislative committee overseer of a
projected road from Willamette Falls to Tualatin Plains,
intersecting the road from Linnton to "Yam Hill Falls."
On June 3, 1845, he was a judge of the election held at
Charles McKay's residence. In that same year, neighbors
whom he had often helped, assisted him in raising the first
frame barn in Tuality District.[15] On April 27, 1846, the
Tuality County grand jury indicted William Johnson for
". . . retailing ardent spirits . . . being seduced
by an evil heart . . . to one Caleb Wilkins."[16] Thus

14 *Ibid.*, 96-97, 292; George Schreiber and Esther L. Plumer, eds., "Provisional
Government Papers and Miscellaneous Documents from Archives, Oregon State
Capital, 1913," MS, 38; Alvin T. Smith "Diary," Oregon Historical Soc., Dec. 26,
1841, Mar. 5, 1842, Aug. 7, 1843; Victor, *op. cit.*, 285-87.

15 Tobie, *op. cit.*, 126; E. E. Rich, ed., *Letters of John McLoughlin, Third Series,
1844-46* (London, 1944), 244, 249-50; Albert Tozier to S. A. D. Meek, Jan. 25, 1928;
Scott, *op. cit.*, II, p. 228.

16 Tobie, *op. cit.*, 134; "Tuality District Archives, 1842-63," WPA inventory, no.
34, entry 126, p. 15.

did the community exercise a well-intentioned but negative spirit of cooperation.

In addition to operation of his well-stocked farm, Wilkins, a hatter by trade, with fellow Wyeth-man Joe Gale acted as agent for D. H. Lownsdale's Portland tannery, receiving hides to be paid for in leather, shoes or "store pay" by the following fall.[17] On May 20, 1847, Cale and "Squire" Ebbert filed a joint claim to their splendid 1280-acre farm. That was also the year of the terrible Whitman Massacre, followed by the Cayuse War in which Wilkins served briefly.

In December 1848, Cale lost his Nez Perce princess, Catherine, and assumed a widower's burden of raising seven children, including two sets of twin girls – infants and two year olds – a four-year-old girl, and boys of six and ten.[18] On March 28, 1850, with Rev. J. S. Griffin officiating, Cale married Mrs. Miriam (Marian) Enyart, who brought into the overcrowded household seven-year-old Abner. The 1853 enumeration credited the Wilkins family with five sons and five daughters.[19]

At the April, 1850, term of circuit court, Wilkins and others were ordered to appear at the October session to show why they should not be fined for failure to serve as jurors. Wilkins was a Whig; the court was that presided over by excessively-partisan Democrat, Judge O. C. Pratt. Together with neighbors, including Joe Meek and George Ebbert, Wilkins was indicted in October 1850, for playing monte in his own dooryard on April 10. At the April, 1851, term of court, all the defendants except Ebbert threw themselves on

---

[17] Oregon *Spectator,* Feb. 18 to Apr. 15, 1847.

[18] Oregon State Archives, "Index to Oregon Donation Land Claims," IV, p. 302; Oregon Statesman, Nov. 1, 1853; Oregon Census of 1850; "Provisional and Territorial Papers," Oregon Historical Society, 3450; "Genealogical Material in Donation Land Claims, Abstracted from Applications," Genealogical Forum of Portland, 1959, VII, p. 3089 states that there were five children. Catherine died in childbirth. Goldman, *op. cit.,* 58.

[19] "Provisional and Territorial Papers," 5290; *Spectator,* May 2, 1850.

the mercy of the court, whereupon their cases were dismissed after payment of costs. That Cale was by that time well able to pay any and all fines is indicated by the fact that on July 2, 1850, he furnished a bond of $7000 for David T. Lenox and Henry Black, to guarantee performance of duties by the county treasurer.[20]

Wilkins was politically too consistent and independent to be generally successful in election races of his own. He ran unsuccessfully for county treasurer in 1851, but he was supervisor of public roads for east Tuality County in that year, and a biographer says that he served as treasurer of his county in 1852. Standing as a Whig but with Knownothing support, in a day when Democrats were ascendant, he ran a strong race for coroner in 1853. In 1851 he was a director of "The Mutual Insurance Office." [21]

It was Baptist neighbors who complained of Wilkins' monte party. Those good people outdid the Puritans and their descendants in their disciplinary rectitude. Though Cale continued in his independent way, he must have understood his censors, for he seems to have cherished no hard feelings. In fact, when a committee called on him in September 1852, he offered to donate a lot on his place for a Baptist meeting house. The committee accepted the gift, but ". . . the building cite [sic] upon Caleb Wilkins claim did not take well" with a majority of the congregation. The famous West Union Baptist Church was built, therefore, on land offered by David T. Lenox. On May 8, 1854, Mrs. Wilkins was received ". . . as a sister and member of the church by relation having formerly been Baptised [sic]." [22]

20 Washington County (Oregon) Court House, "Circuit Court Record, 1849-1852," book no. 1, pp. 9, 19, 24; Washington County "Deed Book," A, p. 14; "Provisional and Territorial Papers," 6437; Tobie, op. cit., 206, 303.

21 Oregonian, May 21, 1853; Oregon Statesman, June 6, 1851, June 11, 1853, July 12, 1853; Spectator, May 22, 1851, Mar. 16, 1852, June 5, 1851; Dobbs, op. cit. 150.

22 J. Orin Oliphant's transcription of "The Minutes of the West Union Baptist Church in Oregon," 1935, pp. 31-35, 37; Tobie, op. cit., 207, 304.

During the fifties there were increases both in the Wilkins assets and in the size of his family. By 1857, though there had been losses, he had six girls and two boys, all under ten years of age. The 640 or so acres which remained after division of the claim formerly held jointly with the "Squire" was valued by the assessor in 1858 at $5000, while personal property on the well-stocked ranch was listed at $3000. He paid a poll tax of $1, school and territorial taxes of $8 each and a county tax of $40, or a total of $57.[23]

During the decade of the Civil War, the Wilkins household was struck by calamities nearly as overwhelming as the sudden sufferings of Job. In September 1859, a committee was sent from the West Union church "requesting" Mrs. Wilkins to attend the next church meeting. In other words, an ultimatum was delivered. Disciplinary action was canceled only after her death on December 20, 1860. Four children less than ten years old were left motherless. The next spring, Caleb's third child and eligible housekeeper, Elizabeth, died. Of greatest assistance in the family emergency was Mrs. Isaac Butler, whose unparalleled neighborliness was appreciated. Mrs. Butler's daughter remembered that Cale, in his gratitude, offered her mother half his entire farm. On January 26, 1864, Wilkins did sell to Butler forty acres for a recorded $700, but it is possible that receipt of the actual cash was not expected. On August 20, 1869, Wilkins deeded to Butler 41.576 acres adjoining the earlier purchase for a recorded $1000. In 1870, Cale's real estate was valued at $10,000, personal property at $17,000.[24]

Overheated by war frictions and alcohol, Cale became involved in an incident that could have been extremely serious. On July 19, 1862, Wilkins drank a tavern health to McClellan, and John Thorp, ex-Mountain Man and a leader of

[23] "Provisional and Territorial Papers," 6914, 12279 A, B, and C.
[24] Interview with Mrs. E. A. Bloyd, July 23, 1946; Oliphant, *op. cit.*, 58, 87; Washington County "Deed Book," D, p. 795, L, p. 229, G, p. 92; Census of 1870.

the 1844 immigration, responded ". . . to the health of Beauregard and to hell with the McClellan fraternity." As Thorp spoke, he lunged at Wilkins with his bowie knife. The extraordinarily quick reactions which had kept Cale alive in Indian country brought his pocket knife into lightning play and into Thorp's left side. "NOT SO BAD," commented the *Oregonian* on learning that Thorp's wound was superficial.[25]

The war ended. "Doc" Newell died in 1869 in Idaho, William Doughty in 1872 at Wapato Lake, and Joe Gale in 1881 in eastern Oregon. Courtney Meek was acquitted of murder; his father's life was published; and in 1875, Joe Meek died. "Squire" Ebbert then stepped affably into limited spotlights, but Cale remained in the background until the end of his days. Of the original group which planned and founded the "Rocky Mountain Retreat," Cale and "Squire" stayed on until 1890. Before the time Wilkins died on October 5, 1890, five days after Ebbert's passing, he was no longer a newsworthy personality. The *Oregonian* called him a "landmark" and had little else to say.[26] He had indeed been a man who could not be moved, at least not against his will. The Hudson's Bay Co., muddy or non-existent roads, Baptist busybodies, the Salem clique, secessionists – none of those forces could overturn the firm landmark of the Tualatin Plains. By such men, no less than by more flamboyant individuals, has the stability of the commonwealth been preserved.

[25] Oregon *Statesman,* July 28, 1862; *Oregonian,* July 24, 1862; Robert Glass Cleland, *This Reckless Breed of Men* (New York, 1950), facing p. 202.

[26] *Oregonian,* Oct. 7, 1890.

Dick Wootton

by Harvey L. Carter
Colorado College, Colorado Springs

Richens Lacy Wootton was born on May 6, 1816, in Mecklenburg County, Virginia, the son of David C. Wootton, who moved to fertile Christian County, Kentucky, in 1823. When he was eighteen he left his father's tobacco farm and joined an uncle on a cotton plantation in Mississippi. In the spring of 1836, he took a trip to Independence, Missouri, where he yielded to the lure of the Rocky Mountains and hired to a Bent Brothers and St. Vrain wagon train.[1] Thus was begun a long and eventful career in the West.

Twenty years old, of an open and frank countenance, well muscled, and above the average in height and weight, Dick Wootton could handle a gun and a team and take care of himself. The small train of seven wagons overtook a train of fifty-seven, and he soon learned the essential military precision of a large wagon train. Before the small train was dropped off at Bent's Old Fort on the Arkansas, within sight of the Rockies, he had shot his first buffalo and participated in a brush with the Comanches. He was then sent, with thirteen men and ten wagon loads of goods, to trade among the Sioux. After a profitable trade, somewhere north of Fort Laramie, he returned to Bent's Fort in the early months of 1837 and, except for a quick trip to Taos with

---

[1] Howard Louis Conard, *Uncle Dick Wootton* (Chicago, 1890), 28-29. *The Denver Republican*, Aug. 23, 1893, in an obituary article states that the Woottons were a Scottish family in origin. Conard's work is essentially Wootton's autobiography, since it was written from interviews during which he told his life story. It has been cited in preference to Henry Inman, *The Old Santa Fe Trail* (New York, 1898) and Glenn D. Bradley, *Winning the Southwest* (Chicago, 1912), both of which contain chapters on Wootton which are almost wholly based on Conard.

Ceran St. Vrain, spent the rest of the winter at the fort.[2] In the summer of 1837, he went down the Arkansas to the Pawnee Fork to meet a wagon train and, with eight men, killed thirteen of sixteen Pawnees.[3]

Deciding now to strike out for himself, he got up a party of seventeen free trappers, upon his return to Bent's Fort, and headed into the Colorado Rockies. On Grand River they had a fight with a band of Snake Indians, killing twenty of them. The trapping was good and he sold his peltry in Westport for over $4,000. With great optimism, he wrote to his mother that he would soon be rich and would be home in a year or two![4]

In the fall of 1838, he set out upon one of the most extended trips of which there is any record in the annals of the fur trade. Nineteen free trappers, accompanied by six or seven Shawnee and Arapaho Indians, left Bent's Fort in September, 1838. It was nearly two years before they returned. Their route lay up the Arkansas to its source; thence northward over the mountains and up the Green; thence over the Wind River range to the Big Horn; down that stream to the Yellowstone and westward along its course; thence over the continental divide to the Salmon and the Snake and on to the Columbia. At Fort Vancouver, they sold their furs to the Hudson's Bay Company and passed across Oregon and into California by an unspecified route, except that they struck the Pacific Ocean near San Luis Obispo and continued on to Los Angeles. Then heading east, they trapped the Gila and the Colorado, catching plenty of beaver but of inferior quality; thence into Utah and back to Bent's Fort by an undetailed route. The party had traversed the great western circuit which Jedediah

---

[2] *Ibid.,* 41-44. Wootton's story that he shot a mule, thinking it was a skulking Indian, on his first trip west was the stock story told on all greenhorns and need not be credited as true. It may also be doubted whether Wootton was in charge of his first trading venture as he claims to have been.

[3] *Ibid.,* 46-51.   [4] *Ibid.,* 54-62.

Smith had covered twelve years earlier, but in a counter-clockwise direction.

Five of the trappers were killed on this circuit, three by the Bannocks on Green River and two by the Pah-Utes. La Bonte, a noted character among the early trappers, was cut off by the Pah-Utes when he lagged behind the main party. His bones were found and buried by his companions but most of the flesh had been taken off and eaten by his slayers. Le Duc was shot by a poisoned arrow and died after twenty-four hours of agony. The Snake Indians also beat in the skull of August Claymore (Clermont), but he recovered, surprisingly, and lived for many years. Another French-man, Charlefoux, was chased by Nez Perces and fell into a fissure, breaking both legs. He was rescued and carried in a litter for two months, but the notched stick, whereby he kept track of the days for the party, was lost.[5] For most of the trappers this trip was a last fling; for some it was their swan song; for young Dick Wootton it was his first great adventure. Henceforth, he could regard himself as a seasoned Mountain Man.

During the final stage of this trip, Wootton had sent furs to Taos by some Mexican slave traders who had been encountered. So, in the fall of 1840, he went from Bent's Fort to Taos to collect his money. On his return trip, he rescued an Arapaho woman who had escaped from her Ute captors but who was nearly naked and perishing from cold. Her kinsmen gave him two ponies as a reward and the Arapahoes

---

[5] *Ibid.*, 65-82. *The Denver Republican*, Aug. 23, 1893, refers to Wootton's having trapped on the Yellowstone and his having visited Fort Vancouver. It does not refer to the further excursion into the Southwest. There seems to be no positive evidence upon which it may be questioned, although it seems strange that no other reference to so extensive a trip by so large a party seems to exist. Wootton's account to Conard is a sketchy one, fifty years after the event, but the newspaper reference indicates that he had talked of it before and that it had become a matter of commonly accepted knowledge. Conard attributes the death of the three unnamed men to the "Monarch" Indians but he obviously misunderstood Wootton or did not hear him clearly. The Bannocks lived in the area west of Green River which is the locality of the incident in question.

were always his friends thereafter. Their name for him was Cut Hand, because he had lost two fingers off his left hand in an accident during childhood. On one occasion, some years later, he was pursued by a band of nineteen Pawnees, who came upon him after his horse had given out and he had walked over twenty miles. They chased him for six miles until he reached an Arapaho village near where Greeley, Colorado, now stands. Wootton had killed one Pawnee but was too exhausted to mount and go with his Arapaho friends, who killed and scalped all but one of his pursuers.[6]

Falling prices had dealt the fur trade a heavy blow by 1840, so, for the next two or three years, Wootton made his living by contracting to supply buffalo meat to Bent's Fort. This, he felt, was combining business with pleasure, for he considered buffalo hunting to be the finest of sports. Around this time, he built a corral where the city of Pueblo, Colorado, is now located, and used forty cows to raise buffalo calves for him. He claimed that, when they were three years old, he broke several to work as oxen and drove them to Kansas City, where he sold them for shipment to zoos in the East.[7]

In 1842, he is said to have run a weekly express for a time between Bent's Fort and Fort St. Vrain, with an occasional trip from Bent's Fort to Taos, sometimes carrying as much as $60,000 in silver on pack mules. In the winter of 1843, he got a license to trade with the Utes. With only a Delaware Indian as a helper, he made a successful trade with an Indian village on the Canadian River in the Texas Panhandle region, but his profits were lost when Comanches killed and robbed a man named Tharp, by whom he had

---

[6] Ibid., 91-95; 315.

[7] Ibid., 88-89. This tame buffalo story has a most improbable sound. However, other similar claims have been made. It is likely that all such accounts are basically true but exaggerated as to detail.

sent his robes and skins to Kansas City. Next, he traded
with Yellow Wolf's Cheyenne band in northern Colorado;
then, after supplying meat again for Bent's Fort, he traded
with the Utes in New Mexico. He paid ten to twelve dollars
for mules and a little less for ponies, in trade goods. This
trade was always rather dangerous. On one occasion, a
Shawnee Indian employed by Wootton killed a Ute, and
Wootton and his party of eight men had to hold off a large
number of Utes who sought revenge.[8] At another time, Jim
Walters [Waters] was wounded while in company with
Wootton and Old Bill Williams, but they were able to bring
him safely in to Bent's Fort.[9]

In the fall of 1846, Wootton was in and out of Taos a
good bit, but he was not there when the famous Taos uprising occurred in January, 1847. He was at the old Pueblo on
the Arkansas when John Albert brought the news of the
massacre. Wootton and four others set out at once for Taos
and kept watch on it from the mountains to the east until
Captain Burgwin, with two companies, and St. Vrain, with
sixty volunteers, appeared on February 3, 1847. They joined
this force during the night and engaged in the fight next day
which ended the rebellion. Wootton said that St. Vrain,
seeing a supposedly dead Taos Indian, dismounted, when
the Indian wrestled with him until Wootton intervened on
St. Vrain's behalf with an ax. His estimate of the losses in
the battle, on both sides, is probably too high.[10]

Immediately after this, Wootton received a letter from
Colonel Doniphan requesting his services as a scout. By
hard riding, he overtook Doniphan's column south of El

8 Ibid., 98-108. Wootton's dates are frequently in error. Here he may have confused the order of his trading with the Cheyennes and the Utes, as Bill Tharp was
killed in 1847.

9 LeRoy R. Hafen, "Colorado Mountain Men," in Colorado Magazine, XXX, p. 26;
Conard, 147-48.

10 LeRoy R. Hafen, "Mountain Men – John D. Albert," in Colorado Magazine, X,
pp. 60-61; Conard, 178-84.

Paso and was present at the battle of Sacramento on February 28, but was sent back to Albuquerque by Doniphan with dispatches telling of his success. He reached there in nine days and this ended his service in the Mexican War.[11]

In March, 1848, and for four months thereafter Wootton and Antoine Leroux acted as guides for Colonel Newby and Major Runnels against the Navajos.[12] In common with other Mountain Men, Wootton felt that army officers paid little heed to experienced advice. This impression was strengthened in October, 1849, when word was received in Taos of the capture of a Mrs. White and her child by Jicarilla Apaches in eastern New Mexico, where the Santa Fe stagecoach had been ambushed. Soldiers, under Colonel Greer, set out to attempt a rescue, accompanied by Kit Carson, Antoine Leroux, Tom Tobin, and Dick Wootton. These scouts located the Indian encampment undetected, but the rescue could only have been effected by a sudden onset, which was rendered impossible by Colonel Greer, who decided to parley before fighting. The Indians had time to kill their captives and Wootton and the other scouts were thoroughly disgusted.[13] In this period, also, Wootton and others set out from Taos to rescue Lucien Maxwell and a party who were beleaguered by Utes and met them, in bad condition, about thirty miles from Taos.[14]

In 1848 Wootton was married to Dolores, daughter of Manuel Le Fevre, a French-Canadian, of Taos.[15] The

[11] *The Denver Republican,* Aug. 23, 1893, says he "worked as scout for Colonel Doniphan's army down in Old Mexico." Also Conard, 189-97.

[12] Conard, 218-32.

[13] *Ibid.,* 205-14. Henry Inman, *The Old Santa Fe Trail,* 161, gives January, 1847, as the date for the White tragedy. Neither Wootton nor Carson could possibly have been along with Greer at that time. Jacob Piatt Dunn, *Massacres of the Mountains,* 374, gives the correct date.   [14] Conard, 214-17.

[15] *Ibid.,* 235, 320. Lewis H. Garrard, *Wah-to-Yah and the Taos Trail* (original edition, 1850) in Ralph P. Bieber and LeRoy R. Hafen, *Southwest Historical Series* (Glendale, 1938), VI, pp. 246-47, refers to Señorita LeFevre, the daughter of Manuel LeFevre. This was about a year before her marriage to Wootton. Garrard was much taken by her appearance and is highly complimentary in his remarks.

English traveler, George F. Ruxton, who had become acquainted with Wootton in 1847, endowed him with a bride from Sonora in his book, *Life in the Far West,* but this is a work of semi-fiction.[16] By reason of his being newly married, Wootton escaped the worst of the California gold fever, contenting himself with unsuccessful searches for lost Spanish mines in the Sandia Mountains.[17] He made his home at Taos until 1854 but spent a part of his time at the old Pueblo on the Arkansas. He is said to have turned back from Fremont's ill-fated expedition of 1849 when he saw the unusual amount of snow on the Sangre de Cristo Mountains, and he seems to have been in Taos when the demoralized survivors of the winter disaster straggled in.[18]

Faced with the necessity of providing for a family, Wootton extended and diversified his business operations.[19] In the winter of 1849-50, he conducted a trade with the Comanches at Adobe Walls, one of the few trading ventures to this hostile tribe, and got twelve old-fashioned Pennsylvania (Conestoga) wagons full of robes and skins.[20]

Then came two long trips. In 1851, he went to St. Louis

---

16 George F. Ruxton, *Life in the Far West* (New York, 1849), 178-79, 186, 193, 199. Ruxton calls his character "Young Ned Wootton" in the first two citations, and "Young Dick Wootton" in the other two. Wootton was thirty-one, but he was five years older than Ruxton, who also adds six inches to Wootton's stature. Joseph Wootton, a younger brother of Dick, was in the West with him only in 1857-59, and so could not have been the original of Ruxton's "Ned" Wootton. Dick Wootton's eldest daughter told F. W. Cragin that there was no truth in Ruxton's story of how her father got a wife by abduction. See below, note 19, for Cragin Papers.

17 Conard, 236-38.

18 *Ibid.,* 197-200. The statement that Wootton turned back was made by Thomas E. Breckenridge, "The Story of a Famous Expedition," in *Cosmopolitan,* XXI, p. 400. Conard says nothing of this and it is obvious from what he does say that Wootton had no first-hand knowledge of this expedition.

19 The Francis Whittemore Cragin Papers, "Interview with Eliza Ann Walker (née Wootton), widow of William R. Walker, December 4, 1907," in Notebook XI, p. 5. There were five children by Wootton's first marriage, of whom those reaching maturity were Eliza Ann, born February 1, 1850; Richens Lacy, Jr., born March 26, 1851; Frances Dolores, born April 14, 1853. – Cragin Papers, Pioneer Museum, Colorado Springs.

20 Conard, 241-44.

to buy goods. He won a bet with Colonel Greer as to who would arrive first, covering the distance between Taos and Westport in a little over seven days on horseback and continuing by river steamer to St. Louis. On his return to Westport, he learned of a cholera epidemic and set off at once for the mountains, leaving his goods to come later.[21] In 1852, he bought nine thousand sheep around Watrous, New Mexico, and drove them to California, thus preceding the famous drives of Carson and Maxwell by one year. He employed fourteen Mexicans and eight Americans and used mules instead of horses. Starting on June 24, 1852, he arrived in Sacramento 107 days later on October 9, with a loss of only a hundred sheep. When the Ute chief, Uncotash, disputed his passage in western Colorado, Wootton grappled with him and forced his consent at knife point. In Salt Lake City, he met Ben Holladay and Brigham Young and, in Sacramento he witnessed the famous fire and flood. Taking a steamer from San Francisco to Los Angeles, he bought some mules and traveled home via Yuma and Tucson to avoid the Apaches, arriving back in Taos on January 8, 1853, after thirty-three days on the road. He brought with him $14,000 in gold and more than twice that amount in drafts on a St. Louis bank.[22]

----

[21] *Ibid.*, 245-46. It seems most probable that the well-known picture of Wootton in trapper's costume (Conard, 64), was made while he was on this trip. This portrait is reproduced herein at page 19.

[22] *Ibid.*, 249-62. Wootton's claim that Brigham Young served him some very good wine may, perhaps, be open to question. See also the letter written by Wootton, dated at Don Fernandez de Taos, New Mexico, October 22, 1853, and published in the *Missouri Democrat*, November 28, 1853. This letter is reproduced in LeRoy R. and Ann W. Hafen, *The Far West and the Rockies Series* (Glendale, 1957), VII, pp. 269-72. Wootton recommends the route to California which he had recently traveled, via Robidoux (Mosca) Pass, Cochetopa Pass, and the Old Ute Trail, and takes occasion to advertise the settlement at the mouth of the Huerfano, which he was then in the process of establishing. Wootton was the active partner in the sheep venture. He and Charles Williams furnished $3,143.23 and Jesse B. Turley furnished $6,132.12 of the capital. The agreement of the partnership, formed June 26, 1852, and dissolved Feb. 9, 1853, is in the Scrapbook of Jesse B. Turley, in the possession of the Missouri Historical Society.

During these years he also kept cattle at the junction of the Huerfano and Arkansas rivers. In July, 1854, he moved his family to this location, where he and his partner, Joseph B. Doyle, built houses about one hundred yards apart. They also built a blacksmith shop and operated a mill and an irrigation ditch.[23] At Christmas time, the Utes wiped out the old Pueblo settlement, but they did not attack the Wootton-Doyle ranch.[24] Doyle now moved to Fort Barclay, New Mexico, but Wootton stayed on, raising some corn and wheat and trading one sound ox for two sore-footed ones when California-bound emigrants came by.[25] However, Doyle persuaded him to engage in the freighting business. Just as the Woottons prepared to move to Fort Barclay, Dolores Wootton died, May 6, 1855. Her husband took the children to their grandfather, Manuel Le Fevre, in Taos [26] and joined Doyle in freighting goods between Kansas City and Albuquerque, via Fort Barclay, near which the army established Fort Union.

While in this business, Wootton became acquainted with A. S. Johnston, H. H. Sibley, and E. R. S. Canby, among other army officers. Wagons going east were only half loaded, but those coming west carried from six to ten thousand pounds each. The freighters received eight dollars per hundred pounds. The train had thirty-six wagons, each pulled by five span of oxen. On one occasion, Wootton raced William Bent to Fort Union, winning by a day and a half. He played cards with Bent while his men moved their train ahead of Bent's at night. In 1857-58, Wootton made his longest freighting trip, covering the 1225 miles between Fort Atkinson, Kansas, and Salt Lake City in ninety-seven days. Doyle was along on this trip and, after they started

[23] Cragin Papers, Notebook II, p. 61.

[24] Conard, 282-307.   [25] Cragin Papers, Notebook II, p. 61.

[26] Conard, 320; Cragin Papers, Notebook II, p. 32; XI, p. 5. Dolores Wootton died in childbirth. The infant also died. Interview of Wootton by a reporter for the *Chicago Inter-Ocean,* reprinted in *The Denver Republican,* March 18, 1888, p. 21.

back, Wootton sold out to him and went on horseback to
Taos to visit his children.[27]

Returning to Bent's Old Fort (abandoned by Bent), he
married Mrs. Mary Ann Manning, a widow from Pike
County, Missouri, who was with an emigrant train. They
were married there by contract and later by a priest at
Mora, New Mexico.[28] Leaving his wife at Fort Barclay,
Wootton decided to make a last trading trip among the
Cheyennes and Arapahoes, after which he would take his
family "back to the States." [29]

However, he reached the Arapaho village on the Platte
to find that gold seekers had established the infant settlements of Denver and Auraria. This was in December 1858,
and the settlers persuaded him to remain and set up a trading post by giving him a quarter-section of land. For the
next three years, he ran a saloon and a hotel, as well as a
general trading and loan business. The hotel failed because
he would never turn a man away hungry, whether he had
money or not.[30] In the loft of one of Wootton's cabins, W. N.
Byers brought out the first issue of his newspaper on April
23, 1859.[31] His brother Joseph returned to Kentucky in this
year, taking with him Dick Wootton, Jr., who returned to
his father in 1865.[32] His wife joined him in Denver, but

[27] Conard, 323-63.

[28] Cragin Papers, Notebook XI, p. 5. Conard makes no mention of Wootton's second and third marriages. W. J. Ghent in his sketch of Wootton in the *Dictionary
of American Biography,* XX, pp. 525-26, mentions only his first and last wives and
only three children. There were three sons by his second marriage. Those surviving
were: Joseph, born at Barclay's Fort, December, 1858; and William, born at Denver in 1861. Mrs. Wootton died at William's birth.

[29] Conard, 371-72.

[30] *Ibid.,* 372-84; see also LeRoy R. and Ann W. Hafen, *The Far West and the
Rockies Series,* XIII, p. 200.

[31] Wilbur Fisk Stone, *History of Colorado,* I, p. 782. Henry Villard, *The Past and
Present of the Pikes Peak Regions* (original edition, 1860) gives a description of
Wootton's place of business. It will be found in Hafen's edition (Princeton, 1932),
14.

[32] Cragin Papers, "Interview with Maria Paulina Wootton (née Lujan), Dec. 4,
1907, in Notebook XI, p. 3.

died in 1861. It may have been partly for this reason that Wootton sold out in 1862 and built a house at Pueblo and another dwelling eight or nine miles above, on the east side of Fountain Creek, where he farmed till his crops were destroyed by a great flood in May 1864.[33]

Meanwhile, he had married a Miss Fanny Brown in 1863, at Doyle's ranch on the Huerfano, and his older children lived with them. However, his wife died a year and twelve days after the marriage, leaving an infant daughter.[34] After giving up the farm, he kept a store at Pueblo for a time, but all his real estate in this area was confiscated by Colorado Territory because of his pronounced secessionist sympathies during the Civil War.[35] Wootton said his opinions were only natural to one of his Southern antecedents. On one occasion, in 1863, he found it prudent to get out of Denver rather suddenly, having expressed his opinions in a manner that Denver citizens objected to.[36]

In 1865 he decided to engage in a venture that he had been considering for some time – to build a toll road over Raton Pass, on the Colorado-New Mexico line. He secured legal authorization for this project from the Colorado and the New Mexico territorial legislatures and, with George C. McBride as his partner, built twenty-seven miles of road, including many bridges, at considerable expense.[37] They operated it for the next thirteen years. At first, Wootton lived in a tent, then he built a three-room cabin and, in 1869, a comfortable and commodious home, with a veranda

[33] Conard, 403-04. Another reason for his leaving Denver was his opinion "that it would never amount to much."

[34] Cragin Papers, Notebook XI, p. 5. This daughter, named Frances Virginia, married a man named Fitzgerald.

[35] After Wootton lost his property he was overseer on Doyle's ranch until Doyle's death in 1864. Doyle's widow was engaged to marry Wootton but she died the night before he arrived for the wedding. He suspected she had been poisoned to keep him from getting control of Doyle's property. *Ibid.*, Notebook IX, p. 38.

[36] Conard, 395-400. It was at this time that the amusing incident of Fagan's ghost, apparently one of Wootton's favorite yarns, occurred.

[37] *Ibid.,* 417-30.

across the front in the best ante-bellum Southern architectural tradition.[38]

Wootton said that the toll road was a financial success. Wagons were charged $1.50; lesser vehicles, $1.00; horsemen and pack animals, 25¢. Herded livestock on foot passed at 5¢ a head. Indians had to be allowed free passage. Wootton simply tossed the coins into a whiskey keg and, when the keg was full, took it to the bank in Trinidad. However, McBride kept books for a period in 1869-1870, when Wootton was absent. The later years were probably more profitable, but these books show that, for a fifteen month period, the gross receipts averaged over $600 a month.[39]

In 1878, the Atchison, Topeka, and Santa Fe Railroad built over Raton Pass and Uncle Dick "got out of the way of the locomotive." The railroad company allowed him a credit of $50 a month, as compensation for having put him out of business. After his death, this was continued to his fourth wife, Maria Paulina Lujan, whom he had married on June 17, 1871.[40] They continued to live in their mountain home until it burned on March 3, 1890.[41] For some years after the toll gate closed, Wootton enjoyed hunting and engaging in shooting contests with visiting Utes.[42] Then he became nearly blind, but about 1886 an operation partially restored his sight. It was after this that he told his life story to Howard Louis Conard, of Chicago. Wootton died Au-

[38] Cragin Papers, Notebook XI, p. 5. For a picture of the large house at Simpson's Rest, see Conard, 465.

[39] Bess McKinnon, "The Toll Road over Raton Pass," in *New Mexico Historical Review,* II, pp. 83-89.

[40] Cragin Papers, Notebook XI, p. 3; Glenn D. Bradley, *Winning the Southwest* (Chicago, 1912), 101-02. Maria Paulina Wootton was sixteen at the time of her marriage; Wootton was nearly forty years older. She died at the age of eighty, in Albuquerque, in 1935. They had ten children, six of whom survived childhood. Five were living in 1935: Ida (Baca), Fidelis Wootton, and John, Frank, and Jesse Wootton. See obituary article in the *Rocky Mountain News* (Denver) March 3, 1935.

[41] *Ibid.* After the house at Simpson's Rest burned, Wootton lived in Trinidad, Colorado.   [42] Conard, 427-30.

gust 22, 1893, having been bedfast for the last three months of his life.[43]

His familiar title of "Uncle Dick" probably dates from 1858. Though only forty-two when he came to Denver, the newcomers there thought of him as a relic of a bygone age, and he was indeed an old settler, having been in the area for twenty-two years. He was always an active man, of great physical endurance. His temper was somewhat unpredictable. He killed a Mexican teamster who asked him a second time for a hickory shirt when he was reading and did not want to be bothered.[44] He also shot Luke Murray (Moran) in the right arm. Murray was considered harmless and people said Wootton "ought not to have done it" although he considered that Murray was set on killing him.[45] He also had to be restrained from shooting up some troublesome Comanches in Denver.[46] No doubt he mellowed in the last years of his life, for Conard calls him "a genial warmhearted old man" and speaks of his "honesty, simplicity, and candor," his "modest manly manner," and his "tears at his own recollections." [47]

He never softened much toward the Indians. The Comanches he considered the meanest of all, but as merely the worst of a bad lot.[48] He thought the Crows and Cheyennes

---

[43] *The Denver Republican,* Aug. 23, 1893. On the basis of this article, *The Dictionary of American Biography* gives the date of Wootton's death as Aug. 21, 1893. However, his widow said it was August 22. Cragin Papers, Notebook XI, p. 3. Rufus Rockwell Wilson, *Out of the West* (New York, 1936), 29, makes the curious and unwarranted statement that Wootton died in 1908, at the age of ninety-two. Wootton went to Chicago in 1888, where a Dr. Olin removed a cataract from his eye. Details are in an interview given by Wootton to a reporter for the *Chicago Inter-Ocean,* reprinted in *The Denver Republican,* March 18, 1888, p. 21. Where dates given by Wootton in this article conflict with those given in Conard, the latter has been followed.

[44] Cragin Papers, Notebook III, p. 74. This was in 1858; Wootton had been drinking.

[45] Cragin Papers, Notebook VIII, p. 75. Conard, 317-19, gives Wootton's extenuation of his action.

[46] Conard, 383.   [47] *Ibid.,* 469-72.   [48] *Ibid.,* 41.

to be the best fighters and conceded that the Maricopas and Pimas were handsome and intelligent.[49] He was almost the only Mountain Man who defended Chivington's action at Sand Creek in 1864.[50] He was also fond of pointing out that far more Indians were killed by other Indians than were killed by white men.[51] Wootton has been called "second only to Carson as an Indian fighter." [52] Like Carson, he seems to have had a level head in an emergency and a strong element of caution, which was occasionally supplanted by swift, daring action. He passed through so many skirmishes unharmed that he began to feel confident that it was not his destiny to be killed by Indians.

Wootton's business qualities were well developed and, although he never made a fortune, he was never in want and none of his varied enterprises ever failed completely. Better than most of the Mountain Men, he kept abreast of the changing times. He held office as a county commissioner and lived to see his eldest son a respected member of the state legislature of Colorado.[53]

The fact that he reminisced for Conard has provided a detailed record of his life that is unusually complete. His memory was remarkably reliable, and there are only a few instances in which his reputation for veracity can be questioned.[54] The year that marked his death was the same in

---

[49] Ibid., 121; 275-76.   [50] Ibid., 409-11.   [51] Ibid., 118-21.

[52] Henry Inman, The Old Santa Fe Trail (New York, 1898), 341.

[53] The Denver Republican, August 23, 1893. Conard's book is dedicated to Richens Lacy Wootton, Jr., who apparently helped to finance its publication.

[54] Wootton's statement (Conard, 289) that he put Tom Tobin on the trail of the Espinosa bandits is dubious. Conard (149-153) provides an instance of Wootton's having appropriated the story of Thomas Fitzpatrick's escape from the Indians, which was said to have caused his hair to turn white. Wootton tells it of an army officer named Fitzgerald but the fact that he says he was afterward a noted Indian agent is sufficient to identify him as Fitzpatrick, whose adventure occurred before Wootton came west. It was undoubtedly one of the tales he heard in his early days and Conard was thirsting to hear hair-raising adventures. On the whole, Wootton must be accounted a reliable raconteur, except as noted occasionally in these footnotes.

which Frederick Jackson Turner called attention to the disappearance of the American frontier. Uncle Dick would have agreed that the frontier was gone. In fact, he would have placed its passing a few years earlier, perhaps in 1876 when he made his last buffalo hunt in the Texas Panhandle or, perhaps in 1878, when the iron horse came chugging over Raton Pass. The Denver paper, in taking note of his passing said, "He has trapped beaver where Denver now stands; he owned a buffalo farm on the site of Pueblo, and he fought wild animals and Indians where other prosperous communities now are. The pioneer of Colorado pioneers, (he) has been a maker of history." [55]

[55] *Denver Republican*, August 23, 1893.

*The final volume of the series will provide
an index-directory to the biographies
and introductory materials in
all volumes of the work.*

The Series——

THE MOUNTAIN MEN AND THE FUR TRADE OF
THE FAR WEST is a project estimated to run to six or more
volumes of 375 to 400 pages each. The publication will contain carefully prepared biographies of some four hundred Mountain Men.

More than fifty scholars will cooperate in the project through their
signed contributions of biographical sketches of participants in the fur
trade drama. The biographies will run from one to twenty-five pages
each, depending on the importance of the subject and the available
source materials. Each sketch will give not only the subject's experience as a fur man, but a brief account of his full life span, to the
extent that dependable information can be found.

The areas of exploration and activity will include the present states
of California, Oregon, Washington, Idaho, Montana, Wyoming,
Nevada, Utah, Colorado, Arizona, New Mexico, the Dakotas,
Kansas, Nebraska, Missouri, Oklahoma, and Iowa, as well as the
Provinces of southwest Canada.

The volumes will be issued at intervals of approximately six
months, the first volume appearing in early 1965. Subscription orders
for the entire series may be placed, or individual volumes may be
ordered as each is published. The publisher will furnish descriptive
material or other detailed information on request.